THE APOSTLES' CREED

The Apostles' Creed

WILLIAM BARCLAY

WESTMINSTER JOHN KNOX PRESS

LOUISVILLE, KENTUCKY

© The Estate of William Barclay, 1967, 1998

Originally published in 1967 as
The Plain Man looks at the Apostles' Creed

First published in this edition in 1998 by

ARTHUR JAMES LTD
Berkhamsted, Hertfordshire, England

Published in the U.S.A. in 1998 by

WESTMINSTER JOHN KNOX PRESS
Louisville, Kentucky

Scripture quotations are taken, unless otherwise stated, from the
Revised Standard Version of the Bible, copyright 1946, 1952 and © 1971
by the Division of Christian Education, National Council of the
Churches of Christ in the USA, and are used by permission.

The quotation from *Portrait of Glasgow* by Maurice Lindsay
is used by permission of Robert Hale Ltd.

Typesetting by Strathmore Publishing Services, London
Cover design by Jennifer Cox

PRINTED IN GREAT BRITAIN
98 99 00 01 02 03 04 05 06 07 – 10 9 8 7 6 5 4 3 2 1

A catalog card for this book may be obtained from the
Library of Congress

ISBN 0-664-25826-3

Contents

Foreword

by the Archbishop of Canterbury

Whether in his volumes for *The Daily Study Bible*, or in his other works, William Barclay achieved a balance between fine scholarship and popular exposition, which few others have achieved this century. Throughout my own ministry I have found myself turning to his works time and again for clarification of the classical or biblical background to an incident in the New Testament, or for a story that would bring to life the teaching lying behind a complex passage in one of Paul's Epistles.

I am delighted, therefore, that not only does *The Daily Study Bible* remain in print but that steps have now been taken to re-publish these volumes from the series originally titled 'The Plain Man's Guides'. I am quite convinced that each of them still has a great deal to teach a new generation of Bible students, whether lay or ordained, both in what they say and in how they say it.

My hope, then, is that through this re-publication of several of Dr Barclay's works many of our contemporaries will discover the power of the Gospel which inspired him, and – which was his great longing behind everything he wrote – that they should discover for themselves the greatness of the Master.

+ George Cantuar

Lambeth Palace
March 1998

Preface

This book was first published in 1967, and is the third in a series originally titled 'The Plain Man's Guides', which also includes *The Beatitudes*,
The Lord's Prayer and *The Ten Commandments* (originally *Ethics*). It was
always my father's aim to pass on the results of study and scholarship to
the general reader and so this series became a major part of his theology.
Above all, William Barclay wanted to remove jargon, use simple language, and allow everyone to understand more fully the message of the
New Testament.

In his original Foreword, he said: 'I send this book out in the hope
that it will enable people better to understand the Christian faith and
therefore more able to live it and more eager to love its Lord.' And in
that statement you see one of my father's main aims in his work –
understanding combined with action. This book is a call to commitment
and discipleship. William Barclay felt that belief for a Christian can never
be static; it must always be dynamic; it must live. Our understanding of
our faith is an adventure and an exploration. He saw the Apostles' Creed
as a symbol, a picture, a political expression capable of almost infinite
expansion, a vehicle of growing truth which is almost limitless. This
book is an example of my father's belief that 'to think is a necessity of
the Christian life'. Our minds must have room to think and freedom
to move.

I hope that this book challenges you to think and that it brings to you
fresh understanding of the one universal statement of faith in the
Christian world.

RONALD W. BARCLAY
Bedford, March 1998

Acknowledgements

In sending this book out to the public I should like to make certain acknowledgements. In the first place I should like to thank the Reverend Denis Duncan, B.D., Editor of the *British Weekly* for giving me permission to republish this material which has appeared in the pages of the *British Weekly*. In the second place I am under a very deep debt of gratitude to Miss Caroline Scott, who prepared this manuscript for publication. She actually did much more than prepare it in the technical sense of the term. In many places she greatly improved the form of it and in not a few places made valuable suggestions as to the substance of it. I am most grateful to her for the invaluable help that she gave to me.

In a book like this the author must have many debts because he is working over material which has often been worked over before. I have tried to acknowledge all these debts but if I have failed to acknowledge any I hope I shall be forgiven.

WILLIAM BARCLAY
The University, Glasgow, 1967

CHAPTER ONE

Introduction to The Creed

I believe in God
    the Father Almighty,
    Maker of heaven and earth:
And in Jesus Christ
    His only Son our Lord,
    Who was conceived by the Holy Ghost,
    Born of the Virgin Mary,
    Suffered under Pontius Pilate,
    Was crucified, dead, and buried;
    He descended into hell;
    The third day he rose again from the dead;
    He ascended into heaven,
    And sitteth on the right hand of God the Father Almighty;
    From thence he shall come to judge the quick and the dead.
I believe in
    The Holy Ghost;
    The Holy Catholic Church;
    The Communion of Saints;
    The forgiveness of sins;
    The resurrection of the body;
    And the life everlasting.

So runs the creed which is called the Apostles' Creed; and if there is one universal statement of the faith of the Christian Church, it is the statement contained here.

As the basic statement of the Church's faith, the creed is very commonly repeated by the congregation at Church services, and there are not a few people for whom that is a problem, either because they feel that they do not fully understand its affirmations, or because there are certain of its articles which they feel in honesty that they cannot accept.

But it is worth remembering one basic point about the creed. As F. R. Barry points out in his book, *Asking the Right Questions,* 'The original form of credal statement is "We believe", rather than, "I believe".' In saying the creeds, as Dr Barry says, 'we identify ourselves with the total faith and experience of the Church.' In reciting the Apostles' Creed a man is affirming, not so much his own faith, as the faith of the Church. There may be things which are a mystery to him; there may be things which pass his understanding; there may even be things which he has come to the conclusion he cannot personally accept; the fact remains that in repeating this creed he puts himself in line with the total faith of the universal Church. A man will therefore be guilty of no intellectual dishonesty if he unites with God's people in the affirmation of this state-ment of the faith, even if there are parts of it about which he has doubts or reservations or even denials.

We would naturally like to know what right this creed has to be called the Apostles' Creed. What connection has it, if any, with the original apostles? In how far can it be said to state or to reflect their faith and their belief?

The Apostles' Creed did not take the exact and precise form in which it exists today until the eighth century; it is first actually called the Apostles' Creed about AD 390. In the end legend and tradition came to believe that it was literally composed by the apostles. For instance, about the year AD 400, Rufinus of Aquileia wrote his *Commentary on the Apostles' Creed,* and in the second chapter he sets down his account of the com-position of the creed: 'After our Lord's Ascension (so runs the tradition of our forefathers) with the coming of the Holy Spirit tongues of fire settled on the apostles individually. They were thus enabled to speak a variety of different languages, with the result that they found no nation strange to them, and no foreign speech beyond their powers of compre-hension. The Lord then commanded them to journey separately to different countries to preach the word of God. When they were on the point of taking leave of each other, they first settled on a common form for their future preaching, so that they might not find themselves, widely dispersed as they would be, delivering divergent messages to the people they were persuading to believe in Christ. So they all assembled in one spot and, being filled with the Holy Spirit, drafted this short summary, as I have explained, of their future preaching, each contributing the clause he judged fitting: and they decreed that it should be handed out as standard teaching to converts.'

This story has all the marks of legend, but even if we cannot trace the Apostles' Creed right back to the original apostles, how far back in the Church do we find it, or something very like it?

(i) The Apostles' Creed is in fact an expansion of Matthew 28.19: 'Go therefore and make disciples of all nations, baptizing them in the name of the Father and of the Son and of the Holy Spirit.' It is precisely the Church's belief about the Father, the Son and the Holy Spirit that this creed defines, and it is probable that the Apostles' Creed was in fact constructed to state the Church's belief on the great basic matters of the faith, which were the foundations of all missionary preaching.

(ii) Long before Rufinus we find quite unmistakable evidence that the faith of the Apostles' Creed was the faith of the Church. Tertullian, writing in the first half of the third century, describes (*De Virg. Vel. I*) the basic faith of the Church and he says that it means 'believing in one God Almighty, Maker of the world, and in his Son Jesus Christ, born of Mary the Virgin, crucified under Pontius Pilate; the third day raised from the dead, received in the heavens, sitting now at the right hand of the Father, about to come to judge quick and dead, through the resurrection also of the flesh.' Although there are still some statements missing, this is very near to the Apostles' Creed. It takes us back to about AD 230.

(iii) Further, we find that almost as far back as can be traced, the Church at Rome had a baptismal creed in which candidates for full membership of the Church were instructed, and to which they had to profess their allegiance and in which they had to pledge their belief. That old Roman Creed runs:

> I believe in God the Father Almighty:
> And in Christ Jesus his only Son, our Lord,
> Who was born of the Holy Ghost and the Virgin Mary,
> crucified under Pontius Pilate and buried,
> the third day he rose from the dead,
> he ascended into heaven,
> sitteth at the right hand of the Father,

thence he shall come to judge living and dead.
And in the Holy Ghost,
the holy Church,
the remission of sins,
the resurrection of the flesh.

It can be seen that it bears the closest possible resemblance to the Apostles' Creed.

It seems likely, therefore, that these words had, not long after AD 100, become the basic statement of the Church's faith, the statement in which those entering the Church were instructed, and the affirmation of faith which they had to make before they were baptized and admitted to the Sacrament. It is unlikely that it was written down, and it is certain that it would not be known outside the Church, and that it was part of the teaching given only to converts to the faith. It is certain, too, that it would vary slightly in wording from place to place and from time to time. But it was undoubtedly the foundational statement of the Church's faith.

So then, while we cannot state that the apostles were the actual composers and authors of the creed which bears their name, we can state that the Apostles' Creed does stretch a very long way back, and we can feel, when we repeat it, that we are using a statement in which for more than eighteen hundred years the Church has expressed its faith.

THE NECESSITY OF A CREED

It may well be that there are some to whom we would have to justify any connection at all between Christianity and creeds and dogmas. Christianity, it is argued, is a direct experience of God in Jesus Christ. It can no more be reduced to creeds and dogmas than love can, and to attempt thus to reduce it is to petrify and ossify it, and to take the living, throbbing life and vitality out of it. There are always those who plead for a creedless Christianity and a Christianity liberated from the strait-jacket of dogma. But certain basic things must be remembered.

Certainly Christianity is an experience, but equally clearly the validity of any experience has to be tested. There are people in lunatic asylums who have the experience of being the Emperor Napoleon or a poached egg. It is unquestionably an experience, and to them a real experience, but for all that it has no kind of universal validity. It is necessary to go far beyond simply saying that something comes from experience. Before any such thing can be evaluated at all, the source and character of the experience must clearly be investigated.

Further, it has to be remembered that, though Christianity is unquestionably a *personal* experience, it is equally unquestionably not a *private* experience. It is an experience which in the very nature of Christianity has to be communicated and shared. Since the duty of communication is something which is laid on every Christian, there are three necessary steps in the Christian life. First, the power and grace of Jesus Christ and the love of God in him must be personally experienced. Secondly, the validity of that experience must be tested. It must be clear that it is not artificially produced and that it is not a delusion. Thirdly, that experience must be so expressed that it can be transmitted, and that others may be enabled to share it; and immediately that obligation to expression and communication is admitted, the necessity of creed and dogma and doctrine is clear, because that which is to be transmitted must necessarily first be defined and expressed.

Sydney Cave has laid it down that there are three moments in Christian theology. There is *revelation*, when a man is confronted with God's truth and God's love. There is *appropriation*, when a man appropriates the privileges and accepts the responsibilities which are offered to him. From this moment the man is no longer a detached spectator of the revelation; he becomes personally involved in it. There is *interpretation*, in which he has to discover the meaning, in as far as he can, of the event which has happened to him, the moment when, although still vitally concerned with the *what*, he becomes equally concerned with the *why*. And the moment interpretation enters in – and it must, if for no other reason than communication – then the necessity for creed and dogma arises. Dr F. R. Barry is perfectly right when he says, 'Christianity, as I understand it, is not a body of specialized information to which Christians claim privileged access, but an attitude to all thought and experience, built on faith in God through Jesus Christ.' But that attitude is neither intelligible nor obligatory apart from certain truths about the nature and the character of God, and apart from the authority of Jesus Christ to say that God is indeed such as he taught him to be. In other words, at the back of the attitude there must lie certain convictions of the truth of which a man is fully persuaded.

There are then certain reasons why the existence of creeds and dogmas is essential.

(i) A creed is necessary *to define the faith*. The Christian must be able to state what he believes. He must be able to say: 'This is that for which I stand.' This is all the more necessary in a world in which there is blank indifference to Christianity, and in which there are other faiths competing for the allegiance of men. Christianity cannot evaporate in a vague and nebulous feeling or glow. It is all very well to have an open mind, but there is nothing to be said for a mind which is open at both ends. It is related that at a discussion regarding the worship part of a united service on some public occasion, someone finally remarked: 'What we really want is an interdenominational non-religious prayer!' The Christian must be able to say: 'Here I stand!'

(ii) A creed is necessary to provide a *norm, standard and touchstone*. To overstress the overriding rights of experience means in the end to run into all the perils of subjectivism. No one wants a creed which will become the instrument of a heresy hunt. But at the same time it is true that, although the Christian has a wide field in which to move, there are necessarily limits. Unquestionably the Gnostics would have called themselves Christians; unquestionably the Ranters who stressed Christian liberty and freedom considered themselves far more Christian than the Church; but equally unquestionably neither the Gnostics nor the Ranters were Christian. A creed is necessary simply that a man may test his own faith and thought by the faith and thought of the universal Church. It is impossible, to put it at its simplest, to see how a man can be a Christian who cannot with all the New Testament and all the Church say: 'Jesus Christ is Lord,' and who cannot or will not accept the social and personal ethic which the New Testament teaches.

(iii) A creed is necessary *to provide the material of Christian teaching and preaching*. Phillips Brooks defined doctrine as 'truth considered with reference to its being taught'. Missionary work, like teaching, is impossible without a body of defined teaching which is transmitted to those who have decided to enter the Christian faith. It is obviously dishonest to invite a man to enter any society or institution or association or fellowship without clearly telling him what that entry demands from him and offers to him. It was precisely to meet that situation that the Apostles' Creed first came into being. And the same is true of preaching. Preaching cannot be the expression of a man's private views and even prejudices; it can only very seldom be the expression of some revelation which has come directly and personally to the preacher; it must by far the most commonly be the exposition of the faith and belief of the Church. And therefore there must be some statement of belief which defines the territory in which the preacher moves, and which provides him with those revealed principles which he must apply to every event in the human situation.

But in spite of all this, two *caveats* must be entered. It remains true that any creed and any doctrine and any system of dogma must be a guide and not a chain. There are two truths which must be constantly remembered.

(i) *No creed can be complete*. It is not given to the mind of man to imprison the whole of God's truth in any formula of words. And in any event the creed cannot express the experience of which it is the symbol. What is precious is not so much the formula of the creed as the living faith and vital experience which lie behind the words. It is when the creed becomes Christian dogma without Christian experience that it loses its function.

(ii) *No creed can be final*. It must never be forgotten that there is hardly any creed which was not composed in answer to some heresy which was threatening the life of the Church. It might almost be true to say paradoxically that a creed can define heresy but not faith. A creed is always designed to meet some particular situation. Further, a creed is necessarily expressed both in the language and in the categories of thought of the age in which it was wrought out and stated. It will be affected by the world view of the age, the psychology and the philosophy of the age, the particular heretical threat of the age. This necessarily means that it is not the creed which is sacred but the Christian experience which it expressed, and when it is the creed itself which is regarded as sacrosanct then it becomes an idol and not a symbol.

The Church is, then, from age to age faced with a double task and obligation. It must in prayer and devotion keep alive the vital experience of the living God and the Risen Christ, and it must state and restate that experience in the language and the images of the age in which it is confronting men with God in Jesus Christ.

WHAT DO I MEAN WHEN I SAY 'I BELIEVE'?

A creed is a statement of belief; to recite a creed is to engage in an act of belief; a creed therefore necessarily begins with the words: 'I believe.' What do we mean when we use these words? What do we mean when we say 'I believe'? Belief can be arrived at in a variety of different ways.

(i) Belief can come from *experiment and demonstration*. If I wish to make certain that two and two make four, I can take two counters and then another two counters and I can lay them together and actually *see* that they make four. I can by actual experiment prove that hydrogen and oxygen combined as H_2O make water, or that metals expand when heated and contract when the temperature is lowered. There are a number of facts in this world which I can prove by experiment and demonstration. I believe in the result of the experiment because I see it with my own eyes.

(ii) Belief can come from *a process of reasoning*. I can demonstrate by a series of logical steps that the square on the hypotenuse of a right-angled triangle equals the sum of the squares on the other two sides. I can go through the steps of the proof, and can be certain of the result to which they lead me. I can use the processes of logic to arrive at some conclusion in the movement towards which each step in the argument is a cast-iron link.

(iii) Belief can come from *the acceptance of authority*. We do in fact in every sphere of life daily accept things on the authority of those whom we trust; and the more complex life becomes and the wider human knowledge extends, the more we are under the necessity of accepting the word of the expert for facts which we have no means of ascertaining or proving for ourselves. The scientist tells me that light travels at 186,000 miles per second; that the light from Alpha Centauri, the nearest fixed star, takes four and one third years to reach the earth. I believe that this is true though I have neither the knowledge nor the means to prove it. The astronomer tells me that the sun is 92,900,000 miles from the earth, that its diameter is 864,000 miles, that its weight is

2×10^{27} tons, 332,000 times the mass of the earth, that its temperature is 5,800–6,300 degrees. I can only take his word for it! If we are ill we have to accept the word of the doctor or the specialist about what is wrong with us; we have to accept his opinion that such and such treatment and such and such drugs will benefit us; we place so much trust in the surgeon's authority that we will allow him to send us helplessly to sleep, and then to operate on our body. We cannot tell whether the verdict is correct; we cannot decide between various methods of treatment. We have to believe the expert, and on that belief we stake nothing less than our lives.

Now this is the kind of authority that the Roman Catholic Church claims. The Roman Catholic apologists quote the alleged saying in Augustine's sermon (Sermon 131): '*Roma locuta est; causa finita est*', 'Rome has spoken; the case is finished.' It is precisely this attitude to ecclesiastical authority which takes as its principle the famous saying of Cyprian (*Letter to Jubaianus*, Letter 73): '*Salus extra ecclesiam non est*', 'There is no salvation outside the Church.'

Why do we who are Protestants not accept that ecclesiastical authority in these terms? There is obviously an attraction in retiring from the battle of thought and simply accepting authority; clearly such an attitude simplifies life and belief very greatly. Why not accept the word of the expert in this sphere as in almost all other spheres? The reason why we do not accept this form of authority is that we do not believe that the parallel between it and other kinds of authority is real or valid. It is not necessary that every man should know the facts of science and physics and astronomy; he can live quite well without knowing them, and he need come to no personal conclusion about them. All such knowledge is what we might call sectional knowledge: it is the concern of only certain people and certain sections of the community. But a man's relationship to God in Jesus Christ is the concern of every individual. It is not something which he can accept on the authority of someone else; he has to discover and experience it for himself. It is never external to him. It is a universal human concern; and, being universal, it must be subject to a man's own knowledge, experience and judgement. This is something which no man can take on trust and which he must decide for himself, for the simple reason that there is no salvation in a secondhand knowledge of God.

(iv) Belief comes from *the evidence of people whom we can trust*. There are a great number of things in life which we neither prove for ourselves nor experience for ourselves. I cannot prove that the Battle of Hastings was fought in AD 1066, but I accept the evidence of historians. I do not know what Istanbul is like from personal experience, but I accept the description of it given by people who have been there. There are certain things we believe because the evidence seems convincing, and because we accept the knowledge and experience and character of the people who supply the evidence. This also enters into Christian belief. At least in part, Christianity is based on an event in history, on the emergence of Jesus of Nazareth in Palestine centuries ago. The evidence for that fact we must examine and accept, or the basis is taken from our faith. Further, if it is the witness of good men in every generation that they have experienced Jesus Christ, and if there is something in their lives which marks them out from others, then it is an act of folly at least not to examine that evidence, for men like that have a right to speak.

(v) This leads directly to a very closely related source of belief. Belief can come from *seeing the effects of something*, although the thing itself may be beyond our knowledge or understanding. I believe in the existence of electricity, because I have seen and used its power and its effects. We may therefore believe in Christianity simply on the grounds of its personal effect on the lives of men and on the grounds of the demonstrable change it has brought about in human society and conduct. The effects of Christianity are a signpost to belief.

(vi) Lastly, belief may come from *experience*. Experience in fact speaks the last word. As a result of experience a man need no longer say: 'I have heard that this is so'; he can say: 'I know personally that this is so because it has happened to me and I have experienced it.' Experience is the argument to which there is no answer; and since Christianity consists in a personal relationship between a man and God through Jesus Christ, experience is the final argument for Christian belief, for a personal relationship can only be evaluated when it is experienced.

There remains one last thing to say. The word *belief* and the phrase *I believe* can be used in two senses.

(i) There is a belief which consists in the assent of the mind that something is true. But that assent need not have any effect on the action of the person involved. To take a simple example – I may be intellectually convinced that cigarette smoking has something to do with cancer of the lung, and yet I may continue to smoke. My belief has not affected my action. This is a belief which rests only in the mind, and which never expresses itself through the will and through the deed.

(ii) There is a belief which can only be called total belief. In it a man's whole life and every action are dominated by that which he believes. This is a belief which is an act, not only of the mind, but of the total personality. To take a very simple example again – my belief that two and two make four dominates every financial transaction which I make every day.

There is no doubt which is the Christian belief. The Christian belief is not the acceptance with the mind and the intellect of a series of propositions; it is the committal of the whole life to the conviction that certain things which Jesus taught about God and man and the world are true.

THE APPROACH TO STUDY

It is quite obvious that what we get out of anything will very largely depend on the spirit and the attitude of mind with which we approach it. Clearly we will get far more out of something which we approach with eagerness and seriousness than out of something which we approach with lethargy and flippancy. Clearly we will get more out of something which we approach with the conviction that it is of the utmost importance than out of something which we approach with the feeling that it does not really matter. In exactly the same way the spirit in which we approach the study of theology is all important. Let us then discuss the necessary approach to study.

There have always been those who have believed that religion has nothing to do with the mind. There have always been those who made an absolute division between faith and reason. In this position the seeking mind does not enter into religion at all. Tertullian states bluntly that no one seeks unless he has never found or, having found, has lost (*De Praecript. Haer II*). Bernard of Clairvaux dismissed the whole approach of reason to religion as *turpis curiositas,* shameful curiosity. Luther called reason 'the devil's bride'. And even in our own day Karl Barth, at least in his earlier position, denied that there was any such thing as natural theology, in which knowledge of God can be reached through the world and the human situation.

That is in fact an extremely dangerous position, because, if it is pressed to its logical conclusion, and if its presuppositions are examined, it is bound in the end to mean that there is a part of the constitution of man to which religion has nothing to say. It means that to be religious a man must cease to be intellectual; that to enter into what religion has to offer, he must leave his mind behind. Whereas, man was created with a mind which insists upon thinking and searching, and, as J. S. Whale has said, 'it is a moral duty to be intelligent.' 'Christian testimony,' he says, 'which raises no questions for the heart, does raise them for the thought. They may be insoluble, but not to tackle them would be theological suicide; it would be to surrender the citadel of Christian truth to the enemy without and to the Fifth Columnist within.' If it be the very characteristic of the human mind, as the writer of Ecclesiasticus says, that it muses upon many things, then thought cannot be wrong.

If we accept this denial of the mind then Christian truth must for ever remain external to a man; it can never be his own personal discovery; and since it has never become an integral part of himself, the danger will always be that in any time of stress it will collapse. A man will always possess in a much more real sense of the word that which he has struggled and striven and even agonized to possess, than that which has merely come to him from some external source.

Further, there is a very real danger that truth remains static, that it remains for ever simply an unalterable body of things handed down, rather than a dynamic and developing discovery. John Baillie in his posthumous volume, *Christian Devotion*, quoted a passage from Emile Cammaert's *Flowers of Grass* in which Cammaert traces his own progress from atheism to belief: 'The best advice which could be given to any young man or woman would be to urge him not to allow his present beliefs, whatever they may be, to harden into prejudice; to keep an open mind, to watch eagerly what happens to him and around him, and never to close the book of life before reading the past page.... A Christian life compels us to leave the book open to the end.' Unless life is a mental development it is a mental death, and if it is to be a mental development the mind must enter into it. This is not to say that a man can think himself unaided into the Christian conception of God; but it is to say that the revelation which God gives him must be passed through the processes of his own mind and thought.

(i) If it is easy to neglect the mind altogether, it is just as easy to exalt the mind into a position which is quite out of proportion. J. S. Whale has said that one of the greatest dangers that theologians run is that we put a pipe in our mouths and our feet on the mantelpiece and sit down in an armchair to discuss theories of the atonement instead of bowing down before the wounds of Christ, that we scurry round the burning bush taking photographs from suitable angles instead of taking our shoes from off our feet for the place whereon we stand is holy ground. There is a real danger that theological thought and argument are entered into, not so much for the conclusions reached, as for the joy of the mental gymnastics involved, and for what Beatrice Webb called 'the stimulus of the mental hike'.

J. S. Whale wrote: 'You may spend years on the sacred texts, the wearisome minutiae of linguistic and archaeological research, the arguments about the deepest things by which men have lived. But by studying these facts it is easy to lose the life which alone gives them unity and meaning.' There is a very real sense in which the purely intellectual approach can in the end defeat itself and in which questions can end only in an arid desert of still further questions. There is truth in G. K. Chesterton's saying: 'We have asked all the questions that can be asked. It is time we gave up asking questions and started looking for answers.'

(ii) We have now come to see that the approach to theology which denies the mind any place at all is wrong, and that the approach to theology which thinks in nothing but terms of the mind can be equally wrong. How is the mean between the two approaches to be struck? How can faith and reason join hands in the perfect partnership?

My own late chief, that great scholar and man of God, G. H. C. Macgregor, often quoted the great eighteenth-century scholar, classicist and textual critic, Richard Bentley, to his students. Bentley used to warn that the great danger was of losing the *res ipsa,* the thing itself, in the minutiae and technicalities of scholarship. And in the same way the early fathers used to warn how easy it is to lose the *unum necessarium,* the one thing needful (Luke 10.42).

How, amidst the technicalities and the mental activity of theology, shall we firmly retain our grasp upon the *res ipsa,* the thing itself, the *unum necessarium,* the one thing necessary?

There are two sayings, one of Melanchthon, one of Luther, both quoted by J. S. Whale, which will go far to give us our line of safety. Melanchthon said: 'To know Christ is not to speculate about the mode of his incarnation, but to know his saving benefits.' Luther said: 'He who merely studies the commandments of God (*mandata Dei*) is not greatly moved. But he who listens to God commanding (*Deum mandantem*), how can he fail to be terrified by majesty so great?' To these two sayings we may add Paul's great statement of belief: 'I know whom I have believed' (2 Timothy 1.12). To all this we may add the sentence in which John describes his aim in writing his Gospel: 'These are written that you may believe that Jesus is the Christ, the Son of God, and that believing you may have life in his name' (John 20.31).

This is to say that at the end of the search there are two things, *a person and a life*. At the end of all Christian thought there is not an abstract truth but a living person; the aim of all Christian thought is not the acquisition of theoretical knowledge, but the ability to live. That is precisely why two very great theologians could make two very startling statements. Vincent Taylor once said: 'The test of any theologian is, can he write a tract?' James Denney once said: 'I haven't the faintest interest in any theology which doesn't help us to evangelize.' 'If evangelists were our theologians,' he said, 'or theologians our evangelists, we should be nearer the ideal.' This is very far from absolving men from the most intense and rigorous thought. On one occasion Denney rebuked a minister who asked, since he was too busy to prepare a proper address, to be excused for delivering a simple evangelistic sermon. 'As if', said Denney, 'there was any task which could so tax the strength of the Christian preacher as to preach the love of God, and so to preach it that men should commit themselves to it.'

Here we have our answer. The proper approach to theological study is in the spirit which loves God and loves men. Its aim must be that we ourselves should know God better in order to love him more, and in order that we should communicate that love to others. Theology will never go wrong so long as its twin dynamics are love of God and love of men, for in the beginning the *unum necessarium* was nothing other than to sit at the feet of Jesus (Luke 10.38–42).

CHAPTER TWO

I Believe in God

To the mind of the modern man there is one strange omission in the Bible. The Bible is the supreme religious book, and yet it never makes any attempt to prove the existence of God. In the Bible the fool says in his heart that there is no God (Psalm 53.1). But the fool there is not the intellectual fool or simpleton; he is the moral fool, the man who, as we would say, is playing the fool. He is not denying the existence of God on intellectual grounds; he is denying the existence of God because he wishes to deny the commandments of God, and he wishes to live life as he likes. His abolition of God is not the issue of mental despair, but the result of wishful thinking.

The biblical writers did not feel the necessity of proving the existence of God To them God's existence was too vividly experienced, and God's action was too obviously visible for any doubt to arise. It has been truly said that in the Bible God is not merely a character in life and history; he is properly the only character in life and in history. To a biblical writer the existence of God was as self-evident as that of his wife or child.

But the mind of the modern man works differently, just as indeed the mind of the Greek in the ancient world worked differently. 'We feed on questions,' said the old Athenian. 'Curiosity', as Plato said, 'is the mother of knowledge.' Suppose we put our minds to the task of trying to prove the existence of God, how far will they take us? Ritschl said: 'Without Christ I should be an atheist.' Is that a necessary conclusion? Can human thought and the contemplation of the world take us no distance towards God at all?

It is certainly true that the biblical view of life would not rule out such an inquiry. Paul speaks of the people who have turned their backs on God and who have chosen to live in shameless immorality, and of the

wrath of God against them, and of how they can be legitimately condemned: 'For what can be known about God is plain to them, because
God has shown it to them. Ever since the creation of the world his invisible nature, namely, his eternal power and deity, has been clearly per-
ceived in the things that have been made' (Romans 1.18–19). There was
no doubt at all in Paul's mind that it was possible to argue from the
world to God, and to see God in the world. C. H. Dodd has pointed out
that the way in which Jesus uses the natural processes of the world in his
parables makes it quite clear that he too believed that there is a kinship
between the world and God, making it possible to learn of God from
the world and the processes of the world. Suppose then that we try to
see how far our own minds can take us in the search for God, how far
we can go in the direction of proving the existence of God.

(i) There is the argument from cause and effect. Every effect must
have its cause; the cause itself must have its cause; and the cause which
caused the cause must have its cause. And so, if the chain of causation be
followed back and back and back into infinity, it must somewhere come
to a first cause, which is the cause of every other cause. Thus we arrive at
a God who is the First Cause, or, as the Greek called him, 'the unmoved
mover of all things'.

(ii) There is the argument from life. Man can do many things; he can
change and rearrange and alter and develop and elaborate but the one
thing which man has never created is life. He cannot take a dead thing
and make it alive; he cannot take a collection of elements and breathe life
into them. Life must therefore have entered into the world from outside,
and so we arrive at a God who is the source and the fountain and the
giver and the origin of all life.

(iii) There is what is perhaps the most famous of all arguments, the
argument from design. This is an argument for the existence of God
which men have used for thousands of years. A modern example of it is
the parable of Paley. Suppose a man is walking across a moor and he
happens to hit his foot against a watch. He picks it up; he has never seen
a watch before; he examines it. He sees that the hands are moving
round the dial in what is clearly an orderly way. He opens it up and he
finds inside a host of wheels and cogs and levers and springs and jewels.
He discovers that by winding up the watch, you can set it going, and
that the whole complicated machinery is moving in what is obviously a

predetermined pattern. What then does he say? Does he say: 'By chance all these wheels and levers and jewels and springs came together and formed themselves into this thing I have in my hand. By chance they set themselves going. By chance they move in an orderly way. By chance this watch became an instrument which counts the hours and minutes and seconds'? No. If he applies his mind to this problem at all, he says: 'I have found a watch. *Somewhere there must be a watch-maker.*' So then when we discover a world where there is an order more accurate than any watch, where tides ebb and flow according to schedule, where spring, summer, autumn and winter come back in unvarying succession, where the planets never leave their courses, where the same cause always produces the same effect, we are bound to say: 'I have found a world. *Somewhere there must be a world-maker.*'

As we have said, this argument is an argument as old as thought. It was the favourite argument of the Stoics. Cicero's *De Natura Deorum* is full of it. The musical harmony of the world would be impossible without a mind behind it. Poseidonius made an orrery, a working model of the sun and the moon and the five planets. The model implies a mind to make it. How much more does the original from which the model was made imply a mind. You might as well, says Cicero, expect to produce the *Annals* of Ennius by putting the twenty-six letters of the alphabet into a pail, and then shaking them up and pouring them out, as to expect to produce the order of this world by sheer blind chance.

This argument from design can be illustrated by something much closer: by the structure of the human body. Xenophon in the *Memorabilia* tells how Socrates argued for divine *pronoia*, forethought, from the structure of the body: 'Are there not other contrivances which look like the results of forethought? Thus, the eyeballs, being weak, are set behind the eyelids, that open like doors when we want to see, and close when we sleep; on the lids grow lashes through which the very winds filter harmlessly; above the eyes is a coping of brows that lets no drop of sweat from the head hurt them. The ears catch all sounds, but are never choked with them. Again, the incisors of all creatures are adapted for cutting, the molars for receiving food from them and grinding it. And again, the mouth through which the food they want goes in is set near the eyes and nostrils; but since what goes out is unpleasant, the ducts through which it passes are turned away and removed as far as possible from the organs of sense. With such signs of forethought in these arrangements can you doubt whether they are the works of chance or design?'

(iv) There is the argument from purpose. It does seem that the universe is purposely designed to produce certain things. The evolutionary process looks as if it was purposely designed to produce the particular forms of life which it did produce. The very fact that the same effect follows the same cause, the very fact that this is a reliable universe, is the prerequisite of purposeful activity.

The Stoics, again to quote Cicero's *De Natura Deorum*, put this in a special way. There is in the world, plain for all to see, so they claimed, a graduated scale of being. There is the vegetable kingdom, for whose preservation nature provides by nurture and growth. There is the animal kingdom, in which exist sensation, motive, appetite, the impulse to choose what is helpful and avoid what is harmful. There is man who has reason to direct and control his appetites. To complete the scale there must be a fourth scale of beings, consistently good and wise, possessing perfect and absolute reason. This fourth grade must be above the level of human beings and therefore must consist of gods.

There does seem to be in the universe an end and a purpose for each of its parts, which they may or may not achieve and attain; and purpose and plan and end necessarily imply mind. And thus once again we reach God.

(v) There is also what might be called the moral argument. Where does man get his moral sense? Where does he get the values which are moral values? Long ago Epictetus pointed out that no man is born with a knowledge of music or geometry but every man is born with some kind of moral sense, even if he defies it and turns his back on it and perhaps ultimately loses it. There is a kind of innate consciousness of right and wrong. Certainly man cannot live without the natural instincts of self-preservation and of acquisitiveness, but what is it that prevents these instincts from taking control and from dictating the whole pattern of life? What is it, for instance, that makes a man override the instinct of self-preservation and die for a principle, or sacrifice life for a loved one? What is it, for instance, that makes a man realize that in life there is an obligation to give, which controls the instinct to get?

The conclusion is that these things must come from outside humanity. There must be that beyond man which breathes them into man. The moment we use the word 'ought' we arrive at God; the moral imperative implies God. J. S. Whale writes: 'Man's distinctive and imperious sense of "oughtness" has a sanctity which refuses to be bargained with, or to be explained away in terms of any alien principle.' And he goes on to quote a saying of John Oman: 'Whoever says "ought", really meaning "ought", is in that act bearing witness to the supernatural and supra-temporal as the destined home of man.' The very word 'ought' implies a standard given from beyond the human situation, and sanctions imposed by a power above the human situation. The moment we use the word 'ought' we are saying that it is not possible to explain man in exclusively physical terms, and that there is another area of life to which as man he necessarily belongs. The principles, the obligations, the laws, the duties, which are all assumed in the word 'ought' have not emerged from the human situation but have been given from outside it. Thus the moral argument leaves us facing God. This is the argument which is summed up in the famous saying of Kant that two things convince him of God: 'the starry heavens above me, and the moral law within me.'

(vi) There is the argument from the universal belief in God, what the Romans called the *consensus gentium*, the common consent of all people. This again is an argument which has been used for thousands of years. Cicero in the *De Natura Deorum* uses this argument as one of the Stoic proofs of the existence of God. 'The years obliterate the inventions of the imagination, but confirm the judgements of nature,' and, 'the belief in God is only strengthened by the passage of the years, and grows more deeply rooted with each successive generation of mankind.' Men of all nations have 'engraved on their minds an innate belief that the gods exist.' It has been said that there never has been discovered a tribe of men however primitive who did not pray. And long ago Seneca argued that, if there are no gods, prayer would become a kind of 'universal madness', which is incredible.

(vii) We come last of all to the purely logical arguments for the existence of God. The most famous of all these arguments is Anselm's ontological argument. It has been said that either this argument is quite final or else it is merely 'ratiocinative trifling'. It runs in three steps.

- By definition God is a being than which a greater cannot be conceived.
- But an idea which exists only in the mind cannot be as great as an idea which exists in fact as well. An idea which exists only *in intellectu* cannot be as great as an idea which exists also *in re*.
- Therefore, God must be thought of as necessarily existing.

Given the truth of the second step in this argument, the argument is quite undeniable.

To this argument Descartes added another. God is infinite and perfect. Man is finite and imperfect. Now a finite and an imperfect being cannot by himself conceive of that which is infinite and perfect. Therefore the idea of an infinite and perfect being cannot have arisen from the mind of man and must have been put there by God himself. As Galloway puts it: 'Man's knowledge of God is due to God himself. God is the sufficient reason of the idea of himself in man.'

The logical proofs of the existence of God will appear quite differently to different minds. To some they will appear to clinch the matter and to leave no room for doubt; to others they will be quite unconvincing and devoid of reality; but it is Anselm's ontological argument that is the most famous of all arguments for the existence of God.

(viii) There is one argument for God, the validity of which there are at least some who will totally deny. This is the argument from history. There are those who claim that there is design in history just as there is design in the world, and that that design necessarily implies an overruling mind. It may broadly speaking be said that there are three views of history.

- There is the Stoic view that history is circular. The Stoics believed that at the end of the 'great year', when the sun and the moon and the five planets return to the positions relative to each other in which they began, there comes a great conflagration in which all things are burned up. Then after that the world is reborn and things happen all over again in exactly and precisely the same way. As Chrysippus put it: 'Socrates and each individual man will live again, with the same friends and fellow-citizens. They will go through the same experiences and the same activities. Every city and village and field will be restored just as it was. And this restoration of the universe takes place not

once but over and over again, indeed to all eternity without end.'
In this view history is only an endless repetition of itself.
- There is the view that history is planless and senseless, blind and
haphazard. C. M. Trevelyan said: 'Philosophy must be brought to
history. It cannot be extracted from it.' G. N. Clark in his inaugural
lecture at Cambridge asserted that he saw no plan in history: 'I do
not believe that any future could make sense of all the irrationalities
of the preceding ages. If it could not explain, still less could it justify
them.' Herbert Fisher wrote: 'Men wiser and more learned than
myself have discerned in history a plot, a rhythm, a pre-determined
pattern. I can see only one emergency following upon another as
wave follows upon wave.' André Maurois wrote: 'The universe is
indifferent. Who created it? Why are we here on this puny mud-heap
spinning in infinite space? I have not the slightest idea.' There are
many voices to tell us that there is neither sense nor plan in history.
- There is the view that history is the unfolding of a plan, and that
there is a guiding hand and a guiding mind behind it and in it. J. A.
Froude wrote: 'One lesson and one lesson only history may be
said to repeat with distinctness, that the world is built somehow
on moral foundations, that in the long run it is well with the good,
and in the long run it is ill with the wicked.'

This is of course the biblical view of history. The Bible sees
the history of Israel as nothing other than the result of the direct
plan and action of God. If history is the arena of purpose then
history is the arena of God.

(ix) Last of all, there is the argument from experience. That experience may be any one of three different kinds.
- There can be few people who have not at some time or other,
perhaps in the dark on a lonely mountainside, or in a wood, or
an open road, had the eerie sense of something other which can
make the hair literally stand on the head. That is what is known
as the sense of the numinous, the sense that in the universe there
is a power other than human power. That kind of feeling is
indeed the raw material of all religion.
- There are those who at different times in life have been quite sure
that God spoke to them in guidance and in comfort, and who on
looking back are sure that they can trace the guiding hand of God.

– There are the few, the saints and the mystics, to whom the presence of God is the most real thing in the world, and who live in daily communion with God.

In one sense, the argument from experience is the strongest argument of all. In another sense, it is an argument which may be personally undeniable but which cannot be used to convince anyone else because an experience is of necessity incommunicable.

We have looked at the arguments for the existence of God which can be drawn from the world in which we live, and which can be deduced by human reason. We must now ask another question. What kind of a God would these arguments lead us to believe in? Suppose that we had only our reason, and suppose that we did not possess the Christian revelation, what would we say about God?

(i) We could say that God is a God of *law and order*. There is nothing haphazard about the universe. The universe is both far more complicated and far more accurately ordered than any human machine. As one great astronomer put it: 'God must be a mathematician.'

This is a universe in which it is possible to rely on things happening in accordance with the law which governs their movements and reactions. The planet Uranus was discovered in 1781. That planet takes one hundred and sixty-four years to complete its orbit round the sun. When its movement was tracked and studied, it became clear that there must be yet another planet still further in outer space, exercising its influence on Uranus. From the movements of Uranus, calculations were made as to where that further planet must be and when it would come into sight from the earth. A watch was kept at the time calculated, and, promptly on 22nd September 1846 Neptune swam into man's ken.

(ii) We could say that God is a God of *immense power*. The more we know of the universe the more staggering its sheer immensity becomes. Hendrik van Loon in his book, *The Home of Mankind*, presents us with certain figures about the world in which we live. Astronomers speak about stars and planets being so many 'light years' away. Light travels at the rate of 186,000 miles per second. That is to say, in one year light travels 186,000 × 60 × 60 × 24 × 365 miles. So when an astronomer speaks of a star or a planet as being so many light years away, he means that the light from that planet has taken that number of years to reach us, travelling all the time at 186,000 miles per second. The light from Alpha Centauri, the nearest star to this earth, takes four and one third years to reach us. The light from the Pole Star takes 466 years to reach us. That is to say, the Pole Star is 186,000 × 60 × 60 × 24 × 365 × 466 miles away from this earth.

Such figures are frankly inconceivable for the ordinary mind. So Hendrik van Loon has expressed it in a different way. He has expressed it in the time that it would take an express train travelling day and night to reach certain stars and planets. It would need 300 years to get to the sun; it would take 8,300 years to reach Neptune; it would take 75,000,000 years to reach Alpha Centauri, the nearest star; and it would take 700,000,000 years to reach the Pole Star; 25,000,000 generations of men would have lived and died before that celestial train got there. Another way of thinking about it is to say that the light from the Pole Star that we see today, at the end of the twentieth century, left the star some fifty years before the Authorized Version, and has been travelling towards this earth at the rate of 186,000 miles per second ever since.

When we think of figures like that, we can catch some faint glimpse of the sheer majestic and infinite power of the divine mind which created, orders and sustains all that.

Or let us think of this in terms of time. Suppose we take the whole length of Cleopatra's needle, and suppose on the top of it we stick one single postage stamp, the thickness of the postage stamp would represent the time during which man as man has been in being, and the length of the whole monument would represent the probable length of time the world existed before man came into it at all. Human history represents the merest fraction of time. Time like that leaves the human mind baffled and amazed, and yet that is time as God sees it.

It is told that a countryman who knew something of the universe asked a certain preacher to study astronomy. 'Why should I do that?' asked the preacher. 'Because', said the countryman, 'you've an awfu' wee God.' No one can believe in a 'wee God' if he studies the universe around him.

(iii) Although God is so great and powerful, although the universe has its imagination-defying immensities, God is also the God of *the least detail.* To see a snowflake under the microscope is to see a detailed loveliness beyond the skill of man to create. The universe tells not only of the infinite greatness of God; it tells also of the infinite care of God on the smallest things.

(iv) It would be possible to tell from the universe that there is a certain *bounty* and *generosity* in God. In the universe there is enough and more than enough for the needs of men; where there is not enough, it is not God's bounty that has failed but man's distribution of it.

(v) It would be possible to tell from the universe *God's attitude to men.* If the universe tells us one thing more than another, it is that the gifts of God are to those who are prepared to work for them. We can see that God did not design the universe as a cushion but as a challenge. The great things are there, but they are not for the man who is lazy and lethargic; they are there for the man who is prepared to toil for them. Seneca has a great phrase. He says of God that God *fortiter amat* his children. God loves his children *strenuously, gallantly*; he is not concerned to make man into a flabby creature into whose lap things will fall without effort; he is concerned to give men things in such a way that a man will develop strength and courage of mind and heart and sinew in the getting of them. What the God of this universe has given mankind is not so much the ready-made articles as a series of almost limitless potentialities which man by thought and toil must make into realities.

Hesiod, the old Greek poet, said: 'The gods have placed sweat as the price of all things.' Leonardo da Vinci, the great artist and scientist, prayed: 'Thou, O God, dost sell us all good things at the price of labour.' Sir Thomas More prayed: 'These things, good Lord, we pray for, give us thy grace to labour for.' Samuel Johnson began one of his prayers with the address to God: 'O God, who hast ordained that whatever is to be desired should be sought by labour.'

There is a certain grim truth in the idea of the survival of the fittest. The whole lesson of the evolutionary process is that creatures which adapted themselves too completely to circumstances became in the end extinct. They were so dominated by their circumstances that, when the circumstances altered, they perished, for they were unable to survive. The creatures which survived and which rose higher in the scale of being were creatures which not only adapted themselves to the existing circumstances of life but which in some way rose above them. To the element of adjustment, which is necessary, they added the element of mastery, which is ultimately still more necessary. It is possible to see behind the universe a mind which is concerned to make living things move higher or perish, and which has so designed things that the upward movement is not an automatic process but a conscious achievement.

In the universe we can see the law and order of the mind behind it. In the universe we can see a God of infinite power, and yet of a power which does not neglect the smallest detail of the universe. In the universe we see a certain generous bounty, which can be turned into poverty and want by the selfishness or the short-sightedness of men. In the universe we see the action of a mind which has so designed life that lethargy begets disaster and even extinction, while toil of mind and body begets still greater life and still greater gifts.

CHAPTER THREE

I Believe in God the Father Almighty

We have now seen the idea of God which we might gain by the exercise of human reason and by deduction from the world around us and the universe in which we live. We must now turn to the specifically Christian conception of God. It would be true to say that the Christian conception of God is summed up in the statement of the creed: *'I believe in God the Father.'* By the Christian use of that one word Father a new relationship is established between God and man.

Jesus was by no means the first person to apply the word Father to God, but he did fill that word with a new content and a new meaning. Long before Jesus the Greeks had called Zeus the Father of gods and men, but by the word Father they had never meant what Jesus meant. There are two senses in which the word Father may be used. It may be used in the sense of *paternity*. That is to say, it may be used of a person who is responsible for the physical existence of a child. But when it is used in that sense the connection is purely physical. A man may be responsible for the existence of a child in the *paternity* sense of the term without ever having seen the child in his life. But the word Father may be used in the *fatherhood* sense of the term. In that sense the word conveys a relationship of love and care and intimacy, a close bond of love and sympathy and cherishing, which is one of the loveliest relationships in life. In the ancient world men did think of God as Father in the *paternity* sense of the term; they did think of God as the physical begetter of mankind, the one who was responsible for the life and the existence of men; but seldom, if ever, did they think of God as Father in the *fatherhood* sense of the term with all its intimate love and fellowship.

The idea of God as Father has become to us a commonplace in religion. But it was far from being a commonplace when Jesus first brought it to men. At that time it was not a religious cliché, but a religious revelation. We can, therefore, best see the sheer newness of the Christian conception by looking at men's ideas about God before the Christian idea of God emerged with Jesus.

Let us begin by looking at the Jewish idea of God.

In Jewish thought God was certainly the Father of *the Jewish nation* and of Israel as a people. 'Do you thus requite the Lord, you foolish and senseless people? Is he not your Father who created you, who made you and established you?' (Deuteronomy 32.6). 'I am a Father to Israel, and Ephraim is my first-born' (Jeremiah 31.9). 'Thou art our Father, though Abraham does not know us and Israel does not acknowledge us; thou, O Lord, art our Father, our Redeemer from of old is thy name' (Isaiah 63.16). Certainly, God is the Father of Israel. Since the nation is so to speak incarnated in the king, and since the king of the chosen people clearly stands in a special relationship to God, God is said to be the Father of the king. God said to David regarding Solomon: 'I will be his Father, and he shall be my son' (2 Samuel 7.14). Certainly, God is Father of the king. But the fact remains that in the Old Testament, although God is Father of the nation and of the king, he is never said to be the Father of the individual man and woman. The fatherhood of God is never individualized. In so far as it belongs to any individual man at all, it belongs to him, not as a person, but as a member of the nation. It is only in the literature between the Testaments, and then only in brief glimpses, that sometimes the individualized fatherhood emerges. So Ben Sirach in Ecclesiasticus can write: 'O Lord, Father and God of my life' (Ecclesiasticus 23.1, 4). What then were the characteristics of the Jewish belief about God?

(i) Between man and God there is *unbridgeable distance*; there is such *absolute difference* that the approach to God is not simply difficult, it is fatal. Moses hears God say: 'You cannot see my face; for man shall not see me and live' (Exodus 33.20). When Moses came down from the mountain, it was the astonished saying of the people: 'We have this day seen God speak with man and man still live' (Deuteronomy 5.24). When Manoah discovered who his heavenly visitor had been, he said to his wife: 'We shall surely die, for we have seen God' (Judges 13.22).

In the Old Testament the basic description of God is in the word *holy* (Hebrew, *kadōsh* ; Greek, *hagios*); and the basic meaning of that word is *different, separate, other than.* It describes God, in a modern theologian's phrase, as *the wholly other.* The characteristic of God is that he belongs to an other and different sphere of being, to which for man there is no possible approach. The Old Testament is awed by the sheer transcendence of God.

If this holiness is to be approached at all, it can only be approached by a like holiness:

> Who shall ascend into the hill of the Lord?
> And who shall stand in his holy place?
> He who has clean hands and a pure heart,
> Who does not lift up his soul to what is false,
> And does not swear deceitfully.
>
> (Psalm 24.3–4)

A qualification of entry such as that simply shuts the door on all ordinary men and women.

(ii) In the Old Testament God is the God of *unconditioned authority.* The typical picture is the picture of the potter as Jeremiah saw him at work (Jeremiah 18.1–11). Jeremiah saw how the clay with which the potter was working assumed the wrong shape. The potter simply squeezed it into a lump again and started all over again. The clay had nothing to do with it; the clay had no rights; the potter can make or mar it, alter, change, obliterate it, as he wishes. 'O house of Israel,' says God, 'can I not do with you as this potter has done?' God can pluck up and break down and destroy, or build and plant, just as he wishes and wills.

In a way that is a terrible picture, for at the back of it there is the idea that in the divine unconditioned authority *persons* can be treated as *things.* The person has no more rights in the eyes of God than the clay has in the eyes of the potter. A picture of a God like this will certainly produce awe and reverence and fear, and maybe even submission and acceptance and resignation; it could not possibly produce love. Nor could the name Father possibly be given to a God whose treatment of men can be likened to the picture of the potter.

(iii) In the Old Testament God is the God of *ineluctable power.* This is precisely the problem which lies at the back of the spiritual agony of Job. When Job seeks to put his case to God, it is not an answer which he receives; it is a barrage of almost contemptuous questions. 'Where were you when I laid the foundations of the earth? Have you commanded the morning since your days began? Have you entered into the springs of the sea? Have you entered into the storehouses of the snow? Can you bind the chains of the Pleiades, or loose the cords of Orion? Do you know the ordinances of the heavens? Can you lift up your voice to the clouds? Do you give the horse his might? Is it at your command that the eagle mounts up?' (Job 38 and 39). It is tremendous poetry, as great as any in the world. It is an awesome conception of God and of course it is in one sense true. But the whole essence is that God confronts a man in his soul's agony and answers his cry with the question: 'What right have you to speak to me?' A man might well lie prostrate in utter submission to such a God, but he could never cast himself on the breast of a God who regards him like that.

The plain fact is that the might and the majesty and the holiness and the power of God stand out, in the Jewish idea of God, in all their splendour; but the effect is to leave man crushed and bowed beneath the feet of God. There is in God a certain arbitrariness; God does as he likes, and man is without rights and without explanations. The name of God is King and Lord, but not Father; the position of man is slave and servant, but not child. And the truth is that this is precisely the idea of God that any thinking man will arrive at *apart from Jesus Christ*. This is exactly what, humanly speaking, we would expect God to be. By reason we could arrive at this picture of God; it requires more than reason, it requires revelation, to enable men to see that, while all these things are true of God, there is something truer yet – the supreme fact that while God is like that he is also like Jesus Christ.

Now let us turn to the way in which the Greeks thought of God.

(i) Sometimes they thought of God as simply *an abstract idea*. Plato was one of the great thinkers of all time, and the conception which was in many ways his greatest contribution to thought was his conception of forms or ideas. He held that in heaven, in the unseen world, there are laid up the patterns and ideas and forms of which everything in this world is a pale and shadowy and imperfect copy. To take it at its simplest, there is in the unseen world the perfect idea or form of a table of which all material and earthly tables are imperfect copies. Now as Plato saw it, the highest of all these ideas is the idea of the good, of which all earthly goodness is an imperfect and inadequate copy; and that idea of the good and God are one and the same thing. This leaves us with the conception of a God who is literally an abstract idea. There is nothing personal here at all. There is undoubtedly something which the mind can grasp, but there is nothing in which the heart can rest.

(ii) Sometimes the Greeks thought of God or the gods as being *grudging and grasping*. The gods, as they saw it, were determined that men should possess as little as possible; they grudged and resented every upward step that man was able to take. The typical Greek myth is the story of Prometheus, one of the gods. In his time men did not possess the gift of fire, and life without fire must have been a comfortless existence. In his sympathy for men Prometheus stole fire from heaven and gave it to men. Zeus, the father of gods and men, was violently angry. He took Prometheus and chained him to a rock in the middle of the ocean; and he arranged for a vulture to tear out Prometheus' liver, which ever grew again, only to be torn out again. Here, the gods and men are at variance and the aim of the gods is at all costs to keep men in their place and to refuse them any betterment of life.

(iii) Sometimes they looked on the gods as essentially *withdrawn, detached and indifferent*. The Stoics declared that the first and essential attribute and characteristic of God was what they called *apatheia*. *Apatheia* is not apathy. Apathy is the indifference of a man who can feel and should feel, but who refuses to feel. *Apatheia* is an existence devoid of any feeling or any emotion The Greek argument was that if God can feel sorrow or joy, approval or disapproval, pleasure or grief, it means that the action of man can bring God joy or sorrow. That is to say, the action of man can have an influence upon God. But, the Greeks argued, if anyone can influence another person, it means that he has power over that other person; and if he has such a power, then he is, at least temporarily, greater than the other person. But, they said, by definition no one can be greater than God. Therefore, no one can have any influence upon God. And the only way to ensure that is to assume that God must have complete *apatheia*. He must be such that by his very nature he cannot feel anything; he must be totally insulated against all emotion, so that he can remain for ever serene and tranquil, calm, unmoved and detached.

So Greek thought presents us with a God who is an abstract idea, a God who grudges man everything to which he can rise, a God whose deity depends on his insulation from all emotion.

The Jewish and the Greek view of God have only to be stated for it to be seen how far apart they are from the Christian view. Let us then see what the Christian view of God is, and what is contained in the affirmation: I believe in God, the Father.

(i) The Christian does believe in the *paternity* of God; he does believe that God is the source and origin and goal of all life; that God is the One from whom life comes and to whom life goes.

(ii) But even more, the Christian believes in the *fatherhood* of God, that intimate, loving, caring fellowship which goes so much further than paternity can ever go. The intimacy of the relation of the Christian to God is seen best of all in the name which Jesus used for God, and the name which Paul says that the Christians too may use, the name *Abba* (Mark 14.36; Romans 8.15; Galatians 4.6). *Abba* is the name by which a little child addressed his father in the home circle in the time of Jesus, as *jaba* still is in Arabic today. In any secular context it would be translated simply as Daddy. Nothing shows so well the intimate fellowship of the Christian with God. Here is no God transcendent in infinite might and majesty, unapproachable, different and separate; here is no God who is an abstraction or a philosophic idea, or a grudging or a passionless deity. Here is a God who is as near to us as a father is to a little child.

(iii) This means that for the Christian God is *love* (1 John 4.8). It must clearly be understood what this divine love is. The word *agapē*. Greek has four words for love. *Erōs* is the love of a man for a girl, and always has something of sex in it; it does not occur in the New Testament, not because the New Testament in the least despises physical love, but because by New Testament times it had come to mean lust rather than love. *Storgē* is family affection, the love of brother and sister and parent and child; it is the love which characterizes the relationship of those who are kith and kin. *Philia* is the highest Greek word for love, and describes the relationship of body and mind and spirit which unites two people who really and truly care for each other. But the word used of God and of Christian love is *agapē*. The characteristic attitude of the love of God is defined in Matthew 5.43–8. There the distinguishing feature of the love of God is that God makes his sun rise on the evil and on the good, and sends rain on the just and the unjust. That is to say, no matter what a man is like, be he good or bad, just or unjust, God seeks nothing but his highest good and sends nothing but his gifts upon him. In other words, the love of God is all-inclusive. It is not, as human love must so often be, a variable thing, now at one temperature and now at another, or even a fickle thing, altering when it alteration finds; it is a steadfast and undefeatable graciousness to man, which nothing that man can do can ever alter. It is the simple fact of the New Testament that, however often it may speak of the necessity of man being reconciled to God, it never speaks about God being reconciled to man, for in the heart of God there is this unwavering and unconquerable and outgoing kindness to man.

(iv) But there is something to be added to that. We have spoken about the inclusiveness of the love of God; we have spoken about this undefeatable kindness of heart to men. But the love of God for men is no vague, generalized benevolence. It is *detailed and personalized*. All the love of God goes out to each and every man.

There is a saying of Jesus which is related slightly differently by Matthew and Luke, yet the slight difference is very significant. Matthew (10.29) has it: 'Are not two sparrows sold for a penny? And not one of them will fall to the ground without your Father's will.' Luke (12.6) has: 'Are not five sparrows sold for two pennies? And not one of them is forgotten before God.'

Sparrows were two a penny; but, if a man was prepared to spend two pennies, he got an extra sparrow thrown into the bargain, a sparrow which had no human value whatever, a sparrow which was given away as completely worthless. Further, it may well be that in Aramaic Jesus did not speak of the sparrow *falling* on the ground, as if in death, but *lighting* on the ground, as if to say that the sparrow does not even alight and hop on the ground but God sees and knows it.

Here is the unbelievably detailed love of God. Just as a shepherd cannot rest while one sheep of a flock is lost, just as a woman cannot be content when one of her ten coins cannot be found, just as a father cannot be content while there is one vacant place in the family circle (Luke 15), so God cannot rest until the last one of his children return to him.

God loves each one of us, in Augustine's great phrase, as if there was only one of us to love.

(v) This leads us directly to three other great ideas in the Christian conception of God. God, as the Christian knows him, is the *giving* God. In almost every other religion, if not in all other religions, the great characteristic of God is that God demands gifts from men. He demands this or that sacrifice; man cannot come into his presence without this or that gift. God is a demanding God and man must produce the gifts and offerings and sacrifices which God insists upon. But the most characteristic thing that was ever said about the Christian God is that 'God so loved the world that he *gave*' (John 3.16).

God, as the Christian knows him, is far more eager to give than to receive, precisely because it is the characteristic of love that it always wants to give. The only thing which the God who is love desires from the men he loves is their love in return. As the child's hymn has it:

> What can I give him,
> Poor as I am?
> If I were a shepherd,
> I would bring a lamb;
> If I were a wise man,
> I would do my part;
> Yet what can I give him –
> Give him my heart.

(vi) Further, God, as the Christian knows him, is the *forgiving* God. It is natural to think of the holy God as the condemning God. It is natural to think of God as Judge, and to think of man as under the condemnation of God.

It has been said that all Greek tragedy is written on the one text – 'The doer shall suffer.' Deep at the heart of it there is the idea of Nemesis. When a man does a wrong thing, immediately Nemesis, fate, retribution is at his heels, and the pursuit will never stop until the man has paid in suffering for the thing that he has done, even if he has done it unwittingly and in ignorance. The typical text of the Old Testament is: 'The soul that sins shall die' (Ezekiel 18.4). But the God and Father whom Jesus revealed to men is far more eager to forgive than he is to condemn. The Christian knows that he is bound to say, 'Nothing in my hand I bring', and yet that, if he brings a penitent and contrite heart, God will forgive. Any natural human parent would far rather forgive than condemn his child, and God is like that.

(vii) Still further, God, as the Christian knows him, is the *seeking* God. The great liberal Jewish scholar C. G. Montefiore held strongly that this is the one absolutely new thing which Jesus came to say. The idea of a

God who will *invite* the sinner back is not new; the idea of a God who will *welcome* back the penitent sinner is not new; but the idea of a God who will go and seek for the sinner, and who wants men to do the same, is something completely new. Montefiore would find the very centre and soul and essence of the Christian Gospel in Luke 15.1–10, in the story of the shepherd searching for the lost sheep and the woman searching for the lost coin. He writes: 'Jesus sought to bring back into glad communion with God those whom sin, whether "moral" or "ceremonial", had driven away. For him sinners (at least certain types of sinners) were the subject not of condemnation or disdain, but of pity. He did not avoid sinners, he sought them out. They were still children of God. This was a new and sublime contribution to the development of religion and morality…. To deny the greatness and originality of Jesus in this connection, to deny that he opened a new chapter in men's attitude to sin and sinners is, I think, to beat the head against the wall.' 'The virtues of repentance are gloriously praised in the Rabbinical literature, but this direct search for, and appeal to, the sinner are new and moving notes of high import and significance.'

It is not so very difficult to think of a God who will forgive the sinner who comes humbly and penitently back to him on his hands and knees; but no man outside Christianity had ever thought of a God who would deliberately go out and seek for the sinner until he found him and brought him home.

(viii) All this goes to show that in Christianity there is established a quite new relationship between God and man. The relationships of king and subject, master and slave, judge and criminal, immortal and mortal, holy one and sinner, are all obvious and natural. All these relationships are in one way or another based on a relationship whose essence is law. The idea is that God lays down his law; man obeys or disobeys, accepts or rejects; and is accordingly found innocent or guilty. What Christianity does is to remove the fear and the distance in the relationship between man and God, and establish first and foremost a relationship of love, the relationship of father and son.

(ix) This means that there has entered into life a quite new conception of the meaning of sin. It certainly does not make sin any less serious, but it brings it into a different realm of thought. In this relationship sin is no longer a breach of law; sin is a breaking of God's heart; for sin ceases to be simply sin against law and becomes sin against love.

It is precisely that fact which makes sin so serious. It is always perfectly possible to make satisfaction for a sin against law. When the penalty which the law inflicts has been paid, when the sentence has been served, then the law has no more claim upon a man. But a sin against love is a very different thing. Law's claim is always limited; love's claim is always unlimited. A man might well be able to meet the stern severity in the eyes of a judge without flinching, when he could not meet the sorrow and the pain in the eyes of someone whose heart he had broken.

The fact that our relationship with God is not one of law but one of love makes our obligation to God infinitely greater and infinitely more binding, and makes sin not less but far more serious.

But to the word Father, the creed adds one other word, the word *Almighty*. I believe in God, the Father Almighty. Herein three things are conserved.

(i) The word Almighty saves us from ever sentimentalizing the relationship of God to men. God is love, but nonetheless God is the Almighty, infinite in might, majesty and power.

(ii) Yet it still remains true that this might and majesty of God are at all times motivated and directed and used in love. Might and power are always neutral things; the important thing is always the spirit in which they are used and by which they are directed. Here we become sure that the might and the power of God will never be used in any other way than in love for man.

(iii) But there is something even more important. One of the supreme tragedies of human love is frustration – and it is a tragedy which is common. We may love a person and we may yet be quite unable to help that person; we may not have the power or the resources or the ability to do so. Or, we may be quite unable to influence that person in the way he ought to go, and we may have to stand by and see him making ruin and shipwreck of life. But the very fact that the love of God is backed by the power of God is the guarantee that ultimately and in the end the love of God cannot be frustrated. It can be hindered; it can be delayed; it can be grieved; it can be disappointed, but in the end it cannot be defeated, for we must remember that the infinite power of God has not only infinite might, but it has also infinite time, all eternity, in which to work.

When we say that we believe in God the Father Almighty we say that we believe in a God whose infinite might is ever used in his undefeatable love, and whose undefeatable love is ever backed by his infinite might. We therefore believe in a God whose love for us can never come to an end, and whose love for us some time in time or eternity will triumphantly work out its purposes.

CHAPTER FOUR

Maker of Heaven and Earth

The Bible unhesitatingly and unequivocally lays down its belief in God the Creator. The very first words of the Bible are: 'In the beginning God created the heavens and the earth' (Genesis 1.1). Isaiah (42.5) describes the Lord as the one,

> who created the heavens and stretched them out,
> who spread forth the earth and what comes from it,
> who gives breath to the people upon it
> and spirit to those who walk in it.

Isaiah (45.12) hears God say:

> I made the earth,
>   and created man upon it;
> it was my hands that stretched out the heavens,
>   and I commanded all their host.

To the New Testament seer God is the God 'who created heaven and what is in it, the earth and what is in it, and the sea and what is in it' (Revelation 10.6). The belief in God the Creator is an essential part of biblical teaching in both the Old and the New Testaments, as it is an essential part of the creed.

Man's interest in the question of creation is natural and inevitable. It is so for two reasons.

(i) Man is always interested in his own beginnings. Instinctively he knows that to understand himself he has to understand the source and the origin from which he came, as well as the goal and end to which he goes.

(ii) But, even more, man cannot help seeking to understand, and to be sure of, the nature of the universe in which he lives. Lessing once said that if he had one question to ask the Sphinx, that one question would be: 'Is this a friendly universe?' Dick Sheppard somewhere told of an experience of his own. He was out one night on the Downs in the south of England. It was a night of thick, velvety darkness that you could almost feel. He became, he said, suddenly conscious of what he could only call the Spirit of the Universe around him and about him. Somehow his thoughts and memories went back to a time during the war when he was lying in no man's land between the lines in the dark and, when he heard footsteps approaching without being able to see who it was, was consumed with the desire to shout the question: 'Friend or foe?' So that night he wanted to shout out to the Spirit of the Universe the question: 'Friend or foe?'

Thomas Hardy finished his novel which tells of the troubled and the tortured life of Tess with the words: 'The President of the Immortals had finished his sport with Tess.' John Greenleaf Whittier wrote certain stanzas:

> Here in the maddening maze of things,
>   When tossed by storm and flood,
> To one fixed ground my spirit clings:
>   I know that God is good.
> And so beside the silent sea
>   I wait the muffled oar;
> No harm from him can come to me
>   On ocean or on shore.
> I know not where his islands lift
>   Their fronded palms in air;
> I only know I cannot drift
>   Beyond his love and care.

Which kind of world do we believe in? A world where some half-amused President of the Immortals makes his sport with us, or a world in which there is neither any place nor any experience which is outside the love of God? The answer to that question will depend entirely on the conception we have of the creating power which made and sustains this world. So the question of creation is not simply a cosmological speculation, but rather an essential part of that personal faith which either does, or does not, enable us to meet life and all its experiences in confidence, in hope, and in trust.

There are, broadly speaking, three ways in which the relationship of God to the world has been conceived.

(i) There is the way of *pantheism*, which holds that in some sense everything is literally God. In pantheism God *is* the world and everything that is in it. The thought of Stoicism provides an illustration of this. According to the Stoics, God is fiery spirit, far rarer and far purer than any earthly fire. The soul of a man is a spark of that divine fire which has come to dwell in a man's body, and which in the end will return to the divine fire from which it came. Part of that divine fire also became what the Stoic called depotentiated, and began to exist in a form with a much lower tension. When it became depotentiated, it became by descending stages vapour, water, and even stone and earth. In other words, everything in the world, from the soul of man to the sticks and stones of the ground, is in some sense God, and is made out of the being of God.

According to this view we have the picture of a God-filled man living in a God-filled world. This view can be spiritualized into the general idea of a world pervaded with God. Wordsworth, in 'Tintern Abbey', describes how he finds in all of nature,

> A presence that disturbs me with the joy
> Of elevated thoughts; a sense sublime
> Of something far more deeply interfused,
> Whose dwelling is the light of setting suns,
> And the round ocean and the living air,
> And the blue sky and in the mind of man.

But the real teaching of pantheism is rather that the world *is* God. In a sense pantheism shuts God up in his own world. Pantheism identifies the universe and God.

(ii) There is the way of *deism*, which removes God from the world altogether. In deism God is entirely transcendent; he is above, beyond and outside the world. This is of course in reality an overstressing of a very real truth. God is *holy*; and the basic meaning of both the Greek (*hagios*) and the Hebrew (*kadosh*) word for *holy*, is separate, other, different from. God, as a modern theologian put it, is *the wholly Other*. We can see this development in Jewish thought within the Bible itself. In the Old Testament story Moses receives the tables of the Law directly and personally from the hands of God; by New Testament times it has come to be thought that there never could be any such direct contact between God and man, between God and the world, and the Law is handed over to man through the intermediate agency of angels (Galatians 3.19; Acts 7.38). We see this development in the Greek idea of divinity. In later Greek thought there had emerged between man and God a whole host of lesser spiritual beings called *daimons*, through whom God administered the universe, as it were, and who were in charge of the forces of nature, because, as Plutarch said, it did little honour to God to involve him in the things and the affairs of the world.

(iii) There is also the way of *theism*, which thinks of God as being both involved in the world, and yet above and beyond the world. To put it in technical language, it thinks of God as being at one and the same time immanent and transcendent, as being at once in the world and beyond the world, at one and the same time sharing life and directing life. This is the Christian view of the relationship of God and the world. The Christian believes that God is neither contained in the world nor divorced from that world, but that God is at one and the same time in the world and beyond the world.

Having looked at the relationship between God and the world, the first question which rises in the mind is *Who made the world?* As we have seen, the Bible lays great stress upon the fact that God is the Creator of heaven and earth. In the New Testament there is a strong line of thought which connects not only the Father but also the Son with creation. Speaking of the eternal Word, who in Jesus became flesh, the John of the Fourth Gospel writes: 'All things were made through him, and without him was not anything made that was made' (John 1.3). Paul, writing to the Colossians, says of the Son: 'In him all things were created, in heaven and on earth, visible and invisible, whether thrones or dominions or principalities or authorities – all things were created through him and for him' (Colossians 1.16). The writer to the Hebrews, speaking of God, speaks of 'a Son ... through whom also he created the world' (Hebrews 1.2).

The form in which the Church's faith is stated has always been at least to some extent dependent on the background of thought and life against which it was being stated. It is to counteract certain errors that the Church has stressed certain truths; and the Christian doctrine of creation, especially in the New Testament, emerged as a corrective and counterblast to a certain widespread line of thought.

This line of thought goes by the general name of Gnosticism. Gnosticism was founded on a thorough-going and ultimate dualism. It believed that in the beginning there was matter and spirit. Confronted with the sin and the sorrow and the suffering of the world, Gnosticism laid the blame fairly and squarely on matter. If there existed nothing but spirit, then everything would be good; it is in matter that the essential fault lies. But out of this matter the world is made, and since it is essentially bad stuff, the true God who is altogether pure spirit could not defile and pollute himself by working with it. So in order to achieve creation there came from God a series of aeons or emanations, each one in the descending series a little more distant from God. As the aeons grew more distant from God, they also grew more ignorant of God. As the series went on, the aeons became not only ignorant of God, but also hostile to God; and so at the end of the series there emerged an aeon utterly ignorant of God, utterly hostile to God, so distant from God that it could touch and handle evil matter; and it was by that aeon that the world was created. Hence come the sin and the sorrow and the suffering and the evil of the world.

In New Testament times this was a widespread belief, which left men living in an evil world, shut up in an evil body. The answer of Christian belief was that this was not the case but that creation was the direct work of the one true and only God. And when Christian thought connects the Son with the work of creation it means that the fatherly love and care which we see in Jesus Christ, the mind of God displayed in the words and actions of Jesus Christ, is also the power which created this world. It means that the God of creation and the God of redemption are one and the same God.

And, if this is so, it means that we live in what is ultimately and essentially a friendly universe. However hurting life may be and can be, it is not intended to break us but to make us; at the heart of the world there is love.

The second question which rises in the mind is *Why did God make the world?* The world with its disobedience, its rebellion and its ingratitude must have brought infinite sorrow to the heart of God. Why then should God create the world and mankind apparently only to bring himself pain?

That is clearly a question to which we cannot return an easy and a confident answer, for to answer it would involve reading the mystery of the mind of God. But we do have one line to go upon. The essence and the centre of the Christian conception of God is that God is love. Love must love, and furthermore love can never be complete and satisfied until it is loved. We may therefore dare to say that for God creation is a necessity. In his very being he needs persons whom he can love and who will love him. A God of love could not do anything other than create, so that his own love might go out to his creation, and so that the love of his creation might return in answering love to him.

This is what the poet James Welldon Johnson so beautifully expressed in his poem 'The Creation'. The poem begins:

> God stepped out on space,
> And He looked around and said:
> 'I'm lonely –
> I'll make me a world.'

So God made everything, and of everything he was able to say: *'That's good!'* But there was still something missing.

> Then God walked around,
> And God looked around
> On all that He had made.
> He looked at His sun,
> And He looked at His moon,
> And He looked at His little stars;
> He looked on His world
> With all its living things,
> And God said, 'I'm lonely still.'
> Then God sat down –
> On the side of a hill where He could think;
> By a deep, wide river He sat down;
> With His head in His hands,
> God thought and thought,
> Till He thought, 'I'll make me a man!'

A child might have written that, and a child might understand that; but in it it may well be that there is the whole Christian doctrine of creation. God being love created the world and all that is in it in order to have someone to love and someone to love him. Creation is a necessity of the love of God.

The third question which rises in the mind is *How did God create the world?* For many years the first two chapters of Genesis were storm centres of argument. We have come to see that these chapters are poetry and not science, that they are religious symbolism and not cut-and-dried history. They do not tell us anything of God's *method* of creation; they do lay down the one supreme *fact* that life came into being through the power of, and by the will of, God. If we ask any intelligent child to read these chapters and then sum up in one sentence what they teach, he will certainly answer: 'God made the world.' That is the answer; they tell in deathless imagery of the creating power of God, but they do not tell of the scientific method which God used.

In point of fact modern science has clothed the conception of creation with a new wonder. The older story seemed to teach that God created a perfect world, and then that the world fell and degenerated and lost its pristine beauty and goodness. The story as we now know it tells us that life began from the smallest beginnings and climbed upwards and onwards until it is what it is today. In the older story man received things, as it were, ready-made. As we now know the story, man received, not a ready-made world, but a series of infinite potentialities which he can work out or fail to work out, as he puts himself in line with, or refuses to put himself in line with, the will of God. The most tremendous thing that man's increasing knowledge has taught him is that God in his love has given man a share in the work of creation; God did not give men things all complete but made men partners in the work of making a world. So far from destroying belief in God's creating power, the idea of an evolutionary process has lent a glory to the task of creation which it never had before, for it means that God has made man his fellow-worker in the making of a world. As William Herbert Carruth wrote:

> A fire-mist and a planet –
>   A crystal and a cell,
> A jelly-fish and a saurian,
>   And caves where the cave-men dwell;

> Then a sense of law and beauty
>> And a face turned from the clod, –
> Some call it Evolution,
>> And others call it God.

Whatever the method of creation, God remains the Creator without whom life is impossible.

CHAPTER FIVE

And in Jesus Christ, His only Son,
our Lord

With this article of the creed, belief enters the realm of history and of time. When we are thinking of God we are moving in the timeless spheres of eternity; but when we think of Jesus, we think of these historic events which are the basis and foundation of the Christian faith. 'I believe in Jesus Christ,' the creed says, 'God's only Son, our Lord.' In that simple statement there are no fewer than four affirmations of faith about Jesus; or, to put it a little differently, we see Jesus in four different relationships.

First of all, *he is called Jesus*. In this name we see Jesus in relation to the fulness of his manhood. To us Jesus is a sacred name; we would not think of calling one of our children by it. But in the time of Jesus it was one of the commonest of all names, and is in fact the Greek form of the Hebrew name Joshua. At least five Jewish High Priests were called Jesus, and in the works of the Jewish historian Josephus there appear about twenty people called Jesus, ten of them contemporary with our Lord. In the Apocrypha we find the book of Jesus the son of Sirach, the book otherwise known as Ecciesiasticus. In the New Testament itself we find Jesus Justus, and we find the sorcerer of Paphos called Bar-Jesus (Colossians 4.11; Acts 13.6). So the very name marks out Jesus from the start as a man among men. It is significant that the description of our Lord begins with his human name, thereby asserting right at the beginning his perfect and complete manhood.

Secondly, *he is called Christ*. In this name we see the relationship of Jesus to a people's history. The word Christ is the same word as the word Messiah. Christ is the Greek, and Messiah is the Hebrew for *anointed*.

The Messiah is the central figure in all Jewish thought. The Jews never forgot that they were the chosen people and the covenant people, and they were convinced that some day their earthly place would befit their divine destiny and that God would make it clear to all men and nations that the Jews were his people. The agent of that demonstration was to be the Messiah. The Messiah was the Anointed King of God who would bring in the reign of God, and in whom the history of God's people would be consummated and all God's promises fulfilled.

Here then we have the picture of Jesus as the one in whom history finds its consummation, the one for whom throughout all preceding time the world had been prepared, the one who is in himself the supreme event in history, the one in whom God himself enters the arena of human history for the sake of men.

This is why we divide all history by the birth of Jesus. Time before that is BC, *before Christ;* time after that is AD, *in the year of our Lord.* The name Christ marks Jesus as the climax, not only of a people's, but also of a world's history.

Thirdly, *he is called God's only Son.* Here we see Jesus in his relationship to God. It is here that the matter becomes difficult. That which is involved in the name Jesus is easy enough to understand, as is that which is involved in the name or the title Christ. But now we come on something which it must be the for ever unfinished task of the thinkers of the Church to define – the relationship of Jesus to God.

We may start with one perfectly definite and indisputable fact. The creed does not say that Jesus is God's Son; it says that he is God's *only* Son. We can therefore begin by saying that *the relationship between Jesus and God is unique.* There is no one who shares it or can share it; he is God's *only* Son. What then can we go on to say of the meaning of this title of Jesus, the Son of God?

(i) If we were to take into account nothing more than linguistic possibility, we could say that this means that Jesus was *God-like.* The Hebrew language is not strong in adjectives and often as a substitute for an adjective it will use the phrase *son of* plus an abstract noun. Barnabas is a son of consolation, that is to say, he is a consoling man. James and John are sons of thunder, that is to say, they are thunderous characters. So the Beatitude (Matthew 5.9) runs: 'Blessed are the peacemakers, for they shall be called the sons of God' (RSV; the AV 'children of God' is less accurate). This would mean: 'Blessed are the peacemakers, for they are God-like in character', or 'because they are doing a God-like work'.

In Matthew (27.54) and in Mark (15.39) the verdict on Jesus of the Roman centurion who was in charge of the crucifixion was: 'Truly this was a son of God' (RSV; the AV 'the Son of God' is a mis-translation). In Luke (23.47) the verdict is: 'Certainly this man was innocent.' In this use a son of God means a good and innocent man.

Is this then what we are to understand by the phrase the son of God? Are we to take it to mean that Jesus was a good man, a God-like character? One word of the creed forbids that interpretation, the word *only*. It would be possible to say that many men have been God-like in their sacrifice and courage and love and fidelity; but Jesus is not one of many; he is unique. He is not *a son* of God; he is *the Son* of God.

(ii) There is abundant evidence that Son of God was one of the titles by which the Jews called the Messiah. In 2 Esdras this is often the case: 'My Son the Messiah shall be revealed.' 'My Son shall reprove the nations for their ungodliness.' 'No one upon earth can see my Son but in the power of his day' (2 Esdras 7.28, 29; 13.37; 13.52). This even emerges in the New Testament. In Matthew (16.16) Peter's confession of Jesus is: 'You are the Messiah, the Son of the living God' (NEB). When Nathanael was confronted with Jesus, his reaction was to say: 'Rabbi, you are the Son of God! You are the King of Israel!' (John 1.49).

So it is true enough to say that Jesus was the Messiah, but once again this interpretation does not do justice to the *only*. It does not sufficiently mark out the uniqueness of Jesus which lies in this word. What then are we to say?

Before we go on to study the meaning of Son of God in full detail, it is worth noting two quite general truths contained in this description of Jesus.

(i) To call Jesus God's Son is to state that Jesus' relationship with God is not a relationship which is in any sense *achieved*, but one that is completely *personal*. A man cannot *become* a son of his father; he *is* a son. It lays down that Jesus' relationship to God is not *accidental* but *essential*. It is not an *acquired* thing; it is a thing which is his by *his very being*. It establishes that Jesus' relationship with God is not *alterable* but *permanent*. Sonship is not a thing which can ever be lost; humanly speaking a father and son may drift apart, but nonetheless they remain father and son.

(ii) To call Jesus God's Son is to establish, as no other title can do, the double, and almost paradoxical nature of his relationship to God.

In sonship there is at one and the same time *equality* and *subordination*. A son is in a very different relationship to his father from a slave, or even a servant; and yet with all the equality a certain subjection and subordination remain. In sonship there is at one and the same time *identity* and *difference*. No one can be closer to a father than a son; they can be of one mind and one heart; and yet they remain separate persons. The word son sums up in itself a double relationship, a two-sided relationship, which can be expressed through no other word.

We must now go on to see if we can find out in a little more detail what it means to call Jesus the only Son of God.

It is quite true to say that in one sense all men are the sons of God; but it is clear that Jesus used this term of himself, and made this claim for himself, in a quite special way. He himself prays to God as 'My Father', while he teaches men to pray 'Our Father'. The ordinary man's relationship to God is something which he shares with other ordinary men; the relationship of Jesus to God is something which is special and peculiar to himself and which no one else shares. Further, it is equally clear that the Jewish authorities recognized that Jesus did claim a special relationship with God. The Jews were enraged that Jesus called God his Father, for, they said, he thereby made himself equal with God (John 5.18). That Jesus thought of himself in a special relationship to God cannot really be disputed, and this relationship becomes most clear in the Fourth Gospel.

(i) First and foremost, the bond between the Father and the Son is the bond of love. 'The Father loves the Son' (John 5.20; 10.17; 12.49; 15.9).

(ii) The Father has set his seal on the Son. 'On him has God the Father set his seal' (John 6.27). In the ancient world the seal had a very special place. Wine was sealed; consignments of all kinds of goods were sealed; even animals which were sold were sealed. The seal was the sign of ownership; it guaranteed the source from which the thing offered had come, and in so doing it guaranteed its genuineness and its quality. To say that the Father set his seal on the Son is to say that the Father guarantees that the Son comes from him, and that the Son has in himself, and for other people, that very life which comes from God and which is God's.

(iii) The Fourth Gospel sets out a whole series of privileges which belong to the Son because he is the Son.

- The Son has special *knowledge* of the Father. The Son knows the Father as the Father knows the Son (John 10.15). Jesus knows God in a way in which no one else has ever known God, and that knowledge is not intellectual or theoretical or philosophic knowledge; it is personal knowledge. The Son does not only *know about* the Father; he *personally knows* the Father with what we can only call an intimate, face-to-face, personal knowledge.

- To the Son the Father has given a *special revelation* of his purposes, his plans, his actions, and his truth. The Father shows the Son what he is doing (John 5.20); the Father taught the Son (John 8.28); what the Son says is what he has already heard the Father say (John 8.38; 12.50). The Father has revealed his mind and heart to the Son as they have been revealed to no one else.

- To the Son the Father has given *his own life*, and he has made the Son *the agent by which that life comes to men*. The Son like the Father has life in himself (John 5.26). It is the Father's will that it is those who see the Son and who believe in him who should have eternal life (John 3.16). No one comes to the Father in any other way than by the Son (John 14.6). The Son is the way of entry to the presence of the Father and to the life of the Father.

- To the Son the Father has committed the function of judgement. 'The Father judges no man but has given all judgement to the Son' (John 5.22). The real meaning of this is that to be confronted with the Son is in itself a judgement; a man in his reaction to Jesus Christ expresses a judgement on himself. If he feels the attraction of Jesus Christ, if his heart runs out in love to him, if in the presence of Jesus Christ he feels himself in the presence of God, then he is in the right way. If in the presence of Jesus Christ he is left cold, if he is irritated and annoyed by the claim of Jesus Christ, if in his heart of hearts he would like nothing so much as to eliminate this troublesome Jesus, then he has already expressed on himself a judgement of condemnation.

- The privileges of the Son are summed up in the statement that what the Father has is the Son's (John 16.15). So close to the Father is the Son, and so does the Father love and trust the Son, that the Father's possessions belong to the Son as by right.

(iv) Just as the Son has this whole series of privileges in relation to the Father, so he had also a whole series of tasks and responsibilities.

– The thing that is said oftenest of all about the Son in the Fourth Gospel is that he is *sent* (John 6.44; 6.57; 8.16; 8.18; 14.24; 20.21). It is as if the Son is at the disposal of the Father to be sent out, and commissioned for, any task which the Father wishes to assign to him. It is true that the Father glorifies the Son (John 8.54), but the glory is not the glory of honour and of prestige, but the glory of serving God in the world, and bringing God to men and men to God. The glory of the Son is the glory of a servant.

– Another way to put this is to say that the whole life of the Son is lived in willing *obedience* to the commands and the will of the Father. It might well be said that the central and basic saying of the Son in the Fourth Gospel is: 'My food is to do the will of him who sent me, and to accomplish his work' (John 4.34). When Jesus thinks of the death that lies ahead of him he says: 'This charge have I received from my Father' (John 10.18). He would have his followers keep his commandments as he has kept his Father's commandments (John 15.10).

(v) This leads us to the characteristic paradox of the Father–Son relationship in the Fourth Gospel.

– There is a sense in which there is identity and equality between Father and Son, and it is just there that many of the greatest sayings in the Gospel occur. Again and again it is said that the Son is in the Father and the Father is in the Son (John 10.38; 14.10, 20; 17.21). To see the Son is to see the Father. 'He who has seen me has seen the Father' (John 14.9). The Son has come from the Father and goes to the Father (John 16.28). No one has seen the Father except the Son (John 6.46). This arm of the paradox culminates in the saying: 'I and the Father are one' (John 10.30).

– There is a sense in which the Son is completely subordinate to the Father. The Son is sent, as we have already seen; the Son does the Father's will, and the doing of that will is the very centre and soul of the Son's life. The Son prays to the Father as to the one who alone can give him what he needs to face the task that has been given to him. This arm of the paradox culminates in the saying: 'The Father is greater than I' (John 14.28).

(vi) So we come to the final question – Wherein does this unity between the Father and the Son lie? In thinking of a question like this we must begin by remembering that we cannot finally answer it; all we can do is to argue from the known to the unknown, always remembering that there remains a mystery which is not for our solution.

Jesus said: 'I and the Father are one' (John 10.30). But Jesus also prayed of his followers 'that they may be one even as we are one' (John 17.22). Now the basis of the unity which should exist between Christian and Christian is love, for love is the mark of all true discipleship (John 3.34–5). Therefore the basis of the unity between Father and Son is not a matter of metaphysics and abstractions; it is in the last analysis a personal relationship begotten by, based on, and maintained in, perfect love.

Jesus Christ is the Son of God because he is the love of God incarnated in a human person, and because between him and God there is that perfect bond of love which is at one and the same time the bond of perfect unity and the dynamic of perfect obedience.

Finally, in the word *Lord*, the creed lays down the relationship of Jesus to us.

The title Lord became the Church's most universal title for Jesus. Jesus is called by that name almost six hundred times in the New Testament. In Greek the word is *kurios*, and *kurios* expresses four different but closely related things.

(i) *Kurios*, Lord, expresses *absolute ownership*. It describes the owner of a vineyard (Matthew 21.40), the owner of a colt (Luke 19.33). It expresses the kind of ownership which gives a man the absolute right to do as he likes with that which he possesses.

So then the Christian belongs to Christ, and Christ has a right to do with him as he likes. Even the great heathen thinkers conceived of God as having this absolute claim upon them. Epictetus said to God, as he knew him: 'Do with me henceforth as thou wilt. I am of one mind with thee, I am thine. I decline nothing that seems good to thee. Send me whither thou wilt. Clothe me as thou wilt. Wilt thou that I take office or live a private life, remain at home or go into exile, be poor or rich, I will defend thy purpose with me in respect of all these.'

Even so the Christian knows that he is not his own because he has been bought with a price (1 Corinthians 6.19–20). When Paul used that phrase he had in his mind a custom very common in the Greek world, the custom known as sacred manumission. There was one way in which a slave could purchase his freedom. In Greek society the slave had some little time of his own. In it he could work and earn a few pence. Over many years, perhaps over half a life-time and more, he could take these savings and deposit them in the temple of some god. When in the end he had amassed his purchase price he took his master to the temple, the money was paid over, and the slave became the property of the god, and therefore free of all men. The god had bought him for his own. So, as the Christian sees it, Jesus Christ has paid the price on the Cross for his freedom and his redemption and his emancipation from sin; and therefore the Christian becomes the property of Jesus Christ. And all this not because of an ineluctable force, but because of an illimitable love.

(ii) *Kurios*, Lord, expresses *absolute mastery. Kurios* is the word for master as opposed to slave. It is the word which describes the one who has the right to exercise absolute control and to demand absolute obedience. 'No man can serve two masters,' Jesus said (Matthew 6.24).

Looked at from this point of view, a Christian is quite simply a man who can never again do what he likes; he is a man who must always do what Jesus Christ likes. The Christian is a man who knows that he has received his own will only that with it be may accept the will of his Lord for him. In this too the greatest of the heathen thinkers have arrived at the same attitude. 'Merge my ego in thy will,' is the prayer of the Indian mystic Ramakrishna.

But once again this obedience comes from a special source. Of course, Jesus has all wisdom. Of course, Jesus has all power. But our obedience to him springs neither from his wisdom nor his power, but from his love.

It is told that once in the days before the ending of slavery, Lincoln bought a slave girl with the sole purpose of giving her her freedom. She did not realize why he was buying her; she thought that it was simply another transaction in which she was involved as a thing. So he paid the price for her; and then he handed her her papers of freedom. She did not even understand. 'You are free,' he said to her gently. 'Free?' she said. 'Can I go wherever I want to go now?' 'Indeed you can,' he said. 'Then,' she said, 'if I am free to go anywhere I will stay with you and serve you until I die.' Legally she was free; but love and gratitude had bound her in a new and willing service.

The absolute mastery of Jesus Christ is the inevitable consequence of his absolute love. The absolute obedience which we are bound to give him is the response of the heart to the love of him who loved us and gave himself for us.

(iii) *Kurios,* Lord, expresses *absolute royalty. Kurios* is the word of imperial power. By the end of the first century it had become the normal title of the reigning Roman Emperor. It was the word in which the highest power the world knew was summed up.

Kurios is the word which tells us of the victor Christ. There is a real sense in which the life of Jesus was a series of battles and a series of victories. In the beginning he fought the tempter and defeated him. All through his ministry he was fighting the demons and expelling them. In the end he fought the opposition, the hatred, the bitterness, the sin of man, and even death itself and conquered them all. It is the Resurrection, the last and final victory, beyond which victory cannot go, which above all gives Jesus the absolute right to the title of imperial power.

In the latter half of the fourth century AD the Roman Emperor Julian tried to put the clock back; he tried to destroy Christianity, to rebuild the ancient temples, to revive the ancient worship, and to bring back the ancient gods. For a time it looked serious for the Christian Church; but in a campaign in Persia Julian was fatally wounded in battle. The historians tell how, as he was dying, he took a handful of his own blood from his wound and flung it into the air, and said: 'Thou hast conquered, O Galilaean.' As the dramatist made him say: 'To shoulder Christ from out the topmost niche of fame was not for me.' In the end Christ is the victorious Christ, and those who seek to destroy him end only by destroying themselves.

It is precisely this that puts the iron into Christianity. It is possible so to speak of the love of Christ as to sentimentalize the whole concept. But in addition to love there is royalty. As it has been put: 'Jesus did not say discuss me; he said follow me.' We do not make terms with Christ; we surrender to Christ. We do not compromise with Christ; we submit to Christ. Christianity does not mean being interested in Jesus Christ; it means taking the same oath as princes take to the king or the queen in a coronation ceremony and saying, 'I am your liege man of life and limb, and faith and truth will I bear to you against all manner of folk. So help me God.' The very word *sacrament* comes from the Latin word *sacramentum* which means a soldier's oath of loyalty. The Christian is the man who has sworn loyalty and who keeps loyalty to Christ the King.

(iv) *Kurios*, Lord, expresses *absolute deity*. The Septuagint is the Greek translation of the Hebrew Old Testament. By the time of Jesus it was used by Jews all over the world, because many of them had forgotten their original Hebrew; and in it the word *kurios* is consistently used as a translation of Jahweh, the name of God. To call Jesus Lord is to say that human categories are too small to contain him, and to affirm our faith that nothing less will do than to say that God was in Christ (2 Corinthians 5.19). It is to affirm that we believe that in Jesus Christ we are in the presence of God, that through him alone we fully know God, and in him alone we can dare to approach God.

To call Jesus Lord is to affirm that he is our *absolute owner*, and to confess that we must give him our *absolute obedience*. To call Jesus Lord is to affirm that he is our *absolute master*, and to confess that we must give him *absolute submission*. To call Jesus Lord is to affirm that he is our *absolute king,* and to confess that we must give him *absolute loyalty*. To call Jesus Lord is to affirm his *absolute deity*, and to confess that we must give him *absolute reverence.*

I believe in Jesus Christ, God's only Son, our Lord – here is laid down Jesus' relation to manhood, Jesus' relation to the history which led up to his coming, Jesus' relation to God and Jesus' relation to ourselves. He is fully human, a man among men; he is the consummation of history and the supreme event; he is the Son of God in a unique relation with the Father, a relation shared by no one else; he is the supreme Lord and Master of life, to whom we must render our obedience, our submission, our loyalty and our reverence. There is no clause in the creed which is nearer to being a summary of the Christian faith than this.

CHAPTER SIX

Who was Conceived by the Holy Ghost, born of The Virgin Mary

Up to this point the affirmations of the Apostles' Creed find general agreement and little controversy; but this item of the creed reveals wide differences between various schools of thought and attitudes of belief.

With the first part of this statement, with the belief that the Holy Spirit was specially present at, and operative in, the birth of Jesus Christ, almost all Christian thinkers would agree; but on the matter of the Virgin Birth belief is much divided.

There are those who feel that the Virgin Birth must remain an unalterable and essential element in Christian belief. Between 1909 and 1915 there appeared a series of twelve small volumes entitled *The Fundamentals*. It is indeed with that name that the word *fundamentalism* is connected. These volumes sought to expound and support the 'fundamental' Christian doctrines, which, it was claimed, are essential for evangelical Christianity. These doctrines include: the inspiration and infallibility of Holy Scripture; the personal deity of Jesus Christ, and the Virgin Birth as a witness to it; the substitutionary atonement; the physical resurrection of Christ; and his coming personal return.

There have been others who have felt that on historical grounds the belief in the Virgin Birth rests on no sure foundation, and that on doctrinal grounds it actually makes belief in the incarnation in the fullest sense of the term impossible.

Between these two extremes of belief there are many who hold that belief in the Virgin Birth is not essential to Christian faith. These people are not prepared to argue strongly on one side or the other. It seems fair to say that there are today a considerable number of Churches in which, while it may be orthodox to accept the doctrine of the Virgin Birth, it is certainly not heresy to reject it.

Two conclusions follow from this. First, this is just the kind of subject which it is not only legitimate, but even essential, to discuss, so that we may make up our own minds about the two different views. The second conclusion is well stated by Oliver C. Quick in his *Doctrine of the Creed*. After summarizing the arguments on both sides, he goes on to say: 'The chief result to my mind is to suggest that on the subject of the Virgin Birth we ought to be especially tender and sympathetic towards the convictions of those who differ from ourselves.'

Let us then set down the evidence on both sides of the question, and let us begin with the evidence for the Virgin Birth.

(i) The only biblical evidence is in two passages.

– There is the story in Matthew 1.18–24. In that passage the relationship between Joseph and Mary seems curiously complicated. In verse 18 Mary is *betrothed* to Joseph; in verse 19 Joseph is referred to as her *husband*; in verse 20 she is referred to as Joseph's wife; and in verse 19 Joseph is said to be minded *to divorce* her. The apparent inconsistency and confusion is due to the way in which marriage customs normally operated in Palestine. In marriage there were three stages. There was the *engagement*. This might take place when the parties were only a few months or a few years old. It was entered into by the parents or by professional matchmakers, and in due time this was ratified in *betrothal*. Betrothal lasted for one year. During betrothal the couple were known as man and wife. We read in the Jewish law of a betrothed girl whose husband-to-be had died during the year of betrothal and she is called 'a virgin who is a widow'. Betrothal was so binding that it could in fact only be broken by divorce. At the end of the year the marriage proper was carried out.

The incidents in this passage all take place during the year of betrothal. That is why Mary can at one and the same time be said to be betrothed to Joseph and to be his wife; that is why Joseph can be called her husband; and that is why he is said to be intending to divorce her. In that betrothal period Mary is found to be pregnant, and Joseph knows well that the child is not his. It is then that he is told that the child has been begotten by the act of the Holy Spirit, begotten and conceived by nothing other than the action of God.

– The other passage is in Luke 1.26–38. There the angel Gabriel comes to Mary to announce that she will have a child whose birth will be the work of the Holy Spirit.

(ii) Matthew cites the evidence of prophecy. He quotes Isaiah 7.14 in the form: 'Behold, a virgin shall conceive and bear a son, and his name shall be called Emmanuel' as a forecast and foretelling of the virgin birth of the Messiah.

(iii) Whatever else may or may not be certain, it is certain that by early in the second century the Virgin Birth had become a widely spread and widely accepted article of the Christian faith. To cite only one passage from him, Ignatius, bishop of Antioch, who was martyred early in the second century writes to the Church at Smyrna (1.1, 2) that Christians are 'fully persuaded as touching our Lord that he is truly of the race of David according to the flesh, but Son of God by the divine will and power, *truly born of a virgin*, and baptized by John that all righteousness might be fulfilled by him, truly nailed up in the flesh for our sakes under Pontius Pilate and Herod the tetrarch.'

Aristides was one of the earliest defenders of the Christian faith; he wrote his Apology about AD 140. In it he gives a summary of Christian belief: 'The Christians then reckon the beginning of their religion from Jesus Christ, who is named the Son of God most high; and it is said that God came down from heaven, and *from a Hebrew virgin* took and clad himself with flesh, and in a daughter of man there dwelt the Son of God.'

Justin Martyr wrote his defence of the Christian faith about AD 170. *The Dialogue with Trypho* is a dialogue with a Jew whom Justin is seeking to convince of the truth of the Christian faith. In it Justin describes Jesus as 'the first-born of every creature, *who became man by the Virgin*, who suffered and was crucified under Pontius Pilate by your nation, who died, who rose from the dead, and ascended into heaven' (85).

It is clear that by the early second century belief in the Virgin Birth had established itself as a widely accepted article of Christian belief.

(iv) Again it is not a matter to be questioned that the belief in the Virgin Birth found its way into the creeds. It is in the Apostles' Creed. It is in the Nicene Creed (AD 381): 'Incarnate of the Holy Ghost of the Virgin Mary.' It is in the Creed of Chalcedon (AD 451): 'Born of the Virgin Mary, the Mother of God, according to his manhood.' It is in the

Athanasian Creed, although not so definitely; 'God of the substance of
the Father; begotten before the worlds; man of the substance of his
mother, born in the world.'

(v) From the theological point of view it could be argued that if God
was to make a special entry into the world, he might well do so in a special way. Whatever else the doctrine of the Virgin Birth is concerned to
do, it is certainly concerned to conserve the fact that Jesus is the Son of
God, and that he is at one and the same time man and more than man,
that he is at one and the same time human and divine. We need not be
concerned with the matter of possibility. As Luke himself put it (1.37):
'With God nothing shall be impossible.' It is impossible to speak of
impossibilities when the action in question is the action of God.

(vi) Finally, it has to be said that the doctrine of the Virgin Birth has
been dear to Christian devotion in every branch of the Church. There
have been many in every Church who have felt that only through the
Virgin Birth can the claims of reverence and fittingness be conserved,
and who feel that anything else can hardly be contemplated.

Belief in the Virgin Birth goes far back in the Church's faith, it is lodged
firmly in the Church's creeds, and it is for many a precious article of faith
which they would never willingly give up. But there is the other side of
the question still to be looked at.

(i) There are certain curious facts about the story of the Virgin Birth
in Scripture itself. The ancient manuscripts and the ancient translations
of the New Testament often contain different readings. The Syriac translation of the New Testament was one of the very first to be made; it
must have been made as early as the second century; and in it Matthew
1.16 reads: 'Joseph, to whom was betrothed Mary the Virgin, begot
Jesus, who is called Christ.' That statement quite definitely makes Joseph
the father of Jesus, and it could certainly not have been written by anyone who took a literal view of the story of the Virgin Birth. One Latin
fifth-century manuscript, *Codex Veronensis*, entirely omits Luke 1.34:
'And Mary said to the angel, How can this be, since I have no husband?'
and moves into its place Luke 1.38: 'And Mary said, Behold, I am the
hand maid of the Lord; let it be to me according to your word.' In Luke
2.5 most of the manuscripts read that Joseph went to Bethlehem with
Mary *his betrothed* who was with child; but the Syriac Version, and four

Old Latin manuscripts, *Codex Vercellensis, Codex Colbertinus, Codex Veronensis, Codex Corbeiensis II*, all read not *betrothed* but *wife*.

This does not mean that the Virgin Birth is not a fact, but it does mean that there certainly was a strand of early Christian thought which either did not know about it, or did not accept it in the literal sense of the words.

(ii) The evidence from prophecy is very uncertain. Matthew (1.23) quotes Isaiah 7.14 as a forecast of the birth of Jesus: 'Behold, a virgin shall conceive and bear a son, and his name shall be called Emmanuel.'

This translation introduces us to one of the strangest problems of biblical translation. The word translated *virgin* is in the original Hebrew *almah*, which means simply a young woman of marriageable age, whether or not she is a virgin. It is certainly not the characteristic word for virgin; that word is *bethulah*, which Isaiah would surely have used if he had wished to underline the fact that the young woman of whom he writes was a virgin.

Where then does the word *virgin* come from? It comes from the Septuagint, the Greek Version of the Old Testament, which was made in the third century BC. In it the Greek translators for some reason which has never been explained translated the Hebrew word *almah* by the Greek word *parthenos*, which certainly does mean *virgin*. To add to this very odd problem, it must further be noted that there were three later revisions of the Septuagint, by Aquila, Theodotion and Symmachus, and all of them remove the word *parthenos* and substitute the word *neanis*, which does mean a young woman of marriageable age. The strange thing about the Matthew quotation of Isaiah 7.14 is that it is a quotation based on the Greek version of the Old Testament, and not on the Hebrew version, in which the word does not necessarily mean a virgin at all.

To disentangle this, as far as possible – and it is not fully possible – we must turn to the context in the Isaiah passage (Isaiah 7.1–17). The circumstances are as follows. In the days of King Ahaz of Judah, Judah was faced with a terrifying situation. Israel and Syria had combined against her and the future seemed disaster. Isaiah foretold that the nation would quite certainly be delivered. God offered Ahaz any sign that this salvation would come, and Ahaz replied that he would not seek to put God to the test by demanding some miraculous and phenomenal sign. Isaiah then promises him a sign, the sign that an *almah*, a young woman, would

conceive a child and that his name would be called Immanuel. The obvious question is, what does that promised sign mean? There are three
basic interpretations of this passage.

- Amongst the Jews in Old Testament times names were meaningful
  and significant. Sometimes names were, for instance, an affirmation of faith: Elijah means *Jehovah is my God.* Sometimes a name
  was an expression of gratitude: Samuel means *asked for.* A mother,
  then, would be likely to give a child a name which was an expression of her faith and gratitude. So Isaiah may be saying that proof
  of the certainty of God's deliverance of Judah from Syria and Israel
  will be given when mothers, seeing what God has done for them
  and their country, express their faith and gratitude by calling their
  children Immanuel, which means 'God with us'.
- This may be the prophecy that a child is on the way who will turn
  out to be the deliverer of his people. This is the way in which
  Jewish scholarship has usually taken this passage: as the promise to
  King Ahaz of the birth of a son who will be the deliverer of the
  hard-pressed nation, and whose birth is the proof that God is with
  us; and Jewish scholarship usually identified the promised child
  with Hezekiah the good king during whose reign Judah was in fact
  miraculously delivered.
- The third view is that the passage is prophetic in what might be
  called the long-distance sense of the term; that it is not limited to
  the immediate situation in which Isaiah lived, but foretells the coming of God's champion, the Messianic King, who would be the
  great and true deliverer of his people. Then, when the passage was
  read as it is in the Greek with the word *parthenos*, virgin, in it, it was
  taken as a definite prophecy of Jesus and of his birth.

In fact, Isaiah was almost certainly speaking of the immediate situation in Judah, and not of the distant coming of the Messiah at all, and
Christian devotion has simply annexed a prophecy which originally had
no reference to Jesus.

(iii) It is a very significant thing that both Matthew (1.1–16) and Luke
(3.23–38) give genealogies of Jesus which trace his descent *through Joseph.*
These genealogies were clearly compiled by someone who either did not
know about the Virgin Birth or who did not take it literally, for the genealogies become pointless if Joseph was not the father of Jesus.

Further, the point of the genealogies is to prove that Jesus was the Son of David; they are designed to prove his Davidic descent and therefore to further his Messianic claim. Now if Jesus was descended on the human side only from Mary, then he was not of the lineage of David, he was not the Son of David; for Mary was the kinswoman of Elizabeth the mother of John the Baptizer (Luke 1.36), and Elizabeth was one of the daughters of Aaron (Luke 1.5).

So although the genealogies do not disprove the fact of the Virgin Birth, it is evident that those who compiled them did not know of the Virgin Birth in the literal sense of the term.

(iv) The rest of the New Testament makes no reference to the Virgin Birth. There is no mention of it either in Paul's letters or in his sermons as related in Acts. It is sometimes claimed that Galatians 4.4–5 where Paul speaks of Jesus as being *born of a woman*, born under the law, is a reference to the Virgin Birth. But *born of a woman* is the standard description of an ordinary man born in the usual way. 'Man that is born of a woman is of few days and full of trouble' (Job 14.1). 'How can he that is born of woman be clean?' (Job 25.4). Certainly the phrase 'born of a woman' has nothing to do with the Virgin Birth. That Paul does not speak of the Virgin Birth is no proof that he did not know of it and believe in it; but it quite certainly is proof that he did not set either the doctrine or the belief in it in the forefront of his gospel, nor did he regard knowledge of it and belief in it as in any way essential to salvation.

There is no mention of the Virgin Birth in John, but there is a question here. In John 1.12–13 practically all manuscripts read: 'But to all who received him, who believed in his name, he gave power to become children of God; who were born, not of blood, nor of the will of the flesh, nor of the will of man, but of God.' One Old Latin manuscript, *Codex Veronensis*, reads in the last part of that saying, 'who *was* born not of blood...'. If the verb is in the singular, then the reference is to Jesus and the reference could be, and maybe is, a reference to the Virgin Birth. But it must be remembered, as we have already seen, that it is this same *Codex Veronensis* which omits Luke 1.34 and substitutes for it Luke 1.38, and which in Luke 2.5 calls Mary Joseph's *wife* instead of his *betrothed*. The uncertainty of the whole matter is well shown by the fact that the same manuscript in one place seems to go out of its way to stress the Virgin Birth and in another to deny it.

(v) The New Testament writers have a way of speaking about Jesus and of relating incidents involving him which would be very strange, if they did indeed set belief in the literal Virgin Birth in the forefront of their message.

- They freely speak of Mary and Joseph as the *parents* of Jesus (Luke 2.27; 2.41); and they speak of *the father and mother* of Jesus (Luke 2.33). It is significant that the later manuscripts, coming from a time when the Virgin Birth had become a dogma, alter *father and mother* in Luke 2.33 into *Joseph and his mother*, and *parents* in Luke 2.43 into *Joseph and his mother*. The difference may be seen in the translation of these passages in the Authorized Version and the Revised Standard Version:

Luke 2.33 AV: And Joseph and his mother marvelled at those things which were spoken of him.

       RSV: And his father and mother marvelled at what was said of him.

Luke 2.43 AV: The child Jesus tarried behind in Jerusalem; and Joseph and his mother knew not of it.

       RSV: The boy Jesus stayed behind in Jerusalem. His parents did not know it.

There is no doubt that the reading of the older manuscripts is the original reading, and that the later manuscripts have altered it in doctrinal interests.

- The Gospel-writers relate sayings in which Joseph is spoken of as the father of Jesus without any attempt to correct them, and without any hint that they are inaccurate or inadequate.

'Is not this the carpenter's son?' is the question of the people in Nazareth (Matthew 13.55). 'Is not this Joseph's son?' (Luke 4.22). 'Is not this Jesus, the son of Joseph, whose father and mother we know?' (John 6.42). John can show us Philip calling Jesus, 'Jesus of Nazareth, the son of Joseph' (John 1.45). The odd thing about these passages is that these sayings are related as if they were in fact true, and the point of them is that this man whom everyone knew was, astonishingly, also the Messiah and the Son of God.

- There are two incidents involving Mary which are difficult to understand on the assumption of a literal virgin birth. In Mark 3.21,

31–5 we find Jesus' friends, and Mary among them, coming to take him home, because in their opinion he is crazily deluded. Is it likely that Mary would have been a party to any such expedition if the birth of her son had been as physically miraculous as a literal belief in the Virgin Birth demands? When Mary and Joseph did find Jesus in the Temple after their long search for him, Mary's words are: 'Your father and I have been looking for you anxiously' (Luke 2.48). Is it likely that she would so bluntly have called Joseph the father of Jesus, and is it likely that she would have treated Jesus like an ordinary rather disobedient boy, if his birth had really and literally been such an astounding physical miracle? The action of Mary in both these passages is the action of a mother dealing with an ordinary son.

(vi) Oliver Quick in *The Doctrines of the Creed* concludes that the evidence for the Virgin Birth considered purely from the historical point of view is in fact quite inconclusive and that we must therefore base our conclusions about it, not on the grounds of historical evidence, but on the grounds of the logical considerations. In other words, does our theological view of who and what Jesus was necessitate our belief in the Virgin Birth? At first sight that seems a good criterion, but when we begin to examine it we discover that it leaves us in as much doubt as ever.

- As we have already said, if God did decide upon a special and unique entry into the arena of human history, he might well have decided that that entry had to be made in a special and a unique way. This is always an argument which must carry weight. But against it there must be set the argument that it is just as characteristic of God to use the natural and normal human processes and events for his own purposes.

- It is argued that the Virgin Birth is necessary if Jesus is to be really and truly the Son of God. But that is to interpret the word *son* in the most literal and the most physical sense, and it is to forget that sonship is something that is offered and promised to every man who accepts and believes in Jesus Christ.

- It is asked how we are to conserve the sinlessness of Jesus, if he came into the world by the natural and normal processes of human birth, and thereby inherited normal fallen human nature and the taint of sin which attaches to every man. The difficulty of that argument is that if Jesus was fully to escape the taint consequent upon involvement in human nature, then he would need to have entered the world without human parentage at all, for he could just as well have inherited that taint from his mother as from both parents. It is in fact difficult to see how this argument can hold good without proceeding from the Virgin Birth to the Immaculate Conception, and holding that Mary also came into the world in a special and unique way.

— But these are small and comparatively unimportant theological difficulties compared with the difficulty into which the doctrine of the Virgin Birth really runs. The great difficulty is its impact upon belief in the incarnation. If the Virgin Birth is a literal fact, then the conclusion is quite inescapable that Jesus came into the world in a way that is different from that in which every other man comes into the world. This means that he is different from all other men, and that we can therefore no longer hold to his full manhood and his full humanity.

If there is one thing to which all the New Testament writers hold, it is the full and complete humanity of Jesus. 'God', said Paul, 'sent his Son in the likeness of sinful flesh' (Romans 8.3), or as we might put it, with a human nature exactly like our own. Paul speaks of how the sin of one man, Adam, involved the whole human race in sin, and of how the goodness of one man, Jesus, lifted man out of the evil of human sin (Romans 5.15–17), and the plain fact is that Paul's argument collapses unless Jesus was as fully and completely identified with humanity as Adam was. The writer of the Pastoral Epistles says: 'There is one God and one mediator between God and man, the man Jesus Christ' (1 Timothy 2.5), a saying in which the full and complete humanity of Jesus is an absolute necessity. The writer to the Hebrews makes his great statement and makes it with a kind of thrill in his voice: 'He had to be made like his brethren in every respect' (Hebrews 2.17). It was Irenaeus (*Against Heresies* 3.19.6) who put this unforgettably: 'He became what we are to make us what he is.'

The supreme problem of the doctrine of the Virgin Birth is that it does quite undeniably differentiate Jesus from all men; it does leave us with an incomplete incarnation; it does mean that Jesus is not in fact completely like all other men, because it does in fact mean that Jesus came into the world by a way in which no other man ever came into the world; it leaves us with a Jesus who is half-and-between, neither fully divine nor yet fully human.

It is not irrelevant to note that this even impinges on the simple idea of Jesus as our example. If this be true, he cannot be in a full sense our example, for he entered into life with an advantage which is denied to all other men, and we cannot ask men to walk in the steps of him who was not truly and fully a man.

This difficulty will appear quite differently to different people. Broadly speaking, it will always be true to say that the sincere and the devout and the devotional Christian will usually be in danger of emphasizing the deity of Christ at the expense of his humanity. His reverence for his Lord will never allow him to forget that Jesus is divine, although it will sometimes make him underrate the fact that Jesus is truly man.

Having examined the evidence in regard to the Virgin Birth, and found it on the whole inconclusive, let us approach the matter from another angle. In interpreting any Jewish story, when that story is used for religious purposes, it is of the first importance to remember that the first question of any Jew would always be, not, 'Did this actually happen?' but, 'What does this teach?' The Jewish teachers were much more interested in finding out the eternal truth behind any story than in arguing whether or not it was literally true. Let us then apply that principle to the story of the Virgin Birth.

There can be no argument or question about what the story teaches. The story teaches that *the Holy Spirit was specially operative in the birth of Jesus*. In the narrative of both Matthew and Luke there are certain sentences which are, as it were, printed in heavy type and underlined. Before Mary and Joseph came together, Mary was found to be with child of the Holy Spirit. The word of the angel of the Lord to Joseph was: 'That which is conceived in her is of the Holy Spirit' (Matthew 1.18, 20). The word of Gabriel to Mary was: 'The Holy Spirit will come upon you, and the power of the Most High will overshadow you' (Luke 1.35). Whatever else may be doubtful, it is certain that these stories say that the Holy Spirit of God was specially and uniquely the cause of the birth of Jesus. What then does this mean?

It must be remembered that this comes long before Pentecost and before the coming of the Spirit, in the full Christian sense of the term. The Holy Spirit is being spoken of here in terms of the Jewish understanding of the work and function of the Spirit, and it is in this sense that Joseph and Mary would have understood it. In *The Holy Spirit in the Gospel Tradition* C. K. Barrett has pointed out that the Jews thought of the work of the Spirit mainly in two ways.

(i) The Holy Spirit is connected with *the work of creation*. In the Creation story the Spirit of God was moving over the face of the waters (Genesis 1.2). It has to be remembered that both in Greek (*pneuma*) and in Hebrew (*ruach*) the words for spirit, wind, and breath are all the same. 'By the word of the Lord the heavens were made, and all their host by the breath (*ruach*) of his mouth' (Psalm 33.6). 'When thou sendest forth thy Spirit (*ruach*) they are created; and thou renewest the face of the ground' (Psalm 104.30). 'The Spirit of God is in my nostrils,' says Job (27.3), describing the secret of life. 'The Spirit of God has made me, and the breath of the Almighty gives me life' (Job 33.4). In the books between the Testaments we have the same picture. 'Let all creation serve thee: for thou spakest and they were made, thou didst send forth thy Spirit and it builded them' (Judith 16.14). So then the Spirit is intimately and personally involved in the work of creation.

(ii) The Holy Spirit is connected with the *work of re-creation*. Ezekiel sees the grim picture of the valley of dry bones; he sees the bones come to life again; and then he ends the vision: 'I will put my Spirit within you, and you shall live' (Ezekiel 37.1–14). The Rabbis pictured God as saying: 'In this world my Spirit has put wisdom in you, but in the future my Spirit will make you to live again.' So the Spirit of God is the power and the person who can raise to newness of life those who are spiritually dead. The Spirit is God's life-giver.

So then if the Spirit is specially operative in the birth of Jesus, we can say with certainty that in Jesus there entered into this world the creating and creative power of God; the power which made the world and which alone can remake the world; the power which gives life and the power which alone can re-create life when life is lost and dead in error and in sin. In this story we are being told that God's creating and re-creating power came personally to men in Jesus Christ.

If we begin with this certainty, does that help us to penetrate still further into the meaning of this story? Does it help us to find the reason for the story of a *virgin* birth? I think it does.

The Jews believed that no child was ever born without the Spirit of God. Since a child is not born from every act of intercourse, when a child *is* born, the Spirit of God, the Glory, has been present there. The Jewish teachers had many sayings about this, and very lovely sayings they are. Rabbi Simlai said: 'In the past Adam was created from the dust of the ground, and Eve was created from Adam. Henceforward it is to be "in our image and after our likeness" – meaning that man will not be able to come into existence without woman, nor woman without man, nor both without the Glory of God.' 'When husband and wife are worthy the glory of God is with them.' 'There are three partners in the production of any human being – the Holy One, blessed be he, the father and the mother.'

So it is perfectly possible that this beautiful story is not talking about a physical and literal virgin birth, but is saying vividly and pictorially that in the birth of Jesus, and in the coming of the Son of God into this world, the Holy Spirit was specially and uniquely operative.

It would indeed be characteristic of the whole attitude of biblical thought that the Holy Spirit should act through a human agent. In the old story in Judges (6.34) we are told that the Spirit of the Lord took possession of Gideon, or, as it should be even better translated, 'The Spirit of the Lord clothed himself with Gideon.' In the story in Acts (13.2) of the Church's first deliberate expedition to the Gentile world it is said that the Holy Spirit said, 'Set apart for me Barnabas and Saul for the work to which I have called them.' Quite clearly that message must have come from the Spirit through the lips of one of the prophets who were there. Throughout the Bible, the Holy Spirit acts and speaks through some chosen human person, making that person the instrument and the agent of the purposes of God. It may well be that the Holy Spirit took Joseph and acted through him, so that the Son of God should be born into this world.

We need not be tied to any one interpretation of this story. If we choose to take it literally and physically, and if we find that we can rest our faith in such an interpretation, we may certainly do so. Indeed, if we feel that we are led to do so, we must do so. But if on the other hand we feel that the historical evidence is insecure and inconclusive, if we wonder why so great a preacher and interpreter of the Christian faith as Paul never mentions the story, if we feel that the literal and physical interpretation threatens the fulness and the completeness of the incarnation and the manhood of Jesus, then we are quite free to hold that, through the providence of God, the Spirit used the ordinary events in an ordinary home for the glory of God, and that the clue to the story is the special operation of the Holy Spirit through a human agent in the birth of Jesus.

One thing is clear. There are no grounds for controversy here; there is no reason to set this story in the forefront of Christian faith and doctrine. If it forms no part of the message of the supreme mystic John, or of the great thinker Paul, then we need not seek to make it a foundation stone in the edifice of Christian belief. In this story let each of us both intelligently and prayerfully choose our own interpretation, and let us regard with sympathy and understanding those who choose another way of finding God's truth in it.

CHAPTER SEVEN

Suffered under Pontius Pilate

It is an odd thing that the only human name which appears in the Apostles' Creed is the name of a Roman governor who was guilty of agreeing to carry out the most terrible crime the world has ever seen or ever will see. Let us see what manner of man this Pilate was.

Pilate was procurator of Judaea from AD 26 to 36. He was not a governor in the full Roman sense of the office, although he was fully responsible for the administration of Judaea. Judaea was part of the province of Syria, and Pilate was subordinate to the governor of Syria and answerable to him for what he did. There can be no doubt that Pilate must already have shown himself a competent military commander and an efficient administrator or he would never have been chosen to administer and control so notoriously difficult an area as Judaea. Let us begin by looking at his conduct during the trial of Jesus.

In that trial Pilate was inescapably responsible for whatever final decision might be given. Palestine was an occupied country subject to the Romans. It was the Roman custom to allow subject countries very largely to govern themselves, so long as they maintained peace and order, and so long as the taxes were paid. The Sanhedrin was therefore still the effective administrative body in Judaea. But there was one thing the Sanhedrin could not do; it could not carry out the death sentence. That final verdict was the governor's responsibility; nor could Pilate, however much he wished, delegate the decision to anyone else.

John (19.12) says of Pilate that he sought to release Jesus – and that, in one brief sentence, is a summary of Pilate's attitude all through the trial. To Pilate, Jesus seemed quite out of the ordinary run of criminals. Pilate knew men and had administered Roman justice for many years, but he had never encountered anyone like this. He was astonished that

Jesus made no defence (Matthew 27.11–14; Mark 15.3–5). He was accustomed to defiant criminals who even violently defended themselves; he was accustomed to cringing, panic-stricken creatures who plead for mercy; but he had never before encountered a calm, serene, regal figure, before whom he felt not like the judge but the defendant. He wanted nothing to do with the trial. He told the Jews to settle it themselves (John 18.31; 19.6), but Jesus was charged with political insurrection and of conduct calculated to subvert the government (Luke 23.2), and, whether or not he wished to do so, he was compelled to deal with the case.

He was never in any doubt of the innocence of Jesus (Luke 23.4, 13–16, 20; John 19.4–6). This man might claim to be a king, but he was not the kind of king who was in any way a political threat to the power of Caesar (John 18.33–8). Pilate was well aware of the malicious motives with which the Jews had brought Jesus before him (Matthew 27.18; Mark 15.10). Pilate would never have reached the administrative level he had reached unless he had been perfectly capable of reading the minds of men. His gorge must have risen within him when he heard the Jewish leaders protesting their solicitude for Caesar and proclaiming that Caesar was their only king (John 19.12–15). He had cause to know only too well the embittered Jewish hostility to Rome, and he had no delusions about the value of such protestations of loyalty and concern.

He tried every possible way of saving Jesus from his accusers, for he stood for Roman justice and knew it. There was a custom that at the Passover time a prisoner of their own choice was released to the Jews. Pilate offered them the release of Jesus, but they chose the brigand revolutionary Barabbas (Matthew 27.15–26; Mark 15.6–15; Luke 23.18–25; John 18.38–40). He sent Jesus to Herod, because Jesus was a Galilaean, and Herod was king of Galilee, although he was in dependence to Rome, hoping, unsuccessfully, that Herod would take the final decision for him (Luke 23.6–12). He sought, equally unsuccessfully, to appeal to the hearts of the Jewish leaders by presenting Jesus to them, bruised, battered, bleeding, but still calm, and regal. 'Here is the man,' he said. 'Here is your king' (John 19.5, 14).

There were other things too which disturbed and distressed Pilate. His wife sent him a message that in a dream she had been warned that Jesus was innocent (Matthew 27.19). Fear, half religious, half superstitious, entered his heart when he heard that Jesus had claimed to be the Son of God. In his heart of hearts he knew that he was in the presence of divinity (John 19.7–8).

And yet in the end Pilate gave his verdict against Jesus and the ultimate responsibility for the crucifixion of Jesus cannot be removed from his shoulders. Why did he do it?

It so happens that from Josephus and from Philo we know three incidents from Pilate's career as governor of Judaea, and in them there lies the explanation. Early in his office Pilate removed the army headquarters from Caesarea, which was the administrative seat of the government, to Jerusalem. He marched his troops into Jerusalem – although he had to do so under cover of dark – with their standards. Now these standards were little metal images of the reigning Emperor (Tiberius), and the Roman Emperor was officially a god. The standards therefore counted to the Jews as graven images, and their presence in the holy city was an outrage. No governor had ever done this before. A deputation of Jews came to Caesarea to plead with Pilate to remove these blasphemous standards; he refused. The Jews persisted in their entreaties; he threatened them with instant death at the hands of his soldiers. The Jews bade him kill them if he wished; they could do no other than continue their protests. Pilate was defeated and the standards were removed, for it is hardly possible to slaughter a nation (Josephus, *Antiquities of the Jews* 18.3.1–2; *Wars of the Jews* 2.9.2–4).

The second incident was an occasion when he hung in his palace a series of gilt shields bearing the names of the Romans' gods. They too constituted graven images in the eyes of the Jews. Again they protested; on this occasion they took their protest as high as the Emperor Tiberius himself, and Tiberius took their part and ordered Pilate to remove the shields (Philo, *Ad Caium* 38). Pilate was building up a dangerous record for himself, for Rome did not forget the rights of her provincials.

The third incident occurred when Pilate formed an entirely laudable scheme to bring a new and improved water supply into Jerusalem, but he proposed to finance his scheme by taking the money from the Temple treasury. There were immediate riots which were suppressed with undue savagery by troops who had got out of control (Josephus, *Wars of the Jews* 2.9.4.). And in Luke 13.1 we read of the Galilaeans whose blood Pilate had mingled with their sacrifices, a glimpse of another incident, this time otherwise unrecorded, when Pilate's severity seems to have overrun all reasonable bounds.

'If you do not execute Jesus,' the Jewish leaders said, 'you are not Caesar's friend' (John 19.12). The words are nothing less than a threat to report him to Tiberius the Emperor – and Pilate could not afford another such report. If it had gone in, dismissal would have been certain. The plain fact is that Pilate's past gave the Jewish leaders their opportunity to blackmail him into giving them their way.

And now we have the point of Pilate's famous question: 'What is truth?' (John 18.38). He knew the truth very well – but when truth conflicted with policy, truth had to go. As one writer has said of Pilate, he was moved by nothing other than 'a selfish regard for his own security'. To him, 'political success was as the breath of life.' If principle had to be abandoned, if even Roman justice had to be dragged in the mire, then principle and justice must be sacrificed, so long as he remained procurator of Judaea. As it has been put: 'Worldliness, want of principle, are sources of crime no less awful than those which spring from deliberate and reckless violence.'

In one sense at least Pilate is a tragic figure. We may believe that he never meant anything other than well. He had set out to be a governor who put discipline above the prejudices of the troublesome Jews whom he governed. He had set out to improve the life and the welfare of the city of Jerusalem. He had set out to worship his own gods without concealment, and with a strange malignancy of fate, everything he had done had recoiled upon his own unfortunate head. He had got himself into such a position that he had to choose between principle and his own career – and he chose his career. Pilate ordered the crucifixion of Jesus Christ, the Son of God, for no other reason than that he could see no other way to remain procurator of Judaea.

But his tenure of office was not to last for long. In the year AD 35/6 a situation arose in Samaria, which was also in Pilate's territory. A man appeared there claiming that he was able to reveal the sacred treasures which Moses had hidden on Mount Gerizim. It appears that the resulting situation was not a real threat to the Roman authority and that there was very little danger in it. Pilate arrived with his troops and dealt with the situation with characteristic but quite unnecessary severity in which many lives were lost. The consequence was that the Samaritans reported him to Vitellius the governor of Syria, who was his superior. Thereupon Vitellius suspended Pilate from office and ordered him to report to Tiberius in Rome (Josephus, *Antiquities of the Jews* 18.4.1, 2). Tiberius died before Pilate reached Rome, and what happened in the end to Pilate history does not tell, although there is an abundance of legendary material which we shall go on to investigate.

With the name of Pilate the events of Jesus' death are firmly anchored in history. They are not only anchored in sacred history and in Jewish history; they also find their place in Roman history. When Tacitus is describing the great fire of Rome, he tells how Nero the Emperor, who was himself responsible for the fire, fastened the blame on the Christians. Then in connection with the name Christian Tacitus goes on to say: 'Christus, from whom the name had its origin, suffered the extreme penalty during the reign of Tiberius at the hands of one of our procurators, Pontius Pilate, and a deadly superstition, thus checked for the moment broke out again, not only in Judaea, the first source of the evil, but also in the City, where all things hideous and shameful from every part of the world meet and become popular' (Tacitus, *Annals* 15.44.4).

It is in connection with this that we come upon our first piece of legendary material. If the facts concerning Pilate's part in the trial and death of Jesus are true, then he would have sent a report of it to Rome. Such a report is actually mentioned by Justin Martyr (*First Apology* 1.76, 84), by Tertullian (*Apology* 21), and by Eusebius (*The Ecclesiastical History* 2.2). Pilate's report, the *Anaphora*, exists in a legendary form (M. R. James, *The Apocryphal New Testament* pp. 153-5), and along with it there exists a letter which is supposed to have been written by him to the Emperor Tiberius, which runs as follows:

Jesus Christ of whom I recently wrote to you has been executed against my will. So pious and austere a man has never been seen, nor will be again. But there was a wonderful unanimity in the request of the Jews and their leader that he should be crucified, though their own prophets, and the Sibyls, testified against them, and signs appeared at his death which the philosophers said threatened the collapse of the whole world. His disciples who still live do not belie their master's teaching, but are active in good works. Had I not feared a general rising, the man might have been yet alive.

No doubt the original report of Pilate is long since lost, and no doubt this letter is a work of imagination, but nonetheless we may well believe that it does represent Pilate's mind on the matter.

We must go still further into the legendary stories about Pilate. Astonishing as it may seem, in the Coptic Church and in the Church of Abyssinia Pilate has been canonized, and his saint's day is 25th June. Let us see how the story grew.

The simplest and the earliest development of the story is that Pilate, 'weary of misfortunes', ended by taking his own life (Eusebius, *The Ecclesiastical History* 2.7). A later development is that he was banished to Vienna (Vienne) on the Rhône, where for many years the monument of his alleged tomb was shown.

But the story goes on to develop many more elaborations. The first is found in the *Paradosis Pilati*. This story tells how Tiberius, alarmed at the darkness which had fallen over the world at the death of Jesus, put Pilate on trial. Pilate related the mighty works that Jesus had done, and the signs and wonders which had accompanied his death, and blamed the intransigence of the Jews. Tiberius said: 'You should have kept him safe and sent him to me, and not have yielded and crucified one who had done all these mighty works of which you spoke in your report. It was plain that he was the Christ, the King of the Jews.' At the name of Christ all the images of the Roman gods fell down and became as dust. Pilate was then condemned to death and a soldier called Albius was ordered to behead him. As he went out to his death, Pilate prayed: 'Number me not among the wicked Hebrews. Remember not evil against me or against thy servant Procla (his wife) who standeth here, whom thou didst make to prophesy that thou must be nailed to the cross; but pardon us and number us among thy righteous ones.' Then a voice from heaven came: 'All the generations and the families of the Gentiles shall call thee blessed, because in thy days were fulfilled all these things which were spoken by the prophets concerning me; and thou shalt also appear as my witness at my second coming, when I shall judge the twelve tribes of Israel and them that have not confessed my name.' Pilate was then beheaded, and an angel received his head, and Procla died with him.

The second and even more elaborate form of the legend is connected with the Veronica story, and centres round Mount Pilatus in Switzerland.

Pilatus really means 'cloud-capped', but the name came to be connected with Pilate. Tiberius the Emperor was ill, and sent a messenger to ask him to send Jesus to Rome to heal him. Pilate had to confess that Jesus had been crucified. But the messenger met Veronica in Jerusalem. Veronica was the kindly lady in the legend who saw Jesus on the way to Calvary bearing his cross, and who gave him a napkin to wipe the sweat from his brow. When Jesus handed her back the napkin, the picture of his face was printed on it. Veronica gave the messenger the towel and by it Tiberius was healed. Tiberius then sent for Pilate to put him on trial for his crime, but Pilate arrived wearing the seamless robe which Jesus had worn, and the sight of the robe turned the wrath of Tiberius into gentleness for the moment. He sent Pilate away, but later called him back, stripped him of the robe, and sentenced him to death. Pilate thereupon killed himself. Tiberius tied a millstone round the neck of Pilate's dead body and threw it into the Tiber, but the demons caused such storms and tempests that it had to be taken out. It was sent to Vienna and flung into the Rhône, but the same disasters followed. Finally it was taken to Losania (Lausanne or Lucerne), and there flung into a pool surrounded by lonely mountains, and the pool still bubbles and boils, and is overlooked by Mount Pilatus. In *Anne of Geierstein* Sir Walter Scott referred to this legend and this pool. 'A form is often seen to emerge from the gloomy waters, and go through the action of one washing his hands; and when he does so, dark clouds of mist gather first round the bosom of the infernal lake (such it has been styled of old), and then, wrapping the whole upper part of the mountain in darkness, presage a tempest or hurricane, which is sure to follow in a short space.'

The figure of Pilate has always exercised a strange fascination over the minds and the imaginations of men. And the strange and curious and moving thing is that the reaction of men has been at least as often pity as much as hatred. Tertullian, stern rigorist though he was, said of Pilate that he was *iam pro sua conscientia Christianus*, as far as his conscience went a Christian (*Apology* 21). In the apocryphal *Gospel of Nicodemus* (1.12) it is said of Pilate that he was 'uncircumcised in flesh, but circumcised in heart'. No one has wished to take Pilate's guilt away, but men have always felt that Pilate was in the grip of forces far greater than himself, and that the inevitable horror which his action awakes, cannot be other than tinged with sympathy.

Pilate did the wrong thing because he was afraid to do the right thing. He sacrificed Jesus in order to keep his position and to further his ambition. Pilate was not the first who, on being confronted with the choice between worldly ambition and obedience to Jesus Christ, chose worldly ambition. So, far from condemning Pilate in self-righteousness, we would do well to say: 'There but for the grace of God go I.'

CHAPTER EIGHT

Was Crucified

'And when they came to the place that is called The Skull, there they crucified him, and the criminals, one on the right hand and one on the left' (Luke 23.33; John 19.18). The Gospels tell the story of the crucifixion of Jesus with the most astonishing restraint. They simply state the fact, and leave it at that with no description at all.

The reason for this is that the Gospel-writers did not need to describe crucifixion; their readers knew all about it, for crucifixion was too tragically common in the ancient world to need any description. After the siege of Tyre, Alexander the Great crucified two thousand Tyrhians. During the Jewish civil wars Alexander Jannaeus crucified eight hundred men on one single occasion (Josephus, *Antiquities of the Jews* 13.14.2). In Sicily Augustus on one occasion crucified six hundred men (Orosius 6.18). Hadrian crucified five hundred in one single day. Varus, in crushing the revolt in Galilee within the actual life-time of Jesus, crucified two thousand people (Josephus, *Antiquities of the Jews* 17.10.10). In Titus' final campaign in which the Jews lost their freedom for ever and in which the Temple was destroyed, it was said of Titus that he crucified so many men 'that there was no space left for crosses, and no crosses for the bodies' (Josephus, *Wars of the Jews* 6.18). No one in the ancient world needed to be told what crucifixion was like. They were perfectly familiar with its agonizing details.

The custom of crucifixion was widespread. We find it in Egypt, Phoenicia, Carthage, Persia, Assyria, Scythia and even India; and we find it in Greece and Rome. It is likely that the Romans took it over from the Phoenicians and the Carthaginians. Cicero says that it was introduced into Rome by Tarquinius Superbus (*Pro Rab.* 4); but Pliny has the story that at that time it was the dead bodies of suicides which were fixed to crosses as a deterrent (*Natural History* 36.15.24).

Crucifixion was not a Jewish practice. The Jews had four ways of carrying out the death sentence: by the sword (Exodus 21.14), by strangling (Numbers 25.4), by fire (Leviticus 20.14), and by stoning (Leviticus 20.27). When the Jews did use anything in the nature of crucifixion, it was the dead body of a criminal that was thus exposed after execution (Deuteronomy 21.22–3)

There was never any doubt in the minds of the people of the ancient world that crucifixion was the most terrible and the most shameful of deaths. The 'unhappy wood' or 'the unhappy tree', they called the cross (Livy 1.26; Cicero, *Pro Rab.* 3; Seneca, *Letters* 101). The most cruel and the vilest punishment, Cicero called it (*Verrines* 5.66); the ultimate penalty, Apuleius called it (*The Golden Ass* 10); the penalty of slaves, it was commonly called (Tacitus, *Histories,* 4.11; Juvenal 6.218; Horace, *Satires* 1.3.8). It was a punishment which could only be inflicted on slaves and noncitizens. Even a freedman was exempt, and by the right of citizenship (*ius civitatis*) no Roman citizen could be killed in that way (Cicero, *Verrines* 2.1.3). Even in a grim world which knew little of mercy the word cross was a word of horror, and crucifixion was a fate which a man would hardly wish for his worst enemy.

The Greek word *stauros* is a word with a fairly wide range of meaning. It is the normal word for *cross*, but it can very often mean a *stake* as well. There were, remembering that double meaning, four kinds of crosses.

(i) There was the *crux simplex*, which was simply a stake on which a man was impaled. The stake might be driven through his breast; he might be tied to it with his hands upstretched; it might be driven right through his body emerging through his mouth.

(ii) There was the *crux decussata*. It was shaped like a capital X, and is commonly known as St. Andrew's Cross because of the legend that Andrew was crucified on a cross of that shape. The early fathers loved to search the Old Testament for 'types' and 'symbols' of the Christian faith and of the events in the life of Christ. They found this kind of cross prefigured in three things. When Jacob blessed Manasseh and Ephraim, the sons of Joseph, in doing so he crossed his hands, so that his right hand was on the son on Joseph's right, and his left hand on the son on Joseph's left (Genesis 48.12–14). He blessed them, as the old story has it, 'crossing his hands'. In Jewish ritual it is said that priests, when they were ordained to office, were anointed *in modum chi*, in the form of the Greek letter *chi*, which is the same shape as a capital X. In the ritual for the Day of Atonement the priest laid both his hands upon the head of the scapegoat, crossing them so that they formed once again the X cross. In all these things the early fathers saw a prefiguring of the cross of Jesus.

(iii) There was the *crux commissa*. It was shaped like a capital T, and is generally known as St. Anthony's Cross. Here there was even more room for ingenuity and for fertility of imagination. In Greek, T is *tau* and the shape of the letter is exactly the same as it is in English, the shape of the *crux commissa*. Now Greek has no separate signs for numbers, which are represented by the letters of the alphabet, so that A is 1, B is 2, and so on. In Greek, T (*tau*) is the sign for 300. Therefore, wherever the fathers came across the number 300 in the Old Testament they took it to be a mystical prefiguring of the cross of Christ. So they find the prefiguring of the cross in the fact that the length of Noah's ark was 300 cubits (Genesis 6.15). In Genesis 14.14 we are told that Abraham had 318 servants, which gives scope for even greater skill in interpretation! The 300 is represented by T, which, of course, equals the cross. But it so happens that the Greek for 10 is I, and the Greek for 8 is *ēta*, which is one of the two Greek letters for E. 18 is therefore IE which are the first two letters of the name of Jesus! Therefore the 318 stands at one and the same time for the cross and for the name of Jesus! Once again the fathers saw the prefiguring of the cross in the Old Testament.

(iv) There was the *crux immissa*. This is the cross with the projecting top piece, and this is the shape of the cross as it appears on the coins of Constantine It is the traditional shape of the cross as we know it; and tradition is almost certainly right, for it is only to a cross of this shape with its projecting upper arm that the board bearing the charge could have been affixed.

This cross too had its symbolic meaning for the fathers. Its four arms point north, south, east and west, and so it embraces the whole world. With its vertical piece and its horizontal piece, it symbolizes the length, breadth, depth and height of the love which died upon it (Ephesians 3.18).

The cross was not high; it would not lift the feet of the criminal more than a foot or two above the ground. Half way up it or thereabouts there projected a piece of wood called the *pēgma*. This fitted between the victim's legs, and on this, as on a saddle, his weight rested, for no body could have been supported, resting only on 'four great wounds' in the hands and feet.

There were many traditions in regard to the wood of the cross. Bede says that the upright was of cypress, the cross-piece of cedar, the head-piece of fir, and the saddle of box. The best-known legend is that the cross was made of the wood of the aspen tree, which is why the aspen always shivers. One thing is certain: so many crosses were used that they must have been made of the commonest and the cheapest wood, and it is perhaps likeliest of all that the cross was made of oak wood, for the oak was common in Palestine.

The charge against Jesus was written on a board and affixed to the cross (Matthew 27.37; Mark 15.26; John 19.19). The board was whitened with gypsum, and the lettering was in black. The description of guilt was usually as simple and brief as possible. Eusebius (*Ecclesiastical History* 5.1) tells of such a board which said simply: 'This is Attalus the Christian'. The charge (*titulus, epigraphē*) was either hung round a man's neck, or was carried in front of him by a herald to the place of execution.

The place of execution was outside the city gates, or outside the camp, and often in as conspicuous a place as possible, in order that all might see and profit by the dreadful warning.

We must now follow the process of Jesus' crucifixion step by step.

When the verdict of death had been passed, there came the order: '*Summove, lictor, despolia, verbera*' (Livy 1.26). The lictor was the attendant or the court officer, and the order means: 'Remove him, lictor, strip him, and scourge him.' The scourging was of the most severe kind. It was not with the *virga*, the rod, but with the *flagellum*, the lash. The lash was a long leather thong, often studded with nails and pieces of bone and sharpened pellets of lead. The prisoner was bound to a pillar in such a way that his back was exposed and he was unable to move, and then the lash was laid on. The victims usually lost consciousness under this scourging; many of them emerged from it raving mad; and not a few died under it.

Jesus was scourged; but his scourging had a special character. As we have seen, the condemned criminal was normally scourged before crucifixion, and that is what Matthew and Mark both imply (Matthew 27.26; Mark 15.15). But in both Luke and John the impression is of something different. In Luke and John it seems that Pilate had Jesus scourged in the hope that the Jews would be satisfied with that, and that he might save him in this way from the still worse fate of death. John even seems to imply that Pilate had Jesus scourged and then brought him out to the people to excite their pity, but to no avail (Luke 23.22; John 19.1–5). In any event, Jesus had to submit to this terrible ordeal.

The prisoner was then marched to the place of execution; he was placed in the middle of a hollow square of four Roman soldiers, with, as we have seen, a herald going in front carrying the board on which the charge was written. The criminal was compelled to carry his own cross to the place of execution, or at least to carry the cross-beam of it. So accepted a part of crucifixion was this that *furcifer*, cross-carrier, is one of the Latin words which mean criminal. Jesus went out carrying his own cross (John 19.17), but the weight of it must have been too heavy for him after all that he had gone through, and on the way the soldiers compelled Simon of Cyrene to carry it for him (Matthew 27.32; Mark 15.21; Luke 23.26). Sometimes a criminal was lashed and literally goaded along the road that led to the place of execution.

For this part of the story too the fathers found forecasts in the Old Testament. They found one in the wood for the sacrifice laid on the shoulders of the young Isaac (Genesis 22.6), and they took Isaiah 9.6, 'The government will be upon his shoulder', as a further prophecy.

When the party arrived at the place of execution, the criminal was stripped naked. It was the Roman law, laid down in the Digest, that the prisoner's clothes were the perquisite of the party of soldiers in charge of the execution. So the soldiers drew lots for Jesus' clothes. The necessity for drawing lots came from the fact that there were four soldiers and five articles of clothing. Every Jew had five articles of clothing, four of which were of equal value – the tunic, or undergarment, the belt, the sandals and the turban. But the fifth was in a different class. It was the great outer cloak, which was a Jew's principal article of clothing by day and his covering at night. It measured as much as seven feet by three feet; it was much more valuable than the others; to cut it up would be to ruin it, and so the soldiers drew lots to see who would receive it (Matthew 27.35; Mark 15.24; Luke 23.34; John 19.23–4). For this too the early writers found a forecast in the words of Psalm 22.18: 'They divide my garments among them, and for my raiment they cast lots.'

At this point there came the only tinge of mercy in the agonizing process: sometimes the prisoner was stunned with a blow before he was actually affixed to the cross. We read, for instance, that Julius Caesar dealt thus mercifully with certain pirates whom he had captured and who were being executed (Suetonius, *Caesar* 74). It was the custom generally, and particularly among the Jews, to give the criminal a drink of medicated wine to dull the pain. This was offered to Jesus, but he refused it (Matthew 27.34; Mark 15.23). This is not to be confused with the drink of vinegar which was also offered to him (Matthew 27.48; Luke 23.36; John 19.29). The vinegar was the *posca,* the bitter, sour wine which was the ordinary drink of the Roman soldier, and which, of course, was not drugged at all.

Next came the affixing to the cross. There was no one way of doing this. Sometimes the cross was first placed in its socket, so that it stood upright, and then the prisoner was lifted up and fixed to it, with the projecting saddle between his legs. Sometimes the cross was laid flat on the ground, and the prisoner affixed to it; and then, with the prisoner on it, the cross was lifted upright and placed in its socket. Sometimes the prisoner was only bound to the cross with his hands and arms out-stretched. This may sound the most merciful form of crucifixion. In point of fact it was in many ways the most terrible of all, for the prisoner was then left hanging, to die slowly and agonizingly of hunger and thirst and exposure, a lingering death which might last for many days, and in which many a man went raving mad. Far more usually nails were driven through the hands of the prisoner, fixing them to the cross-beam of the cross. Sometimes the feet were only loosely bound; sometimes they were crossed and a nail driven through both feet into the wood of the upright of the cross. We know that Jesus' hands were nailed to the cross, but it seems likely that his feet were only bound to the cross, for in the Thomas incident there is reference to the print of the nails in Jesus' hands and to the spear thrust in his side, but not to any nail prints in his feet.

When the nails were driven through the hands and the feet, they were driven through the places where the most delicate nerves and tendons are. When a man was fixed on his cross, he was left hanging in a completely unnatural position, of which the tension increased every moment. The result was that every smallest movement of the body became an increasing agony. There was no way in which a man might rest or ease his body to gain relief from the pain. The longer a man hung – and he could hang on the cross for as long as a week – the more inflamed his wounds became, until in the end they could even become gangrenous. The position in which a man hung affected the natural flow of blood in his body; the blood flow was constricted and the blood vessels especially in the head became distended, with accompanying agony. In addition to all his other tortures, a man was consumed with raging thirst. There can have been few more agonizing deaths, and for Jesus the one merciful fact in the whole terrible process was that he died soon.

Matthew says of the soldiers who carried out the crucifixion: 'Then they sat down and kept watch over him there' (Matthew 27.36). There had been occasions when crucified men had been taken down from their cross, and had still survived and the Roman authorities probably still thought that there was some possibility that Jesus' followers might stage an attempt to rescue him from the cross.

In John 19.31 we read that the Jewish authorities came and asked that the legs of the criminals might be broken in order to hasten their death, so that the bodies might not hang on their crosses over the Sabbath day. John tells that this was done for the brigands, but that Jesus was already dead. No detail shows more vividly the agony of crucifixion than the fact that this fracture of the legs was actually considered a merciful mitigation, and was sometimes even purchased at a price (Cicero, *Verrines* 2.45). Sometimes, with the almost incomprehensible savagery which was characteristic of that age, a fire was lit under a man's cross, so that he was burned as well as crucified, and sometimes wild beasts were let loose upon him, so that in his helplessness he was torn to pieces, as if he had been flung to the beasts in the arena.

When Jesus had died, Joseph of Arimathaea begged his body from Pilate, and so he was given decent burial (Matthew 27.57–61; Mark 15.42–6; Luke 23.50–4; John 19.38–41); but the ordinary custom was for the body to hang rotting on its cross until the action of the wind and the rain and the elements destroyed it, or until it was devoured by vultures and carrion crows and pariah dogs and beasts. The wood of the cross was usually burned in the end, for a cross was an accursed thing.

Such then was the terrible process of crucifixion. The cross was the symbol of ultimate shame and humiliation, but the day was to come when it was to be the most precious and sacred symbol and sign in the world. The day was to come when the cross was to be the very sign of the Roman Empire itself.

The Battle of the Milvian Bridge on 27th October 312 was one of the great decisive battles of history. It won freedom from persecution for the Christians, and was the first step towards making Christianity the religion of the Roman Empire. It was won by a man who took the cross for his standard, and who also banished crucifixion as a legal punishment under Roman law. The name of this man was Constantine.

At that time the Roman Empire was split under four leaders. There was Licinius, who was not an active persecutor, but who was not sympathetic to Christianity; there was Maxentius who was actively opposed to Christianity; there was Maximin who was the persecutor in chief; and there was Constantine who was a monotheist, a good man and a good governor. Constantine's sphere of influence was in Gaul; he marched on Maxentius in Rome. Somewhere on the way something happened to him, the story of which he himself afterwards told to Eusebius (*The Life of Constantine* 1.28). Just where the thing happened is not certain, but: 'About noon, when the day was beginning to decline, he saw with his own eyes the trophy of a cross of light in the heavens above the sun, and bearing the inscription, CONQUER BY THIS.' From that moment Constantine took the cross as his standard. When he reached Rome, Maxentius came out to meet him, and at the Battle of the Milvian Bridge, Constantine defeated him and thus took the greatest step to becoming the master of the Empire. The criminal's cross had become the imperial sign.

It was inevitable that long before this the cross and the sign of the cross had become interwoven with Christian practice and devotion. The Christians loved to point out that the sign of the cross was stamped on the very universe. A bird flying, a man swimming, a ship sailing, a crossbeam against an upright, a man with outstretched hands offering worship to God – in these and in many another thing they saw the sign of the cross (Minucius Felix, *Octavius* 29.6–8). 'At every forward step and movement,' writes Tertullian, 'at every going in and out, when we put on our clothes and shoes, when we bathe, when we sit at table, when we light the lamps, on couch, on seat, in all the ordinary actions of daily life, we trace upon the forehead the sign of the cross' (*The Soldier's Crown* 3).

Sometimes indeed the heathen said the Christians worshipped the cross; but the Christians were careful to point out that it was neither the wood of the cross nor the sign of the cross that they worshipped; what was dear to them was all that the cross stood for and all that it reminded them of. The sign of the cross showed that they were Christians; when they made it, it reminded them of their faith; it put the devil to flight, and made them remember the almighty resources they had with which to fight the battle of temptation. It was the sign which brought them nearer their master who had died on it for them.

It is easy to see how such reverence for the cross and for the sign of the cross could turn into superstition and even into a kind of idolatry; but it is also easy to see what memories the cross could awake, and how close it could bring him who hung upon it. If the Roman Catholic Church has gone too far in the use and veneration of the cross, it may well be that the Protestant Church has lost something of infinite value to devotion by going too far in the opposite direction.

The legends which grew up around the cross were many, and they have left their mark in ceremonies and festivals observed by certain branches of the Church. The most famous of them all is the story of the discovery of the cross by the Empress Helena, the mother of Constantine (*The Ecclesiastical Histories of Socrates,* 1.17; Theodoret 1.17; Sozomen 2.1). The story is that Constantine in his zeal for Christ was determined to find the site of the Holy Sepulchre in which the body of Jesus had been buried, in order to build a church upon it. This much is true, but while he found the site, in the earliest account of the story there is no word of the finding of the cross (Eusebius, *Life of Constantine* 26–32). According to the later stories, Helena went to Jerusalem to seek for the site. From the time of Hadrian it had been covered over with a huge mound of earth on the top of which had been erected a Temple to Aphrodite. There had been a deliberate attempt to obliterate the site of the Sepulchre. Helena was able to find the place with the help of a Jew who possessed special documents and information. When the mound had been cleared the Sepulchre was found, and in it three crosses, together with the trilingual inscription upon them. It was uncertain which had been the cross of Jesus. Macanus, the Bishop of Jerusalem, settled the matter by taking the crosses in turn to a lady of Jerusalem who was dying. When she was touched by the first two crosses, it had no effect; but when she was touched by the third cross she was immediately cured. And so the third cross was taken to be the cross of our Lord.

Part of the wood of the cross, the greater part of it, was encased in a silver chest and left at Jerusalem. Part of it was sent to Constantine, who incorporated it into his own statue in Byzantium. The nails which had pierced Jesus' hands were also found; they were sent to Constantine who had one worked into his helmet and one into his horse's bridle, so that the prophecy of Zechariah might be fulfilled and even the bells of the horses should be holy to the Lord (Zechariah 14.20).

The legend grew ever more miraculous and wonderful. Fragments of the alleged cross found their way all over the world. The number of the fragments would make a large number of crosses, but the legend was that the wood of the cross had a self-multiplying power. Paulinus of Nola at the beginning of the fifth century sent a piece to Sulpicius Severus, saying at the same time that, though the pieces were continually taken from it, it grew no smaller (*Letter* 31). In certain branches of the Church the Festival of the *Inventio Crucis*, the Invention or Finding of the Cross, is observed on 3rd May each year.

But the whole story is obvious legend and cannot have any foundation. That Constantine wished to build the Church is certain; that he did search for the site of the Holy Sepulchre and that he did believe that he had found it is also certain. But it must be noted that in the earliest account of Constantine's plan there is no mention of the finding of the cross. And what is even more damaging to the legend is the custom we have already mentioned of destroying criminals' crosses by fire. The probability is that the cross of Jesus was destroyed long before.

Two other great festivals, the *Exaltation of the Cross* and the *Adoration of the Cross*, also began very early on in the Church's history. They find no place in Protestant or Reformed worship but are dear to certain great branches of the Christian Church and are intensely dramatic and moving in character.

Certainly there are dangers here, of turning a reverence into a superstition and the cross into an image. But it may well be argued that there are some of us who have gone too far in the direction of the rejection of all symbolism.

Once I was at a conference held in a diocesan retreat centre. In my bedroom there was fixed to the wall, not a cross, but a crucifix with a prayer desk before it, and I am bound to say that Jesus Christ was very near; and into life there came a new awareness of that figure on the cross, and a new sense of obligation to make life fit for him to see.

James Denney was no ritualist, and no one would ever accuse him of flirting with Roman Catholicism. But Denney once said that he could find it in his heart to envy the Roman Catholic priest who could go to a dying man, when that man was beyond hearing the help that words could give, and who could hold the crucifix in front of the dying man's eyes, as they closed on time and began to glimpse eternity, and say: 'God loves you like that!' There is everything to be said for a symbol which in one vivid picture confronts the sinner in life and in death with the suffering, dying, redeeming love of God.

Gossip somewhere tells of an experience that Sir George Adam Smith once had. He was travelling in a train with a young Roman Catholic priest who was dressed in a cassock with the crucifix at his waist. They got into talk and it emerged that the young priest was about to go as a missionary to a place where at that time the life of a white man had to be counted not in years but in months. The young priest was a splendid figure of radiant young manhood, and to Smith this seemed a tragic waste of a life to be thrown away. He tried to dissuade him; he tried to argue that there must be some other sphere of service where life would not be recklessly expended like that. They came to the station at which Adam Smith was to get out, while the young priest continued his journey. Even at the carriage door Adam Smith still continued his plea. But the young priest's decision was made; his mind was made up. And just as the train was moving away, he lifted up the silver crucifix at his belt and held it up and looked at it with glowing eyes. 'He loved me,' he said, 'and he gave himself for me, and I – can I hold back?' There are times when the crucifix is the perfect image of the Christian faith, and when it reminds a man as nothing else can of the awful obligation of love that is laid upon him.

It may be that in our austerity, and in our reaction from things which were quite certainly superstitious and almost idolatrous abuses, we have been so conscious of the danger of the symbol of the cross that we have forgotten its immense value.

We need not and cannot believe in the legends of the cross; but – who knows? – there might be more devotion in our lives if we saw the cross oftener and if we looked oftener at the picture of the Son of God on it, who loved us and gave himself for us.

Interesting as it may be to study the process of crucifixion, moving as it may be to look at the cross and the crucifix as a means of devotion, it is far more essential to try to see what the cross of Jesus has done for us and means for us. On that the New Testament is not in doubt. 'Christ died for our sins' is the New Testament affirmation (1 Corinthians 15.3). Before we go any further, it is worthwhile to pause for a moment and to look at the preposition in that sentence. In Greek the *for* is *huper*, and the meaning of *huper* is *on behalf of*. The basic New Testament statement is therefore very wide; it does not tie us to any theory of the Atonement; it simply says that Jesus Christ died to do something for our sins, to do something to help our sinful condition. That is one good reason why the Church has never had any one orthodox theory of the Atonement. Within that great and wide statement of the New Testament there is room for many ways of appropriating the saving benefits of the cross of Christ.

Different men will find different ways to peace with God through the cross of our Blessed Lord, and we do well to refuse to treat our own experience as the norm and standard and to deny the validity of the experience of others. But on the whole there are three different ways of regarding the cross and the death of Christ. Of course, they are not mutually exclusive, but it is fair to say that almost all the theories of the Atonement travel in one or other of these three directions.

(i) There is the line of thought which thinks in terms of *Christus Victor*, the victorious Christ. The great merit of this line of thought is that it refuses to separate the death and the resurrection of Jesus. It sees Christ as the conqueror for all time of the embattled forces of evil, and his victory as open for all men to share.

So Paul writes in the Letter to the Colossians: 'On that cross he [Jesus] despoiled the cosmic powers and authorities, and boldly made a spectacle of them, leading them as captives in his triumphal procession' (Colossians 2.15, NEB margin). So the ancient hymn has it:

> Sing my tongue, how glorious battle
> > Glorious victory became;
> And above the Cross, his trophy,
> > Tell the triumph and the fame:
> Tell how he, the earth's Redeemer,
> > By his death for man o'er came.

Or again:

> Thine was the warfare with his [man's] foe,
> The Cross of pain, the cup of woe,
> > And thine the victory.

It is a great thought to see in the cross a death-grapple with all the forces of evil and to see in the Resurrection their ultimate and final defeat. There is no doubt that this was an idea dear to the early Church, indeed dear to every age of the Church. But it encounters one difficulty. We have only to look out into the world, and into our own hearts, to see that the power of evil is *not* broken, that in fact evil is as rampant and demonic as ever it was. It is doubtless true that Jesus won his own personal victory, but the fact is that that victory is very far from obtaining in the world.

(ii) There is the line of thought which sees in the cross either a sacrifice which atoned for the sins of men, or a moment in which Jesus Christ literally bore the pain and the punishment which should have fallen on us. We may see in the cross a sacrifice which made it possible for the Holy God to forgive sin and yet at the same time not to infringe his own holiness. Or we may think of God as the Judge; of man as the criminal upon whom no verdict but a verdict of guilty is possible; and of Jesus as bearing for us the penalty that should have fallen upon us.

Mrs Cousin's hymn has it:

> Jehovah lifted up his rod;
> > O Christ, it fell on thee.
> Thou wast sore stricken of thy God;
> > There's not one stroke for me.
> > Thy tears, thy blood,
> > Beneath it flowed:
> Thy bruising healeth me.

> Jehovah bade his sword awake;
>> O Christ, it woke 'gainst thee!
> Thy blood the flaming blade must slake,
> Thy heart its sheath must be,
>> All for my sake,
>> My peace to make:
> Now sleeps that sword for me.

Here is the thought that in the most literal sense Jesus Christ bore the divine punishment that should have fallen on us, and gathered to himself the divine wrath which should have been directed against us.

There is a certain moving magnificence in this thought. This is the kind of action which moves the hearts of men. David Smith quotes a human example of this spirit: Fergus MacIvor, as Scott tells in *Waverley*, was sentenced to death at Carlisle for his part in the 1745 rebellion. In the court was one of his clansmen, Evan Maccombich. Evan addressed the judge: 'I was only ganging to say, my lord, that if your excellent honour and the honourable court would let Vich Ian Vohr go free just this once, and let him gae back to France, and no' to trouble King George's government again, that ony six o' the very best of his clan will be willing to be judgified in his stead; and if you'll just let me gae down to Glennaquoich, I'll fetch them up to ye mysell, to head or hang, and you may begin wi' me the very first man.' There was a titter in the court at this extraordinary offer, but the judge silenced it. Evan went on: 'If the Saxon gentlemen are laughing because a poor man, such as me, thinks my life, or the life of six of my degree, is worth that of Vich Ian Vohr, it's like enough they may be very right; but if they laugh because they think I would not keep my word and come back to redeem him, I can tell them they ken neither the heart of a Hielandman nor the honour of a gentleman.' And then Scott ends the story: 'There was no further inclination to laugh among the audience, and a dead silence ensued.'

There is nothing moves the heart like the picture of a man ready to lay down his life for his friend, the picture of a man with such a love that he will willingly bear what someone else should have borne. And that is the picture of Jesus our substitute.

And yet there are certain things in this line of thought which raise vast questions.

– It does seem to imply that Jesus did something to alter the attitude of God to men, that he did something to make God withhold his hand. It seems in this way to show God as the one who punishes and Jesus as the one who bought men off. And yet the whole New Testament scheme of things insists that everything began in *the love of God,* 'God shows *his love* for us in that while we were yet sinners Christ died for us' (Romans 5.8). It was never God who needed to be reconciled to men; it was always men who needed to be reconciled to God. Yet this line of thought suggests a God who must be placated and satisfied before he can forgive.

– It seems to say that forgiveness became possible only through an act of injustice. If God punished Jesus instead of us, then God's justice and holiness were satisfied by punishing the only perfect person in all the world, an action which justice could not in fact tolerate. David Smith illustrates this with an incident which George Fox relates in his Journal. Fox was lying in the filthy prison of Doomsdale at Lancaster. He goes on: 'A friend went to Oliver Cromwell and offered himself, body for body, to lie in Doomsdale in my stead, if he would take him and let me have liberty. Which thing so struck him [Cromwell] that he said to his great men and council, "Which of you would do as much for me, if I were in the same condition?" And though he did not accept the friend's offer, but said he could not do it, *for that it was contrary to the law,* yet the truth thereby came mightily over him.' The fact is that justice and holiness are not satisfied by the penalty of being inflicted on, and paid by, the wrong person, even if he voluntarily accepts it.

– This difficulty was faced by James Denney in his exposition of the meaning of the death of Christ. To put his view briefly – it is wrong to isolate any one attribute of God. God is justice *and* love. In his justice God cannot allow sin to go without its penalty; in his love God must forgive. Therefore God in the death of Christ says: 'I myself in my love will pay the price of forgiveness which my holy justice necessitates.' It is thus God himself who pays the price of the forgiveness of sin. There is no doubt that that is a view which can only be regarded with reverent wonder. But does it not leave a picture of a God who in the last analysis is a split personality, torn between the claims of his holy justice and his divine love? Must there not finally be one dominating characteristic in the personality of God? And must this not be, 'God is love' (1 John 4.8)?

Far be it from any man to lay unsympathetic hands on a line of thought which is life to thousands of people, but it is a line of thought which at least for some has difficulties which are hard to overcome.

(iii) So we arrive at the third line of thought about the cross and the death of Jesus. This sees in the death of Jesus the ultimate and final demonstration of the love of God. The concept of God as love is a difficult one. We more naturally think of God as Judge, as King, as Lawgiver, as justice, as holiness, as perfect goodness, as wrathful with the sinner and determined upon his punishment. Men had always thought of God in this way. No man had ever dreamed of a God who was suffering, redeeming, yearning love. Without Jesus Christ it would have been impossible. But in Jesus we see what God is like, and in Jesus we see love: love for the sick, the hungry, the sad, and above all love for those with whom respectable people would have nothing to do.

But why the death of Christ? If Jesus had stopped before the cross, it would have meant that there was some point beyond which the love of God would not go, some limit to his love. But in Jesus God says: 'You may disobey me; you may grieve me; you may be disloyal to me; you may misunderstand me; you may batter me and bruise me and scourge me; you may treat me with savage injustice; you may kill me on a cross; I will never stop loving you.' This means that the life and death of Jesus are the demonstration and the proof of the limitless, the undefeatable, unchangeable, unalterable, infinite love of God. If this is so, the cross and the death of Jesus show us certain things.

– They show us what God is *always* like. They do not in any sense change the attitude of God; they show what the attitude of God always and for ever was, is, and will be. Ibsen makes Julian, the arch-enemy of Christianity, say, as he thinks of Jesus and his cross: 'Where is he now? Has he been at work elsewhere since *that* happened at Golgotha?... Where is he now? What if *that*, at Golgotha, near Jerusalem, was but a wayside matter, a thing done as it were in the passing? What if he goes on and on, suffers and dies and conquers again and again, from world to world?' There is this much truth in that: what happened in Palestine, and above all what happened on Calvary, is in fact a window into what is always going on in the loving, suffering, redeeming heart of God. The cross shows us the limitless and unalterable love of God, which will accept that and still love. This *is* God, as God was, as God is, and as God ever will be.

– Clearly this sheds a new and blazing light on the character of God. This is staggeringly and astonishingly new. No man and no religion has ever had a vision of God like this. Leconte de Lisle, the French writer, makes two of his characters talk together. Says one: 'Science will not suffice; sooner or later you will end by coming to your knees.' 'Before what?' says the other. And the answer is: 'Before the Darkness.' But in Jesus Christ the last word is not Darkness; it is love. The unknown God has become known – and he is revealed as love. The God whom men had seen as law and justice and holiness is astonishingly and amazingly revealed as unalterable love. This indeed is revelation.

– From all this one thing emerges. Through the life, and especially through the death of Jesus Christ, there is established a completely new relationship between man and God, a relationship which was not previously possible, and which would be possible in no other way. Through Jesus Christ men know that they can come to God with childlike confidence and boldness, as children come home to a father, knowing that his love will be great enough to welcome them in spite of what they have done. Because Jesus showed us God as he is, the fear has turned to trust, the distance has turned to intimacy, the estrangement has turned to love.

– And, finally, we must see the cost of that new relationship. Man's sin had created a situation in which he was estranged from God: it took the life and death and agony on the cross of Jesus to show men what God is like and so to bridge that otherwise unbridgeable gulf. The agony of Jesus, and the sorrow in the heart of God are the price of our new peace with God. Only through that agony could God make himself fully known to men, and so bring men to himself.

The meaning of the word Atonement is at-one-ment; it is making man and God *at one* in a new relationship. There is no single way in which we must think of the work of Christ, and the Church has never said that there is only one way. We must take the way that our heart finds best.

CHAPTER NINE

Dead and Buried

It is extraordinary how both the New Testament itself and the creeds insist with the greatest possible deliberate emphasis and reiteration that Jesus was really and truly dead.

'Jesus', says Matthew, 'cried again with a loud voice and yielded up his spirit' (Matthew 27.50). The centurion saw Jesus breathing his last (Mark 15.39). Luke tells of the moment of death and then goes on to tell of the heart-broken grief of the spectators (Luke 23.46–9). The two in the story of the walk to Emmaus had not the slightest doubt that Jesus had been crucified until he was dead (Luke 24.19–21). John goes further; he also tells of the thrust of the spear into Jesus' side, as if unwilling to leave out any detail, however grim, of the story of Jesus' death upon the cross (John 19.30, 34).

Not only do the New Testament writers tell of the death of Jesus; they also tell in the greatest detail of his burial. They tell how he was laid in the tomb, how the body was wrapped in the grave-clothes and the shroud, how it was embalmed with the perfumes and the unguents used to prepare the bodies of the dead, how the stone, which, as one manuscript says, not twenty men could move, was rolled against the door of the tomb (Matthew 27.57–60; Mark 15.42–7; Luke 23.50–5; John 19.38–42). And these facts become all the more significant when we remember that they had to pick and choose what they would include and what they would omit, because they were strictly limited in space by the standard length of the papyrus roll which they had to use.

Still further, when the early preachers began to tell the story of Jesus, they did so with a kind of grim insistence on his death. 'This Jesus', says Peter, 'you crucified and killed' (Acts 2.23). 'You killed the Author of life' (Acts 3.15). The Righteous One was betrayed and murdered, declares

Stephen (Acts 7.52). 'They put him to death by hanging him upon a tree,' Peter tells the party who came from Cornelius (Acts 10.39). The Jews killed Jesus, says Paul at Antioch, and took him down and laid him in a tomb (Acts 13.28–9). Christ died, says Paul, and was buried (1 Corinthians 15.3).

Everywhere we turn in the New Testament there is this insistence on the death and the burial of Jesus. Why should this be? It cannot be accidental. This is not simply a luxuriating in horrors; there is aim and purpose here.

We are back here at that heresy called Gnosticism which is never far behind New Testament thought. Gnosticism, as we have seen, saw the universe in terms of a thorough-going dualism in which spirit and matter struggled against each other, a universe in which spirit was altogether good and matter essentially evil. Clearly, in such a universe, God, who is pure spirit, could have no contact with matter. There could therefore be no such thing as an incarnation; the very thought of God really becoming man is ruled out. Furthermore, if God were insulated from the universe and from all the life of this world, then he could not suffer; suffering and God become opposites. Therefore in so far as Jesus Christ was in any sense divine he could not possibly have suffered. Irenaeus summarizes these beliefs as follows: 'The world was not created by the first God, but by a power distant and separate from the divinity who is over all, and ignorant of the God who is above all things. He [Cerinthus, the Gnostic teacher] added further that Jesus was not born of a virgin, but that he was the son of Joseph and Mary, born like all other men, and that he became more righteous and wiser than any other man, and that after the baptism there came down on him from the Power which is over all, the Christ in the form of a dove; that he then preached the unknown father, and performed miracles, but that at the end the Christ departed from Jesus, and that it was Jesus who suffered and was raised, but that the Christ remained incapable of suffering, because he was an entirely spiritual being.'

Here then is the Gnostic view. Jesus was a man into whom at his baptism the eternal Christ came, only to leave him before the agony and the pain of the cross, the pain of the death and the burial.

In the apocryphal and Gnostic Gospel of Peter the cry of Jesus on the cross is: 'My power, my power, why have you forsaken me?' It is the cry of the man Jesus forsaken by the divine Christ. In the apocryphal and Gnostic Acts of John, Jesus holds a conversation with John on the

Mount of Olives at the very time of the crucifixion, telling John that the crowds think he is being crucified, but in reality he is not suffering at all. According to Cerinthus, it was Simon of Cyrene who died on the cross, not Jesus at all.

It is precisely this heresy that John is refuting in 1 John 5.6: 'This is he who came by water *and* blood, Jesus Christ, not with the water only but with water and the blood.' The Gnostic was willing enough to agree that the Christ, the Divine One, came with the *water*, that he entered into the man Jesus at baptism, but he would never agree that the Christ came with *blood*, in the suffering of the cross. This is why the Gospels and the New Testament writers insist again and again that Jesus Christ was *dead and buried*. He truly suffered death with all its agony; he truly lay in death in the grave.

The Gnostics erred in two things. *They had the wrong idea of God.* They saw God as detached and isolated insulation; the Christian sees God as involved and caring love. *They had the wrong idea of Jesus.* They refused to take the humanity of Jesus seriously enough, whereas the true Christian belief is that Jesus' entry into the human situation was complete. There are at least three reasons why Jesus had really and truly to die.

(i) *He had to suffer the ultimate crime.* If Jesus came into the world to deal with the sin of man, then he had, so to speak, to meet sin at its worst in a head-on collision. The crucifixion of the One who is incarnate love is the ultimate in sin; Jesus had to meet that sin and to show that it could neither break his love nor destroy his life.

(ii) *He had to suffer the ultimate human experience.* In regard to death, Epicurus said, all men live in an unfortified city. The experience of death is the universal and the ultimate human experience. If Jesus was truly to enter into the human experience, and truly and completely to become man, then he had to experience death.

(iii) *He had to win the ultimate victory.* If he was able to suffer the ultimate crime, and emerge from it with his love undefeated and his life undestroyed, if he could face death and death at its worst and its bitterest, then indeed he had faced and conquered all that life and death could do to him. His greatness lay not in isolation but in victory. Yet he was more than conqueror; and for that very reason there is no situation in life or in death in which he cannot make those who have joined their lives to his more than conquerors too.

CHAPTER TEN

He Descended into Hell

He descended into hell. It would surely be true to say that this is the most neglected sentence in the Apostles' Creed. Even the books which deal with the creed pass it quickly by, and there can be very few who can recollect hearing a sermon on this particular article.

Its history is in keeping with the neglect which it has suffered. It was late gaining entry into the creed. As we saw in the beginning, the Apostles' Creed is to all intents and purposes the baptismal confession of faith of the Church in Rome, and Rufinus, writing about AD 400, tells us that it was omitted from that creed which ran:

> I believe:
> In Jesus Christ his only begotten son our Lord,
> who was born of the Holy Ghost and the Virgin Mary,
> crucified under Pontius Pilate, and buried;
> the third day he rose from the dead;
> he ascended into heaven and sitteth at the right hand of the Father:
> from thence he shall come to judge the quick and the dead.

Quite often we come on statements in the early Christian writers, which are not what we would technically call creeds, but in which their beliefs are set down. We get such a statement, for instance, in *Ignatius's Letter to the Trallians* (9):

> Be deaf therefore when anyone would speak to you apart from
>   Jesus Christ,
> The Son of God,
> who was descended from the family of David,
> born of Mary,

who was truly born both of God and of the Virgin;
who truly took a body,
for the Word became flesh and dwelt among us without sin;
truly ate and drank;
truly suffered persecution under Pontius Pilate;
was truly crucified and died;
who was also truly raised from the dead,
his father raising him up ...
And after having spent forty days with the apostles,
was received up to the Father,
and sits on his right hand,
waiting till his enemies are put under his feet.

Here is a full statement of faith, and yet it contains no mention of the descent into hell, and this statement can be paralleled from the statements of faith both of Irenaeus and Tertullian. All three of these writers certainly knew about the descent into hell, and all three accepted it and believed in it, but it is clear that they did not regard it as something which ought to be inserted into an official creed.

It is not in the Nicene Creed, which says simply:

He was made man,
and was crucified also for us under Pontius Pilate.
He suffered and was buried,
and the third day he rose again, according to the Scriptures.

But it is in the Athanasian Creed which says of Jesus:

Who suffered for our salvation:
descended into hell,
rose again the third day from the dead.

Its first actual appearance in a credal statement is in the Symbol of Sirmium in AD 359/60, and its first appearance in the Apostles' Creed is in AD 570. We must remember that this does not mean that it was not part of the Church's belief long before that. It was, but it does not seem to have been regarded as suitable for insertion into a credal statement of the faith.

We shall divide our treatment of it into four different sections: what it really originally meant; what the New Testament evidence for it is; what developments in meaning it underwent; and finally its meaning and relevance for us today.

First, then, we look at the original meaning of the statement. 'He descended into hell', is liable to mislead us straightaway. It should read, 'He descended into *Hades*.' We have a similar necessary correction in Acts 2.27 which is a quotation of Psalm 16.10. In the Authorized Version that is cited in the form: 'Thou wilt not leave my soul in hell', but the Revised Standard Version and the New English Bible both have correctly: 'Thou wilt not abandon my soul to Hades', and Moffatt in his translation simply uses the word 'the grave'.

The word in Hebrew is *Sheol*; and Sheol is not hell; Sheol is simply the land of the dead. The Jews had no full doctrine of immortality or of a life after death. They believed that the souls of all men, or rather all men themselves, went to Sheol which was a grey, shadowy land, in which men moved like ghosts, in which there was neither light, nor colour, nor joy, and in which the shades of men were separated alike from God and from their fellow-men. Sheol is simply the place of the dead, with none of the connotation of torture and punishment which the word hell includes.

In the Authorized Version this word Sheol is translated by three different words.

- It is often translated as 'hell', wrongly, as we have seen, as in the Psalm (16.10) that we have just cited.
- It is sometimes translated as 'the pit'. Of Korah, Dathan and Abiram it is said: 'They and all that pertained to them went down alive into the pit, and the earth closed upon them' (Numbers 16.33).
- It is sometimes translated as 'the grave'. It was Jacob's lament for the lost Joseph: 'I will go down into the grave unto my son mourning' (Genesis 37.35).

The Greeks had the same idea, and Hades in Greek was also the place of the dead. To be quite accurate, it is likely that Hades was not originally a place but a person, for the original phrase is 'the House of Hades', and certainly in the Revelation Hades is a person. 'And I saw, and behold, a pale horse, and its rider's name was Death, and Hades followed him'

(Revelation 6.8). 'And the sea gave up the dead in it, Death and Hades gave up the dead in them' (Revelation 20.13). 'Then Death and Hades were thrown into the lake of fire' (Revelation 20.14). Hades was the king of the dead and it was to his shadowy house all men went.

When the New Testament wishes to express the place of punishment it uses the word Gehenna. It is better to lose your hand or your eye than with your whole body to be thrown into Gehenna (Matthew 5.29–30). It is not necessary to fear those who can kill the body; it is necessary to fear him who can cast soul and body into Gehenna (Matthew 10.28).

Now Gehenna is Ge Hinnom, the Valley of Hinnom outside Jerusalem. It was in that valley that in the ancient days those who worshipped Moloch the fire-god had burned their children in the fire as an offering to him. Josiah had stopped that impious worship and had made the Valley of Hinnom desecrated territory (2 Kings 23.10). It had then become the official rubbish dump, the public incinerator, of Jerusalem. It smouldered continuously, and in it a loathsome species of worm bred and multiplied. That terrible valley, a kind of valley of destruction, stood as the popular idea of hell.

The two words are quite distinct. Sheol is simply the place of the dead. Gehenna is the place of the punishment of the wicked. Sheol is not hell, but Gehenna is.

This sentence of the creed therefore had originally nothing to do with hell. It simply meant that Jesus went to the place of the dead. In other words, it was merely another and vivid way of saying again that he was really and truly dead. In point of fact when Rufinus wrote his commentary on the creed, and noted that this phrase was absent from the Roman creed, he went on to say that its absence made no difference because it was exactly the same as 'dead and buried', and it is a fact that the creeds often have one or other, but not both statements. It is also of interest to note that in the American editions of *The Book of Common Prayer* the priest, when reciting the creed, can use the word *hell*, or he can use the phrase *the place of departed spirits*, which is more correct. The American custom might well be copied everywhere.

Now, in the second place, we turn to look at the New Testament evidence which can be cited in support of this article of the creed. There are eight New Testament passages which are quoted as evidence.

(i) There is the quotation from Psalm 16.10 in Acts 2.27, to which we have already made reference. It runs: 'Thou wilt not abandon my soul to Hades, nor let thy loyal servant suffer corruption.' From this it is quite clear that Peter thought of Jesus as being in the place of the dead, in Hades, in Sheol, during the time between his death on the cross and his resurrection.

(ii) Romans 10.6–7 runs: 'Do not say in your heart, "Who will ascend into heaven?" (that is, to bring Christ down), or, "Who will descend into the abyss?" (that is, to bring Christ up from the dead).' The abyss, the pit, is another name for Sheol. So it seems that Paul also thought of Jesus as being in Sheol between his death and his resurrection

(iii) This line of thought is closely repeated in Ephesians 4.8–10. There Paul quotes Psalm 68.18: 'When he ascended on high, he led a host of captives, and he gave gifts to men.' He then goes on to comment, as it were in parenthesis: 'In saying, "He ascended", what does it mean but that he also descended into the lower parts of the earth? He who descended is also he who ascended far above all the heavens that he might fill all things.' 'The lower parts of the earth' is yet another name for Sheol, and here again the assumption is that, just as Christ ultimately ascended into the heavenly places, so he first descended into Sheol.

(iv) There are certain passages which speak of the universal triumph of Christ in every part of the universe. Philippians 2.9–11 reads: 'Therefore God has highly exalted him, and bestowed on him the name which is above every name, that at the name of Jesus every knee should bow, in heaven and on earth and *under the earth*, and that every tongue should confess that Jesus Christ is Lord, to the glory of God the Father.'

(v) There is a very similar passage in Revelation 5.13: 'And I heard every creature in heaven and on earth and *under the earth*, and in the sea, and all therein saying: To him who sits upon the throne and to the Lamb be blessing and glory and honour and might for ever and ever.' In both of these passages the triumph of Christ extends to *under the earth*, that is to Sheol and to the realm of the dead.

(vi) There is a passage in the Fourth Gospel which may have fitted into this pattern. In John 5.25 we read: 'Truly, truly, I say to you, the hour is coming, and now is, when the dead will hear the voice of God, and those who hear will live.' As we shall see, it became an essential part of this doctrine that Jesus did not only go to the place of the dead, but that he also preached to the people who were there. This may be a reference to the preaching to the dead, but in the Fourth Gospel it is more likely to be a reference to the preaching to those who are spiritually dead, those who are dead in their sins and trespasses, and who are raised to newness of life by the preaching of Jesus Christ.

(vii) The final two passages come close together and must be taken close together, and it is on them that this doctrine mainly depends. They are the proof texts for it. They are both from the First Letter of Peter. The first is 1 Peter 3.18–20:

> Christ also died for our sins once and for all, the righteous for the unrighteous, that he might bring us to God, being put to death in the flesh but made alive in the spirit, *in which he went and preached to the spirits in prison*, who formerly did not obey, when God's patience waited in the days of Noah, during the building of the ark.

The second is in 1 Peter 4.6:

> For this is why *the gospel was preached even to the dead*, that though judged in the flesh like men, they might live in the spirit like God.

The first of these two passages in particular has always been a storm centre of interpretation. On the face of it it says that Jesus preached to the spirits in prison, that is, to the dead. There have been several unconvincing attempts to explain it completely away.

If we read the passage again, we shall see that it contains the words 'When God's patience waited in the days of Noah'. If we go back to near the beginning of the Letter (1.10–12) we find that Peter holds that it was the spirit of Christ who spoke within the prophets. Now still further in 2 Peter 2.5, Noah is called a herald of righteousness. So it is argued that this preaching actually took place *in the days of Noah*. Perhaps through the lips of Noah, the spirit of Christ preached to the men whose spirits are *now* in prison, because they did not listen to this preaching. But they were actually on earth in the wicked days before the Flood. This, of course would completely eliminate the doctrine, for the preaching would have been in this world and not in the world of the dead at all.

There are those who hold that *the spirits in prison* are not men at all, but that they are the wicked, rebellious and disobedient angels. In 2 Peter 2.4 we read that God did not spare these angels but threw them into

Tartarus (that is, hell), and committed them to pits of nether gloom. If Peter's statement is taken this way, it means that Jesus proclaimed final and irrevocable doom to the rebellious angels.

Anyone who uses Moffatt's translation must have been puzzled by it. It runs:

> Christ himself died for our sins, once for all, a just man for unjust men, that he might bring us near to God; in the flesh he was put to death, but he came to life in the Spirit. It was in the Spirit that Enoch also went and preached to the imprisoned spirits who had disobeyed at the time when God's patience held out during the construction of the ark in the days of Noah.

We are at once compelled to ask, Where did *Enoch* come from? How does Enoch get into Moffatt's version of this passage?

In the earliest days of the transmission of the New Testament, of course, all copies of it were laboriously transcribed by hand. Anyone who copies makes mistakes and the early copyists made their quota of them. One of the commonest kind of mistake was that words which sounded the same, or words which looked the same, often got missed out. Further, it must be remembered that in the early manuscripts there was never any space between the words. Now we write this passage with the English in the Greek order and with the Greek in English letters above:

Thanatōtheis		*men sarki*	*zoopoiethēis*	
Having been put to death		in the flesh	having been raised to live	
de pneumati	*en hō*	*kai*	*tois en phulakē pneumasi*	*ekēruxen*
in the Spirit	in which	also	to the in prison spirits	he preached.

Now in that passage we have the Greek *en ho kai* which sounds almost exactly the same as *Enoch kai*. Moffatt therefore held that after *en ho kai* the word *Enoch* had got missed out because the sound was so similar and that the passage should read

en ho kai	*Enoch*	*tois en phulake pneumasi*	*ekeruxen*
in which also	Enoch	to the in prison spirits	preached.

It so happens that Enoch was a very prominent figure in Jewish literature between the Testaments and it was said that he did pronounce the doom of the fallen angels. But it is really quite impossible to accept

Moffatt's guess; there is no evidence that Enoch ever stood in the text of the passage. We must discard that solution.

We will be wise to take the Peter passage in its obvious sense. Peter meant it to mean that Jesus preached to the shades of men in the world of the dead.

We have looked at the original meaning of this doctrine, and at the evidence for it which can be produced from the New Testament. We must now go on to look at the way in which it developed and was elaborated in the thought of the Church.

(i) We begin by again reminding ourselves that the original intention of this phrase in the creed was to affirm that Jesus was really and truly dead, in answer to those who held that he was so holy and so divine that he could feel no pain and experience no death.

(ii) Calvin took it to mean that Jesus went to hell to bear the penalties and the pains and the tortures and the punishments in our stead. He wrote: 'If Christ is said to have descended to the dead, it is nothing to be surprised at, since he bore the death which is inflicted by God on sinners.' Parker is even more definite, 'What then? Christ in his own person, according to his humanity, suffered the penalties of hell which we should have suffered.'

However moving and dramatic that interpretation may be, it cannot be the correct one, for, as we have seen, the original reference of the statement is not to hell, the place of the punishment of sinners, but to Hades, the place which, according to Jewish thought, was the shadowy home of all the dead. So this is an interpretation which we must discard.

(iii) By far the commonest development, one which became to all intents and purposes orthodox belief, is that which stresses the preaching of Christ. The Peter passage says: 'He went and preached to the spirits in prison' (1 Peter 3.19). In the early Church it came to be held that it was for this preaching that the descent was made. In the first elaboration of this line of thought the preaching was not to everyone in Hades. It was to the patriarchs, the saints, the prophets and the martyrs of the Old Testament. Jesus preached the gospel to them, and then led them with him out of Hades into heaven.

This is repeated again and again by the early thinkers. Irenaeus says: 'It was for this reason that the Lord descended into the regions beneath the earth, preaching his advent there also, and declaring the remission of sins, which is received by those who believe in him.' He goes on: 'Now all those who believed in him, who had hope towards him, that is, those who proclaimed his advent and submitted to his dispensations, the righteous man, the prophets and patriarchs, to them he remitted sins in the same way as he did to us. The death of the Lord became the means of healing and remission to them.' Tertullian says that he descended to Hades that 'he might make the patriarchs and prophets partakers of himself.' The Syrian *Didaskalia* says quite definitely: 'Jesus was crucified under Pontius Pilate, and departed in peace in order to preach to Abraham, Isaac and Jacob, and all the saints, concerning the end of the world and the resurrection of the dead.'

In connection with this there is one interesting fact which no one has ever been able to explain. The early Christian thinkers always aimed to clinch every argument with a quotation from Scripture. In particular they were always eager to produce a passage from the prophets which the actions of Jesus fulfilled. Now when Justin Martyr and Irenaeus speak about this doctrine between them they quote no fewer than six times a proof text, attributing it sometimes to Jeremiah, sometimes to Isaiah. The text is: 'The Lord God remembered his dead people of Israel, who lay in the graves, and he descended to preach to them his own salvation.' That indeed would be a precise prediction of this interpretation of the descent; but the odd thing is that that text occurs in no known part of the Old Testament in any language or in any manuscript. Where Justin Martyr and Irenaeus got that text is one of the unsolved mysteries.

We may cite one more interesting appearance of this interpretation. In the statement of the explication of the articles of belief of the Church of England after the Reformation, in the form produced in the fourth year of the reign of Edward the Confessor in 1552, it is said of Christ that his body lay in the grave until the Resurrection, while his spirit was with the spirits who were detained in hell, and preached to them. This belief is then put into rough verse:

> And so he died in the flesh,
> But quickened in the spirit;
> His body then was buried,
> As is our use and right.

His spirit did after this descend
Into the lower parts,
Of them that long in darkness were
The true light of their hearts.

In the 1562 version of the explication both the reference to the preaching and the verses about it are removed.

So it can be seen that the idea of Jesus preaching to the Old Testament saints in Hades and leading them out of it into heaven was deeply rooted in the thought of the Church.

(iv) We come now to what in many ways is the most interesting and the most attractive development of all, a development which is connected with the name of Clement of Alexandria. Clement was a very great scholar; he was steeped in the wealth of Greek and Latin literature. Had he not been a Christian teacher, he would have been one of the great figures in the culture of the Graeco-Roman world. Now Clement was persuaded that Greek philosophy was in its own way just as much a preparation for Christianity as Jewish religion had been. He saw the Spirit and the Word of God moving in men like Plato and Socrates too. And Clement's idea was that the preaching of Jesus Christ in the realm of the dead was not only to the Jewish prophets and saints but also to all the Gentiles who, according to the light that was in them, had lived and walked in loyalty and obedience to the will of God as they knew it.

Clement had sympathy as wide as the world. He believed in what he called 'a universal movement and translation'. It is a very beautiful and a very gracious conception, and one which very much appeals to the modern mind, but the Church never accepted it as orthodox belief.

(v) We come finally to the last elaboration of this belief, one which became popular both in legend and in art. This is known as the Harrowing of Hell. In this idea Jesus Christ did not so much descend to hell as invade hell. He came as the conqueror. Hell is harrowed; death is vanquished; the bars of iron yield; the saints and the martyrs and the prophets, and they are named in a long catalogue, crowd to him as the victorious king. Satan is conquered for ever and committed to his own hell. The story is told in full in the apocryphal book called the Gospel of Nicodemus or the Acts of Pilate. Death is terror-stricken and conquered.

Satan is for ever subdued and eliminated; the faithful have the gates of heaven opened to them. 'Then each of the just said, "O death where is thy sting? O Grave, where is thy victory? For the conqueror has redeemed us."'

This is the vivid, pictorial, dramatic representation of the final triumph of Jesus Christ in all parts of the universe, and with it the elaboration of this doctrine reaches its peak.

We must bring our study of this article of the creed to an end by asking what it means today, and what its relevance for us is. This we are bound to do because it is a part of the creed which is the basic statement of Christian belief, and which many of us regularly recite in church. That it is beset with all kinds of difficulties is clear; it is indeed so difficult that there is little wonder that it is largely neglected, and hardly ever finds its way into a sermon. But the difficulty does not absolve us from inquiring into its meaning and relevance; rather it makes such an inquiry all the more necessary and all the more a matter of duty.

(i) We must begin by remembering the basic fact that, as it stands, the wording of this article of the creed is quite misleading. We would do much better to say quite simply: 'He descended to the place of the dead.' That initial restatement is absolutely necessary.

(ii) It also labours under another obvious difficulty. It is expressed in terms of a world view and a cosmology which have been long since left behind. The very word *descended* is proof of this. This sentence clearly suggests a three-storey universe with heaven above and the earth in the centre and the subterranean abode of the dead below. It could hardly have been expressed in any other terms for that was the way the age in which it was first set down saw the world; but it does mean that these terms are no longer acceptable or even possible for a twentieth-century man. We are therefore once again faced with the necessity of restatement.

(iii) Furthermore, the conception behind it is that of Jewish rather than of Christian eschatology. Suppose we do restate it in terms of Jesus Christ going to Hades or to the abode of the dead, then we have more or less committed ourselves to a picture of the life after death in which the dead are in some vague, ghostly, shadowy, nebulous place, existing in a kind of intermediate state in which they have left this life but have not yet entered fully into the life to come. This approach is far more Jewish than it is Christian.

(iv) This article of the creed certainly remains subject to all these difficulties and problems and disadvantages; and yet there may be found in it a symbolism which has much beauty and not a little value.

As we have repeatedly said, we must start from the fact that its original intention was to emphasize that Jesus was really and truly dead. It also gives rise to the question: What was Jesus doing and experiencing in the period when from the human point of view he was dead? What was he doing when, to use the language of the creed itself, he was in the place of the dead? As we have seen, the answer that the thinkers of the early Church gave to that question was a twofold answer. At first they were content to say that he preached the gospel to the people in the place of the dead, either limiting the preaching to the Jews who had walked in the ways of God, and who had been expecting and longing for the Messiah, or extending the preaching to the much wider circle of those of all nations who had served and obeyed God to the utmost of their understanding, and who were true to the highest that they knew. Later on men were to think of the action of Jesus at that time as the invasion of hell, the shattering of Satan's power, the liberation of Satan's captives, and the final destruction of Satan himself.

- Here in symbolic language and picture is the answer to the question that has always exercised the minds of thinking people: What happens to the millions upon millions of men who never heard of Jesus Christ? What happens to the great and good figures of the past who in every age and generation and in every race and nation lived nobly, but never had the opportunity to receive the Christian gospel, because they lived before Jesus came?

  This doctrine means symbolically that either in this life or in the life beyond death all men are offered the gospel of the truth and the love of God.

- There is another and a more inclusive way of putting this: it means that there are no limits in space and time to the grace of God, indicating symbolically that the grace of God continues to operate in whatever other world and whatever other life there may be.

  Here there is surely something to make us think. What right have we to set limits to the operation of the grace of God?

Whatever other world there is, and whatever other life there is, surely still belong to God; the whole universe in time and in eternity, here and hereafter, is the Lord's. In this doctrine we may at least glimpse the truth that the sphere of operation of the grace of God is illimitable; that God has not only time but also eternity to win men to himself.

– If we look at this from still another angle, from that of the later versions of the doctrine, we see that this doctrine does symbolically lay it down that the triumph of Jesus Christ is destined to be complete. It is the affirmation that it is true that at the name of Jesus every knee shall bow in heaven and on earth and under the earth (Philippians 2.10). In other words, we may believe encouragingly in the universal hope that in the end all men will be saved. Origen, who was in many ways the greatest and the most adventurous thinker the Church ever produced, took the idea of the final and ultimate triumph of Christ so seriously and so completely that he believed that in the end even Satan himself would submit to the love and power of God in Jesus Christ and would be saved.

There are tremendous reaches of thought in this apparently unpromising article of the creed. But the more we think of it, the more we come to the conclusion that it belongs far more to the poetry of thought than to the theology of thought. If we take it quite simply to mean that Jesus underwent the death which all men undergo, then no doubt it is a statement which ought to be included in the creed, but the wording does need clarification. But, if we go further, and if we allow it to lead us on to these thoughts and speculations amid which we have been moving, this is not material which can be crystallized and stereotyped in a creed. This is the language of hope and of devotion and of vision and of poetry. And therein lies the value of this article of the creed – it states a fact, but it opens a vision. The fact the mind can accept; of the vision the heart may dream.

CHAPTER ELEVEN

The Third Day He Rose Again
from the Dead

The claim that Jesus rose from the dead is a claim so vast and far-reaching in its importance and in its implications that there is no half-way house about it. It is either the greatest single fact in history, or, if it is not true, it is the greatest deception in history. That is the reason why the Church's belief in the Resurrection must be submitted to the most stringent examination. The Resurrection is not one of the Christian beliefs which can be left in suspense.

That the Resurrection was an unvarying element in early Christian preaching is beyond all doubt. There is scarcely a sermon in the Book of Acts which does not state the Church's belief in the Resurrection (Acts 2.24–36; 3.15; 4.10; 7.56; 10.40; 13.30–7; 17.31). If the Resurrection is removed from the messages of the early Church, then that message loses its centre and its soul. The claim on which all other claims were based is invalidated, and there is very little left.

It must at once be admitted that it is not possible to demonstrate the fact of the Resurrection as one would demonstrate the truth of a theorem in geometry. We cannot produce a neat series of steps in an argument, and finish with QED at the end. If the fact of the Resurrection is true, it is also unique. There are no parallels. It is easy to believe in the historicity of a repeated event. It is much more difficult to attain to anything like certainty about an event which stands alone.

The movement of men's minds has changed. A modern man does not think in the same terms and categories as his forefathers did. Arguments which convince one generation are ineffectual in another. We must nonetheless look first at the arguments for the Resurrection which were valid in New Testament times and in previous generations.

(i) First, there is the argument from prophecy. The classic exposition of the creed is that written by John Pearson, the then Bishop of Chester, and first published in 1659. Pearson found three prophetic passages which seemed to him convincing arguments for the Resurrection.

The first is from Psalm 2. In the second verse we read: 'The kings of the earth set themselves, and the rulers take counsel together, against the Lord and his anointed.' The word for *anointed* is in Hebrew *Messiah* and in Greek *Christ*. Here is foretold the human enmity which brought Jesus to the cross. But the Psalm goes on (verses 6 and 7): 'I have set my king (that is, my anointed) on Zion, my holy hill. I will tell of the decree of the Lord. He said to me, You are my son, today I have begotten you.' This foretells the honour and exaltation of God's Anointed One, in spite of all that cruel and wicked men could do to him. Thus, in the Psalm, Pearson sees foretold both the cross and the resurrection of Jesus – God's Anointed One, God's Messiah, God's Christ.

Pearson finds an even clearer statement in Psalm 16.10: 'For thou dost not give me up to Sheol, nor let thy godly one see the pit.' This text was in fact a favourite proof text in the early Church (cf. Acts 2.30–1; 13.35). It was not true of David who in fact did die and who, so to speak, stayed dead; it must therefore refer to the Messiah; and therefore it guarantees the fact of the Resurrection.

To this Pearson adds still a third text. On the basis of the first two texts it could be argued that Jesus Christ rose from the dead, but it could not be argued that he is alive for evermore. He might have risen, as it were, temporarily, and then afterwards have died. So Pearson adds Isaiah 55.3: 'I will make with you an everlasting covenant, my steadfast, sure love for David' (cf. Acts 13.34). This is taken as the proof that the effect of the Resurrection is everlasting.

Here then is the argument from prophecy. It is an argument which both Peter (Acts 2.24–31) and Paul (Acts 13.33–7) use. There are many people for whom this kind of argument may still hold good today; but equally there are very many for whom it is quite unconvincing, and it will undoubtedly have little or nothing to say to the man outside the Church.

(ii) There is also the argument from Old Testament typology, which is closely related to the argument from prophecy. Pearson finds in the Old Testament two figures whose experiences typified and prefigured the death and rising again of Jesus. Joseph was ordained to save his brothers who would have killed him (Genesis 37.18); in the same way

Jesus Christ saves those who killed him. Joseph was put into the dungeon and then brought out of it (Genesis chapters 39 and 40), which prefigures Jesus being put into the grave and brought out again. The experience of Isaac also prefigures the experience of Jesus. True, Abraham in the end did not sacrifice Isaac, but he was willing to do so (Genesis 22), and this incident is in fact used by the writer to the Hebrews (11.19): 'Abraham considered that God was able to raise men even from the dead; hence, figuratively speaking, he did receive him back.'

There are three further Old Testament passages which are pressed into this kind of service. First, there is Isaiah 53.12, which tells of the ultimate triumph and honour of the one who was the Suffering Servant. Secondly, there is Hosea's promise of the restoration of Israel (6.2): 'After two days he will revive us; and on the third day he will raise us up, that we may live before him.' Thirdly, there is God's promise to the stricken Hezekiah (2 Kings 20.5): 'Behold, I will heal you; on the third day you shall go up to the house of the Lord.'

Again, there are those who find this convincing, and those who find it quite unconvincing. It may in any event be true to say that no one who did not already believe in the Resurrection would find in these sayings and incidents any kind of proof.

(iii) There is also witness to the Resurrection, human and divine. There is the witness of the disciples. In the apostolic company the traitor Judas had to be replaced by one who was to be a witness of the Resurrection (Acts 1.22). 'To this', says Peter, 'we are witnesses' (Acts 3.15). We shall return to this, for it is a line of thought which cannot be disregarded. And to it the older line of argument would have added the witness of angels. In the First and the Fourth Gospel it is an angelic messenger who gives to the first visitor to the tomb of Jesus the message that Christ is risen (Matthew 28.2–7; John 20.11–13). We may nowadays find the angelic witness difficult, but the idea of witness to the Resurrection is clearly something which we must investigate further.

(iv) There are the words of Jesus himself. Not once or twice but many times Jesus foretold his Resurrection according to the story of the Gospels. He foretold his suffering and death, but always he foretold his Resurrection too (Mark 8.31; 9.31; 10.34; Matthew 16.21; 17.23; 20.19; Luke 9.22).

There is unquestionably a difficulty here. As the record stands, the sayings of Jesus are clear and unmistakable; and yet the fact remains that the disciples were quite unprepared for the death of Jesus, quite without hope of the Resurrection, and completely astonished when Jesus did come back to them. Either the disciples were so obtuse that they completely failed to understand – which is in itself likely enough – or the words of Jesus were in the light of subsequent events made more clear and definite than they actually were – which is by no means impossible.

There is indeed one case in which we can see the latter happening. In both Luke and Matthew, Jesus is recorded as using Jonah as an illustration of himself. In Luke the passage runs: 'As Jonah became a sign to the men of Nineveh, so will the Son of Man be to this generation' (Luke 11.30). Here the idea is that just as Jonah and his preaching confronted Nineveh with God, so Jesus and his preaching confront the Jews with God. The sign *is* Jesus. But in Matthew this is completely altered, and the sign is that just as Jonah was three days and three nights in the belly of the whale, so Jesus will be three days and nights in the earth (Matthew 12.40). In point of fact Jesus was *not* three nights in the grave, but only two; and it is clear that Matthew had used a forecast which was not originally intended as such, and that Luke's version is correct. We need not doubt that Jesus foretold his ultimate triumph, but it may well be that his words were not so definite as they were afterwards made to be.

It will be best at this point to tabulate the Resurrection appearances of Jesus as they are contained in the New Testament, because the attack on the historicity of the Resurrection is based on certain features within the record. We shall tabulate the material in each Gospel under three headings: the place where the appearance took place; the people to whom it was made; the messenger or messengers at the tomb who gave the news of it to the first visitors to the tomb.

The Gospel	The People	The Place	The Messenger
Matthew	The Women (28.9, 10)	Jerusalem	An angel of the Lord (28.2–7)
	Eleven Disciples (28.16–20)	Galilee	
Mark	No recorded appearances		A young man in a white robe (16.5)

Luke	Two travellers on the road to Emmaus (24.13–31)	Jerusalem	Two men in dazzling apparel (24.4)
	Peter (24.34)	Jerusalem	
	The disciples (24.36–50)	Jerusalem	
John	Mary (20.11–18)	Jerusalem	Two angels in white (20.11–12)
	Ten disciples (20.19–23)	Jerusalem	
	Eleven disciples (20.26–9)	Jerusalem	
	Seven disciples (21)	Galilee	

In addition to the list of appearances as recorded in the four Gospels there is a much earlier record of Resurrection appearances of Jesus in Paul's first letter to the Corinthians (1 Corinthians 15.1–8). There, five appearances are recorded: to Peter, to the Twelve, to more than five hundred Christians, to James, and to Paul himself. Here then is the recorded evidence as we have it. What are the objections to it?

The first objection is quite simply that such things do not happen. There are some people who dismiss the whole matter simply on the grounds that it could not have happened, and therefore did not happen. That is clearly a quite unscientific approach; that is simply to refuse to consider the evidence and to foreclose the whole question on no better grounds than that of personal opinion. Even a century ago – to take only the most obvious instances – almost anyone would have said of television, of thoracic surgery, of nuclear weapons, that such things do not happen. But the fact remains that time was to prove that they do happen. A man may examine the evidence and come to the conclusion that it does not support the claims made for it; but to refuse even to look at the evidence is neither an honest nor a reasonable nor a scientific approach.

But there is a series of objections founded on the evidence.

(i) It is objected that the Pauline list omits a good deal of the material in the Gospels. For instance, the women at the tomb are absent from the Pauline list, as are Mary Magdalene and the two travellers on the road to Emmaus. There is in fact a good and sufficient reason for this. What Paul is handing down is, so to speak, the official tradition of the Church (1 Corinthians 15.3). Now that official tradition of the Church was naturally and properly and inevitably concerned with what we might call *apostolic* appearances of Jesus. The great concern of the early Church was with evidence which could be traced back to an apostle, or at least to the associate of an apostle, and the tradition which Paul had received is confined to such appearances.

(ii) It is objected that the place of the appearances varies, that in some cases it is Jerusalem and in others it is Galilee. On the whole it is true to say that in Matthew the main appearance is in Galilee; in Luke all the appearances are in Jerusalem; and in John the appearances are both in Jerusalem and in Galilee (but in John the question is complicated by the fact that scholars are largely agreed that John 21 is not part of the original Gospel, but rather an appendix to it).

It is further argued that on the Gospel evidence one would expect the appearances to be in Galilee. Mark reports Jesus as saying: 'But after I am raised up I will go before you to Galilee' (Mark 14.28).

But again this is not an entirely valid objection. It may be that perhaps quite unconsciously we tend to think of the Resurrection appearances of Jesus as being concentrated into a very few days, as if they all followed immediately on his death. But in fact they were spread over the seven-week period between the Passover and Pentecost (Acts 1.3). Given that period, there is ample time for both Jerusalem and Galilee appearances.

(iii) There is in the Gospel record one quite clear and obvious discrepancy in the matter of messenger or messengers at the tomb. In Mark the messenger is one young man (16.5); in Matthew, an angel of the Lord (28.2–7); in Luke, two men in dazzling apparel (24.4); and in John, two angels (20.11–12). But is this in any sense a serious discrepancy? The central fact of the Resurrection and of the empty tomb remains constant and unvarying; it is only this piece of dramatic apparatus which varies. Surely there is no difficulty in holding that an event of such supreme wonder as the Resurrection would tend to acquire still more wonder in its accompanying detail. It is no unusual thing for a story to improve and to develop in the telling and in the repetition, and what is after all a very slight difference in detail cannot invalidate the unchanging evidence for the central fact.

It is perhaps a mistake to demand from any set of accounts of an event an absolute and precise identity. It might well be held that, if four people tell the same story without the slightest variation in detail, that is not so much evidence of absolute honesty as it is evidence of collusion. Slight differences are rather a proof of the essential honesty than they are of fictional dishonesty.

(iv) R. M. Grant, in his section on the Resurrection in *A Historical Introduction to the New Testament*, raises a very interesting point. He holds that it is possible to discern in the three accounts of Matthew, Mark and Luke certain objects which each of the Gospel writers had in mind.

When we read Matthew's account (27.62–28.15) it does seem clear that Matthew is concerned to deny the Jewish explanations of the empty tomb. No one denied that the tomb was empty. The Jews suggested that the disciples had stolen the body of Jesus; the Christians answered that the tomb was sealed and guarded. The Jews suggested that the soldiers had been asleep; the Christians answered that the soldiers had been in fact bribed to say so. At the back of Matthew's account there is the intention of proving the falsity of Jewish attempts to explain away the empty tomb, which they could not deny.

When we read Luke's account there are three appearances, on the road to Emmaus, to Peter, and to the disciples. The appearance on the road to Emmaus underlines the presence of Jesus in the Lord's Supper. 'He was known to them in the breaking of bread' (24.35). The special appearance to Peter underlines the primacy of Peter in the apostolic company, and counterbalances the tragic story of his denial. The appearance to the disciples underlines the reality of the Resurrection body of Jesus (24.39).

The narrative of John once again stresses the reality of the Resurrection body of Jesus, but also stresses the fact that Jesus was now independent of time and place. Closed doors were no barrier to him. He was real, yet he could appear when he would and to whom he would.

One thing is perfectly obvious. The Gospel writers were not really interested in their story simply as a report; they were telling it to beget faith in their readers, and to answer the false stories which circulated partly from heretics within the Church and partly from enemies outside the Church.

But the significant thing is that, whatever the purpose, the central fact remains the same.

Matthew 27.63); or they speak of it as being *on the third day* (Matthew 16.21; 17.23; 20.19; Luke 9.22; 18.33; 24.7; 24.46; Acts 10.40; 1 Corinthians 15.4). Both these ways are perfectly in accordance with the facts as stated, and there is no difficulty there.

But we do find a difficulty in a passage to which we have previously referred. In Matthew 12.39–41 Jesus is reported as saying: 'An evil and adulterous generation seeThere remain two further lines of attack at which we must look. One of them is particular and the other is general; and we shall look first at the particular.

(v) It is alleged that there is an actual or an implied discrepancy in different accounts of the time that the body of Jesus lay in the tomb.

The general course of events is clear, though one thing is always to be remembered when we are thinking of time and days in the Jewish part of the New Testament. For the Jew the new day begins at 6 p.m. on the old day. For instance, to take the best known and the most important instance of that, the Jewish Sabbath begins at 6 p.m. on the Friday evening.

Jesus was crucified on the Day of Preparation (Matthew 27.62; Mark 15.42; Luke 23.54; John 19.31, 42). The Jewish Sabbath is the Christian Saturday; therefore, the Day of Preparation for the Sabbath is Friday. The preparation of Jesus' body and the placing of it in the tomb were in fact a race against time, for all this had to be done before 6 p.m. when the Sabbath began, and after which no work could be done. Jesus' body lay in the tomb all through the Friday night, all through the Saturday, all through the Saturday night, and it was early on the Sunday morning when the women came back to the tomb, that is, on the first day of the week (Matthew 28.1; Mark 16.2; Luke 24.1; John 20.1). Then they found the tomb empty, and slowly they realized that Jesus had risen.

Now the Gospels have two ways of expressing this period in the tomb. They speak of the Resurrection of Jesus as being *after three days* (Mark 8.31; 9.31; 10.34; ks for a sign; but no sign shall be given to it except the sign of the prophet Jonah. For as Jonah was three days and three nights in the belly of the whale, so will the Son of Man be three days and three nights in the heart of the earth. The men of Nineveh will arise at the judgement with this generation and condemn it; for they repented at the preaching of Jonah, and behold, something greater than Jonah is here.'

If Jesus did say that, then his prediction was certainly not fulfilled because on no possible reckoning can Jesus be said to have been three *nights* in the earth, since he was only in the tomb for the Friday and the Saturday night. But this same saying of Jesus is reported again in Luke 11.29–32: 'This generation is an evil generation; it seeks a sign, but no sign shall be given to it except the sign of Jonah. For as Jonah became a sign to the men of Nineveh, so will the Son of Man be to this generation. … The men of Nineveh will arise at the judgement with this generation and condemn it; for they repented at the preaching of Jonah, and behold, something greater than Jonah is here.'

In these two passages the Jonah parallel is used for two quite different purposes as we explained earlier; in the Matthew passage the parallel is the three days and the three nights Jonah was in the belly of the great fish, and that is taken as a forecast and symbol of the Resurrection. In the Luke passage the parallel is Jonah himself and his preaching. God sent Jonah to Nineveh and at his preaching Nineveh repented; God sent Jesus to Palestine and at his preaching the men of Palestine did not repent; Jesus is far greater than Jonah; the Jews were confronted with something far greater than the men of Nineveh, and yet they failed to recognize it; therefore, even the men of Nineveh will at the judgement day condemn the Jews for their blindness. There is no doubt at all that it is Luke's version which makes sense.

What has happened is that both Matthew and Luke knew that Jesus had used Jonah as an illustration and a parallel of his own work. Matthew, being in any event characteristically fond of wonder stories, mistakenly took the parallel to be between the time in the tomb and the time in the whale's belly. Luke, being a better historian and maybe having access to a better tradition, rightly took the parallel to be between the preaching of Jonah and the preaching of Jesus. Matthew's version is a misinterpretation of a saying of Jesus; Luke's version is the correct interpretation, and with this version no difficulty at all arises.

The significance of Jesus' three days in the tomb is that the three days in Jewish eyes proved him really and truly to have passed through the experience of death. The Jews believed that the spirits of the departed hovered around the body for three days, and during that time might just possibly come back, but after that time they permanently departed. For that reason the Jews visited a grave for each of the three days after burial to see if the spirit had returned; after that they had no hope that life would return. So, to underline the fact that the body of Jesus lay in the tomb for three days is to underline the fact that he really did pass through the experience of death.

(vi) The more general objection to the Resurrection story is of a different kind, and is in some ways more serious. It is quite correctly pointed out that the ancient world in the time of Jesus was full of stories of dying and rising gods. A great many of the myths of the ancient world were based on the events of nature. Now the greatest event in nature is the death of the world in winter time and its resurrection each spring time. As an illustration of the kind of resurrection myth that came out of this we may remember the Demeter story. Demeter was the goddess of the harvest; her daughter Persephone was snatched away by Pluto the god of the underworld. Demeter in her grief caused the harvest to fail and the earth gave no crops. It was not possible for Persephone ever to return altogether to the upper world, for in the lower world she had eaten some pomegranate seeds and no one who has eaten in the underworld can wholly escape from it. But the gods came to an arrangement that Persephone should spend half the year with her mother Demeter and half the year with Pluto, as it were, dying and rising each year with the rhythm of the seasons.

The obvious question, asked in the ancient world, and sometimes asked to this day, is: Is the story of Jesus no more than another nature myth? Is this simply an addition to the many stories of dying and rising gods? Is this history or is this myth?

Now this is why the motive of *witness* is so important in the early Church. Judas is to be replaced by another apostle who 'must become with us a *witness* to the resurrection' (Acts 1.22). 'This Jesus God raised up, and of that we all are *witnesses*' (Acts 2.32). The Jews killed the Righteous One and the Author of life, but God raised him from the dead. 'To this we are *witnesses*' (Acts 3.15). 'We are *witnesses* of these things' (Acts 5.32). Paul speaks of the five hundred brothers who saw the risen Christ. 'Most of whom', he says, 'are still alive'; as if to say: If you want evidence for the claim that Jesus rose from the dead, go and cross-question them.

Unless we are prepared to say that the claim of the earliest apostles to be witnesses of the Resurrection is either a delusion or a complete fabrication, we cannot in any sense rank the Resurrection stories along with the stories of the dying and rising gods of pagan mythology. No one would ever have claimed those stories as historical events; the Christians on the other hand claimed that the Resurrection was something which they had witnessed; and it is very difficult to dispose of that claim.

In addition to the detailed attacks on the evidence for the Resurrection, there have been many and varied attempts to explain it away altogether. These so-called explanations are based not so much on the evidence or lack of evidence as on the presupposition that things like the Resurrection simply do not happen. Let us look at some of them.

(i) It is suggested that Jesus did not really die on the cross, but that he lost consciousness in a swoon, and that, when he was laid in the cool of the tomb, he revived, and somehow made his escape, and that from this the whole Resurrection story developed.

As we have already seen when we were studying the cross, it is true that there were cases of people who were taken down from the cross and who did survive; but that was the exception rather than the rule. We have seen how Jesus was scourged and buffeted until he was so weakened that he was unable to carry his own cross to Calvary. On the face of it, the chances of his survival were small indeed. And undoubtedly the body of Jesus must have been handled when it was taken from the cross and when it was being prepared for burial (Matthew 27.59; Mark 15.46; Luke 23.53; and especially John 19.39–40).

There is a curious unexplained difference in the stories here. Matthew, Mark and Luke all use the word *sindōn* for the shroud in which the body of Jesus was wrapped. This word means a sheet and it is the word used in Mark 14.51–2 for the sheet which the young man in the Garden wore over his naked body, and which he left in his pursuers' hands when he wriggled out of it and escaped. On the other hand, John used the word *othonia*, which is the word used for the long, bandage-like linen strips in which a mummy was wrapped in the Egyptian tombs and which was the usual material in which a body was buried. The Jewish custom was to put perfumes and spices between the folds of these as they wrapped them round the body.

The difference makes little effect on the facts of the story, but nonetheless it has its own importance. If John is right, and there is always a curious convincingness about John's details, then the fraudulent nature of the shrouds which are sometimes shown as relics and which are claimed to be the shroud in which Jesus was buried, is completely exposed. It may well be that only the most credulous relic-reverencer would accept the shrouds anyway, but if John is right, there never was a shroud, but only the normal linen bandages.

When the body had been prepared for burial it was laid in a rock tomb (Matthew 27.60; Mark 15.46; Luke 23.53; John 19.41). In these tombs the body was not buried; it was laid on a shelf hollowed out in the rock. Such tombs had no door; they were closed by a great stone which was as big as a cartwheel and which ran in a groove in front of the opening. After Luke 23.53 one famous manuscript of the New Testament adds that the stone which closed the opening of the tomb was so large that twenty men could not have rolled it away.

The simple statement of these facts demonstrates the extreme improbability that Jesus swooned and escaped. It is difficult to believe that, after the treatment he received, he did survive. It is difficult to believe that those who handled his body and who prepared it for burial would not have noticed some sign that life was not extinct, a sign for which they must eagerly have looked. It is difficult to see how Jesus in his weakened state could have extricated himself from the enveloping linen bandages, if John's version of the preparation of the body is right. And it is impossible to see how Jesus could have moved the great stone from the door from the inside and escaped. The swoon theory involves difficulties which are to all intents and purposes insurmountable.

(ii) There are two suggestions both of which involve the suggestion of theft of the body.

– The first is that the disciples stole away the body of Jesus, and concealed and disposed of it, and then claimed that he had risen from the dead. This would mean that the whole edifice of the Christian faith is founded on a deliberate act of deception. Even Klausner, the great Jewish scholar who does not accept the claims of Christ and of Christianity, recoils from any such theory. 'That is impossible,' he writes in his *Life of Jesus*. 'Deliberate imposture is not the substance out of which the religion of millions of mankind is created.'

Further, there is this to be remembered. Within forty years of the cross the majority of the apostles had died martyrs' deaths. It is perfectly possible that men might die for a delusion, but not for something which they knew to be a deliberate lie. There are hints in the New Testament itself that this was a very early attempt to explain away the Resurrection (Matthew 27.62–6), but it bears its impossibility on its face.

— The second is that the Jews stole the body away, lest the tomb of Jesus should become a martyr's shrine, and lest he become even more famous in death than in life.

The complete answer to that suggestion is simply this. Every Christian sermon in the early days in Jerusalem and elsewhere had as its peak and its climax a statement of the Resurrection faith. The only thing that the Jews would have needed to do to discredit the story once and for all, if they had stolen the body, was to produce it, or to produce convincing evidence that they had done so. And that they never did.

(iii) The third theory is that the Resurrection stories are all the product of hallucination. It is suggested that the disciples were perfectly genuinely convinced that they had seen Jesus, but that what they had seen was quite unreal and was only the product of a self-deceived mind.

In point of fact this theory can be put very beautifully. It can safely be assumed that Jesus was for ever in the thoughts of the disciples. As they thought of him, they must – so runs the theory – have remembered how in the history of Israel and in the providence of God time and time again seeming disaster had turned to triumph, and the good man and the good cause had been vindicated. So, perhaps unconsciously, they reasoned: 'He *must have risen*'; and from that they moved on to the conviction: 'He *has risen.*' And once they had reached that stage love did the rest – and they saw that which they had become convinced had happened. As someone has put it: 'It was unconquerable love which resurrected Jesus.'

This suggestion, attractive as it may sound, breaks down on one fact. If the narratives have any truth in them at all, the Resurrection appearances of Jesus were made oftener to groups of people than to single individuals. He appeared to the ten (John 20.19–23) in the absence of Thomas; he appeared to the eleven in the presence of Thomas (John 20.26–9). He appeared to the eleven in Galilee (Matthew 28.16–20). He appeared to more than five hundred disciples at the one time, most of whom, says Paul challengingly, are still alive, and therefore, he implies, available for cross-examination (1 Corinthians 15.6).

Individual hallucinations would be possible; but collective hallucinations on a scale like that are very difficult to believe. The hallucination theory does not solve the problem.

(iv) The last theory is the most surprising of all. It is connected with the name of Kirsopp Lake and is contained in his famous book *The Historical Evidence of the Resurrection of Jesus Christ*. His suggestion is that what happened was this: the disciples went to Galilee after the death of Jesus and there they had the experiences which made them believe that Jesus was still alive. They returned to Jerusalem and found the story of the empty tomb current. That story was due to the fact that certain women had gone to the Garden and had there met a young man, when they were looking for the tomb. He directed them with the words: 'He is not here.' And then he pointed to another tomb and said: 'See the place where they laid him' (Mark 16.6). In this theory the words, 'He has risen' are a later addition. In the grey light of the early morning the women mistook the directions and went to the wrong tomb. This wrong tomb they found empty and so arose the story of the empty tomb. Apart from anything else, it is difficult to see how the women could have made this mistake when they had seen the body of Jesus being laid in its tomb only three days before (Matthew 27.61; Mark 15.47; Luke 23.55).

The swoon, the theft, the hallucination, the mistake – these are the alternative explanations of the story of the Resurrection, and the plain fact is that not one of them will stand up to investigation, and not one of them makes sense. Wherever the truth lies, it does not lie there.

It may be said that up to now we have been dealing largely with the negative side of the matter. We have been looking at the arguments against the Resurrection and the attempts to explain it away. We must now turn to the positive evidence for the Resurrection.

(i) The existence of the Lord's Day is positive evidence. Christianity was born in Judaism, and the Jewish sacred and holy day was the Sabbath. The Sabbath is our Saturday, the last day of the week. The characteristic of the Sabbath was that it was a day when all work was forbidden. The explanation of that particular way of keeping the Sabbath was: 'In six days the Lord made heaven and earth, the sea, and all that is in them, and rested the seventh day; therefore the Lord blessed the sabbath day and hallowed it' (Exodus 20.11). The Sabbath commemorated the rest of

God after the work of creation. To the Jew the Sabbath was one of the most sacred institutions in all the world; and yet very early in the history of the Church we find that the great Christian day is not the last day of the week but the first day of the week, not the Sabbath but the Lord's Day.

This begins to emerge very early. Paul preached in Troas on the first day of the week, when they were gathered to break bread (Acts 20.7). Clearly, we have here the picture of something which even by that time had become a custom in the Christian Church. When Paul was making the necessary arrangements for the taking of the collection which was to go to help the poor Christians at Jerusalem he wrote to the Christians of Corinth: 'On the first day of every week, each of you is to put something aside' (1 Corinthians 16.2). We have here again the indication that the first day of the week was the regular meeting day for the Christian fellowship. This takes us back to a time about AD 55.

The first reference to the Lord's Day in literature is in Revelation 1.10 where the John of the Revelation begins his vision by saying: 'I was in the spirit on the Lord's Day.'

It is not very long before the observance of the Lord's Day is the standard practice of the Christian Church. Dionysius of Corinth tells how the congregation met to hear sacred books read on the Lord's Day (Eusebius, *The Ecclesiastical History* 4.23.11). The *Didachē*, The Teaching of the Twelve Apostles, the church's first service order book, says: 'On the Lord's Day of the Lord, come together, break bread and hold Eucharist' (*Didachē* 14.1). Ignatius writing to the Magnesians says that 'those who walked in ancient customs came to a new hope, no longer living for the Sabbath, but for the Lord's Day' (*To the Magnesians* 9.1). These references come from early in the second century.

Here is something which demands explanation. Here is a radical change in the calendar by which men ordered their lives. It is no small thing to switch your holy day from the last to the first day of the week. Institutions, sanctified by the law of God, and hallowed by centuries of observance, are not easily or lightly changed. Only a life-shaking event can explain such a change. And the Lord's Day is the day on which the Church remembered and commemorated the Resurrection of her Lord.

(ii) The existence of the Church is positive evidence for the Resurrection. If there is one thing which is quite certain, it is that the crucifixion came to the disciples as a shattering blow. The arrest left them terrified. They all forsook Jesus and fled (Mark 14.50; Matthew 26.56). They huddled together in terror behind locked doors (John 20.19). To the disciples the cross seemed the end of their world yet there can be no doubt that if the cross had been the end, then we would never have heard of Jesus today, except perhaps as a martyr whose story was dimly remembered. All that would have been left for the disciples would have been to go back home and try to pick up the threads of life again, and put behind them an episode which had promised a glory and which had ended in tragedy.

We have only to put two sets of events side by side. On the one hand we see Peter denying that he had ever known Jesus, and concerned only to dissociate himself from one with whom to have been friendly was now a source of danger. Peter was prepared to go to any depths of disloyalty to sever all possible connection with Jesus. Just seven weeks passed and this same Peter is preaching this same Jesus to the crowds in Jerusalem. So far from trying to save his own skin now, so far from disclaiming all connection with Jesus, he welcomes arrest. He is arraigned before that same Sanhedrin which had condemned Jesus to death, and his only reaction is a defiance in which there is no tinge of fear and which is the product of an almost reckless courage.

Why the change? How did the coward become the hero? How did the man who had denied that he knew Jesus become the man prepared to be faithful unto death? There can only be one explanation. Something must have happened in these intervening weeks; and that something must have been the Resurrection.

On the facts, there is no real doubt that there never would have been a Christian Church had there been no Resurrection. The event of the Resurrection, or at least belief that there had been a Resurrection, is necessary to explain the existence of the Christian Church. If belief in the Resurrection is removed, then there is no adequate explanation of the pre-Pentecost and the post-Pentecost events. The Resurrection is the only thing which can explain the transformation of the disciples and the rise of the Church. For the disciples, he whom they had thought to be no more than a tragic memory had become a triumphant and ever-living presence.

(iii) The apostolic preaching is evidence for the Resurrection. It is, as we have seen, a fact that almost all apostolic preaching culminates in the proclamation of the Resurrection. But what is perhaps not sufficiently realized is the extraordinarily early nature of that evidence.

R. M. Grant in his *A Historical Introduction to the New Testament* (p. 368) has something to say about this. The earliest statement of the Resurrection, much earlier than any of the Gospels, is that in 1 Corinthians 15.3–8. That chapter was probably written about the year AD 54. Paul begins the section (1 Corinthians 15.1) by saying that he is about to repeat what he had already taught them on his previous visit. This will take the matter back to about AD 50. Now, if Paul could preach this statement of the Resurrection about AD 50, it must mean that the statement had been in existence and in a stereotyped form in the 40's. This would mean that the written evidence for the Resurrection goes back to very little, if any, more than ten years from the event itself. Further, Paul cites as witnesses of the Resurrection Peter (Cephas) and James. These were the two apostles whom Paul had met on his first visit to Jerusalem (Galatians 1.18–19). He says, when he is writing to the Corinthians, that he is passing on what he received; and the word he uses for *receiving* is the technical word for receiving an authoritative oral tradition. It was on that visit that Paul must have received that tradition, and that visit must have been about AD 34. The conclusion therefore is that the evidence for the Resurrection in 1 Corinthians 15.3–8 goes back to about five years after the Resurrection itself, and if we are prepared to place any reliance on the New Testament documents at all, this means that the evidence for the Resurrection is eye-witness evidence and dates to a time as nearly as possible contemporary with the event.

As far as the Resurrection evidence is concerned, there are therefore only a limited number of positions which we can take up. We can hold that it is fiction, and, if so, that it is inescapably deliberate fiction. We can hold that it is a record of delusion, and, if so, that the Church is founded on a hallucination. We can hold that the facts as stated in the New Testament are to be accepted literally and verbatim – in which case difficulties of harmonization will certainly occur. Or we can hold – and this last view best explains the facts – that the Christian writers are passing on in the only terms available to them an account of an experience which in the end baffled language to express. All of which means that we need never have any doubt about the reality of the Resurrection, though we are not absolved from the task of seeking to find out, as far as we can, what really happened.

There are quite a number of other points which we can consider here.

(i) Whatever happened, the event carried with it absolute conviction. From that time, rightly or wrongly, the disciples had not the slightest doubt that the crucified Jesus had become the Risen Lord. They made that claim the centre of their preaching (Acts 2.24–36; 3.15; 4.10; 7.56; 10.40; 13.30–7; 17.31). That faith they proclaimed; in that faith they lived; and for that faith they were willing to die. Whatever the experience was that they had, it left them with no doubts at all.

(ii) It is a notable fact that all Jesus' resurrection appearances were to those who loved him, and who were thinking of him. The love might be tragic and despairing and broken-hearted, but it was love. They might be talking of what they thought was the death of their hopes, but they were thinking and speaking about Jesus. If someone had invented the story, he would surely have shown the Risen Christ returning to confront in his risen glory Annas or Caiaphas, Pilate or his executioners. Such an appearance would indeed have been devastating and dramatic. But it was not so. It was to Mary Magdalene (John 20.11–18); to Peter (Luke 24.34); to the ten and the eleven disciples (John 20.19–29); to the two who were talking about him as they walked the road to Emmaus (Luke 24.13–21); to the women who had come to perform the last offices of love (Matthew 28.9, 10). Even in the case of Thomas (John 20. 26–9) the appearance was to one whose heart had been broken because he had loved so much. Maybe it is not too much to say that men and women had to love Jesus before they could see him.

(iii) Further, the New Testament writers clearly regarded the Resurrection as an act of God. They do not usually say that Jesus rose from the dead; they regularly say that Jesus was raised from the dead (Acts 3.15; 4.10; 5.30; 10.40; 13.30, 37; Romans 4.24; 6.4, 9; 8.11; 10.9; 1 Corinthians 6.14; 15.4, 20; 2 Corinthians 4.14; Galatians 1.1; Ephesians 1.20; Colossians 2.12; 1 Thessalonians 1.10; 2 Timothy 2.8; 1 Peter 1.21). To them the Resurrection was less a triumph and achievement of Jesus than it was an act of God. God, they seem to say, was active in the birth of Jesus and in the life of Jesus, but he was supremely active in the Resurrection of Jesus.

This, however, is not exclusively true. The New Testament writers, for instance, regularly use the word *anastasis* for the Resurrection, and *anastasis* is an active word and means *a rising again* (Acts 1.22; 2.31; 4.33; 17.18; Philippians 3.10; 1 Peter 1.3; 3.21). But the power behind that rising again is the power of God. Here supremely in the universe is demonstrated the undefeatable power of God.

(iv) There is one very unusual view of the fact of the Resurrection. In John 19.33–4 two things are said. First, it is said that when the soldiers came to kill the crucified victims so that they might be dead and removed from their crosses before the Sabbath came, they found that Jesus was dead already. Secondly, it is then said that one of the soldiers pierced Jesus' side with a spear, and there came out blood and water. That is a very odd fact because of the physical fact that with death bleeding at once stops. There are, therefore, those who have held not that Jesus died and rose again from the dead, but that by the power of God he was miraculously kept alive in a series of physical and mental experiences which would quite certainly have normally and universally produced death.

What the explanation of this is is quite unclear. Quite certainly neither John nor any of the Gospel writers intended this interpretation; they were not in any doubt as to the reality of the death of Jesus. John is always full of symbolism, and it may well be that he does not intend us to take this as a physical incident, but that in it he is symbolically speaking of the blood of the atonement and the water of baptism, which, as it were, both flowed from the life and the death of Jesus.

(v) We go on to the view which at first sight – but only at first sight – is the simplest of all. This is the view that the Resurrection was at least in one sense a completely physical event, that Jesus literally rose from the dead with as flesh and blood a body as he had died. There is no doubt at all that this view does seem to receive support from certain passages in the Gospels (e.g. Luke 24.39; John 20.27; 21.13). But there is equally no doubt that that view encounters as many difficulties as it solves.

– One of the strangest things about the Resurrection appearances of Jesus is the fact that there were times when he was not recognized.

Mary Magdalene, who loved Jesus more than anyone else, did not recognize him (John 20.14). The two on the road to Emmaus walked with him for miles and did not know that it was he (Luke 24.13–31). It has been suggested in explanation that Jesus was so altered by the horror of the experience through which he had passed that he was almost unrecognizable, that the horror and the agony of the cross had marked him indelibly. That will hardly do, for it is the triumph and the victory and the glory of the Risen Christ which are foremost in the minds and the memories and the teaching of the disciples.

– The Resurrection stories seem to indicate that the Risen Christ came and went at will, independent of time and space. When the doors were locked, suddenly there he was in the midst of them (John 20.19, 26). He does not seem to have been subject to the limitations to which an ordinary flesh and blood person is subject.

A physical resurrection will not entirely explain the way in which Jesus came and went at will. Nor does this explain what ultimately happened to his physical body.

(vi) One of the most famous of all theories is that which is connected with the name of Keim who wrote one of the great nineteenth-century full-length lives of Jesus. He spoke about the 'telegram from heaven'. What the disciples needed above all was an experience which would convince them once, finally and once and for all that Jesus was alive. So, according to this theory, God sent them an objective vision of the Risen Christ. It was a vision; but it was not the product of their own minds; still less was it the product of any hallucination. It was an absolutely factual, objective, real vision of the Risen Lord. It was a vision which was there just as really and truly and objectively visible as any physical, flesh and blood presence. On this theory the Resurrection appearances of Jesus are visions deliberately sent by God and objectively seen by the disciples.

But we have not yet called the most important, the most impressive, and the most relevant evidence of all, and that we must now go on to do.

In all the difficulties of the Resurrection stories and the Resurrection reality it may well be that there is one key and one clue. In 1 Corinthians 15.5–8 Paul gives the earliest list of the Resurrection appearances of the Risen Christ. He tells how he appeared to Peter, to the Twelve, to more than five hundred Christians at the one time, to James and to all the apostles. Then he brings the record to its conclusion: 'Last of all he was seen by me.'

Now, if there is one thing that is clear about this list, it is that Paul places the appearance made to him on the same level as the appearances made to all the others. He makes no distinction between his Resurrection experience of Jesus and the experiences of all the others. In fact we know more about the appearance to Paul than we do of any of the other appearances; it will therefore surely be correct to use the appearance to Paul to interpret the others.

The story of the appearance to Paul on the Damascus road is told three times in Acts, twice by Paul himself and on the first occasion by Luke (Acts 9.2–9; 22.6–10; 26.12–18). The first thing we note is that the appearance to Paul was some years after the others, and yet Paul regards it as completely the same in kind and in meaning. There are slight discrepancies in the three accounts in Acts, but basically the story remains the same. It begins with a blaze of light (9.2; 22.6; 26.13). It goes on to a voice, asking a question and giving a command (9.4–6; 22.7–10; 26.14–6). It is after that that the discrepancy comes. In Luke's account those with Paul heard the voice but saw no person; in Paul's two accounts those with him saw the light but did not hear the voice (9.7; 22.9; 26.13–14). This is quite definitely stated in the first of Paul's two accounts, and it is implied in the second.

The fact that the Risen Christ was experienced only by those who loved him and who were thinking and talking of him is still basically true of the experience of Paul. The voice said to Paul: 'It is hard for you to kick against the pricks' (26.14). When a young ox was yoked to a cart or a plough, it was his first instinct to resent it and it was his first action to try to kick the plough or the cart to pieces with his hooves. To teach him not to do this there was affixed at the front of the plough or cart a row of sharpened goads on a cross-bar; and the more the ox kicked, the more he hurt himself, until in the end he learned not to kick. The implication is that the event on the Damascus road was no new invasion of the life of Paul by the divine presence, but that it was something against which he had been fighting for a long time. The implication is that Paul had long felt the fascination of the spell of Christ and had battled against it, and was now finally compelled to succumb to it.

Now this appearance to Paul on the Damascus road is clearly not a flesh and blood appearance; it was beyond doubt real, as real as anything could possibly be; but it was not a physical appearance. There is something else to be noted. On two later occasions Paul had memorable experiences of direct contact with the Risen Lord. The first was in Corinth when Paul found himself in a situation which must have seemed impossibly hard and difficult, and there the Lord came to him in a vision by night and told him not to be afraid and not to keep silent, but to go on, for not a hand would be laid on him to harm him, and there were many people in the city to be won (Acts 18.9–10). Quite clearly, that experience was imprinted on Paul's mind and memory as a real experience. The other experience was in Jerusalem on the occasion when Paul's life was in danger and when life was full of threats. There again in the night the Lord came to him and told him that it was quite certain that he would bear his witness in Rome as he had done in Jerusalem (Acts 23.11) It was this experience which in the midst of the peril of the storm made Paul certain that all would be saved (Acts 27.23–4). Again, that experience was clearly something so real that Paul was prepared to stake his whole future upon it.

The question which demands an answer is obviously: What, if any, is the difference between Paul's experience of the Risen Christ on the Damascus road, and his experiences of him in Corinth and in Jerusalem? We believe that the answer is that there was no difference in the *nature* of the experiences, although it might be argued that there was a difference in the *objects* of the experiences. It could be said that the object of the experience on the Damascus road was evidential, and that its aim was to convince Paul of the fact of the Risen Christ, while the object of the experiences at Corinth and Jerusalem was to strengthen and nerve him for his task.

The conclusion we reach is that in the stories of the experiences which the disciples had of the Risen Christ the physical details are not at all important; they are in fact just the kind of details which would be added to the stories with the idea of enhancing verisimilitude. The really important thing is a spiritual experience of the power and the presence of the Risen Christ in such a way as to make it certain that he is alive for evermore.

In the last analysis there are two ways of reading the New Testament.

It may be read in literal and physical terms. If we do so read it, we can hardly escape a wistful regret that things like that do not happen now, and that we live in a time in which the supreme experiences of the Christian life are bluntly no longer possible. But if we read the New Testament as a book of spiritual truth, often symbolizing in a series of pictures that which is not the event of a moment but a continuing possibility, if we read it as a book of pictures written by men who could not write theology or philosophy in the modern sense of the terms, but who were thinking and writing in the childlike way which was all that they knew – and how great it was! – then we have the triumphant radiant certainty that whatever happened in the early days can and does still happen to us and for us.

He would be a bold and reckless man who would say that he knows everything about the Resurrection of Jesus Christ, but, when we probe to the essential meaning of the fact and of all the stories which have gathered round it, we come to the certain truth that Jesus Christ is such that it is open to those who know him and love him to experience his for ever living presence and his for ever living power. The basic meaning of the Resurrection is the liberation of Jesus Christ. John Masefield in his play tells in imagination how Procla, the wife of Pilate, sent for Longinus, the centurion in charge of the crucifixion, and asked him what had happened. 'He was a fine young man,' said Longinus, 'but when we were finished with him he was a poor broken thing on a cross.' 'So you think', said Procla, 'that he is finished and ended?' 'No, madam, I do not,' said Longinus. 'He is set free throughout the world where neither Jew nor Greek can stop his truth.'

We may argue for long enough about the details, and about how it happened. We may argue for long enough about the empty tomb and about the physical character of the Resurrection body of Jesus. In the last analysis these things are not important. What is important is that the Christian is sure that he possesses a Lord who is not a figure in history who lived and died and whose story we tell, but one whom we can daily meet and experience and who is alive for evermore, present to comfort and mighty to help.

For the Christian the Resurrection necessarily means two things: First, he never lives life alone. In every problem the Risen Christ is there to consult; in every effort he is there to help; in every sorrow he is there to comfort; on every dark road he is there to banish fear, and in the sunshine he is there to make joy doubly dear. He has at his side one who has fulfilled his promise to be with his people to the end of time and beyond.

Secondly, he has the knowledge that there is nothing he does which his Lord does not see, and nothing he says which his Lord does not hear. He has therefore in the memory of that presence an antiseptic against all evil, and a warning and an inspiration to make life fit for those eyes to see.

Whatever be the problems of the Resurrection, about which the historian and the theologian may argue, the Christian knows the certainty of the continued presence and power of his Lord, a presence and a power which even death cannot take away.

CHAPTER TWELVE

He Ascended into Heaven

The Ascension is far and away the most difficult incident in the life of Jesus either to visualize or to understand. There are three facts which prove that. First, no one has ever succeeded in painting a picture of the Ascension which was anything other than grotesque and ridiculous. In films of the life of Christ, if the Ascension is portrayed, the whole matter descends into sheer bathos. Secondly, it is astonishing to see how little time and space the Lives of Jesus give to the Ascension. To take some typical examples of the older, uncritical Lives of Jesus, David Smith gives the Ascension four lines of type and Farrar eleven lines. Edersheim gives it rather more than twenty lines. Of the more liberal Lives, Warschauer does not mention it at all, nor does Holtzman, or Klausner, the Jewish writer. Of the highly critical writers, Strauss gives it seven pages. Thirdly, it is extremely unusual to hear a sermon on the Ascension. It is one of the neglected parts of the life of Christ in the ordinary teaching of the pulpit.

In spite of this neglect the Ascension is firmly anchored in the creeds. It has its place in the Apostles', the Nicene, and the Athanasian Creeds. If not in the very earliest writings, certainly by the second half of the second century the Ascension had become what A. J. Maclean calls in his article in *Dictionary of Christ and the Gospels*, 'a widespread crystallized tradition.' It is there in Justin Martyr's Dialogue with Trypho the Jew. Trypho says that the Christians wished to persuade men that Jesus became man, was crucified and ascended up to heaven (*Dialogue with Trypho* 38). The curious thing there is that in this summary it is actually the Ascension rather than the Resurrection which is included. Irenaeus speaks of the birth from a virgin, the passion and the resurrection from the dead, and the ascension into heaven in the flesh (*Against Heresies*

1.10.1). Three times at least Tertullian mentions the Ascension in statements of belief, and, oddly enough, he uses three different words to describe the experience of Jesus. In his treatise on the Veiling of Virgins (1) he says that Jesus was born of the Virgin Mary, crucified under Pontius Pilate, raised again the third day from the dead, received (*receptum*) into the heavens. In his work on the Prescription of Heretics, he says of Jesus that, having been taken up (*ereptum*) into the heavens, he sat down at the right hand of God (13). In his work against Praxeas (2), he says that Jesus, after he had been raised by the Father, was taken back (*resumptum*) into heaven. As we saw at the very beginning of our study, there was an ancient legend that each of the apostles contributed one article of the Apostles' Creed. One of the earliest versions of that legend says that Thomas said, 'He rose from the dead', and James said, 'He ascended to heaven.' There is then no doubt at all that the statement of the Ascension lodged very early in the creeds and in the beliefs of the Church.

When we turn to the New Testament itself we find that the direct evidence for the Ascension is very scanty. It is stated in Mark 16.19: 'So then the Lord Jesus, after he had spoken to them, was taken up into heaven, and sat down at the right hand of God.' But it is one of the assured results of modern scholarship that the last twelve verses of Mark's Gospel, as it now stands, were not part of the original Gospel. It is stated in Luke 24.51, as the Authorized Version has it: 'And it came to pass, while he blessed them, he was parted from them, and carried up into heaven.' But in both the RSV and the NEB the phrase 'and was carried up to heaven' is not given as part of the text, although its existence is mentioned in a footnote. So then there is only one New Testament passage in which the Ascension is definitely described and stated, and that is in Acts 1.9–11, where it is said: 'As they were looking on, he was lifted up, and a cloud took him out of their sight.'

But there are many passages in which it may be said that the Ascension is implied. There is more than one reference to the Ascension in the Fourth Gospel. In the Nicodemus story there comes the saying: 'No one has ascended into heaven but he who descended from heaven, the Son of Man' (John 3.13). We find Jesus saying: 'Then what if you were to see the Son of Man ascending where he was before' (John 6.62). In the Garden Jesus tells Mary that she must not hold him. 'I have not yet ascended to the Father,' he said, 'but go to my brethren and say to them, I am ascending to my Father and your Father, to my God and your God' (John 20.17). In Ephesians 4.8–10 Paul quotes Psalm 68.18 and applies it to Jesus: 'When he ascended on high he led a host of captives, and he gave gifts to men.' The writer to the Hebrews speaks of a High Priest 'who had passed through the heavens' (Hebrews 4.14), and of a High Priest exalted above the heavens (7.26). 1 Timothy 3.16 speaks of Jesus being taken up in glory. Peter speaks of Jesus 'who has gone into heaven and is at the right hand of God' (1 Peter 3.22).

Quite clearly, the idea of an ascent is there, but it may well be that many of these passages do not necessarily imply a visible ascent, such as the story in the first chapter of Acts portrays, but intend rather the unseen exaltation of Jesus Christ into the glory of heaven.

Once the Ascension had become part and parcel of Christian belief, the Christian thinkers were not long in finding forecasts and prophecies of it in the Old Testament, with all their accustomed ingenuity. Rufinus in his Commentary on the Apostles' Creed, and Cyril in his Catechetical Lectures to those preparing for Church membership, both go to the Old Testament and find there types and foretellings of the Ascension. The early theologians found in the Old Testament three especially telling examples.

The experience of Enoch was taken as a type of the Ascension. In the Old Testament itself it is said of Enoch: 'Enoch walked with God; and he was not, for God took him' (Genesis 5.24). In the Apocrypha in the book of Ecclesiasticus the parallel becomes even closer. Ben Sirach writes: 'Enoch pleased the Lord, and was taken up.' 'No one like Enoch has been created on earth, for he was taken up from the earth' (Ecclesiasticus 44.16; 49.14). And this form of the story comes into the New Testament in the honour roll of Hebrews: 'By faith Enoch was taken up so that he should not see death' (Hebrews 11.5).

The experience of Elijah was also used. The story not so much of the death of Elijah as of his departure from this earth as told in 2 Kings 2.4–12: how the chariot of fire came for him and how he went up by a whirlwind to heaven. Ben Sirach brings this story even closer to the picture of the Ascension. Addressing Elijah, he says: 'You were taken up by a whirlwind of fire, in a chariot with horses of fire' (Ecclesiasticus 48.9). In 1 Maccabees it is said: 'Elijah because of great zeal for the law was taken up into heaven' (1 Maccabees 2.58). The parallel between the Ascension of Elijah and the Ascension of Jesus was closely worked out. Elijah went up in a chariot; Psalm 68, which was very closely tied to the Ascension, as we shall see, talks of the Lord coming with twice ten thousand chariots (Psalm 68.17). Elijah went up from the East of Jordan; Jesus went up from the East of Kedron. The going up of Elijah brought the Spirit to Elisha (2 Kings 2.9, 10); the Ascension of Jesus brought the Spirit to the disciples (Acts 2). The early thinkers found one curious parallel in the Elijah story. Elisha asked for the Spirit. Elijah answered: 'You have asked a hard thing; yet, if you see me as I am being taken from you, it shall be so to you; but if you do not see me, it shall not be so' (2 Kings 2.10). It is strange how the matter of seeing is stressed in the Elijah story; and in the same way in the Acts story the Ascension happened as the disciples were looking on (Acts 1.9). There are scholars who think that the Elijah story has had its influence on the Ascension story.

The last parallel is not found in the Old Testament but in the apocryphal book Bel and the Dragon, which expands the Daniel story. The character involved in this parallel is Habakkuk. There the story is that Habakkuk had made potage and bread and was about to take them to the reapers in the field. He was told by the Spirit to take them to Daniel in the lions' den in Babylon. Habakkuk protested that he knew neither Babylon nor the place of the den. The story goes on: 'Then the angel of the Lord took him by the crown of his head, and lifted him by his hair and set him down in Babylon, right over the den, with the rushing sound of the wind itself' (Bel and the Dragon 33–6). In that apocryphal story we are in the realms of the fantastic rather than the historical, but the argument went that if the power of God could do that to the prophet Habakkuk, how much more could it take the Messiah up to heaven.

The early thinkers of the Church also exercised their ingenuity to find actual prophecies of the Ascension. Often the particular form of translation which they used served their purpose better than a modern translation would have done, for the Greek or Latin translation of the Old Testament, that is, the Septuagint or the Vulgate, were far better known and far more widely used than the original Hebrew.

One of the favourite texts was: 'When he ascended up on high he led captivity captive; he gave gifts to men' (Psalm 68.18). Rufinus quotes Acts 2.33 in a compressed form: 'Being exalted by the right hand of God he has poured forth the gift of God which you see and hear.' He then goes on to quote Psalm 24.7–10 which bids the gates lift up their heads that the king of glory may come in, and says that this is the cry of the astonished door-keepers of heaven, when they saw in the ascended Christ 'the fleshly nature penetrating the sacred recesses of heaven.' Psalm 47.5 is quoted: 'God is ascended with jubilation, and the Lord with the sound of trumpets.' Psalm 18.10 is quoted in the Vulgate version which speaks of him who has ascended upon the cherubim, and who has flown upon the wings of the winds. Amos 9.6 is cited. In the Revised Standard Version and the Revised Version this is part of an address to God who builds his chambers in the heavens. The AV noted the alternative meaning *spheres* and says that the Hebrew literally means *ascensions*. So then this is taken to be an address to the one who builds his ascensions in the heavens.

It may well be doubtful if modern scholarship would look on any of these texts as references to the Ascension of Jesus Christ, but to the exegesis of their day they were relevant and effective.

Although the Ascension was part of the faith of the Church, presaged, as they believed, by Old Testament events and buttressed by Old Testament prophecy, it nevertheless was not without its difficulties.

One of the main difficulties was to be certain of the time at which it happened. The ecclesiastical date of the Ascension was fixed by the fourth century when it came to be regularly observed on the sixth Thursday after Easter – as it still is. This date was arrived at by taking literally the forty days mentioned in Acts 1.3, but it did not meet with unanimous acceptance.

If we read Luke 24 in the AV, and retain the Ascension statement in verses 50–1, the story runs as follows: 'And he (Jesus) led them out as far as Bethany, and he lifted up his hands, and blessed them. And it came to pass, while he blessed them, he was parted from them, and carried up into heaven.' In that whole chapter there are no marks of time, apart from reference to times of the day; and, if we only possessed that chapter and had no other accounts of the Resurrection and the Ascension, at least at a first reading we would quite certainly assume that the Resurrection and the Ascension took place on the same day.

When we turn to one of the earliest references to the Ascension in the Letter of Barnabas (15) we encounter a problem, no matter what we take the meaning to be. Barnabas is speaking about the Lord's Day as opposed to the Jewish Sabbath; he says that Christians observe the Lord's Day for joy, the eighth day on which Jesus rose from the dead, and, after he had been plainly seen, went up into heaven. That may mean either of two things. It could mean that the Resurrection and the Ascension took place on the same day. Or, and this is on the whole more likely, it could mean that both the Resurrection and the Ascension took place not on the same Lord's Day, but on the day which is called the Lord's Day. In either case it would mean that the forty days of Acts 1.3 is not to be taken literally, and it would mean that the traditional ecclesiastical date of the Ascension, the Thursday, is wrong. There were in fact certain sections of the early Church in which the Ascension was commemorated on Whitsunday, and not on the Thursday.

The Gnostic sect of the Valentinians held that there were eighteen months between the Resurrection and the Ascension. It has been suggested that the reason for this date is that the conversion of Paul on the Damascus road probably took place eighteen months after the Resurrection. If this is so, then the appearance to Paul on the Damascus road can be ranked exactly the same as the other appearances, can in fact be looked upon as the culminating appearance, with the Ascension coming after it.

Eusebius (*The Demonstration of the Gospel* 8.2) records the odd view that Jesus' risen life after the Resurrection lasted exactly the same time as his physical life before the crucifixion, which would mean that there must have been three years between the Resurrection and the Ascension.

Certain Gnostics, who were of course heretics, held that the time between the Resurrection and the Ascension was no less than twelve years. They maintained that one of their most sacred books, the *Pistis Sophia*, was given by Jesus to them in the twelfth year after the Resurrection. But the length of time which these Gnostic heretics postulated was really due to the fact that they wished to have a long period during which Jesus could be claimed to have given to certain chosen disciples a special revelation, far greater and fuller than that given to ordinary Christians and the orthodox Church. We can certainly discount the idea of years between the Resurrection and the Ascension as something introduced to suit the purposes of those who claimed special revelations.

When we discuss the length of the period between the Resurrection and the Ascension in the intention of the Gospel story we must remember that in Jewish usage forty days stands for a period which is quite lengthy but has a definitely limited duration. In English we use the phrase ten days in much the same way. If we say: 'I'll see you in ten days' time', we mean that we will see the person quite soon, without tying ourselves to a definite date.

In the same way the rains preceding the flood were said to have lasted for forty days (Genesis 7.4). Moses was on Mount Sinai for forty days (Exodus 24.18). Elijah went in the strength of the divinely prepared meal for forty days (1 Kings 19.8). Within forty days Nineveh is to be overthrown in the Jonah story (Jonah 3.4). Jesus was in the wilderness at the time of the temptation for forty days (Mark 1.13)

If we accept this approach, and it fits the facts, then we will not argue about the definite date of the Ascension. We will simply take Luke's forty days to mean that Jesus was with his disciples for a considerable but a limited time, and we will not argue as to whether the present date of Ascension Day is accurate or whether it ought to be commemorated on Whitsunday. We will know that we are not trying to draw up an hour-to-hour timetable but that we are speaking in general terms.

The difficulty about the Ascension which the modern mind will most readily seize on lies in the word itself. It will be claimed that if we speak of an Ascension we are still thinking in terms of a world in which heaven is up and hell is down and the earth in between. But we surely know quite well when we speak like this that we are speaking in symbols, and not imagining that if we sent a rocket up far enough into the sky it would actually reach heaven. It is in any event far more natural to think of one who departs to God as going up than as going down or going across. It is simply the natural human instinctive way of saying that Jesus left the human scene to enter into the life which is superhuman and which is with God. The plain fact is that it is difficult to see how, if we are to put the matter pictorially, we can put it any other way. We are not thinking literally; we are only using the only pictures we can use – and we know that we are doing so.

But in spite of all these difficulties and uncertainties, there are certain great truths symbolized in the Ascension. We may have to say that it is difficult or even impossible to say what literally happened; but we need not be in doubt as to the spiritual truth that lies behind the story.

(i) There is a sense in which the Ascension looks back. F. F. Bruce rightly points out in his *Commentary on Acts* that the Resurrection and the Ascension cannot be separated. The Resurrection and the Ascension form two parts of one continuous movement; and that movement is what we might call a process of glorification. The words which the Fourth Gospel puts into the mouth of Jesus in the scene with Mary Magdalene are surely very significant. Jesus' message through her to his disciples is neither, 'I have ascended', nor yet, 'I will ascend'. It is 'I am ascending'. It is the present tense of the verb which is used *(anabainō)*.

Language and words always have associations. In the Acts story the scene closes with the words: 'He was lifted up, and a cloud took him out of their sight' (Acts 1.9). We find this cloud idea also in the Transfiguration story. 'A bright cloud overshadowed them' (Matthew 17.5; cf. Mark 9.7; Luke 9.34). For a Jew the cloud had a meaning. The Jew spoke of the *Shechinah,* meaning the manifestation of the glory of God. The Shechinah took the form of a kind of luminous, glowing cloud which rested where the presence of God was. The idea goes back to the cloud which was the guide of the children of Israel in the desert journeyings (Exodus 13.21-2). In particular that pillar of cloud settled upon the Tabernacle to show that God in his glory was there. When the tent of the Tabernacle was pitched Moses would go into it. 'When Moses entered the tent the pillar of cloud would descend and stand at the door of the tent, and the Lord would speak with Moses.' And when the people saw the pillar of cloud, they worshipped, each man at the door of his tent (Exodus 33.9-10). When the Tabernacle was completed, equipped and dedicated, 'Then the cloud covered the tent of the meeting, and the glory of the Lord filled the Tabernacle. And Moses was not able to enter the tent of the meeting, because the cloud abode upon it, and the glory of the Lord filled the Tabernacle' (Exodus 40.34, 35). At the dedication of Solomon's Temple it is said: 'And when the priests came out of the holy place, a cloud filled the house of the Lord, so that the priests could not stand to minister because of the cloud; for the glory of the Lord filled the house of the Lord' (1 Kings 8.10-11). The cloud and the glory of God are synonymous.

So then any Jew, and anyone who knew the Old Testament, would see at once in the Ascension story, with the cloud into which Jesus was received, the reception of Jesus into the glory of God.

We see too how the Resurrection and the Ascension are inextricably linked together. They are milestones in that process whereby Jesus, crucified, risen and ascended, entered finally into the glory of God.

(ii) This is to say that the Ascension also looks forward. J. A. Selbie in the *Dictionary of the Bible* calls the Ascension 'a point of transition'. A. S. Martin in the *Dictionary of Christ and the Gospels* says: 'The Ascension has no substantial independence. It closes the public ministry; it opens the continuation of that ministry in the new age of the Spirit.' As Milligan put it: 'The Ascension is a transition from one condition to another, rather than from one place to another.'

If we put it this way, we might even say that the Ascension stands for the final liberation of Jesus from all limitations of space and time, so that he is freed to be lovingly and powerfully present with every man, in every place, in every age.

A. J. Maclean in the *Dictionary of the Apostolic Church* writes of the work of the Ascended Christ, and shows how it still marks Jesus out in his three great roles – Prophet, Priest and King.

– The Ascended Christ is still priest. It has been pointed out that the Jews had the idea of the Ascension of the Messiah. Thus they saw in the High Priest the type of the Messiah. Christian scholars took and Christianized this idea. On the Day of Atonement the High Priest offered the sacrifices which made atonement for the sins of the whole people. Just so Jesus Christ made propitiation for the sins of the world. On the Day of Atonement and on that day alone, and alone of all men, the High Priest entered into the Holy of Holies (Leviticus 16.2). Now in Jewish thought the Tabernacle symbolized the world; and the Holy of Holies symbolized the highest heaven. So, then, just as the High Priest made his sacrifices and entered into the Holy of Holies, so the Messiah, Jesus Christ, offered his sacrifice and entered the highest heaven. They saw in the entry of the High Priest into the Holy of Holies a symbol and type and forecast of the Ascension of the Messiah into the heavenly places.

Now a priest is above all the person who effects the link between God and man; it is through his work that man is enabled to enter into the presence of God. So Christian thought has always seen the ascended Christ as the eternal High Priest for ever bringing men into the presence of God. Paul speaks of 'Christ Jesus who died, yes, who was raised from the dead, who is at the right hand of God, who indeed intercedes for us' (Romans 8.34). The writer to the Hebrews says that Jesus always lives to make intercession for those who come to God through him (Hebrews 7.25). We have, he says, a great High Priest over the house of God (Hebrews 10.21). So then the ascended Christ is still in love bringing men into the presence of God.

– Obviously – and to this we will return – the Ascended Christ is still King. If the Ascension is the Ascension into glory, then clearly the Ascended Christ is the regal Christ. He is the ruler of the kings on earth (Revelation 1.5). To him the great doxologies of praise are sung by the whole of creation (Revelation 5.11–12). He must reign until he has put all his enemies under his feet (1 Corinthians 15.25). He is far above all rule and authority and power and dominion (Ephesians 1.21). He has the name which is above every name (Philippians 2.9–11). All power is given to him (Matthew 28.18). Clearly, the Ascended Christ is the Christ who has entered into his royal power.

– The Ascended Christ is still the prophet. The prophet is the man who, being in the counsels of God, speaks for God. This the Ascended Christ does through the gift of the Spirit, who could not come in all his fulness until Christ was ascended (John 14.26; 16.13–14). It is in fact significant that the Ascension and the gift of the Spirit are closely inter-related (Acts 1.8–12).

(iii) There are certain writers who see in the Ascension an event which happened not only for the sake of Jesus, but also very definitely for the sake of man. On the human side Jesus is the ideal of manhood. In him manhood reaches its peak and its crown and becomes what God meant it to be. So, J. A. Selbie argues, if Christ is the ideal man, then the Ascension shows that man was made, not for the grave, but for exaltation. The Ascension of Jesus is the type and the pattern of the ascension of all believers.

A. S. Martin sees in the Ascension the guarantee that for man too there is a life beyond and a life in the glory of God. 'There is', he says, 'practically universal remonstrance of the human heart against the grave.' And he sees in the Ascension a guarantee of immortality. 'It furnishes the proof of it, and is the illustration of man's final destiny.'

If the Christian is one with Christ and if the Christian shares the experiences of his Lord, and if his Lord is exalted into glory, so is he.

CHAPTER THIRTEEN

And Sitteth on the Right Hand of
God the Father Almighty

One might say that if the event of the Ascension had not appeared in the story of the life of Jesus, any dramatist would have been bound to invent it. The Ascension is a dramatic necessity; it supplies the only fitting end to the earthly life of Jesus. For some time, as we have seen, Jesus had been appearing to his disciples. Clearly, he could not die again. Equally clearly, the time of special revelation had to come to an end, so that the time of perpetual presence could begin. The time of special revelation could not peter out in a series of less and less frequent appearances. There had to be an end to this act of the drama, and the Ascension supplies it.

But the Ascension is not the end of the whole story; it is merely the end of a chapter. And the continuing of the story is symbolically represented in this article of the creed.

There can be few Old Testament texts which have so stamped themselves on the language and the imagery of the New Testament as Psalm 110.1: 'The Lord says to my Lord, Sit at my right hand till I make your enemies your footstool.' If we accept the Gospel record at all, Jesus himself used that text of himself to prove that he was more than the son of David (Matthew 22.44; Mark 12.36; Luke 20.42). And this picture of Jesus Christ at the right hand of God runs right through almost the whole New Testament.

It is there in the first Christian sermon, when Peter drew the picture of Jesus being exalted at the right hand of God (Acts 2.33). It occurs in Peter's defiant speech to the Sanhedrin: 'God exalted him at his right hand as Leader and Saviour' (Acts 5.31). It is there in the dying vision of Stephen who saw the Son of Man standing at the right hand of God (Acts 7.56). It goes back to Jesus' own warning to his enemies when he warned them that the day would come when they would see him at the right hand of God (Matthew 26.64; Mark 14.62; Luke 22.69). It is in the thought of Paul. In Romans he speaks of Christ Jesus who died, yes, who was raised from the dead, who is at the right hand of God (Romans 8.34). Christians are advised to seek the things which are above, where Christ is seated at the right hand of God (Colossians 3.1). God raised Christ from the dead and made him sit at his right hand in the heavenly places (Ephesians 1.20). It is there in the thought of the writer to the Hebrews. When Jesus had made purification for sins, he sat down at the right hand of the Majesty on high (Hebrews 1.3). For the joy that was set before him, Jesus endured the cross, despising the shame, and is seated at the right hand of the throne of God (Hebrews 12.2). It is there in the thought of Peter who speaks of Jesus Christ who has gone into heaven, and is at the right hand of God (1 Peter 3.22). The phrase runs all through the New Testament.

Of all phrases, it is clear that this one cannot he taken spatially and literally. It is thoroughly anthropomorphic with its picture of God as a kind of colossally magnified human figure on a throne, with Jesus on another throne beside him. But, however impossible the literal picture may be, its symbolic meanings are clear and unmistakable. Pearson on the creed writes suggestively on the symbolism of this article.

(i) The Hebrew verb *to sit* has certain characteristic meanings. It implies settled possession. In the poem which describes how the ten tribes settled into Palestine it is said of Asher that 'he sat still at the coast of the sea, settling down by his landings' (Judges 5.17). If Jesus Christ is pictured as sitting at the right hand of God, it means that that is his permanent abode.

(ii) To sit in Hebrew implies rest and quiet. In the vision of the golden age it is said that 'they shall sit every man under his vine and under his fig tree, and none shall make them afraid' (Micah 4.4). Here is a picture of the rest after the battle, the harbour after the tempest, the peace after the pilgrimage.

(iii) But the picture here is not simply one of sitting; it is one of sitting at the right hand of God. That is a picture of indestructible joy. It is the picture of the Psalmist: 'In thy presence is fulness of joy, in thy right hand are pleasures for evermore' (Psalm 16.11). Here is the joy after the sorrow, the ease after the pain, the happy ending to the tragedy, the rest after the cross.

(iv) The most obvious of all meanings is that the right hand of God is surely the place of supreme honour. When Bathsheba came into the presence of Solomon, he rose to greet the royal mother and had a seat brought for her, and 'she sat on his right' (1 Kings 2.19). The picture represents too the vindication of Christ. The pain and the humiliation and the rejection and the disloyalties are all at an end and there is what we might call the public vindication of the Son. The place which the Son holds in the heart of the Father is made evident to heaven and to earth.

(v) It may be that there is still one other symbolic meaning. There may well be the thought that the place on the right hand of God gives to the Son the right of judgement. He is no longer the judged, but the judge. He is no longer the condemned, but the one who metes out judgement. He is no longer on trial before men, the universe is on trial before him.

Pearson sums it up by saying that the picture of the Son taking his seat on the right hand of the Father is the picture of Christ entering upon his regal office as King of kings and Lord of lords.

Amongst all the passages which speak of Jesus at the right hand of God there is one that is unique. Almost always Jesus is pictured as *sitting*, which stresses the royalty, the honour and the glory. But there is one passage in which he is seen standing. That passage is the Stephen passage. 'Behold,' said Stephen, 'I see the heavens opened, and the Son of Man standing at the right hand of God' (Acts 7.56). Certain commentators have seen a special meaning in that picture of the standing Christ. They have thought that the picture may be that of the Christ at God's right hand rising to come to the help and assistance and comfort of his own, when they are suffering for his name's sake. Certainly it must be true that we cannot think of the Christ of glory as sitting detached and insulated at the right hand of God. He is still mighty and powerful to help, and in his exalted royalty he has not forgotten his own.

There is one last curious thing left to note. There is the connection of the Ascension with joy. Whether or not we put in the actual words in Luke 24.50–1 there is little doubt that it is the Ascension which is in Luke's mind. And then the story closes: 'And they returned to Jerusalem with great joy.' One thing is crystal clear: the disciples did not see in the Ascension a final separation and parting, but rather the means of preventing any further separation from Jesus for ever.

We began our study of the Ascension by saying that there was no more difficult incident in the life of Jesus to visualize and to understand; but that is only half true. It is only true when we think of the Ascension and the sitting on the right hand of God in literal and physical terms. If we think of this whole story as a vivid pictorial way of saying that there came a time when this person Jesus was no longer shackled by the limitations of humanity, but entered into a new life and a new existence in which he was present everywhere with those who loved him, then the story becomes both clear and precious, for then the Ascension becomes the symbol of that new life through which it becomes possible for Jesus to fulfil his promise to be with us always to the end of the world and beyond.

CHAPTER FOURTEEN

From Thence He shall Come to Judge
the Quick and the Dead

This article of the creed brings us face to face with two different items of
Christian belief. These items are very closely connected, but we shall try
to deal with them separately. Here we have first the statement of belief in
the Second Coming of Jesus Christ, and then the belief that he is coining
in judgement on the living – which is what *quick* means – and the dead.

First, then, we must think of the Christian teaching concerning the
Second Coming of our Lord, and we will see that in modern times it has
undergone a curious experience. For some people it is a belief which
simply vanished from the forefront of their minds, taking its place on
the circumference, and even among the eccentricities, of Christian doctrine. They seldom preach on it, and simply lay it aside. For other people
it is the very centre of Christian belief. It dominates their whole thought
and their whole thinking, and it is not far from being the culmination of
every sermon which they preach. Thus it is strangely difficult to get a
balanced view of the doctrine of the Second Coming.

Let us, so far as we can, examine this belief as it emerges in the life and
thought of the early Church, as it stands in the teaching of Jesus. Then let
us go on to see the undoubted difficulties which emerge, and finally let us
try to see the meaning of the doctrine and its permanent value for
Christian belief. First, then, let us look at the thought of the early Church.

Foremost among the many contributions of C. H. Dodd to New
Testament scholarship is his definition of the New Testament *kērugma*.
The word *kērugma* literally means a herald's announcement or proclamation; and the *kērugma* is the basic and essential New Testament proclamation of the gospel which underlies the many different expressions and
presentations of it in the New Testament. It is the underlying unity
behind the diversity. The *kērugma* is expressed in the following terms:

The prophecies have been fulfilled, and the New Age has been inaugurated by the coming of Jesus Christ.

Jesus was born of the seed of David.

He died to deliver us out of this present evil age.

He was buried.

He rose again on the third day.

All these events of his life, his death, and his Resurrection are the direct fulfilment of Scripture.

He is exalted at the right hand of God, as Son of God and Lord of the living and the dead.

He will come again as Judge and Saviour of men.

Here then is the basic Christian proclamation, and, as we can see, it contains the announcement that Jesus will come again, and that Jesus is Judge of men. The Second Coming and the fact of judgement are integral parts of it. Let us see what part the idea of the Second Coming plays in the thought of the New Testament books and writers.

In the Book of Acts there are two definite references to the Second Coming of Jesus and two to the fact that he is Judge. The message of the two angels after the Ascension is: 'This Jesus, who was taken up from you into heaven, will come in the same way as you saw him go into heaven' (Acts 1.11). The same thought occurs again in Peter's sermon after the healing of the lame man at the Temple gate: 'Repent, therefore, and turn again, that your sins may be blotted out, that times of refreshing may come from the presence of the Lord, and that he may send the Christ appointed for you, Jesus, whom heaven must receive until the time for establishing all that God spoke of by the mouth of his holy prophets from of old' (Acts 3.19–21). In his sermon to Cornelius, Peter says: 'He commanded us to preach to the people, and to testify that he is the one ordained by God to be judge of the living and the dead' (Acts 10.42). In his sermon to the Athenians on Mars' Hill, Paul says: 'God has fixed a day on which he will judge the world in righteousness by a man whom he has appointed, and of this he has given assurance to all men by raising him from the dead' (Acts 17.31).

It can be seen that the Second Coming is indeed an essential part of early Christian preaching, but it can also be seen that it is not so prominent and so continuously stated as, for instance, the fact of the Resurrection or the coming of the Spirit.

When we turn to the Letters of Paul the situation is very different. The idea of the Second Coming comes to the fore, and is stressed in every letter of Paul, with the exception of Galatians and Ephesians and Philemon. It is true that as Pauline thought goes on developing there is a change of emphasis, but the Second Coming is never anywhere else than in the foreground. It was part of Paul's essential gospel. He speaks of 'that day, when, according to my gospel, God judges the secrets of men by Christ Jesus' (Romans 2.16). He begs the Thessalonians to let nothing, and to let no one's teaching, move them from an unshakeable belief in the coming of the Lord (2 Thessalonians 2.1–2). Let us then look at Paul's Letters in chronological order.

We begin with the Thessalonian Letters. The Thessalonians have turned from idols to serve a living and true God and to wait for his Son from heaven (1 Thessalonians 1.10). They are to be Paul's hope and joy and crown at the coming of the Lord (1.2.19). So real is the belief in the Second Coming that the Thessalonians stand about in excited groups waiting for it, abandoning their ordinary day's work, and have therefore to be recalled to the ordinary duties of life and living (1.4.11–12). So immediate is their expectation of the Second Coming that they are worried at what will happen to those who die before Christ appears, an anxiety which Paul allays by assuring them that the dead will be raised to share in the glory (1.4.13–17). That day will come as a thief in the night (1.5.2). It is Paul's prayer that God will establish them unblamable in holiness at the coming of the Lord Jesus (1.3.13). When Jesus Christ comes the wicked will be punished and the righteous will find rest and reward (2.1.5–10). In these Letters the Second Coming is at the very heart of Paul's thought, and it is expected immediately and at any moment.

We turn now to the Corinthian correspondence. The Corinthians are waiting for the revealing of our Lord Jesus Christ (1.1.7). The whole point of 1 Corinthians 7 is that the Christian must form no earthly ties whatever because the appointed time has grown very short (1.7.29). It is better not even to enter into marriage but rather to concentrate absolutely on preparation for the coming of the Lord. Paul's one desire

is that he may be proud of them, and they of him on the day of the Lord
(2.1.14). But most illuminating of all is the ending of 1 Corinthians
(1.16.22). There both the AV and the NEB retain the original Aramaic
phrase *Marana tha,* although the RSV translates it. It means, 'Come, O
Lord!' Two things emerge from the use of that phrase. First, it is clearly
the culmination of the whole letter; this is the phrase which Paul wishes
to leave ringing in their ears and imprinted on their memories. Secondly,
here we have very oddly an Aramaic phrase occurring as the climax of a
Greek letter. There is no evidence at all that the Corinthian Church was
predominantly Jewish; all the evidence is that it was in fact predominantly Greek. To the Greeks, Aramaic would be an unknown and an unintelligible tongue; and yet this Aramaic phrase occurs as the summation
of the whole letter. There can only be one explanation; it must have been
a slogan and a watchword. Maybe it was a kind of secret password and
identification which Christians whispered to each other and by which
they recognized each other. It must have been the password of the early
Church, an Aramaic phrase embedded into their thought, much as a
Latin motto might be amongst English people. And, if that is so, then
the hope of the Second Coming must have been the characteristic and
distinguishing mark of the early Church.

Now we turn to Romans, the great central Letter. We have already
seen that in Romans (2.16) Paul speaks of the Second Coming as being
an essential part of his gospel. In Romans 13.11–12 there is a great
sonorous passage which presses upon the Roman Christians the duty of
living in honour and in purity. In it the Second Coming is not mentioned
in so many words, but clearly it is the Second Coming which is at the
back of it: 'Besides this you know what hour it is, how it is full time now
for you to wake from sleep. For salvation is nearer to us now than when
we first believed; the night is far gone, the day is at hand. Let us then cast
off the works of darkness and put on the armour of light.' Here then is
the conviction of the reality and the imminence of the Second Coming.
But with this Letter there enters into the picture another element. In
Romans 9–11 there is the picture of how Paul looks forward to the conversion of the Gentile world, and through it to the conversion of the
Jews, so that all men will come to know and to love God (11.32). Now
quite clearly this is going to take time; such a universal salvation cannot
happen overnight; long years will need to pass. Here is the change. Paul

did not cease to believe and to believe intensely in the Second Coming, but he no longer expected it with the immediacy of his earlier Letters. The Second Coming was to be longer delayed than once he had thought.

However, it remained very much in the forefront of his mind and thought. It is commonly said that there is no reference to the Second Coming in Ephesians, but it is possible that there is one such reference in Ephesians 4.30: 'Do not grieve the holy Spirit of God, in whom you were sealed for the day of redemption.'

The hope of the Second Coming is prominent in Philippians, and there even the idea of immediacy may well have reappeared. The true citizenship of the Christian is in heaven, and from heaven we await a Saviour, the Lord Jesus (3.20). The Lord is at hand (4.5). He pleads with them to live the Christian life so that he may be proud in the day of Christ that all his labour has not gone for nothing (2.16). He is sure that God will complete at the day of Jesus Christ the good work that he has begun in them (1.6). He urges them to live so that they will be pure and blameless for the day of Christ (1.10). In the Letter to the Philippians Paul uses the Second Coming as the inspiration and the dynamic of the Christian life.

In Colossians Paul encourages the Christians by saying: 'When Christ who is our life appears, then you will also appear with him in glory' (3.4).

It is then clear that the idea of the Second Coming remains a constant in the thought of Paul from the beginning to the end of his Letters. The only thing that changes is that experience has projected it further into the future than the original expectation.

It is not likely that the Pastoral Epistles come in their present form from the actual hand of Paul, but it is highly probable that there is at least Pauline material in them; so this is the place to examine their evidence also. Timothy is urged to keep the commandment blamelessly until the appearing of our Lord Jesus Christ (1.6.14). The writer is sure that God can guard what has been put into his trust until that day (2.1.12). He prays that Onesiphorus may find mercy on that day for all the service he has rendered (2.1.18). He charges Timothy to be faithful in the duty of preaching by his appearing and his kingdom (2.4.1). He expects the crown of righteousness to be awarded to him on that day (2.4.8). The Christian must live a sober, upright and godly life, awaiting our blessed hope, the appearing of the glory of our great God and

Saviour Jesus Christ (Titus 2.12–13). The Pastoral Epistles, as we have them now, will probably have to be dated late in the first century, perhaps round about AD 100, and the hope of the Second Coming is still burning as brightly as ever.

We also find the idea of the Second Coming in the Letter to the Hebrews. Christ will appear a second time, not to deal with sin – that he has already done – but to save those who are eagerly waiting for him (9.28). The writer to the Hebrews quotes Habakkuk (2.3–4): 'For yet a little while, and the coming one shall come and shall not tarry', and applies the quotation to Jesus (10.37).

The idea also appears in James. The farmer sows his seed and patiently waits for his crop; so the Christian must patiently wait, for the coming of the Lord is at hand (5.7–8).

In the First Letter of Peter, God's people are guarded through faith for a salvation ready to be revealed in the last time (1.5). A faith tried, tested and purified in the fire will bring praise and glory at the revelation of Jesus Christ (1.7). Christians must gird up their minds and be sober, setting their hopes fully upon the grace that is coming to them at the revelation of Jesus Christ (1.13). They must keep sane and sober for the end of all things is at hand (4.7). When the Chief Shepherd is manifested, they will obtain the unfading crown of glory (5.4). The Christian life is still, in this Letter, the life that awaits the appearing of its Lord.

One of the main aims of Second Peter is to rebuke those who have come to feel that the Second Coming is so long delayed that it is not going to happen at all; those who say: 'Where is the promise of his coming? For ever since the fathers fell asleep, all things have continued as they were from the beginning of creation' (3.4). The only reason for the delay is that men may have a chance to repent (3.9), but 'the day of the Lord will come like a thief, and then the heavens will pass away with a loud noise, and the elements will be dissolved with fire, and the earth and the works that are upon it will be burned up' (3.10). Second Peter is almost certainly the latest book in the New Testament, and the Second Coming is still in the very forefront of Christian thought.

We turn now to the Fourth Gospel, and it is here that we will come on the tensions and the paradoxes which distinguish this matter of the Second Coming. In the Fourth Gospel there are two distinct strains of thought. There are those who think that the Fourth Gospel had as one of its aims the complete spiritualizing of the idea of the Second Coming. According to this view the John of the Fourth Gospel wished to get completely away from the crude and literal idea of a Messiah coming down again on the clouds of heaven, to the idea of the advent of the Messiah into the human heart. In other words, it is argued that John saw the Second Coming realized in the coming of the promised Holy Spirit, and that the Second Coming happened at Pentecost. At Pentecost Jesus came again in the Spirit, as he had promised that he would do.

So in the Fourth Gospel Jesus says: 'He who has my commandments and keeps them, he it is who loves me; and he who loves me will be loved by my Father, and I will love him and manifest myself to him' (14.21). And even more directly Jesus said: 'If a man loves me, he will keep my word, and my Father will love him, and we will come to him and make our home with him' (14.23). That indeed is a promise of a coming of Christ and of the Father to the heart of the loving and obedient man. Just so, in the Fourth Gospel Jesus says: 'He who hears my word and believes him who sent me, has eternal life; he does not come into judgement, but has passed from death to life' (5.24). So there is a sense in which for the believer judgement is over and eternal life has come.

If we follow the argument that the Fourth Gospel has spiritualized the whole matter, and that in the coming of the Spirit the Second Coming is an already existing event, this makes the Second Coming an event which every individual person can for himself experience and enjoy.

That is a lovely idea; and it is true; but in the Fourth Gospel there is another strain of thought. Jesus tells his disciples that, if he goes away, he will come again (14.3); that there will be a little while when they do not see him and that then they will see him again and be glad (16.16–22). The function of judgement belongs to the Son of Man and the day will come when he will judge the living and the dead (5.26–9). Jesus will lose none of those whom his Father has given to him, but will raise them up again at the last day (6.39).

There are thus two quite distinct strains of thought here. One strain, like the Pauline thought, thinks in terms of a visible future Second Coming and a visible future judgement; and the other strain sees that judgement for the Christian is past, and thinks of the Second Coming as having been realized and accomplished in the coming of the Holy Spirit, which would in effect identify the day of Pentecost and the day of the Second Coming. At the moment we are not going to discuss this paradox and this tension. It is sufficient to note that in the New Testament itself the physical and the spiritual ideas of the Second Coming both appear.

In this survey of the evidence of the New Testament, we have ignored two sections of it. We have said nothing about the Revelation, because it is unnecessary to do so, since the whole book is about the last times; and we have, as yet, said nothing about the Synoptic Gospels where the teaching of Jesus is most directly contained. So far it has been apparently plain sailing, but before we come to study the words of Jesus, let us pause to see just where the complications and the problems emerge.

(i) There is one difficulty which lies plain upon the surface. for all to see. We take a passage like 1 Thessalonians 4.13–17. There we read of the Lord himself descending from heaven, and the dead and the living being caught up together in the clouds to meet the Lord in the air. It is clear that we have here a picture in terms of a world view which is simply no longer tenable. It is seen in terms of a universe where heaven is somewhere above the sky, and from which the Lord comes down and to which he and his people go up. However we are going to interpret this, and whatever be the truth behind it, it must be clear that we can no longer take this picture literally in the spatial sense of the term. The truth which this picture contains cannot be literal and must be symbolic.

(ii) This leads directly to the second difficulty. The whole picture of the Second Coming in the New Testament is rooted in Judaism. There is a Jewish belief and a Jewish set of pictures with which the Second Coming has become inextricably entangled. That Jewish picture is the picture of the Day of the Lord.

In their earlier days the Jews, conscious of being God's chosen people, dreamed that their ultimate triumph and vindication would be achieved by the rise of a king of David's line, under whose reign and leadership they believed they would rise to the greatness which was rightly theirs. 'My servant David shall be king over them, and they shall all have one shepherd' (Ezekiel 37.24). 'In that day I will raise up the booth of David that is fallen and repair its breaches and raise up its ruins and rebuild it as in the days of old' (Amos 9.11). This dream never really died, but it did assume a new form.

It began to be clear to the Jews that they could never reach their true condition by human means. Humanly speaking, the opposition was too strong and they were too weak. So their thought went along a new line. They began to see time in terms of the two ages. There is this present age which is wholly bad and wholly given over to the domination of evil, and which is past all remedy and reform. There is the age to come which is the golden age of God, in which the righteous will be vindicated and in which God will reign and his people with him. But how was the one age to turn into the other? The change was impossible by any earthly agency, and so the conviction came about that God himself would come striding into history and would intervene directly. The change was to come about not by human but by superhuman power, not by natural but by supernatural agency. And the day of God's intervention would be the Day of the Lord.

In the prophets and in the intertestamental literature the Day of the Lord acquired a kind of standard apparatus. All the elements in the picture go back to three essentials. First, this present age cannot be mended and can only be obliterated; secondly, the age to come is the age of God; thirdly, the change will be effected by the direct intervention of God, by, we may almost say, the Second Coming of God, if we take the initial creation of the world as his first coming.

It was to be a day of utter destruction. 'Wail, for the day of the Lord is near; as destruction from the Almighty it will come!' (Isaiah 13.6). It was to be a day of cosmic disintegration and disaster. The sun will be turned into darkness and the moon will be turned into blood (Joel 2.30–1). It will come with the suddenness of the thunder clap. It will be a day when human relationships will be destroyed. 'From dawn to sunset they shall slay each other' (Enoch 100.2). It will be a day of moral chaos. Honour is to be turned to shame and beauty into ugliness (2 Baruch 48.35–7). It will be a day when the Gentiles are either subjected or destroyed. God will pour out the heat of his anger upon the nations (Zephaniah 3.8); they will become the servants and the slaves of Israel (Isaiah 45.14). Sometimes, but much more rarely, the ends of the earth are to be saved (Isaiah 45.22–3; Zechariah 8.20–3). From the ends of the earth, Israel will be ingathered again into Palestine (Isaiah 11.11–12; 27.12–13). There will be a new and a restored and a transcendently beautiful Jerusalem (Isaiah 54.12; 60.11, 13, 17). And the dead will be raised up. 'The dead shall live and their bodies shall rise. O dwellers in the dust, awake and sing for joy!' (Isaiah 26.19, RSV). 'Many of those who sleep in the dust shall awake, some to everlasting life, and some to shame and everlasting contempt' (Daniel 12.2). Above all, it will be a time of judgement and of the total destruction of the wicked. God is coming like a refiner's fire and who can stand when he appears? (Malachi 3.1–5).

Such in brief is the picture of the Day of the Lord, and we shall never rightly understand the New Testament picture of the Second Coming of our Lord unless we realize that it is painted in pictures which are not specifically Christian at all, but fundamentally Jewish. There is a complete identification of the Old Testament Day of the Lord and the New Testament idea of the Second Coming.

So once again we are back at the same conclusion. Whatever be the truth behind all this, and whatever its interpretation, we cannot think in terms of literalism.

(iii) The third difficulty will not now in the least surprise us. This is that in the main New Testament passage which deals with the times to come there is an amalgam of all kinds of different pictures of the future all fused into one. This is perfectly clear when we examine the great apocalyptic chapter Matthew 24, with its parallels in Mark 13 and Luke 21. Sometimes these chapters are read as if they referred only to the Second Coming, but there are in fact five different strands interwoven together. We shall take our references all from Matthew 24, which is the fullest of the three accounts.

- One strand deals with the foretelling of the fall and destruction of Jerusalem which happened in AD 70. That strand is in verses 15–22, with its foretelling of the destruction of the Temple, its advice to flee immediately to the mountains, its pity for those who at that time are with child, and its hope that the terrible days of the siege do not happen in the winter time. These verses have nothing to do with the Second Coming for clearly it would make no difference whether Christ came again in winter or in summer, and still more clearly no one could evade the Second Coming by fleeing to the mountains. This is a prophetic forecast by Jesus of the coming fall and agony of Jerusalem.

- The second strand has to do with the prediction of the persecution of the Christians. That strand is to be found in verse 9 which tells how the Christians will be persecuted, killed, and universally hated.

- The third strand has to do with the rise of heresy in the time to come. This strand is in verses 4–5, 11–12, 23–6, which tells how false teachers will arise and will deceive many.

- The fourth strand is composed of signs and manifestations of the end which are taken directly from the Jewish picture of the Day of the Lord. Personal relationships will be destroyed (verse 10). The world will be shattered and shaken and the universe will disintegrate (verse 29). The truth will be told to all nations (verse 14). Israel will be ingathered from among all the nations (verse 31). We have already seen that all these were part and parcel of the Jewish picture of the Day of the Lord.

- Finally, the fifth strand has to do with the Second Coming. It will be sudden and terrifying (verses 27 and 30); it will be a shattering inbreak of God on those who were never expecting it (verses 37–9); it will be a time of separation (verses 40 and 41); and the time of its coming is completely unknown (verse 36), except only to God. In view of this, endurance (verse 13), wisdom to read the signs of the times (verses 32 and 33), and constant vigilance are urged upon the Christian (verses 42–51).

It is easy to see that this chapter, so far from being a straightforward connected forecast of the Second Coming, is in fact an amalgam of different strands of thought, whose one connection is that they all have to do with an uncertain and a terrifying future.

Now we come to the most important part of all, the words of Jesus himself; and we shall find that here the problem becomes more complicated and more acute than ever.

At first sight it would seem that Jesus undoubtedly did speak about his coming again; but we shall see that time and again a doubt creeps into the evidence. In Luke 9.26 a saying of Jesus is recorded: 'Whoever is ashamed of me and of my words, of him will the Son of Man be ashamed when he comes in his glory and the glory of the Father and of the holy angels.' On the face of it this would seem to be a clear reference to Jesus' coming again. But we turn to Matthew's version of that saying in Matthew 10.33: 'Whoever denies me before men, I will also deny him before my Father who is in heaven.' That saying reads far more like a statement about what is to happen in the heavenly judgement after this life is ended, than a statement about the Second Coming on this earth. In Matthew 7.21–3 Jesus says that *on that day* many will claim to have been his followers but that he will reject and disown them. The same saying is recorded in Luke 13.26–7, but there it is recorded without the phrase *on that day*, and once again it gives the impression of being rather a judgement saying than a Second Coming saying. We do have agreement in the saying of Jesus as he looked down at Jerusalem: 'I tell you, you will not see me until you say, Blessed is he who comes in the name of the Lord!' (Luke 13.35; Matthew 23.39). Once again we have the same kind of doubt in the story of the ambitious request of James and John. In Matthew the request is that the two of them should sit one on the right and one on the left of Jesus *in his kingdom* (Matthew 20.21). This could well mean a request for the first places in an earthly kingdom, and would come from the fact that James and John and their mother were still thinking in terms of a nationalistic and a political Messiah. But in Mark 10.37 the request is that these places should be given to James and John *in Jesus' glory*, which reads more like an expectation of a supernatural coming again.

The more we study these sayings, the more the impression is borne in upon us that there are very few sayings of Jesus which speak unequivocally about his coming again. There are still greater difficulties. There are certain sayings of Jesus, which, if they are taken to refer to a literal and earthly Second Coming, were certainly not fulfilled, for on the face of it they refer to an immediate coming again. In Matthew 10.23 it is recorded that, when Jesus sent his disciples out on their mission, he said: 'You will not have gone through all the towns of Israel, before the Son of Man comes.' If that is taken literally, then it was certainly not true. In the apocalyptic chapter a saying of Jesus is recorded: 'Truly, I say to you, this generation will not pass away till all these things take place' (Matthew 24.34; Mark 13.30; Luke 21.32). Once again, if this is taken literally, then the words of Jesus were not fulfilled; and yet in Matthew in the very same chapter (24.14) it is said: 'This gospel of the kingdom will be preached throughout the whole world, as a testimony to all nations; and then the end will come.' And it is quite clear that the universal proclamation of the gospel throughout the world would necessarily take far longer than the life-time of the first disciples.

It becomes clearer and clearer that there is something here which requires explanation. It begins to look as if there were two strands of thought, held as it were simultaneously. We now therefore turn to two sets of parallel passages which have in them both the problem and the key.

There are three different versions of a certain saying of Jesus. It is clearly the same saying; in each case the occasion is the same, and yet in each case the saying is different. Let us set down the three versions:

> Truly, I say to you, there are some standing here who will not taste death before they see the kingdom of God come with power (Mark 9.1).

> But I tell you truly, there are some standing here who will not taste death before they see the kingdom of God (Luke 9.27).

> Truly, I say to you, there are some standing here who will not taste death before they see the Son of Man coming in his kingdom (Matthew 16.28).

Here is a case where harmonization is not really possible. One or other of these versions represents the words of Jesus. Which? Of the three versions only the version of Matthew introduces the Second Coming at all, and, if the Matthew version is to be taken literally, then the promise of Jesus was not fulfilled, for he did not come in the life-time of that generation. On the other hand, the versions in Mark and Luke which speak not of the Second Coming but of the *kingdom*, were gloriously true. For nothing could be truer than that in the life-time of that first generation the kingdom did come with power, and the message of the gospel had swept triumphantly through Palestine and Asia Minor and Europe until it had reached Rome.

Now, it is relevant to note that Mark is the earliest of the Gospels, and that therefore there is every probability that this version is nearest the words of Jesus, and the Mark version speaks in terms of the kingdom. We can therefore draw the conclusion that sayings which had originally to do with the kingdom tended to be turned into sayings which spoke of the Second Coming, and sayings which foretold the glorious growth and coming of the kingdom tended to be altered into sayings which foretold the coming again of Jesus. To put it in another way, sayings which spoke of his coming with spiritual power tended to become sayings which spoke of his coming in physical form.

We now turn to the second of our parallel passages. It is the passage which follows Jesus' claim to be the Christ at his trial before the High Priest. Again we set down the three versions.

I tell you that hereafter you will see the Son of Man seated at the right hand of power, and coming on the clouds of heaven (Matthew 26.64).

You will see the Son of Man sitting at the right hand of power, and coming with the clouds of heaven (Mark 14.62).

From now on the Son of Man shall be seated at the right hand of the power of God (Luke 22.69).

The significant fact about these three versions of the one saying is that Luke completely omits the reference to the Second Coming. Now in this passage what was Jesus doing? He was quoting Daniel 7.13–14, and without doubt he knew what he was doing. Let us set out the Daniel passage in full:

I saw in the night visions, and behold with the clouds of heaven there came one like a son of man, and he came to the Ancient of Days and was presented before him. And to him was given dominion and glory and kingdom, that all peoples, and nations, and languages should serve him; his dominion is an everlasting dominion, which shall not pass away, and his kingdom one that shall not be destroyed.

What is described in that passage? What is described is *an arrival in heaven*, and not a descent upon earth. The passage describes a glorious and splendid and honoured and majestic arrival in the presence of God. Surely in this passage what Jesus is foretelling is his arrival in the presence of the glory of God. He is saying to these Jewish rulers and leaders: 'You think you are eliminating me. You think you are disposing of me once, finally and for all. You think you are humiliating me upon a cross. Very well! Remember this! You will see me again, and the next time you will see me will be as a partner in the very glory of God. You will see me sharing the throne of God.' What a warning is there! It is as if Jesus said: 'You think of me as a criminal on the way to a cross over which you will gloat. But in fact I am the Son of God on the way to glory before whom you will appear for judgement.' The judged is to become the judge. In other words, this passage has nothing to do with the Second Coming; it has everything to do with Jesus' enthronement in glory.

The facts of the case lead us to our conclusion. Jesus very seldom, perhaps never, spoke of a physical Second Coming. What he did speak of was the triumphant spread of his kingdom and his own ultimate and certain glorification.

In the early Church, sayings which had to do with the Kingdom became personalized into sayings which had to do with a physical Second Coming. It was natural that it should be so. The early Church was a persecuted Church. In their agony they looked for release, and they turned sayings about the Kingdom into sayings about the coming again of Jesus. In point of fact they were mistaken; Jesus did not come at once; and the inevitable result was that they pushed the date of the Second Coming further and further into the future; but the whole process had begun because in their agony they had taken Kingdom sayings for Second Coming sayings.

Even though we have to abandon the literal and the physical idea of the Second Coming there is nonetheless a very great symbolic truth enshrined in that doctrine.

(i) It will be best to begin by reminding ourselves of one unquestionable fact. Speculation as to the time and the date of the Second Coming is absolutely forbidden. Jesus himself said: 'But of that day or that hour no one knows, not even the angels in heaven, nor the Son, but only the Father' (Mark 13.32; cf. Matthew 24.36). It is surely blasphemous for any man to seek to know, or to pretend to know, that which was hidden even from Jesus himself. Those who try to draw up celestial time-schemes and schedules of the future are surely engaged on a task which is futile and even forbidden, for they are seeking to know what even their Lord did not know.

(ii) We may have to abandon much of the imagery of the Second Coming; we may even have to abandon the idea of some visible catastrophic event and think rather in terms of the growth of the Kingdom; but no matter how much should be regarded as local and temporary in the expression of those doctrines, one permanent truth remains at the heart of it – the truth that *history is going somewhere*. The supreme truth expressed in the idea of the Second Coming is that history is not a mere chance succession of events, that history is not an aimless and purposeless journey to nowhere, but that there is an ultimate purpose and an ultimate goal in the universe. And that is a faith which is distinctively Christian, as it was distinctively Jewish, and it is a faith that must be held on to.

It was not characteristically the faith of the ancient world. The two great Greek schools of philosophy contemporary with Christianity were strangely pessimistic. The Epicureans, as we have seen, saw everything as a fortuitous conglomeration of atoms, which would simply disintegrate into atoms again. They could see no plan or purpose in the world. The Stoics believed that history was an eternal repetition without variation, world without end. And there are many modern historians who are just as pessimistic. G. N. Clark said in his Cambridge inaugural lecture: 'There is no secret and no plan in history to be discovered. I do not believe that any future consummation could make sense of all the irrationalities of the preceding ages. If it could not explain, still less could it justify them.' Herbert Fisher said: 'Men wiser and more learned than myself have discerned in history a plot, a rhythm, a predetermined pattern. I can see only one emergency following upon another as wave upon wave.' André Maurois said: 'The universe is indifferent. Who created it? Why are we here on this puny mud-heap spinning in infinite space? I have not the slightest idea, and I am quite convinced that no one has the slightest idea.' J. H. Withers in one of his broadcast sermons quotes a passage from Gerald Healy's play, *The Black Stranger.* It tells of the happenings during the Irish potato famine of 1846. As part of the relief work men were set to making roads which had no real function. One evening Michael came home to his father with the tragic and poignant cry: 'They're makin' roads that lead to nowhere!' So many people feel that history is a road that leads nowhere, but whatever else the doctrine of the Second Coming says, it says above all else that there is an end and goal to history, and that history is going somewhere – and the corollary of that is that a man may be on the way or in the way.

(iii) The doctrine of the Second Coming goes a step further than that. It says that history is going somewhere, and that that somewhere is a situation in which the kingdoms of the world will become the kingdom of the Lord. The doctrine of the Second Coming expresses the conviction that in the end Jesus shall reign.

(iv) We may well ask what all this means for us. The theologians use the word eschatology to describe the Second Coming and the events of the last days. Now it may be said that there are three kinds of eschatology.

- There is eschatology which is entirely futurist. This kind sees the Second Coming as a definite single catastrophic event some time in the future, distant or near, an event in which in some way Jesus Christ will literally appear again. If that is the case, then there is little that we can do about it other than watch and pray and prepare ourselves to be ready for it if and when it comes.
- There is what C. H. Dodd in a famous phrase calls realized eschatology. Realized eschatology means that with Jesus Christ the last days came; with him the final time of God's inbreak into the world arrived; that through him the new creation is here and now (2 Corinthians 5.17). This belief teaches that we do not need to look to some distant future, for the end of time; it is here, arrived in Jesus Christ.

  The only trouble about that belief is that all the facts seem against it. Evil is just as rampant; sin is just as dominating; men are just as un-Christlike as ever they were. If the end time has come, then there seems to be strangely little difference.
- But there remains another possibility. What if we are to think not of futurist eschatology, not of realized eschatology, but of personalized eschatology? What if the truth is that we are to think of the Second Coming of Jesus Christ not as some distant, future, cosmic, world-shaking event, but as an event which takes place in each individual heart and soul and mind of man? What if we are to think of the Second Coming not as one single event, but as an infinitely repeated event in the soul of each individual man?

The events of the life of Jesus are certainly historical events; but they are different from any other historical events. The ordinary historical event must be recorded and it may be memorized; it must be examined and tested and interpreted; a conclusion may be drawn from it and a lesson may be learned from it. But there is also something else. The events of the life of Jesus are such that they have an effect on the life of every man in time or in eternity; but for this to be so, there must always be a personal appropriation of each event. Now what if that be supremely true of the Second Coming? What if it be true that the key to the correct understanding of the Second Coming is indeed to be found in John's

Gospel in the words which tell how Father and Son will come and make their dwelling in the loving and the obedient heart? (John 14.23). The cosmic upheaval may well stand for the destruction of the old life and the creation of the new when Christ enters into life. The judgement may well stand for the confrontation of the soul with Christ. The blessedness may well stand for the new life which is the life lived in Christ. For us it may well be that the Second Coming is not meant to be a dream of the future but a challenge to each individual Christian to make that act of submission which will bring the coming again of the Spirit and the presence of Jesus Christ into his own soul.

CHAPTER FIFTEEN

To Judge the Quick and the Dead

Divine judgement is something from which the human mind tends to recoil. We would all like to water down the idea of judgement as much as possible. And yet the fact remains that judgement is one of the inescapable doctrines of the Christian religion.

The idea of judgement has existed in almost every religion, and it existed in Judaism. One of the sayings of the Fathers (3.22) runs: 'The world is ruled by goodness, yet all is according to the amount of work.' And then this saying is expanded into a kind of rabbinic parable: 'Everything is given on pledge (i.e. on pledge of repayment). And the net (i.e. of destiny) is spread over all the living. The shop is opened and the shopman (or money-lender) gives credit; the account book is opened and the hand writes; anyone who desires to borrow comes and borrows; but the collectors (i.e. the angels) go round continually every day and exact payment from a man whether he knows it or not (i.e. whether or not he is aware that calamity and sorrow and sickness are the result of, and the payment for man's debt); and they have that on which they rely; and the judgement is a judgement of truth (i.e. accurate and fair); men have to pay what they owe and no more.' Since Judaism was a religion of merit, judgement was inevitably a part of it.

There is a perfectly general reason why Christianity involves judgement. Christianity is an ethical religion. And any ethical religion involves sanctions. If a religion demands obedience to certain laws of life then it can only be those who keep those laws who will be rewarded with true happiness. And, further, since it is clear that the rewards and punishments are not correctly allocated in this life, the judgement must take place when life is ended, when the faithful will be rewarded for their fidelity, and the disobedient punished for their disobedience.

The idea of judgement runs all through the Letters of Paul. He speaks of the day of wrath when God's righteous judgement will be revealed (Romans 2.5); of the day when God judges the secrets of men by Christ Jesus (Romans 2.16). He speaks of the folly of human judgement in view of the fact that God will bring to light the things hidden in darkness and the secret purposes of every man's heart. 'Then every man will receive his condemnation from God' (1 Corinthians 4.5). Every man will receive his reward or his punishment and there is no favouritism with God (Colossians 3.24–5). He pleads for fine living from master and servant alike, for every man of every station will receive the reward for what he has done (Ephesians 6.8). The day will make manifest each man's work (1 Corinthians 3.13). We must all appear before the judgement seat of Christ, so that each one may receive good or evil, according to what he has done in the body (2 Corinthians 5.10). We shall all stand before the judgement seat of God (Romans 14.10).

It is clear how again and again the parables of Jesus involve judgement. Failure to use the talent is condemned (Matthew 25.14–30); failure to help human needs ends in judgement (Matthew 25.31–46). The parable of Dives and Lazarus shows Lazarus in bliss and Dives in torment (Luke 16.19–31). Judgement is an essential element in the teaching of Jesus.

We have here an initial problem. How can a religion of grace be a religion of judgement? James Moffatt summed up the whole teaching of Paul in one epigrammatic sentence: 'All is of grace and grace is for all.' Jesus teaches the fatherly love of God for all men (John 3.16). How can this be reconciled with judgement? No reconciliation is really necessary. The salient fact is that any offer brings with it the responsibility of acceptance or refusal. Every offer is at once a privilege and a responsibility, and to refuse an offer and to evade a responsibility necessarily involves a man in judgement.

In this doctrine of judgement there are many things which are uncertain and many things which are problems; but we must start with the certainties before we reach the problems. However many things may remain doubtful, we are left in no doubt as to what the standards of judgement will be. Again and again Jesus makes clear the ways of life for which a man stands condemned in the sight of God.

(i) As it has been well put, Jesus teaches that uselessness invites disaster. The servant who refused to use his one talent is condemned. Better to risk it and lose it than to keep it safely and uselessly buried in the earth (Matthew 25.14–30). The fig-tree which received every chance and which still bore no fruit will in the end be cut down. It will not be allowed to fill a place in the orchard, draw nourishment from the ground and give nothing in return (Luke 13.6–9). Usefulness does not necessarily mean a life of energy and action; a person who is physically helpless may by prayer unleash a floodtide of energy into life; a person for whom the days of action are past can still be a focus of spiritual strength and light. But the person who takes and who never gives, the person who makes no contribution to life, the person who has talents and who allows them to rust is under condemnation.

(ii) It might well be said that the supreme standard of judgement is reaction to human need. He who can see human need and listen to human appeal without doing anything about it stands condemned; he whose hand is instinctively stretched out to help is honoured by God. In the parable of the sheep and the goats the standard of judgement is not theological orthodoxy; it is not even what we might call intensity of devotion; it is quite simply response to the appeal of human need (Matthew 25.31–46). One of the sternest parables of Jesus is the parable of Dives and Lazarus. What in the last analysis was the crime of the rich man? He was not deliberately cruel to Lazarus; he did not order him to be removed from his gate; he was quite willing that Lazarus should have the food that was thrown away from his table. His crime was that he accepted Lazarus as part of the landscape, that he saw him with his emaciated body, hungry and diseased, and did nothing about it. As it has been said, it was not what Dives did do that got him into gaol; it was what Dives did not do that got him into hell. It is the teaching of Jesus that we serve God by serving our fellow men, and especially those in need.

(iii) The condemnation of those who lead others into sin is specially stern. The worst of deaths is better than the fate which awaits those who make 'one of these little ones to sin'. Temptation is inevitable in this world, but the man who is the cause and the means of temptation stands condemned (Matthew 18.3–7). Everyone bears with him an intangible influence for good or for evil. Everyone 'pipes for the feet of someone to follow.' It is bad to sin oneself; it is worse to teach someone else to sin.

(iv) Profession without practice is sternly condemned (Matthew 7.21–7). Protestations of loyalty with the lips are useless and worse than useless unless life in action guarantees their reality and their sincerity.

(v) It may be said even more widely that it is by ordinary everyday life that a man will be judged. Men will render account for every word they utter, even the words they utter when they are not thinking what they are doing (Matthew 12.36–7). A man's real character and nature are shown precisely by the things which he says and does quite unconsciously, when he is off his guard, when he is most naturally being himself. A man's day-to-day actions, and a man's day-to-day words will be the witness for his reward or for his punishment. It is the fact that out of the common stuff of life we make or mar a destiny and we win or lose a crown.

(vi) Men will be judged according to their willingness or their unwillingness to accept the offer of God made to them in Jesus Christ. One of the great characteristic features of the teaching of Jesus is the amount of it that is couched in invitations and commands – and invitations and commands are things which necessarily demand a response. The invitation of God in Jesus is likened to the invitation to a marriage banquet (Luke 14.15–24; Matthew 22.1–10), an invitation which the invited guests refused.

And the significant thing in these parables is the things which the invited guests put forward as excuses for not coming. One had bought a field and had to go and see it; another had bought five yoke of oxen and was going to try them out; one went to his farm, and another to his business; and one had married a wife and could not come (Luke 14.18–20; Matthew 22.5). The point is that the things which kept them from coming were good enough things in themselves. There is nothing wrong with being diligent and conscientious in business; in many a parable Jesus used that conscientiousness as the model of what life ought to be. Still less is there anything wrong in giving the claims of home and family life a high priority. But what Jesus is saying is that there is nothing in life which can take priority over the duty of accepting the invitation and the command of God. These are simply a pictorial and dramatic way of saying that devotion to Jesus Christ must take precedence over the closest and the dearest ties on earth (Matthew 10.37; Luke 14.25–7). Nothing in this world must interfere with a man's acceptance of the invitation and command of God in Jesus Christ.

(vii) A man will be judged by his loyalty or his disloyalty to Jesus Christ. Jesus will acknowledge before God all those who acknowledge him before men, and he will deny before God all those who deny him before men (Matthew 10.32–3; Mark 8.38; Luke 9.26). To be ashamed of Jesus Christ is to be liable to judgement. As it has been well put, there is no such thing as secret discipleship, for either the secrecy kills the discipleship, or the discipleship kills the secrecy.

Disloyalty can finally issue in betrayal. Jesus said of Judas the traitor: 'It would have been better for that man if he had not been born' (Matthew 2624; Mark 14.21; Luke 22.22). The Christian can still betray Christ by that disloyalty of life and action which turns men against Jesus Christ, and which makes them refuse the Master because of the unsatisfactoriness of the servant.

(viii) What we may call materialism renders a man liable to judgement. This is the lesson of the parable of the rich fool (Luke 12.13–21). This is the story of the man whose harvests were so plentiful that he had to build new barns to hold them. The future seems to him so well cared for that all he had to do was to eat and drink and be merry; but that very night his soul was required of him, and he was but ill able to meet God.

It is the story of a man who by any worldly standard was an unqualified success, but who on God's standards was a total and abject failure. The fault of the man was that he had concentrated so efficiently on this world that he had completely forgotten that there was any other world; he had been so immersed in time that he had forgotten that eternity existed. He is the brilliant example of a man who had lived in a way that made him completely unprepared for judgement. J. S. Whale put it in this way: 'The only true evaluation of this world is one which recognizes the impermanence of this world.' 'The true evaluation of this world must rest against the background of its impermanence.' 'Other-worldliness is the differentia of the Christian life in this world.' That man is clearly unprepared for judgement who has forgotten that there is such a thing as judgement.

(ix) The refusal to repent involves a man in judgement. In one passage Jesus cited two notable disasters, and then went on to say: 'I tell you that unless you repent you will all likewise perish' (Luke 13.1–5). The sole passport to forgiveness is sorrow for sin. 'The sacrifice acceptable to God is a broken spirit; a broken and a contrite heart, O God, thou wilt not despise' (Psalm 51.17). Without repentance there can be no forgiveness; the unrepentant sinner is committed to judgement.

This comes to its peak in the sin against the Holy Spirit (Matthew 12.22–32; Mark 3.20–30; Luke 12.10). Jesus spoke of the sin against the Holy Spirit, the sin for which there is no forgiveness, when the Jews had described his healing of a demon-possessed man as being due to his alliance with the prince of devils and not to his alliance with God. That is to say, these orthodox Jews could look at the incarnate grace of God and call it the work of the devil. Now one thing is to be noted. When on this occasion Jesus spoke of the Holy Spirit, he could not have been using that name in the Christian sense of the term, for Pentecost and the Christian conception of the Spirit had not yet come. He was speaking to Jews who knew nothing of the Christian conception of the Spirit, and he therefore must have been using that name in the *Jewish* sense of the term. In Jewish thought the Holy Spirit had two characteristic functions. The Holy Spirit revealed God's truth to men, and, equally important, *the Holy Spirit enabled men to recognize that truth when it was revealed*. It is a grim law of life that, if we refuse to use any faculty, we will in the end lose it. And, if we refuse to accept the guidance of the Spirit, we will in the end be incapable of recognizing it when it comes. That is what these Jews had done. They had so consistently refused the guidance of the Spirit, and they had so consistently preferred their way to God's way, that in the end they could not recognize the action of God when they saw it. They had reached such a stage of self-induced blindness that they could look on incarnate goodness and call it incarnate evil. That is the sin against the Holy Spirit. And why is it unforgivable? For this very simple reason that, when a man can no longer recognize goodness when he sees it, when he has come to such a stage of blindness that he confounds goodness and evil, he can no longer repent, for he can no longer recognize sin and desire goodness. And, when the possibility of repentance is gone, then the possibility of forgiveness is also gone.

He who cannot repent has judged himself; and God's judgement simply confirms what a man has made himself.

(x) Lastly, the severest judgement that Jesus passed on any group of people is passed on the Pharisees in Matthew 23.13–33. But this passage must never be read as if it had been spoken in an accent of searing anger. The word for *Woe!* is *ouai*, and the very sound of the word is tears.

This is far more a lament than a savage condemnation; its whole tone is tragedy rather than wrath. It is not so much *Woe!* as it is *Alas!*

The faults which brought the heart-broken judgement of Jesus on these Pharisees were basically three:

– They set their own, man-made rules and regulations above the commands of God.

– To put the same thing in a wider way, they loved systems more than they loved God. Religion to them consisted of their own rules and regulations far more than of obedience to the word and the command of God.

– The result was that they completely externalized religion, until it became a mere observance of regulations, and the state of the heart did not come into the matter at all. The inevitable result of this was a loveless legalism, far from the love of God and the love of man.

And, when we remember this, we are bound to see that so much of modern so-called Christianity is exactly the same.

We have now to discuss some of the many problems and questions which have to do with the idea of judgement. But it will be well to look first of all at the background of Jewish thought out of which Christian thought grew. For even if Jesus and the early Christian teachers filled already existing ideas with a new content and richness, they still had to talk in language and in ideas which their hearers could understand, and use the pictures and the ideas available to them. Four things have to be remembered about earlier Jewish thought.

(i) The conviction that they were the chosen people of God never faltered and never failed in the Jewish mind. They were the *hagios laos*, the holy people, the people who were different, the people who had a special and unique place in the heart and in the plan of God.

(ii) At this stage the hope was corporate and national. It was the *nation* which was chosen, it was the *nation* which would be vindicated, it was the *nation* which would in the end experience the victorious triumph given by God. They were not at this stage concerned to think in terms of the sorrows and the sufferings and the rewards and the punishments and the vindication of the individual; the nation, not the individual, was the unit in the plan and in the purpose of God.

(iii) The teaching of the prophets had laid fast hold of the moral holiness of God. God's standards of judgement were ethical standards. The old pagan ideas of the arbitrariness of the gods were in Judaism long left behind. God was just and righteous, and the law of the universe was a moral law. They were convinced that 'justice held the scales with an even and a scrupulous balance', and that 'in the end it was well with the righteous and ill with the wicked'.

(iv) So at this stage of Jewish belief – and it lasted long – the most important single fact is that they had no real belief in any life to come. We shall discuss this more fully in Chapter 21, but at this point we must take note of it. The Jews did not believe in the complete annihilation of the soul, but they did believe that all souls, good and bad alike, went to Sheol, the place of the dead. 'I am thy passing guest,' sighs the Psalmist, 'a sojourner like all my fathers. Look away from me that I may know gladness, before I depart and be no more' (Psalm 39.13). 'In death there is no remembrance of thee; in Sheol who can give thee praise?' (Psalm 6.5). 'Sheol cannot thank thee, death cannot praise thee; those that go down to the pit cannot hope for thy faithfulness' (Isaiah 38.18). After death there was nothing to look forward to except the shadows.

There was one logical and inevitable conclusion of this. If there was no life to come, then it followed that rewards and punishments and vindications must take place *in this world*. It is here that the righteous must be vindicated and it is here that the wicked must meet their terrible end. The effect of this on Christian thought has been profound, far-reaching, and in a very real sense disastrous.

The idea at its widest was that those who accepted the Messianic kingdom would be blessed and happy, and those who rejected it and rebelled against it would be accursed and obliterated. And that obliteration was connected directly with the idea of Gehenna. Gehenna, as we have seen, was not initially and originally symbolic, but was literally the Valley of Hinnon, *Gē Hinnom* in Hebrew. It lay outside the walls of Jerusalem, the public incinerator for the refuse of the city, and over it hung a pall of loathsome smoke, and in it the worms bred. And since this was the place where the bodies of the worst criminals were thrown, if was natural and inevitable that Gehenna, the Valley of Hinnom, the hateful rubbish dump, should become the final destination of the bodies of the enemies of God. To be flung into Gehenna was the worst fate which could befall any criminal; therefore, since it was believed that all punishment must come on this earth, Gehenna became, literally and physically, the place to which the persistently wicked and rebellious were doomed (Jeremiah 7.30–3; 19.1–9). This is exactly the picture in Isaiah 66.24: 'And they shall go forth and look on the dead bodies of the men that have rebelled against me; for their worm shall not die, their fire shall not be quenched, and they shall be an abhorrence to all flesh.'

But into Jewish thought there came a change. It became increasingly obvious that the vindication of the righteous and the destruction and punishment of the wicked were not happening, and indeed could not happen, within this present time scheme. Therefore the vindication of the righteous and the punishment of the wicked had to be moved forward into the world after death. As W. Morgan writes in the *Dictionary of the Apostolic Church*: 'Their faith, finding nothing in the present to which it can attach itself, takes refuge in the future and becomes eschatological.' The new world of the time beyond the grave has to be called in to redress the balance of the old.

This shift of emphasis and this shift of the time scheme had one supremely important consequence. With it there comes inevitably another shift, the shift from the nation to the individual. This is a quite new and a vastly important alteration.

The alteration comes in Daniel: 'And many of those who sleep in the dust of the earth shall awake, some to everlasting life, and some to shame and everlasting contempt' (Daniel 12.2). There is a foretaste of this in Isaiah, in a passage in which the translation is a little uncertain: 'Thy dead shall live, their bodies shall rise. O dwellers in the dust, awake and sing for joy!' (Isaiah 26.19). This hope is going in the days to come to take many forms, but the sheer force of historical circumstances, the ineluctable logic of inescapable facts, had compelled them to admit that the plan and the purpose of God needs another world. It is true that it will take a long time, a very long time, for the conviction of a future life to become effective and universal, but the process has begun.

With it, this new line of thought was bound to bring another alteration. Clearly, the character of Sheol is changed. If there is to be this judgement in Sheol, if there is to be bliss for the righteous and punishment for the wicked, then Sheol can no longer be the grey, shadowy, indeterminate place that once it was. Instead of being simply a region where the souls of all men dragged out a spectral existence, a kind of hovering between life and death, Sheol must become the scene of eternal destiny, a state, in other words, in which there is heaven or hell.

What happened was that the literal physical Gehenna picture was carried over to the other world. The smouldering flames of Gehenna were, so to speak, transferred lock stock and barrel to the other world; and so was born the popular picture of hell. Hell with its flames and its torture is simply the picture of the Valley of Hinnom projected from time into eternity.

That simple historical fact is the proof of how little the popular picture of hell is to be taken literally.

The word Gehenna is regularly translated as hell in the Gospels (Matthew 5.22, 29, 30; 10.28; 18.9; 23.15, 33; Mark 9.43, 45, 47; Luke 12.5), and through forgetting the simple historical fact about the background of the word Gehenna, there have entered into the text of Scripture, especially in the Authorized Version, translations which have completely misleading overtones. We may take one passage to illustrate this. In Matthew 23.33, in Jesus' condemnation of the Scribes and Pharisees, we have the question: 'How can you escape the damnation of hell?' In the first place, the word *damnation* is, at least in any modern translation, an entirely unjustified translation; it is indeed unjustified even on the grounds of the practice of the Authorized Version itself. The word translated *damnation* is the Greek word *krisis,* which is the normal word for *judgement.* In the Greek New Testament it occurs forty-nine times. In the Authorized Version it is translated *accusation* twice, *condemnation* three times, *damnation* three times, and *judgement* forty-one times. It is for instance the regular word in the Fourth Gospel for Jesus judging the world (cf. John 8.16), and in the phrase 'the Day of Judgement (cf. Matthew 10.15). To translate it by the word *damnation* is to introduce into it an overtone which does not in the least exist in the Greek word. In the second place, hell, in this passage which we are discussing, is *Gehenna.* The question then really means: 'How can you escape being sentenced to Gehenna?' which in turn means, 'How can you escape the sternest judgement of God?'

The New Testament itself is reticent, except in the Revelation, in its descriptions of punishment and penalty after death. As we have seen, such references as there are, are in the Valley of Hinnom symbolism. But it so happens that there was one book, written in the second century, which did a very great deal to fill in the popular idea of hell. This book is the Apocalypse of Peter, which in the late second century was accepted by some as part of the New Testament, and was read in the Syrian Church on Good Friday as late as the fifth century. As an Apocalypse, a revelation of the future, its reputation in the early Church was second only to the Apocalypse of John, which did finally lodge in the New Testament.

In this Apocalypse there are visions of the punishment of sinners in the world to come. 'Some there were hanging by their tongues; and these were they that blasphemed the way of righteousness, and under them was laid fire, flaming and tormenting them. And there was a great lake full of flaming mire, wherein were certain men that turned away from righteousness, and angels, tormentors, were set over them.' Murderers were 'cast into a strait place full of evil, creeping things, and so turning themselves about in that torment.' 'Other men and women were being burned up to their middle and cast down in a dark place and scourged by evil spirits, and having their entrails devoured by worms that rested not. These were they that had persecuted the righteous and had delivered them up.' 'And in another great lake full of foul matter and blood and boiling mire stood men and women up to their knees. And these were they that lent money and demanded usury upon usury.' 'And yet others near to them, men and women burning and turning themselves about and roasted as in a pan. And these were they that forsook the way of God' (Apocalypse of Peter 22–34). It can be seen that this idea of hell is in fact a further elaborated development of the Valley of Hinnom idea.

Before we leave the Jewish ideas there is one last idea to note. We have already seen the importance of the Day of the Lord in Jewish thought. It was the day when this present age, evil and incurable, would, with explosive suddenness, be destroyed, and when the new age, the age of God, would begin. And in particular it would be a day of judgement.

Now the significant thing to note is this. It was believed that until that day the dead were asleep, but that then there would be a great awakening and a general resurrection at which the righteous would enter into bliss and the wicked would perish miserably. This belief became standard Jewish belief between the Testaments. 'The righteous ones shall rise from the sleep of death, and Wisdom will rise up and be accorded to them' (Enoch 91.10). 'In those days the earth will give back those who are treasured up within it, and Sheol will also give back those whom it has received, and hell will give back that which it owes' (Enoch 51.1–2). 'The earth gives up again they that rest in her, the dust returns them that sleep in her, the chambers deliver up the souls that were committed to them. The Most High appears upon the judgement seat' (4 Esdras 7.32–3). Here there is the full doctrine of the general resurrection and the last judgement.

In all this there is something of the greatest significance. The simple truth which the facts demonstrate beyond any question is that the early Christian eschatology was almost entirely in Jewish pictures. It is from Jewish belief that there comes the idea of the sleep of the dead, the general resurrection and the final judgement. The conclusion is certainly not that we must dismiss these things because they are essentially Jewish and not Christian in origin, but that we must be careful not to insist on a literal interpretation of statements which are demonstrably using an already existing symbolism. We must be much less concerned with the pictures themselves than with the eternal truth which lies behind them.

The first of the problems which meet us when we think of judgement is the question of the time when judgement is going to take place. On this there is more than one view within the New Testament and within the various expressions of the Christian faith.

(i) We shall begin by looking at what is called Millennarianism or Chiliasm. We do not take this first either because it is the most orthodox or the most important expression of Christian eschatology, but simply because, although it was once strong within the Church, and although there is one part of the New Testament which, if taken literally, seems to teach it, it has now become more one of the eccentricities of Christian belief than part of the main stream.

The word *millennium* is a Latin word which means a thousand year period; the word *chiliasm* is derived from the Greek word *chilios* which also means a thousand. Therefore by derivation Millennarianism or Chiliasm is a doctrine which has something to do with a period of one thousand years.

The basis of Millennarianism is to be found in Revelation 20. There is a great cosmic battle in which the Devil is defeated (19.17–21). The Devil is then bound for one thousand years (20.1–3). The martyrs and only the martyrs are resurrected; for the time being all the rest of the dead sleep on; and the martyrs enjoy one thousand years of unalloyed bliss with the Messiah (20.4–6). This thousand year period is the Millennium. At the end of this period the Devil is loosed and there is a final battle after which the Devil and all his angels are flung for ever into the lake of fire (20.7–10). There then follows the general resurrection and the final judgement, with eternal punishment for the wicked and the new Jerusalem for the good (20.11–15; 21).

Apart from these few verses of the Revelation there is no evidence whatever in Scripture for this conception of the Millennium, but it is extraordinary what a fascination this idea has exercised on the minds of men, and it is equally remarkable how on the whole orthodoxy has recoiled from it. There are certain things to be noted about this Millennarian teaching.

– Its origins are fundamentally Jewish. It was common belief in the Jewish world – and it was a belief which transferred itself to Christianity – that the age of the world would correspond to the days of creation, each day being taken as a thousand years, for a thousand years are as a day in the sight of God (Psalm 90.4). This meant that the world would go on for six thousand years; that the Messiah would come at the end of the six thousand years; that the seventh thousand would be the reign of the Messiah; and that then the end would come. Christian Millennarianism is an adaptation of this belief.

– Christian Millennarianism from the beginning lent itself to the danger of making the Millennium a period of material happiness and prosperity. It had a tendency to become a purely material vision of bliss conceived in earthly terms.

– It may be said that the deathblow to Millennarianism was dealt by Augustine. Augustine spiritualized the whole idea. He held that the first resurrection, the resurrection of the saints, is the resurrection which the Christian undergoes when he is buried with Christ in baptism and when he rises to life with Christ. The thousand years' reign began with the Resurrection of Jesus, and is the reign of Christ in his Church, and at the end of the thousand years Jesus will come again and there will come the judgement. In so far as Millennarianism continued to exist in the mainstream of Christian thought at all, it was in this form.

(ii) We may look next at what we may call the idea of the intermediate sleep and the final judgement. It is in the thought of Paul that we find this conception. Paul was certain that there would be a day of wrath when God's judgement would be revealed (Romans 2.5). That day he identifies with the Day of the Lord Jesus Christ (1 Corinthians 1.8; 5.5; Philippians. 1.6, 10; 2.16; 1 Thessalonians 5.2; 2 Thessalonians 1.10). The day is the day when Jesus will come again in power and glory, for it is to Jesus Christ that judgement is entrusted (Romans 2.16). The time of that day is as unpredictable as the coming of a thief in the night (1 Thessalonians 5.2), although it is clear that at least in his early thought Paul looked for that day within his own generation. It will be a day where every man's work will be revealed for what it is (1 Corinthians 3.13), and the only thing which will enable a man to face it is Christian character and Christian holiness (Philippians 1.10)

As we have said, it is part of Paul's belief that the time of that day is unpredictable. What is to happen to those who die before that day arrives, or in what state are they? As we shall see, it is not quite certain what Paul's thought on this was. But there are sometimes indications that he thought of them as asleep until that great day. If the resurrection is not a fact then those who have fallen asleep in Christ have perished (1 Corinthians 15.18). Repeatedly in 1 Thessalonians he speaks of those who are asleep (1 Thessalonians 4.13–17).

Once again we are here in the sphere of Jewish thought. Speaking of the resurrection of the dead, the Book of Enoch (91.10) says: 'The righteous ones shall arise from the sleep.' In 4 Esdras 7.32–3 it is said that, 'The dust returns them that sleep in her.' In the Apocalypse of Baruch (30.1) it is said that at the resurrection, 'Then shall all those rise who slept having their hope in him.'

It may well be that here Paul was using ideas and pictures with which he was very familiar. In this view there is a kind of pause between this world and the next. There comes death; and after death there comes sleep; the sleep lasts until Jesus Christ comes again in power and in glory; then there come the general resurrection and the final judgement, in which Jesus Christ is judge, and at which men's deeds are revealed for what they were, and only those who have found their holiness and their righteousness in Christ shall enter into bliss.

The one special thing to note here is that for Paul the sleep of the

Christian is still in Christ. Neither death nor this in-between time separate the Christian from Christ. Even the waiting is waiting in Christ. It is the sleep of security and of peace, like the sleep of a little child in the room of the parent whom he trusts and loves.

(iii) We come now to a view which for a great many of us, whether we are aware of it or not, is in fact the orthodox view. This is the view of the Westminster Confession. We might call it the view of preliminary and final bliss and curse. Chapter 32 of the Westminster Confession is headed *Of the State of Men after Death, and of the Resurrection of the Dead*, and runs as follows: 'The bodies of men after death return to dust, and see corruption; but their souls (which neither die nor sleep), having an immortal subsistence, immediately return to God who gave them. The souls of the righteous, being then made perfect in holiness, are received into the highest heavens, where they behold the face of God in light and glory, waiting for the full redemption of their bodies; and the souls of the wicked are cast into hell, where they remain in torments and utter darkness, reserved to the judgement of the great day. Besides these two places for souls separated from their bodies, the scripture acknowledgeth none.'

'At the last day such as are found alive shall not die, but be changed; and all the dead shall be raised up with the selfsame bodies and none other, although with different qualities, which shall be united again to their souls for ever.' Chapter 33 is headed *Of the Last Judgement*, and the earlier part of it runs: 'God hath appointed a day wherein he will judge the world in righteousness by Jesus Christ to whom all power and judgement is given of the Father.'

Here then is what we may call official Protestant doctrine. We might call it a kind of two-stage eschatology. Immediately after death soul and body are separated. The soul goes to bliss or punishment as the case may be. This is a kind of preliminary classification. Then later there comes the general resurrection of the bodies of men; the bodies are joined with the souls, and there comes the final judgement.

As Vesey, the old commentator on the Catechism, has it: 'My soul, then, being freed from this body of sin, shall immediately be taken up into the paradise of God, there to live for ever with Jesus Christ.... My body, though it be laid for a time to rest in the grave, yet shall it one day be raised up and be joined to my soul to live together in everlasting glory.'

It is not easy to find any direct evidence in Scripture for this view. Like so many statements of belief, it has both negative and positive aims; and one of its main aims is to deny the Roman Catholic doctrine of purgatory by laying it down that even before the general resurrection of the bodies of men and their final judgement the destiny of men is fixed. And yet it is odd to find even Calvin allowing for the idea of progress in the intermediate time between death and judgement. He writes: 'Although those who have been freed from the mortal body do no longer contend with the lusts of the flesh, and are, as the expression is, beyond the reach of a single dart, yet there will be no absurdity in speaking of them as in the way of advancement, inasmuch as they have not yet reached the point at which they aspire, – they do not enjoy the felicity and glory which they have hoped for, and, in fine, the day has not yet shone which is to discover the treasures which lie hid in hope. And in truth, when hope is spoken of, our eyes must always be directed forward to a blessed resurrection as the great object in view.'

(iv) In all the views that we have so far looked at there has been an interval between death and judgement, but there are certain passages of Scripture in which it does seem that judgement follows immediately upon death, and in which a man seems to go straight to appear before God. The writer to the Hebrews says: 'It is appointed to men to die once, and after that comes judgement' (Hebrews 9.27). Paul, writing to the Philippians, speaks of the difficult choice that lies before him; he is not sure whether he wants to go on with the battle of life or to lay his armour down. 'My desire', he says, 'is to depart and be with Christ, for that is far better' (Philippians 1.23). And there surely the implication is that after death he would enter straight into the presence of his Lord. And again: 'We would rather', he writes to the Corinthians, 'be away from the body and at home with the Lord' (2 Corinthians 5.8). Jesus says to the dying thief: 'Truly, I say to you, today you will be with me in paradise' (Luke 23.43). It is true that the meaning of the word paradise is not completely certain and that Origen does, as we shall see, use it of an intermediate state, but in the context in which it is used here it does seem to mean blessedness with Christ, and blessedness to be entered into with no delay.

(v) We have finally to look at this matter of judgement in the words and the teaching of Jesus, and we must do so in two different places, first in the first three Gospels, and then in the Fourth Gospel.

On the face of it the first three Gospels look forward to a definite day of judgement in the future. In the interpretation of the parable of the tares, the harvest, which is the judgement, the separation of the good from the bad, is to come at the end of the age (Matthew 13.39). The devils fear that Jesus has come to torment them before the time (Matthew 8.29). When the Son of Man comes with his angels he will repay every man for what he has done (Matthew 16.27). On the day of judgement men will give account for every careless word they utter (Matthew 12.36). There will come a day when Jesus will disown many who have claimed to have spoken and acted in his name (Matthew 7.22). There are here three interconnected possibilities.

- Judgement is connected with the end of the age. As we have seen more than once before, Jewish thought held the doctrine of the two ages, this present age, which is wholly bad, completely incurable and doomed to destruction, and the age to come which is the blessed and perfect age of God. The change from the one to the other was to come about by the direct intervention of God on the Day of the Lord.
- Judgement is connected with the Second Coming of Jesus. It is when the Son of Man comes in his glory with all the holy angels that he will sit on his throne and judge the nations (Matthew 25.31). This is to all intents and purposes the Christian version of the Jewish Day of the Lord.
- There are some who have seen this picture in terms of death. They have taken death to be the equivalent of the coming of the Lord and the end of the world, and so have thought of judgement as coming at death.

In whatever way this is taken it places judgement in the future.

(vi) Last of all we come to the quite unique conception of judgement in the Fourth Gospel, and here there is an apparent contradiction. In it Jesus says: 'For judgement I came into this world' (9.39). The authority to execute judgement has been given to the Son of Man (5.27). The judgement of the world has come (12.31). But equally Jesus says: 'I did not come to judge the world but to save the world' (12.47). God did not send his Son into the world to condemn the world but that through him the world might be saved (3.17). The two sets of sayings seem to contradict each other, but in fact they do not.

The coming of Jesus into the world happened through nothing other than the love of God (3.16). But nonetheless, in the moment of confrontation with Christ there is inevitably judgement, for when a man is confronted with Jesus, he necessarily experiences a reaction. If he reacts in love, then it is well with his soul. If he reacts in indifference or anger or dislike or hatred, then it is ill with his soul. But whatever his reaction, in that moment of confrontation a man is self-judged. This is why in the Fourth Gospel Jesus says: 'Truly, truly, I say to you, he who hears my word and believes him who sent me, has eternal life; he does not come into judgement but has passed from death to life' (5.24).

So here judgement is seen as a continuous process. It is not postponed to some distant moment but takes place in every confrontation with Jesus Christ. A man's destiny is settled by his reaction here and now to Jesus Christ, the touchstone of God. This thought of the Fourth Gospel is perhaps the greatest and the truest of all thoughts.

Now we have to turn our thoughts to an even more important aspect of this matter; we have to ask what is the nature of judgement. What is the reason for judgement? What, if we may put it so, is God's intention and purpose in judgement? To ask this question is really to ask whether judgement and its consequent punishment are retributive or remedial. Are judgement and punishment the vindication of the offended justice and the outraged majesty of God? Or, are even judgement and punishment designed in some way to do something for men? Are they simply punishment or are they in some sense cure? There are three main ideas about this. All of them can be supported from Scripture and all of them have had and still have their place in the thought and the belief of Christian people.

There is the belief in everlasting punishment; the belief that men are judged, and that if at judgement a man is sent to hell, in hell he will remain and in hell he will suffer torment throughout all eternity, world without end.

It may be said that that is strictly orthodox belief, for the thirty-third chapter, *Of the Last Judgement*, of the Westminster Confession, runs: 'God hath appointed a day, wherein he will judge the world in righteousness by Jesus Christ, to whom all power and glory is given of the Father. In which day not only the apostate angels shall be judged; but likewise all persons that have lived upon earth shall appear before the tribunal of Christ to give an account of their thoughts, words and deeds; and to receive according to what they have done in the body, whether good or evil. The end of God's appointing this day is for the manifestation of the glory of his mercy in the eternal salvation of the elect; and of his justice in the damnation of the reprobate who are wicked and disobedient. For then shall the righteous go into everlasting life, and receive the fulness of joy and refreshing which shall come from the presence of the Lord; but the wicked who know not God and obey not the gospel of Jesus Christ, shall be cast into eternal torments, and be punished with everlasting destruction from the presence of the Lord, and from the glory of his power.'

The terrible thing about this doctrine lies not only in the grim awfulness of the prospect of which it speaks, but also in what can only be called the savagery with which it has so often been presented by those who accepted it.

It has actually been the case that for some people a very real part of the joy of heaven is to be the sight of the sinner in hell. For Tertullian it would be the joy of heaven to see great kings groaning in the depths of darkness, persecuting magistrates liquefying in fiercer flames than ever they kindled against the Christians, sages and philosophers blushing before their disciples as they burn together, poets trembling before the judgement seat not of Rhadamanthus but of Christ, actors and players and athletes burning and twisting in hell (Tertullian, *De Spectaculis* 30). Thomas Aquinas says that the nature of anything is best seen by its comparison with its opposite, and the bliss of the saints will find its completion, and their grateful thanks will find their greatest inspiration in the sight of the punishment of the wicked. Jonathan Edwards can write: 'The damned shall be tormented in the presence of the holy angels, and in the presence of the Lamb; so will they be tormented also in the presence of the glorified saints. Hereby the saints will be made more sensible of how great their salvation is. The view of the misery of the damned will double the ardour and the gratitude of the saints in heaven.' It may be possible to understand the feeling of Tertullian, for he wrote in a day when the blood of the martyrs was the seed of the Church, and when Christians suffered terribly and agonizingly at the hands of the state; but it is very hard to understand how those who claim to be disciples of the

Lord who taught us to love and to forgive our enemies can anticipate the delight of seeing even the blackest sinner agonize in hell.

Furthermore, those who have held this doctrine have often drawn a picture of God which makes the heart shudder. Jonathan Edwards has a sermon 'Sinners in the hands of an angry God'. In it he says: 'The God that holds you over the pit of hell much in the same manner as one holds a spider or some loathsome insect over the fire, abhors you and is dreadfully provoked.' Even Thomas Boston in the *Fourfold State* speaks of God holding the wicked in hell with one hand while he torments them with the other. F. W. Farrar in his book, *Eternal Hope*, makes these quotations and has also a quotation from one of Spurgeon's sermons:

> Thou wilt look up there on the throne of God, and it shall be written, 'For ever!' When the damned jingle the burning irons of their torment, they shall say, 'For ever!' When they howl, Echo cries 'For ever!'
>
> > 'For ever' is written on their racks,
> > 'For ever' on their chains;
> > 'For ever' burneth in the fire,
> > 'For ever' ever reigns.

One can well understand the woman, of whom Farrar tells, who, listening to a certain Dr Nathaniel Emmons preach in such a strain, rose up in the congregation and cried aloud: 'Oh, Dr Emmons, Dr Emmons, has God no mercy at all?'

Still further, many of those who most wholeheartedly preach this doctrine have gone to the most astonishing lengths in their physical presentation of it. To them the flames and the torture have been absolutely physical and absolutely literal. Farrar cites a terrible passage again from Jonathan Edwards: 'The world will probably be converted into a great lake or liquid globe of fire, in which the wicked shall be overwhelmed, which shall always be in tempest, in which they shall be tossed to and fro, having no rest day or night, vast waves or billows of fire continually tolling over their heads, of which they shall ever be full of a quick sense, within and without; their hands, their eyes, their tongues, their heads, their feet, their loins, and their vitals shall be for ever full of a glowing, melting fire, enough to melt the very rocks and elements. And they shall be full of the most quick and lively sense to feel the torments, not for ten millions of ages, but for ever and ever, without any end at all.' The more we read of this particular line of thought, the more difficult it is to effect any connection between it and the Jesus Christ of the Gospels.

Also, when we read passages like that, we can hardly help asking how any bodies could undergo physical torture like this and continue to exist. To put it crudely, why are they not burnt to a cinder? Even that question was not forgotten. It is held that the fire of hell is a special kind of fire. In the *Octavius*, Minucius Felix writes: 'And to these torments there is neither bound nor end. The fire has skill to burn and remake, to riddle and yet nourish, the limbs committed to it. As lightning strikes without consuming, and as the fires of Etna and Vesuvius, and volcanoes in other lands, burn on without exhaustion, so the penal fire does not undo those whom it burns, but feeds on the mangled fuel of bodies unconsumed' (Minucius Felix, *Octavius* 35). Tertullian sees in the volcanoes whose blasts of flame blot out cities small vent-holes of the treasure-house of eternal fire, mere missiles and sportive darts of the inestimably large centre of fire which awaits the condemned in the lower regions of the earth.

Thomas Aquinas has a very different approach to this eternal punishment. He held that character is fixed at death; therefore there can be no alteration of state in the world to come. There are three kinds of punishment: physical punishment by fire, intellectual punishment by regret for the consequences of sin, and spiritual punishment by being spiritually deprived of God. For Thomas there were two kinds of sin. One is 'a turning away from the immutable good which is infinite', which is therefore an infinite sin. The other is 'an inordinate turning to the mutable good which is finite', which is therefore a finite sin. The finite sin is punished by a finite penalty, by physical torture in the fire. But being finite it will end. And the punishment which is eternal and everlasting is the spiritual deprivation of God, the utter and absolute separation from God.

What are we to say about this doctrine of eternal punishment? Must we accept it, or are there grounds for questioning it, if not for absolutely rejecting it? It is quite clear that no wise man will be dogmatic about this, and that no reverent man will speak about what God must or must not do. But it yet remains true that neither human ignorance nor human reverence can absolve us from the search for truth.

(i) It quite clearly begins with one basic difficulty. It leaves an eternally divided universe. To all eternity there will be a heaven and a hell; and to all eternity there will be those who are gathered into the love of God and those who are subject to the wrath of God. God, said Paul, had a plan to unite all things in heaven and on earth in Christ (Ephesians 1.10). If there is such a thing as eternal punishment that dream can never come true. There will come a day, Paul sees in his vision, when every creature in heaven and on earth and under the earth will confess that Jesus Christ is Lord (Philippians 2.11).

(ii) It might be argued that although this dualism remains, nonetheless the victory of God is absolute. His friends are gathered into heaven; his enemies are committed finally and for ever to hell. God stands the undefeated and undefeatable victor in the battle of the universe.

This is perfectly true – but what a victory! If God were simply might, majesty and power, if the only name of God were King, then this victory might be tolerable and desirable. A conquering king might well be content to see his enemies shattered, brought to hell, permanently imprisoned and enslaved and crushed. But God is not only king, he is also Father; God is not only justice, he is also love. It was the world which God so loved (John 3.16). If God is love, a situation in which the greater part of his world is damned in hell must leave God for ever with a sorrow in his heart.

Paul sees in the end a universe in which all things will be put under God, and in which God will be everything to every one (1 Corinthians 15.28). The words *put under* will mean very different things to a king and to a father, to avenging justice and to seeking love. A king may well be content when his enemies are in chains; a father cannot be content until his sons come home. Justice may be content with breaking resistance; love can only be content with being loved.

This is true, however the idea of eternal punishment is interpreted and pictured. There will be few who will think now in literal terms of fire and brimstone. But, even if we grant that this literalism is no longer a living issue, and even if the whole matter is spiritualized and we think in terms of deprivation of God, isolation from God, banishment from God, the problem is not any less. There is still the problem of thinking of the God who is Father and the God who is love being satisfied with an ultimate state and condition of the universe in which vast numbers of his children are still alienated from him. As J. H. Leckie has said, some theologians do not feel any difficulty in the doctrine of eternal punishment and even torment, because they see in it 'a glorious necessary manifestation of the justice of God'. And, if God were simply justice, there would be no difficulty. But how the picture of God as love is to be fitted into this is something which is an insoluble problem for both the mind and the heart. The doctrine of eternal punishment would seem to leave God for ever a split personality, in his justice glorying over the defeat of his enemies, in his love mourning for the members of his family who refuse his love.

(iii) The doctrine of eternal punishment seems to do two closely related things. First, it seems to impose on sinners a quite disproportionate penalty. For the sin of a life-time it imposes the punishment of eternity. It is hard to see even recognizable justice in so infinite a penalty for that which was done in so finite a time. Secondly, the doctrine of eternal punishment undoubtedly imposes limits on the operation of the grace of God, or at least implies that there are limits to the time in which God chooses to exercise his grace. Have we any indisputable reason to believe that the operation of the grace of God is confined to this world and to this life? Is not the so-called doctrine of the descent into Hades a symbolic statement that the grace of God and the offer of God does extend beyond time as we know it? Are we to assume that after seventy years of life in this world we reach a stage in which the grace of God has become impotent or in which God has given up men as hopeless? These are not questions to which any man can give a sure answer, but they do raise the question whether it can be right to limit the grace of God in such a way.

(iv) Finally, we must look at the New Testament evidence which, it is claimed, makes this doctrine essential. The most definite evidence is at the end of the parable of the sheep and the goats, which, after the separation of the approved and the condemned, ends: 'And they will go away into eternal punishment, but the righteous into eternal life' (Matthew 25.46). It is to be noted that here the AV is quite misleading. It has: 'These shall go away into *everlasting* punishment; but the righteous into life *eternal*.' There is no justification whatsoever for using two different words; in the Greek both the punishment and the life are *aiōnios*. Let us then look at the two words, 'punishment' and 'eternal'.

- The word for punishment is *kolasis*. This word was originally a gardening word, and its original meaning was *pruning trees*. In Greek there are two words for punishment, *timōria* and *kolasis*, and there is a quite definite distinction between them. Aristotle defines the difference; *kolasis* is for the sake of the one who suffers it; *timōria* is for the sake of the one who inflicts it (*Rhetoric* 1.10). Plato says that no one punishes (*kolazei*) a wrong-doer simply because he has done wrong – that would be to take unreasonable vengeance (*timōreitai*). We punish (*kolazei*) a wrong-doer in order that he may not do wrong again (*Protagoras* 323 E). Clement of Alexandria (*Stromateis* 4.24; 7.16) defines *kolasis* as pure *discipline*, and *timōria* as the return of evil for evil. Aulus Gellius says that *kolasis* is given that a man may be corrected; *timoria* is given that dignity and authority may be vindicated (*The Attic Nights* 7.14). The difference is quite clear in Greek and it is always observed. *Timōria* is retributive punishment; *kolasis* is remedial discipline. *Kolasis* is always given to amend and to cure.

- The word *aiōnios* is difficult to translate. It is used in the Old Testament to describe Israel's possession of the holy land (Genesis 17.8; 48.4); Aaron's priesthood (Numbers 25.13); regulations about blood in the sacrifices and about the day of atonement (Leviticus 3.17; 16.34); great mountains and hills (Habakkuk 3.6). Now *aiōn* literally means *an age*, and *aiōnios* is literally *age-long*. In all the cases we have quoted the translation is *everlasting* or *for ever*, but in every case the thing described is a human thing, and will sometime come to an end. In every case *aiōnios* means lasting for a very long time; it can even mean lasting as long as the present world lasts; but it does *not* mean lasting for ever and ever throughout eternity.

The Greek usage of *aiōnios* is even more suggestive. Plato in the *Laws* (10.12) says that body and soul are indestructible (*anōlethron*), but they are not eternal (*aiōnios*) like the gods. In the *Timaeus* he says that time as we know it in this world is formed on the model of the nature which is *aiōnios*, eternal. The fact is that in Greek *aiōnios* can properly only describe *that which is divine*; in the true sense of the term only God is *aiōnios*. *Aiōnios kolasis* is therefore the disciplinary punishment, designed for the cure of men, which may last throughout many ages, and which only God can give.

It can therefore be seen that the phrase in Matthew 25.46 does not commit us to a doctrine of eternal punishment in the sense in which it is usually taken. It may well describe a disciplinary, curative punishment, and it certainly describes the punishment which only God can inflict.

Both on general and on particular grounds the validity of the doctrine of eternal punishment in the sense of endless retributive punishment is of very questionable validity.

The second view of what is to happen after death is called the doctrine of conditional immortality. This view holds that the soul is not naturally and inherently immortal, but that man is what Petavel called 'a candidate for immortality'. Immortality is not, as it were, a right; it is not something which man as man possesses. It is the gift of God in Jesus Christ, and comes to us only through a connection with Jesus Christ. According to this view the soul lives or dies according as it accepts or rejects the grace of God in Jesus Christ. A man chooses life or chooses obliteration and annihilation.

This idea emerged very early in the thought of the Church; the idea was that it was Jesus who brought life and immortality and that without him the soul of man is not immortal (2 Timothy 1.10). In this view the reward of goodness is life, and the judgement and the punishment of sin is extinction.

This idea emerged as early as the second century. Tatian (*To the Greeks* 13) says that if the soul remains solitary and apart from the Word, 'it tends downwards towards matter and dies with the flesh; but if it enters into union with the divine Spirit, it is no longer helpless, but ascends to the regions to which the Spirit guides it.' 'Souls', said Justin Martyr, 'both die and are punished' (*Dialogue with Trypho* 5). Theophilus of Antioch (*To Autalycus* 2.27) says that a man was made neither mortal nor immortal but capable of both, so if he inclined towards the things of immortality and kept the commandments, God should give him immortality as a reward, and so that he should become God; but if he turns to the things of death, he is the cause of death to himself. The same idea recurs in Irenaeus (*Against Heresies* 2.34.3–4). He says that God imparts continuance for ever on those who are saved; but the man who does not recognize God deprives himself of continuance for ever and ever. In these writers the idea of conditional immortality is implicit rather than explicit, but in Arnobius it is fully stated (*Against the Nations,* 2.26, 27, 30, 36).

According to Arnobius man is no more than the highest of the animals and owes his creation, not to the supreme God, but to some lesser deity. Man is not naturally immortal, and left to himself will completely perish. The soul of the unbeliever may simply perish with the body, but more likely there is no sudden annihilation, but a long process of punishment which finally destroys the soul. The soul can only become immortal by the miracle of the grace of God. Here, even in one of the fathers of the Church, is a fully developed doctrine of conditional immortality.

Among the churches or sects today the Christadelphians hold this view as their official doctrine. The fullest modern exposition of this doctrine, and the most famous, is Edward White's *Life in Christ*. White held that man was created immortal, but that he lost that immortality at the Fall, and that all the sons of Adam are doomed to death. Jesus Christ came to restore the lost gift. 'The object of the incarnation was to immortalize mankind.' White did not believe that existence ended with death; he believed that after death there was still the opportunity for the unrepentant to repent at least for a time, and that only those who reject every possible offer of salvation will be destroyed. 'After God has gathered out of the world's population by methods of grace, on earth or in Hades, all salvable persons, there will remain for the judgement of the last day those alone who will deserve some terrible positive infliction as the antecedent to destruction.' So White's view was that those who stubbornly refused the offer of God in this life and in the first stage of the life to come would, after terrible punishment, be finally and utterly destroyed.

There is no doubt that this doctrine of conditional immortality has been widely held even by people who would have called themselves both evangelical and orthodox. Is there then any scriptural evidence for it? Can it be supported from biblical teaching?

There is strong evidence for it on one condition – on condition that a great many references to death and to destruction are taken physically and literally and not spiritually. We set down a selection from this evidence. It was the warning of Ezekiel that the soul that sins shall die (Ezekiel 18.20). There is a wide and easy way that leads to destruction (Matthew 7.13). The fate of the sinner is like that of a tree which is cut down and thrown into the fire (Matthew 7.15–19; John 15.6). The weeds in the harvest field are burned in the fire (Matthew 13.40). A man can gain the whole world and forfeit his soul (Matthew 16.26). Unless men repent, they will perish like men involved in some fatal disaster (Luke 13.4, 5). It is only the one who hears and receives the word of Jesus Christ who has passed from death to life (John 5.24). The end of the things of sin is death; the wages of sin is death, but the free gift of God is eternal life in Christ Jesus our Lord (Romans 6.20–3). To set the mind on the flesh is death (Romans 8.6). If you live according to the flesh you will die (Romans 8.13). There are those whose end is destruction (Philippians 3.19). Those who do not obey the gospel will suffer the punishment of eternal destruction (2 Thessalonians 1.9). Sin when it is full grown brings forth death (James 1.15). Whoever brings back a sinner from the error of his way will save his soul from death (James 5.20).

If we are to take all these passages, and many others, in the sense of physical death and destruction, then it might well be held that the argument for conditional mortality and for the ultimate destruction of the adamant sinner is unanswerable. But it is very doubtful indeed that they can so be taken. When the whole thought of many of the writers who are quoted is considered, it becomes clear that they did not think in terms of the annihilation of the soul, but did in fact believe that the soul was immortal. It is fairly certain that it is spiritual death of which they are speaking. What then are the virtues of this doctrine and what are the objections to it?

(i) This doctrine has what might be called a *natural* advantage. Suppose we accept the theory of evolution, as on the evidence we are bound to do; suppose we agree that life has developed from the lower to the higher. Then immediately one question must come in – *when did living creatures, so to speak, acquire immortality?* At what stage does the soul become immortal? What are we to say about animals, about, for instance, a faithful and intelligent dog? This is a question which has long been discussed, and on which there has always been speculation. On the basis of the doctrine of conditional immortality it simply does not arise. No living creature is naturally immortal. Immortality comes, and comes only to those who accept the offer of God in Jesus Christ.

(ii) This theory has what might be called a *human* advantage. A feature of modern life is that there are a great many people who do not want immortality; they would in fact regard life which goes on for ever as a kind of hell. They are so weary of life and living that all they want is to lay life down. Now the fact is that only the person who has really experienced eternal life in the here and now desires life in the there and then. In other words, it is the desire for Jesus Christ which begets the desire for that life which only Jesus Christ can satisfy.

(iii) This theory has what might be called a *cosmic* advantage. Unlike the doctrine of eternal punishment it does not finish up with an eternally divided universe; it ends with a unified universe in which God is all in all, and in which all that has refused God has simply ceased to exist. It ends up with a universe in which there is nothing except those who love God and God himself.

Why then do we not accept this theory? And why in spite of the fact that it has been largely held has it never really laid hold on the minds and hearts of men? There are two reasons which prevent its total acceptance.

(i) When all is said and done, it is the instinctive Christian view that the soul is naturally immortal, that there is a part of man which lasts for ever. This at least is quite certain – Jesus Christ spoke to men as children of eternity.

(ii) It is quite true that this theory leaves us with a unified universe – but at what a cost! It leaves us with such a universe at the cost of annihilation – even if it is the self-annihilation of those who have resisted God. And in the last analysis can we believe that the God whose name is Father and whose nature is love can consent to a final situation in which his supremacy involves the annihilation of so many of his family? For a God of power doubtless that would be enough, but is it enough for the God of love?

We come now to the last of the views of what happens after death. It is the view known as universalism, or perhaps better, as universal restoration. This view teaches 'the final salvation of all mankind'. It holds the belief that 'evil will finally pass away through the reconciliation of all souls to God'. This has never been what might be called the ortho-dox Christian belief; but neither has it been branded as a heresy which divides a man from the Church.

As J. H. Leckie reminds us, H. R. Mackintosh once wrote 'If at this moment a frank and confidential plebiscite of the English-speaking min-istry were taken, the likelihood is that a considerable majority would adhere to universalism.' But it may be true to say that for many universal restoration is a hope rather than a conviction. As the poet Crabbe wrote:

The view is happy; we may think it just.
It may be true; but who shall say it must?

As one might well expect this is a belief which has appealed to the poets.
Tennyson wrote in 'In Memoriam':

The wish, that of the living whole
    No life may fail beyond the grave,
    Derives it not from what we have
The likest God within the soul?
I stretch lame hands of faith and grope,
    And gather dust and chaff and call
    To what I feel is Lord of all,
And faintly trust the larger hope.
Behold, we know not anything;
    I can but trust that good shall fall
    At last – far off – at last, to all,
And every winter change to spring.

Whitman wrote in 'Leaves of Grass':

What ever else withheld, withhold not from us
Belief in plan of thee inclosed in time and space,
Health, peace, salvation universal.
Is it a dream?
Nay but the lack of it a dream,
And, failing it, life's lore and wealth a dream,
And all the world a dream.

Belief in universal restoration is no new belief and no modern heresy. It has always been deeply rooted in the thinking of the Church. The first great exponent of it, and perhaps he remains the greatest exponent, was Origen. He had to meet the attack of the pagan Celsus on Christianity. Celsus charged the Christians with believing that they alone would be saved and that all others would be thrown into everlasting fire. Origen held that the fire was a purifying fire, and that the souls of men are purified by their torments; and he quoted in support of his belief Malachi's saying: 'The Lord cometh like a refiner's fire, and like fuller's soap; and he shall sit as a refiner and purifier of silver and gold' (Malachi

3.2–3). He neither denied the fire nor the torture, but he held that they were purification as well as punishment.

He states his belief much more fully and much more sympathetically in his great work on Christian doctrine, *De Principiis*. He says that a time will come when God will bestow on every creature what he deserves; but in spite of that believes that God through his Christ may recall all his creatures to one end. Christ must reign until he puts all things under his feet (1 Corinthians 15.25; cf. Psalm 110.1); but Origen insists that this is a voluntary subjection in which all men will submit to God. The end, he argues, must be like the beginning. As the world began by being God's world, so ultimately it must end by being God's world in all its completeness.

He quotes the words of Jesus about all being one (John 17.20–1); he quotes Paul's words about *all* coming in the unity of the faith to a perfect man (Ephesians 4.13). He insists that in the world in which the new heavens and the new earth come it is the destiny of the human race to be restored to this unity of which Jesus speaks. But Origen was far from removing penalty and punishment. After death, he believes, the souls of men must pass through order upon order and discipline upon discipline, as each needs, until they reach the highest. They go to that part of eternity which they deserve, and they are punished as they deserve, so that, 'having undergone heavier and severer punishments, endured for a lengthened period and for many ages, so to speak, improved by this stern method of training and restored at first by the instruction of the angels and subsequently by the powers of a higher grade, and thus advancing through each stage, reach even to that which is invisible and eternal having travelled through by a kind of training every single office of the heavenly powers.' Origen does not believe that even the rebellious angels are irrecoverably lost. He believes that 'being remoulded by salutary principles and discipline, they may recover themselves and be restored to their condition of happiness.' He takes a colossal leap of the imagination and sees a time when even Satan, the devil himself, will be saved and brought into willing subjection to God. (Most of Origen's teaching on this subject is in the *De Principiis* 1.6.1–3). No man ever had a fuller vision of the final triumph of the love of God than Origen had, and at the same time no man ever took the reality of future punishment and discipline more seriously.

The other great exponent of the doctrine of universal restoration is Gregory of Nyssa. J. H. Leckie in *The World to Come and Final Destiny* summarizes Gregory's teaching. Gregory believed in universal restoration for three reasons. He believed in it because of *the character of God*. Because God is good he has pity for fallen man; and because God is wise he knows the means to man's recovery (*The Great Catechism* 21). He believes in it because of *the nature of evil*. Evil is negative; evil does not exist in the same essential sense as good exists. 'In any and every case evil must be removed out of existence, so that the absolutely non-existent should cease to be at all' (*Concerning the Soul*).

He believes in universal restoration because of *the nature of punishment*. For Gregory punishment was always disciplinary and remedial. Its nature is 'to get the good separated from the evil and to attract it into the communion of blessedness'. Punishment is part of the process of redemption, and in it 'the divine force of God's very love of man drags that which belongs to him from the ruins of the irrational and material' (*Concerning the Soul*). Just as gold with alloy is put into the fire to be cleansed of the alloy, so the soul with its sin is put into the purgatorial fire 'until the spurious material alloy is consumed and annihilated.' He speaks of punishment being like the surgeon's knife or the cautery, painful but nonetheless curative and salutary (*The Great Catechism* 26). So Gregory looks forward to a time when every soul shall be wrought into conformity with the divine image and will be clothed with the beauty of the Lord, a time when 'a harmony of thanksgiving will rise from all creatures, as well from those who in the process of the purgation have chastisement, as from those who have needed no purgation at all.'

Gregory argues that whether you approach the matter from the nature of God, the nature of evil, or the nature of punishment, you are led to a belief in universal restoration.

One thing is to be noted now, although we shall return to it again. There were certain universalists who believed that sin receives all the punishment it will receive within this world, and that after death there is nothing but happiness and blessedness for all. The great classical exponents of universalism were very far from believing that. It would not be wrong to say, however paradoxical it may at first sound, that the great universalists believed quite as strongly in hell as they did in universal restoration. It never occurred to them that sin would be without its penalty; it never occurred to them that there was an easy way to eternal blessedness. The discipline of God was to them no small thing; the stubborn soul might well have to go to heaven via hell. But the universalists did strenuously believe that any punishment God inflicts must in the end be not merely retributive but also remedial.

Let us now see whether there is any scriptural evidence for universal restoration.

Jesus said: 'I, when I am lifted up from the earth, will draw *all* men to myself' (John 12.32). Paul said, 'As in Adam *all* die, so also in Christ shall *all* be made alive' (1 Corinthians 15.22). 'God has made known to us in all wisdom and insight the mystery of his will, according to his purpose which he set forth in Christ as a plan for the fulness of time, to unite *all* things in him, things in heaven and things on earth' (Ephesians 1.10). 'This is good, and it is acceptable in the sight of God our Saviour, who desires *all* men to be saved and come to the knowledge of the truth. For there is one God, and there is one mediator between God and men, the man Christ Jesus, who gave himself as a ransom for *all*' (1 Timothy 2.3–5). 'We have set our hope on the living God who is the Saviour of *all* men, especially of those who believe' (1 Timothy 4.10). 'The grace of God has appeared for the salvation of *all* men' (Titus 2.11). 'The Lord is not slow about his promise as some count slowness, but is forbearing towards you, not wishing that any should perish, but that *all* should reach repentance' (2 Peter 3.9). 'He is the expiation for our sins, and not for ours only but also for the sins of *the whole world*' (1 John 2.2). 'As one man's trespass leads to condemnation for *all men*, so one man's act of righteousness leads to acquittal and life for *all men*' (Romans 5.18). 'We see Jesus, who for a little while was made lower than the angels, crowned with glory and honour because of the suffering of death, so that by the grace of God he might taste death for *everyone*' (Hebrews 2.9). 'God has consigned *all* men to disobedience, that he may have mercy upon *all*' (Romans 11.32). 'Then comes the end, when he delivers the kingdom to God the Father after destroying every rule and every authority and power. For he must reign until he has put all his enemies under his feet. The last enemy to be destroyed is death. But when it says, "All things are put under him", it is plain that he is excepted who put all things under him. When all things are subjected to him then the Son himself will also be subjected to him who put all things under him, that God may be *everything to everyone*'

(1 Corinthians 15.24–8). It is *all flesh* which is to see the salvation of God (Luke 3.6). Unquestionably the evidence exists, and it is strong.

What then is to be said for and against this belief in universal restoration?

(i) It is argued that a belief in universal restoration takes the nerve and the iron out of religion, and that it removes that salutary threat which eternal punishment undeniably has. If universal restoration is a fact, then why worry, as everything will be all right in the end?

Even Origen with his strong belief in universal restoration felt this. He says that this subject must not be talked about in the presence of everyone. 'It is not unattended with danger to commit to writing the explanation of such subjects, seeing that the multitude need no further instruction than that which relates to the punishment of sinners; for to ascend beyond this is not expedient, for the sake of those who are with difficulty restrained, even by the fear of eternal punishment, from plunging into any degree of wickedness, and into the flood of evils which result from sin' (*Against Celsus* 6.26). But surely if a thing is true, it must be openly stated, and surely if a view is false, it cannot be allowed to continue unamended simply because it happens to be morally useful. To make usefulness rather than truth the test of any doctrine is indeed a cynical approach to truth.

But what are we to say about this argument that belief in universal restoration destroys the impact and the effect of religion? First, it must be remembered that no responsible teacher of universalism ever said that there was no such thing as *punishment*. It is even true, as universalism sees it, that a man might go through a near-eternity of disciplinary punishment before he submitted to God. The plain fact is that the universalist in the realest sense believes in hell *and* restoration. His characteristic belief lies not in the elimination of hell from the scheme of things, but in the belief that punishment is essentially remedial and not simply punitive and retributory. And further, even Origen held that a man might be saved in such a way that the scars, so to speak, will still remain; the necessary punishment will have left its indelible mark. Belief in universal restoration has enough sternness in it to make a man still dread the consequence of sin. Secondly, this objection is based on the assumption that the most effective weapon the Christian preacher has is the weapon of fear; that a man is most likely to be driven into heaven by the fear of hell. As Burns had it:

> The fear o' hell's a hangman's whip
> To haud the wretch in order.

But, if fear is to have the last word, then neither the resultant preaching nor the resultant religion is truly Christian.

Belief in universal restoration does not remove the idea of divine discipline but at the same time it believes that a man can be loved rather than terrified into the kingdom of God.

(ii) It is perhaps a more serious objection that universal restoration might seem to destroy free-will. It does mean that in the end the resistance of every man will be overcome. J. H. Leckie, in answer to this objection, says that it is difficult to believe that the freedom of the will is so absolute as to permit eternal existence in sin. He says that he cannot believe that God has given to any creature the power to perpetuate evil eternally and to work his own everlasting misery. A gift like that would not be a good gift, and all God's gifts are good. And in any event the final effect is to be produced not by coercion, but by 'the persuasive ministry of grace', however long that divine ministry may need to achieve its end. When we think of the persuasion of God, we are not thinking of human persuasion which necessarily has a limited time in which to work. We are thinking of a persuasion which has all eternity to love a man to itself.

Let us now see what we can say in support of the belief in universal restoration.

(i) It is only the belief in universal restoration which can in the end come to think in terms of a universe which is a perfect unity. As we have seen, eternal punishment would leave us with a universe for ever divided; it would mean that there is a dualism at the very heart of things. Only universal restoration could produce a universe in which in the end God is all in all, everything to everyone, a universe which in the realest sense of the term is God's universe.

(ii) Further, it seems to us true that nothing other than, and nothing less than, belief in universal restoration really matches the character of God as he is revealed to us in Jesus Christ.

'God', says J. H. Leckie, 'cannot ultimately be confronted with a power greater than himself.' And yet, if at the end of the day there remains one soul stubbornly unrepentant and adamantly unsubmissive, that soul is greater than God; that soul has defied and defeated God. This situation might be met by the annihilation and the obliteration of such a soul.

But there is another side to this power of God. Ultimately God is love. It is his love which directs his power. Even his holiness and his justice are in the end controlled by his love. Now if God is love God cannot be at peace until the last child in his family has come home, and for God the obliteration and annihilation of the rebellious would be not triumph but tragedy, not victory but final and ultimate defeat. If God were only power, obliteration would meet the case; but if God is love, then it is hard to see how anything less than universal restoration will do.

No one is going to be dogmatic about this. Eternal punishment, conditional immortality, universal restoration – there will be those who will believe in each of these. But it seems to us that if God is the God who is the God and Father of our Lord Jesus Christ, and if the total impression of the Gospel is true, we may dare to hope that when time ends God's family will be complete, for surely we must think in terms, not of a king who is satisfied with a victory which destroys his enemies, but of a Father who can never be content when even a single child of his is outside the circle of his love.

CHAPTER SIXTEEN

I Believe in the Holy Ghost

The creed expresses the belief of the Church, first, in the Father, second, in the Son, and, third, in the Holy Spirit. It is here that we must pause for a moment to look at the doctrine in which as it were, Father, Son, and Holy Spirit are joined together the doctrine of the Trinity. The doctrine of the Trinity says that God is Three in One, and One in Three. The doctrine of the Trinity steers between two dangers. On the one side there is the danger of tritheism, the danger of making Father, Son, and Holy Spirit into three separate and independent entities, and therefore into three gods. On the other hand there is the danger of Unitarianism, in which the Father alone is God, and the Son no more than a supremely great man, and the Holy Spirit no more than an impersonal force and power.

It might well be true to say that the doctrine of the Trinity is the most difficult of all Christian doctrines. It is easy enough to state; it is not difficult to say that God is Three in One and One in Three; it is not difficult to speak of three persons and of one substance in the godhead; but when we try to explain and interpret these statements in intelligible terms, then almost anything that one can say suffers the danger of running into some kind of heresy.

It is important and helpful to remember that the word Trinity is not itself a New Testament word. It is even true at least in one sense to say that the doctrine of the Trinity is not directly New Testament doctrine. It is rather a deduction from and an interpretation of the thought and the language of the New Testament. The most important fact of all to remember is that it was not doctrine which anyone in the Church ever sat down and, as it were, worked out from first principles by a series of logical steps; the doctrine of the Trinity has been from the beginning and must always be seen as an interpretation of actual Christian experience.

The doctrine of the Trinity emerged from facts which Christian experience cannot deny. In the first place, men knew God and never had any real doubt of the deity of God. God, so to speak, is obviously God. Then into the world and into life there comes Jesus Christ. Quite clearly, at least for the Christians, Jesus Christ cannot be explained or interpreted in merely human terms; he too can only be thought of in terms of God. But into Christian experience there also enters the Holy Spirit, guiding, sustaining, directing, controlling, enlightening life. The Christians were certain that the Holy Spirit too could not be explained or interpreted in purely human terms; yet their experience of the Spirit indicated that the Spirit could not be explained merely as an impersonal force or power. The work of the Spirit was far too direct and personal for that. So the Christians as a result of Christian experience had, as it were, to find room in God for the Father, for the Son, and for the Holy Spirit.

It often happens that simple people have to be content with grasping as much of some great doctrine as their minds will take, and as much as will enable them, not so much to understand it fully as to live by it. For most people it will almost certainly be that way with the doctrine of the Trinity, for the doctrine of the Trinity arose out of experience and is something which the heart's experience can interpret when the mind's speculation is unable fully to understand.

No human being can know God as he is in the full sense of the term, for the finite can never fully grasp the infinite, and the creature can never fully comprehend the Creator. But what we can grasp and understand is God in his relationship to us. The being of God is necessarily beyond our comprehension; the love of God is blessedly within our experience. Now it is far from being a full statement of the doctrine of the Trinity, but it is true to say that the doctrine of the Trinity describes God in three relationships to men. God the Father turns our thoughts to God in creation and providence, and makes us think of the God who created life and who sustains life. God the Son turns our thoughts to God in redemption, to the God who forgave and rescued men from their sins and from the consequences of their sins. God the Holy Spirit turns our thoughts to God in revelation, in guidance, in the controlling, the equipping and the directing of life. It is not without relevance to note that we speak of the three *persons* in the Trinity, and the word *persona* in

Latin means a *mask*. It is a word from ancient drama; in ancient drama, especially in ancient comedy, the characters were standardized; each comedy had a set of characters who appeared and reappeared under different names and in different situations in every play. The characters were masked, and the masks were also standardized, so that the minute a character came on to the stage you could tell who he was by the mask which he was wearing. If we connect the word *person, persona,* with that idea, we get the helpful picture that the three persons in the Trinity represent three parts that God plays in the drama of creation and of redemption and of life as we have to live it. God in the divine drama plays the parts of Creator, Redeemer and Sustainer; as God the Father he is Creator; as God the Son he is Redeemer; as God the Holy Spirit he is Sustainer.

But, if we do think in these terms, there is one thing of which we must be careful. It is easy, but it is wrong, to think of God, as it were, playing these parts consecutively, one after another; that is, to think of God as first Creator, then Redeemer, then Sustainer. But what the doctrine of the Trinity says is that God is continuously from all eternity to all eternity creating, redeeming and sustaining. If we think along these lines we will not think of the work of redemption in Jesus Christ as being a kind of desperate emergency measure of God, when the work of creation had gone wrong. We will never be able to present the Atonement as an action in which the Son, as it were, pacified the Father and persuaded him to hold his hand. The doctrine of the Trinity shows us the same God, the One God, for ever at work in Creation, in Redemption and in Providence. The Power which created, the Love which redeems, the Grace which sustains are one and the same, and have been, are, and will be in action from all eternity and to all eternity.

But when we speak like that, we meet something which looks like a difficulty and even a contradiction. In Acts 2 we have the story of the events at Pentecost, which we regularly call the coming of the Spirit. In the Fourth Gospel, chapters 14 and 16 at first sight read as if the Spirit did not come into existence until after the death, resurrection and ascension of Jesus. There is little doubt that the true Greek text of John 7.39 literally translated runs: 'The Spirit was not yet because Christ was not yet glorified,' or, as Moffatt has it, 'As yet there was no Spirit because Jesus had not been glorified yet.'

But this is not really what it means. It is perfectly possible for some great force or power always to have existed, and yet for it to become available to man only at some definite date and time in history. The perfect physical example of that is nuclear energy. Nuclear energy has always existed; it is built into the very structure of the world, but it only became available to man in the twentieth century. So what we are to think is that the Spirit had always existed in all his grace and power, but that the work of Jesus opened the flood gates and the Spirit in all his splendour became fully available to men.

The truth is that everything is dependent on Jesus. Apart from Jesus we could never know what God is like. It is not that God *became* love because of Jesus; the love of God is eternal; but in Jesus Christ the love of God became visible to man and therefore available to man as never before. And what Jesus did for God he also does for the Spirit. 'The Lord,' says Paul, 'is the Spirit' (2 Corinthians 3.17), a saying to which we shall later return. Just as the life and death of Jesus opened to men the love of God, so the resurrection and the ever-continuing life of Jesus open to men the grace and the power of the Spirit. The incarnate Jesus brings us the love of God; the Risen Christ makes available for us the power of the eternal Spirit.

In regard to the idea of the Spirit, the New Testament entered into a rich heritage, for it was an idea already deeply rooted in the religious experience of Israel. In the Old Testament in all the rich variety of the conception of the Spirit one basic line of thought remains constant. As J. A. F. Gregg put it in his commentary on *The Wisdom of Solomon*: 'For the Old Testament writers the Spirit of God denotes God in his activity in the world.' The Spirit is the liaison between God and the world; it is through the Spirit that God acts in the world and in the minds and hearts of men.

(i) We meet the Spirit in the opening words of the Old Testament: 'The Spirit of God was moving over the face of the waters' (Genesis 1.2). This is to say that *the Spirit is God's agent in creation*. Elihu says to Job: 'The Spirit of God has made me, and the breath of the Almighty gives me life' (Job 33.4). The Psalmist says: 'When thou sendest forth thy Spirit they are created' (Psalm 104.30).

The Hebrew word for Spirit is *ruach* and the Greek word is *pneuma;* and it so happens that both these words mean *breath* as well as *spirit*.

The Spirit is God breathing order into chaos and breathing life into that which has no life. The Spirit of God is the person and the power who gives order and reliability to the universe and who puts mind and reason and life and vital breath into man.

(ii) If God created the world, man brought sin and disorder into it. Therefore more than creation is needed; re-creation is also needed. And the Spirit is God's agent in the re-creation of the world and of men. The Spirit is the person and the power through whom God makes all things new. Isaiah writes about present desolation and future glory: 'The palace will be forsaken, and the populous city will be deserted; the hill and the watch-tower will become dens for ever, a joy of wild asses, until the Spirit is poured out on us from on high' (Isaiah 32.14–15). Ezekiel sees the valley of dead dry bones; and then there comes the promise of God: 'I will cause breath, *ruach*, Spirit, to enter you and you shall live' (Ezekiel 37.1–10). It was the promise of God through Samuel to Saul: 'Then the Spirit of the Lord will come mightily upon you, and you shall prophesy with them, *and be turned into another man*' (1 Samuel 10.6).

(iii) In the Old Testament *it is the Spirit who gives a man the gift of leadership*. Pharaoh's tribute to Joseph when he is about to put him in charge of the country is: 'Can we find such a man as this, in whom is the Spirit of God?' (Genesis 41.38). Joshua is chosen as the successor of Moses, because he is a man in whom is the Spirit (Numbers 27.18). The Book of Judges might well be called *The Deeds of the Men of the Spirit*. When a deliverer was needed against Mesopotamia the Spirit of the Lord came upon Othniel (Judges 3.10); in the days when the Midianites were oppressing Israel, the Spirit of the Lord took possession of Gideon (Judges 6.34); when the Ammonites were the threat, the Spirit of the Lord came upon Jephthah (Judges 11.29). After Samuel had anointed David the Spirit of the Lord came mightily upon David from that day forward (1 Samuel 16.13).

It was the Spirit who raised men up as leaders, and equipped them for whatever task God and their country needed them.

(iv) In the Old Testament *the Spirit is especially connected with the prophets*. This is true from the earliest to the latest times. The Spirit of the Lord came upon Saul, and he prophesied among the prophets (1 Samuel 10.10). David says: 'The Spirit of the Lord speaks by me, his word is upon my tongue' (2 Samuel 23.2). Isaiah says: 'Now the Lord

God hath sent me and his Spirit' (Isaiah 48.16). Especially in the case of Ezekiel we can see the Spirit directing every part of a prophet's career. The Spirit gave Ezekiel his commission and his message. 'The Spirit of the Lord fell upon me and said to me, Say, Thus says the Lord' (Ezekiel 11.5). The Spirit gave Ezekiel courage to face the situation and to deliver his message. 'The Spirit entered into me and set me upon my feet' (Ezekiel 2.2). It was the Spirit who would give the will and the ability to obey the message which God had sent. 'I will put my Spirit within you, and cause you to walk in my statutes and be careful to observe my ordinances' (Ezekiel 36.27). Every part of the prophet's call and message is the work of the Spirit.

The message which the Spirit gave the prophets was fitted to the situation. Sometimes it was a message of comfort and of promise. 'The Spirit of the Lord is upon me,' said Isaiah, 'because the Lord has anointed me to bring good tidings to the afflicted; he has sent me to bind up the broken-hearted, to proclaim liberty to the captives, and the opening of the prison to those that are bound' (Isaiah 61.1). Sometimes it is a message of warning and rebuke. 'As for me,' said Micah, 'I am filled with power, with the Spirit of the Lord, and with justice and might, to declare to Jacob his transgression and to Israel his sin' (Micah 3.8). It is always a message which a man neglects at his peril. Zechariah says that great wrath came from the Lord of hosts, because the people adamantly refused to hear the words which the Lord sent by his Spirit through the former prophets (Zechariah 7.12).

(v) We must finish our study of the Spirit in the Old Testament by noting two sets of facts which seem to point in opposite directions. First, in general it is true to say that in the Old Testament *the Spirit is still connected with that which is extraordinary and abnormal*. In Judges, for instance, the extraordinary feats of strength of Samson are connected with the Spirit (Judges 13.25; 14.6, 19; 15.14). The operations of the Spirit are marvellous and wonderful and abnormal. Elijah tells Obadiah to go and tell King Ahab that he is there. Obadiah is very unwilling to do so, because 'as soon as I have gone from you the Spirit of the Lord will carry you whither I know not.' Then Ahab will think the message false and will punish him (1 Kings 18.7–16). Ezekiel's experiences of the activity of the Spirit are repeatedly unusual and extraordinary and abnormal (Ezekiel 3.12, 14; 8.3; 11.1, 24; 43.5).

(vi) But there is another side to this. There are also a number of passages in which the Spirit is brought directly, definitely and simply into the arena of everyday life and living. More than once in the story of the building of the tabernacle there occurs the name of a supreme craftsman called Bezalel. In the story God is depicted as saying to Moses: 'See, I have called by name Bezalel, the son of Un, son of Hur, of the tribe of Judah; and I have filled him with the Spirit of God, with ability and intelligence, with knowledge and all craftsmanship, to devise artistic designs, to work in gold, silver and bronze, in cutting stones for setting, and in carving wood, for work in every craft' (Exodus 31.1–5; cf. 35.31; 36.1). Here quite clearly a great craftsman's skill in wood and stone and metal is ascribed to the Spirit. Here the Spirit is brought out of the world which is narrowly religious into the world of the chisel and the hammer and the saw, out of the Temple and the Church into the factory and the bench. Here is the great thought that all skills are God-given and are mediated to a man by the work of the Spirit of God.

(vii) Another belief of the Old Testament was that when the new age came the Spirit would be poured out on men. 'And it will come to pass afterward', said Joel, 'that I will pour out my Spirit on all flesh' (Joel 2.28). And that prophecy was to come abundantly true.

It would not be possible for us here to give a complete account of the doctrine of the Spirit in the New Testament, but there are two books of the New Testament which give us more information about the Spirit than any others do. These books are John's Gospel and the Book of Acts. We may further say that it is broadly true that Acts gives us the picture of *the Spirit in the Church*, while John gives us the picture of *the Spirit in the individual life*. We shall, therefore, gain a fairly comprehensive picture of the Spirit if we examine what these two books have to say. First then let us turn to Acts.

It has been said that the Book of Acts could well be called the Gospel of the Holy Spirit. It is the record of men of the Spirit and deeds of the Spirit. It begins with the story of the coming of the Spirit at Pentecost, and it goes on to show us the Church as a Spirit-filled and Spirit-guided community.

(i) Acts begins by laying it down that the Spirit is essential to the work of the Church. The expansion of the Church could not begin until

the Spirit had come. Before they began their task the disciples were to
wait until the Spirit had come to them (1.4–5). Later Paul was to say to
the elders of Ephesus that it was the Spirit who had set them apart for
their office and for their duty in the Church (20.28). Without the Spirit
the Church could neither begin nor continue its task. The Holy Spirit is
the very breath of the Church's life.

(ii) It was true, as we shall see, that certain men were uniquely and
specially men of the Spirit; but it is also true that in Acts the Spirit is the
birthright of every Christian. The invitation to receive the gift of the
Holy Spirit is to all who will repent and receive forgiveness (2.38). The
Spirit and the gifts of the Spirit are not the possession of a chosen few;
they are God's gifts to all who will take them.

(iii) Acts is clear about how the Holy Spirit comes to a man.

– It is the lesson of the first two chapters of Acts, which tell of the
    events of Pentecost and of the days which lead up to Pentecost,
    that the Holy Spirit comes to those who wait prayerfully and
    expectantly for him. This kind of prayerful waiting is essential for
    those who wish to receive the Spirit. It is probably true that there
    is too much doing in our lives and too little waiting; we may be in
    such a flurry of business and activity that we simply do not stay
    long enough in the one place to give the Spirit a chance to come
    to us. And it may well be equally true that much of our work is
    frustrated and ineffective just because we do not have that waiting
    for the Spirit before we act. We should perhaps remember the
    prophet's words: 'In quietness and in trust shall be your strength'
    (Isaiah 30.15).

– The Spirit comes from repentance (Acts 2.38). The word for
    repentance is *metanoia*, which literally means *a change of mind*.
    Basically, this change of mind means that we cease to take our own
    way and begin to take God's way, that we cease to look at things
    through the eyes of our own wishes and desires and begin to try to
    see them as God sees them. The Spirit will not come to a man so
    long as he sets himself up against God; he will only come to him
    when he puts himself in line with God. So Peter speaks of 'the
    Holy Spirit whom God has given to those that obey him' (5.32).
    The acceptance of the will of God and the gift of the Spirit of God
    go hand in hand.

- The gift of the Spirit is repeatedly connected with baptism (2.38; 19.2–6). In the early Church, baptism was in the nature of things adult baptism, for a man did not come into the Church from a Christian home. In those days it was not a question of a man confirming a decision to belong to that which he had known all his life, but of making a clean break, an entirely new decision, in which he left behind one religion and entered another, in which he deliberately abandoned one way of life to embark upon another. Entry to the Church was not so much the culmination of a growth as it was the consequence of an explosive revolution in a man's soul. It was in such circumstances that the gift and the help of the Spirit came to the man who had taken the great decision.

- The gift of the Spirit was connected with the work of apostolic men. Philip's preaching in Samaria had to be consummated by the presence of Peter and John, the apostolic men (8.14–17). It was through the agency of Ananias that the Holy Spirit came to Paul (9.17). It is in line with the consistent action of God that he mediates his gifts through men. The preacher and the pastor can still be the agent through whom the Holy Spirit comes.

(iv) Acts leaves us in no doubt about the greatness of the gifts which the Spirit brought;

- The Spirit was to bring power (1.8), especially power for the task that God laid upon his men. The gift of the Spirit is God's way of sending the power with the need.

- In Acts we repeatedly see that the Spirit gave to men both the wisdom to know what to say and the courage to say it. Thus it was with Peter, with Stephen and with Paul (4.8, 31; 6.10; 7.55; 13.9). This was in fact the fulfilment of the promise of Jesus that his followers would be told what to say when they were under arrest and facing their earthly judges (Matthew 10.20).

- The gift of the Holy Spirit is connected with joy (13.52). Into the Christian life there had come a new gladness and it was the Spirit who brought it.

(v) But it may well be that we have left the two greatest functions of the Spirit to the end.

In Acts the leaders of the Church were men of the Spirit. This was the qualification for the Seven, the first office-bearers of the Christian

Church (6.3, 5); and this was the mark of Barnabas to whose great-hearted wisdom it may well be that the Church owed Paul (11.24). Whatever other mental or intellectual qualifications a man might have, he was not equipped for the work of the Church unless he was a man of the Spirit.

(vi) But in Acts the supreme work of the Spirit was the guidance of the Christian Church. No great decision was taken without the guidance of the Spirit; and the most significant thing of all is that every one of the great outgoing steps of the Church, every one of the decisions which turned the Church into a world-wide fellowship, embracing every man irrespective of his colour or his creed, was taken under the guidance of the Spirit and was the work of the Spirit.

It was the Spirit who moved Philip to go and to speak to the Ethiopian eunuch, and thus to make the first missionary advance of the Church (8.39). It was the Spirit who moved Peter, an orthodox Jew, to take the extraordinary step of welcoming Cornelius who was a Gentile (10.19–20; 11.12). It was the Spirit who was the prime mover in the despatch of Paul and Barnabas from Antioch on the first missionary journey, which was the first step towards a world for Christ (13.2, 4). It was the Spirit who guided the Council of Jerusalem to put no obstacles in the way of the entry of the Gentiles into the Church (15.28). It was the Spirit who guided Paul's actions – almost step by step in the events which ended by bringing the gospel out of Asia Minor into Europe, the events which brought the gospel to Macedonia, to Greece, and finally to Rome itself (Acts 16.6–7). In other words, it is directly through the guidance and the influence of the Holy Spirit that we are Christians today.

In the Book of Acts there are almost sixty references to the Holy Spirit. In it we see fully displayed the action of the Spirit in the early and the formative days of the Church. And in these events we see a Church in which the Spirit was the birthright of every man, in which the Spirit took men and gave them the wisdom, the courage and the endurance they needed to do the work of Jesus Christ, in which no man served unless he was a man of the Spirit, and no step was taken except under the guidance of the Spirit.

We now turn to the other New Testament book which tells us much about the Spirit, the Gospel of John, and in it we see *the activity and the operation of the Spirit within the individual life.*

(i) It is in John that we find the title of the Spirit which has been at once a blessing and a handicap. That title is Comforter (14.26; 15.26; 16.7). Nowadays the verb *to comfort* is limited in meaning to giving a person comfort and solace in sorrow. That of course the Spirit does, but the Spirit does far more. In Greek the word is *paraklētos*, which literally means *one who is called in*. In Greek it is used for a witness who is called in to give evidence for the defence, for a counsel who is called in to plead the case for an accused man, for a friend who is called in to give counsel and advice, for a doctor who is called in to give help and healing, for a man of courage who is called in to put fresh courage into those who have become dispirited and afraid. Clearly, the meaning is very much wider and very much greater than simply that of giving comfort and consolation in sorrow. To put it at its widest, a *paraklētos* is someone called in to enable a man to cope with life in any situation when life is too much for him.

The word *comforter* still carried this larger meaning when it first arrived in the English Bible. It was first introduced by Wycliffe in 1386, and the meaning which it had for him is seen in his translation of Ephesians 6.10: 'Be ye comforted in the Lord.' The word Wycliffe there translates as *comforted* is from the Greek verb *endunamoun*, which has in it the root of the word *dunamis*, which means *power*, and from which the English words *dynamite* and *dynamic* come. A *comforter* is really a person who fills others with dynamic power. It would be well if we departed entirely from the translation *comforter* and used quite simply *helper*, as Moffatt does.

(ii) In the Fourth Gospel it is almost true to say that the Spirit was to take the place of Jesus, when he left his disciples in the body. 'It is to your advantage that I go away,' he says, 'for, if I do not go away, the Helper will not come to you; but if I go, I will send him to you' (16.7). The idea is that so long as Jesus was in the body his presence was necessarily intermittent, because he was limited by space and time; but in the Spirit he will come to them in a way in which he and they can never be separated any more. He speaks about 'the Holy Spirit whom the Father will send in my name' (14.26). The phrase 'in my name' can mean, and probably does mean, 'as my representative'. As it has been well put, the Spirit is Jesus' *alter ego*.

(iii) For the Fourth Gospel the Spirit is specially *the Spirit of Truth* (14.17; 16.13). It is in regard to truth that the functions of the Spirit are most specific.

— The Spirit teaches the truth. 'He will teach you all things' (14.26). The Christian is still the disciple, the learner. He will never arrogantly think that his finite and puny mind has compassed all truth; he will ever remember the infinity of God and will ever feel that the great ocean of God's truth lies as yet undiscovered before him, and the Spirit will be his pilot to further and further discoveries.

— The Spirit reminds us of the truth. 'He will bring to your remembrance all that I have said to you' (14.26). Although in one sense it is true that the limitless ocean of God's truth lies before us, in another sense it is true that again and again in life we need more than anything else to be reminded of that which we already know. It may be that in a moment of temptation a text of Scripture, a saying of Jesus, the verse of a hymn, the face of someone we love, has flashed into our minds and saved us; that, too, is the work of the Spirit. It is the function of the Spirit to call to our minds and to our memories the saving truth which we can so easily forget.

— The Spirit interprets truth. 'He will take what is mine and declare it to you' (16.14). The Spirit will show us the true meaning of the things which Jesus said; the Spirit will enable us to apply the teaching of Jesus to life, to work it out in practice, to see its implications and its deeper significances. We might well say that in the beginning it was the inspiration of the Spirit which enabled men to write Scripture, and that now it is the inspiration of the Spirit which enables men to interpret Scripture. The correct interpretation of Scripture, the elucidation of the meaning of Scripture, the preaching of the practical truth of Scripture, is just as much the work of the Spirit as the initial writing of Scripture was.

— The Spirit brings new truth. 'I have yet many things to say to you, but you cannot bear them now. When the Spirit of truth comes he will guide you into all truth' (16.12–13). Here we have the conception not of the Christ who spoke but of the Christ who speaks. Here is the idea of truth not as something static but as something dynamic. Here, as it has been well put, is the eternal protest against all fixity of dogma. To each generation the eternal Christ brings the truth it needs in the form it needs. If we really accept the doctrine of the Spirit we will never have any fear of rethinking and restating and reformulating the faith.

– The Spirit guides men into all the truth. 'When the Spirit of truth comes, he will guide you into all the truth' (16.13). There are two equally valid lines of thought here, between which we do not need to choose because both are true. This could mean that Spirit alone can lead men to the revelation of the whole truth. The truth that men can discover for themselves, the truth that men can come to apart from Jesus Christ, can never be anything but partial and fragmentary. It is only through the guidance of the Spirit that men can enter into the full revelation of the truth given in Jesus Christ. But this could also mean that the Spirit guides men into *all* truth It is not only what you might call theological and religious truth which is the work of the Spirit. *All* truth, every great poem that was ever written, all great music that was ever composed, every discovery of science, every step forward of medicine, every beauty of art is the gift of the Spirit. In the world of truth there is no distinction between the sacred and the secular. All truth in any sphere is the gift of God and comes to men through the Spirit of God.

(iv) The Fourth Gospel has one last series of important things to say about the work of the Spirit. In John 16.8–11 there is a passage which is very difficult, but very important; 'When he (the Helper) comes, he will convince the world of sin and of righteousness and of judgement; of sin, because they do not believe in me; of righteousness, because I go to my Father, and you will see me no more; of judgement, because the ruler of this world is judged.'

The key to this passage lies in the double meaning of the Greek word which is here translated *convince*. The word is *elegchein*; it is the Greek word for to cross-examine, to persuade a man of the truth of something, or to force him to admit some error, by the process of question and answer. Since that is so, *elegchein* represents two English words, the words *convince* and *convict*. And in this passage both words are needed. The work of the Holy Spirit is threefold. It is the Spirit who *convicts* men of sin, and who *convinces* men of righteousness and of judgement. It is the Spirit who *convicts* a man of sin, and who shows him the error and the tragedy of unbelief; it is the work of the Spirit which makes a man realize, which makes him self-convicted, that he is a sinner. It is the Holy Spirit who *convinces* a man of righteousness, and this time the righteousness is the righteousness of Jesus Christ. Jesus was historically a crucified criminal;

it is the Holy Spirit who convinces a man that in this same Jesus there is perfect righteousness, and the means of this conviction is the Resurrection and the Ascension of Jesus to his Father. It is the Holy Spirit who *convinces* a man of the reality and the certainty of judgement to come, by making a man certain that in Jesus Christ the powers of evil are already judged and defeated. In other words, it is the Holy Spirit who is responsible for the beginning, the middle and the end of the process of salvation. It is through the work of the Holy Spirit that a man recognizes and realizes that he is a sinner and that Jesus Christ is a Saviour.

It may be that our ideas of the Holy Spirit have been vague and nebulous, but surely now we can see that in the scheme of salvation there is no more important person than the Holy Spirit.

In the Holy Catholic Church

With this article in the creed we seem to come definitely and directly into our own contemporary human situation. When we speak about the Father and the Son and the Spirit, when we speak about Incarnation, Resurrection and Ascension, we may well seem to be moving in the heavenly places and in the realms of high theology. But when we speak of the Church, the word sounds very differently, for very likely there is a church at the corner of our street, and a church of which we are members, or which we attend; even if we have no personal connection with the Church, the Church is at least a visible part of our contemporary experience. In our attempt to find out something about the character and the meaning of the Church, we cannot do better than begin by simply examining these three words in this article of the creed.

We begin with the word *holy*. In Greek the word is *hagios*; and the basic meaning of this word is *different*. That which is *holy* is *different* from ordinary things. So the Sabbath day is different from other days; the Temple is different from other buildings; and so both the Sabbath and the Temple are *holy*. The Communion Table is different from other tables and the Bible is different from other books, so that table is the Holy Table and that book is the Holy Bible. So then in the first place the Church is different.

It is of the very essence of the Church that the Church is a paradox. The Church is the Church of God (1 Corinthians 15.9; Galatians 1.13). The Church is a divine institution. But the Church is localized here in the world. It is the Church of God 'at Corinth' (1 Corinthians 1.2; 2 Corinthians 1.1). The Church is different, but the difference is to be expressed not by detachment from the world, but by involvement in the world. The Church is a divine institution placed fairly and squarely in the middle of the human situation. Although it is in the world, and although its work lies within the world, it is nevertheless not of the world. While it gathers men into its arms, it always points beyond itself. The Church is in the world precisely to stop men becoming worldly. For a Church to conform to the world and thus to lose its quality of difference, is for a Church to lose that very quality which makes it a Church.

The Church is *catholic*. The word for *catholic* in Greek is *katholikos*, and it means general or universal. So then the Church is the universal Church.

Herein in fact lies one of the distinguishing marks of the Christian Church. It was on the whole true that in the ancient world religion was an erector of barriers rather than a remover of barriers. Both Roman and Greek official religion was state religion. The gods were given their due service and recognition with the intention that they would look after the interests of their own state as opposed to all other states. Religion was a nationalistic thing. The line was rigidly drawn between the Greek and the barbarian, between the slave and the free man. Christianity came on the other hand with the invitation to enter a Church in which there were no barriers. 'Here there cannot be Greek and Jew, circumcized and uncircumcized, barbarian, Scythian, slave, free man' (Colossians 3.11). It was the normal Jewish custom for a man in his morning prayer to thank God, 'that Thou hast not made me a Gentile, a slave, or a woman.' It is with that very prayer in mind that Paul says: 'There is neither Jew nor Greek, there is neither slave nor free, there is neither male nor female; for you are all one in Christ Jesus' (Galatians 3.28).

It may be that we live in a world of barriers; there is more than one kind of *apartheid*. In its very essence the Church should be the one society in which there are no barriers of race, of colour, of caste, of class, or social status, of party or of sect. The greatest condemnation of sects and heresies within the Church is not in fact that they are theologically or intellectually wrong and in error, serious as that certainly is. The greatest condemnation is that they disintegrate the unity of the Church, that they are very often exclusive instead of inclusive, that they split into fragments that which should be united into one. A Church which is less than universal is a contradiction in terms.

So we come now to the third word, the word *Church* itself. In Greek the word is *ekklēsia*; and this word *ekklēsia* came out of two worlds and has two backgrounds.

(i) It has a Hebrew background. In the Old Testament we read frequently, especially in the historical books, of the congregation or the assembly of Israel. We find this expression, for instance, in Deuteronomy 4.10; 18.16; 31.30; Joshua 8.35; Judges 20.2; 1 Samuel 17.47; 1 Kings 8.14; 2 Chronicles 29.28; Psalm 22.22. We quote in full one typical example of this word *ekklēsia* in the Greek Old Testament. 'The Lord gave me the two tables of stone written with the finger of God; and on them were all the words which the Lord had spoken with you on the mountain out of the midst of the fire on the day of the assembly' (Deuteronomy 9.10). Here we have a typical use of the word *ekklēsia*. In its most characteristic usage it describes the nation of Israel met together to receive some message from God, either through the mouth of Moses or of some other great leader. Here then is the first idea of the *ekklēsia*, the Church. *The Church is a body of people who are waiting for a message from God.* The Church is composed of those who have submitted their lives to the guidance and the direction of God.

(ii) It has a Greek background. In its Greek background *ekklēsia* was not a specifically religious word at all; its background was rather political than religious. For the most part the Greek cities were highly democratic in their government; usually the governing body was nothing other than all the citizens who had not lost their citizenship. That body was very often called the *ekklēsia*. It is obvious that such an *ekklēsia* would never meet in its entirety. What actually happened, for instance in Athens, was that the *ekklēsia* met ten times in the year. When it was due to meet, the trumpeter went through the city streets announcing the date, place and time of the meeting, and inviting all citizens who had a right to do so, to attend. The *ekklēsia*, therefore, consisted in fact of those who had heard and accepted the invitation and the summons to be present. We may say likewise that the Christian *ekklesia*, the Church, *consists of those who have accepted the invitation and the command of God, given in Jesus Christ, to come to him.*

We shall have to study the meaning of the Church in much more detail than this; but it is plain that, even if we go no further than a study of the mere words, we do catch something of the greatness of the Church. The Church is *holy*; it is different from merely earthly things; it is the Church of God; and even here in the midst of time it points to eternity, and is always pointing beyond itself. It is *catholic*. Just as God so loved the world, and just as there are no distinctions within the love of God, so the Church stretches out its arms to the world, and within it the distinctions and the differences no longer exist. The Church is the *ekklēsia*. In every one of its local congregations, it is a body of people gathered together to listen for a message from God. That message may come in the words of the preacher. Perhaps, even more likely, it may come in the prayers, in the praises, in the reading of Scripture, and in the silence. But it is for that message, and for no lesser purpose, that the people have come. It is clear from the beginning that the Church is people, people who are aware of the voice of God and people who have responded to the offer and the invitation of God.

There are some further things to note about the way in which the New Testament uses the word *ekklēsia*.

(i) It uses it to describe *the whole Church*. Christ is the Head of the Church; Christ loved the Church (Ephesians 5.23, 25).

When the word *ekklēsia is* used like that, and it very commonly is, it signifies the whole Church, the Church universal, the Holy Catholic Church itself.

(ii) It uses it to describe *the various congregations of the Church*. Thus Paul can speak of the Churches of the Gentiles (Romans 16.4), the Churches of Galatia (Galatians 1.2). Paul goes through Syria and Cilicia strengthening the Churches (Acts 15.41).

(iii) It uses it to describe *a body of Christian people met together for worship*. Paul rebukes the Corinthians that there are sects and divisions among them, 'when you assemble as a Church', or, as the New English Bible has it better, 'when you meet as a congregation' (1 Corinthians 11.18). When Paul is discussing and controlling the gift of speaking with unintelligible tongues, he says that in the Church he would rather speak five words with his understanding than ten thousand in a language that no one can understand (1 Corinthians 14.19). In both these cases the word Church means the congregation in some place, met together for worship and for instruction.

So then we see that in the New Testament the word *ekklēsia* can mean the Holy Catholic Church or any part of it. It may well be that the world in which it lived affected the New Testament idea of the Church. In New Testament times the Roman Empire covered to all intents and purposes the known and civilized world; it would have been difficult ordinarily to move out of the Roman Empire. But in addition to its over-all inclusiveness, there were, so to speak, little pieces of Rome scattered all over the world; in the most important road centres and the most strategic places, Rome had placed colonies. In Roman language a colony was not, as it is in the English language, a piece of unknown territory colonized by pioneers and explorers, but a strategically chosen town in which there was settled a group of Roman citizens, usually soldiers who had served their time and who had won their citizenship. These colonies were the places which, so to speak, joined the Empire together, which ensured its peace, and from which in any emergency action could be taken. And each colony was, as it were, a part of Rome. Roman law and customs were observed; Roman clothes were worn; magistrates had Roman titles; the Latin language was spoken. So far did this go that by a legal fiction even the very soil was Roman soil. The whole Empire was Rome, and every colony throughout the Empire was also a piece of Rome.

It may well be that this became to the Christians a symbol of the Church. It may specially have been so to Paul who was a Roman citizen and proud of his citizenship, and who must have been one of the most far-travelled men of his generation. Paul may well have seen in the all-inclusive Roman Empire and the colonies which were little pieces of Rome, a symbol of the universal Church and of the little separate Churches or congregations scattered up and down the world in increasing numbers. It would have been possible for a Roman to speak of that part of Rome which is at Philippi; and so Paul came to speak of the Church of God which is at Corinth as that part of the vast Empire of God which is the colony of heaven at Corinth (1 Corinthians 1.2).

It is wrong, and even disastrous, when a local congregation becomes identified with the Church and when people begin to look at it as 'the' Church; but it is wholly right when a local congregation regards itself as the Church because it is a living and integral part of the whole Church.

We may deal with one other general aspect of our subject before we come to the details. We are bound to ask the basic and fundamental question: Is the Church necessary? Or, if the Church is necessary, is it necessary for the Christian to enter into the Church? Can he not be a Christian without being a Church member?

There is a sense, and a real sense, in which there is nothing more personal and nothing more individual than a man's relationship to Jesus

Christ. He must meet Christ and he must face Christ and he must confront Christ in the loneliness of his own soul. His decision to accept Christ or to reject Christ is something which no one can take for him. There are some decisions that no one can take for us, and this is one of them.

As J. S. Whale has pointed out, it would not really be the same to sing,

> When we survey the wondrous Cross,

or to sing,

> Were the whole realm of nature ours,
>   That were an offering far too small;
> Love so amazing, so divine,
>   Demands *our* soul, *our* life, *our* all.

Our reaction to Jesus Christ is as personal and individual as falling in love. Wherein then lies the necessity of the Church?

(i) It is within the Church that the story of Jesus Christ and the Christian faith are preserved. The Church is the instrument and the agent through which men meet Christ. The Christian faith, the Christian tradition, the Christian gospel are preserved within the Church. It is the Church which preaches the gospel; it is the Church which goes out in missionary and in pastoral endeavour; it is the Church which, in the spoken word, and in the written word, and in the life and conduct of its members, confronts men with Jesus Christ. It is in the Church that the Christian faith and gospel are contained and transmitted and disseminated among men. In most cases, it is through the agency of the Church that a man is brought face to face with Jesus Christ.

(ii) The Christian faith is meant not to detach and isolate men from each other, but to unite them into fellowship one with another. In Christianity there is a double reconciliation, the reconciliation to God and the reconciliation with our fellow men. If Christianity tells us that God is our Father, then it will also tell us that men are our brothers. The immediate effect of any true Christian experience will be to unite a man in fellowship with his fellow men.

(iii) A Christian will want to worship. He will want to know the joy of learning together, of singing together, of listening together, and of praying together. Certainly he can worship alone; but there are certain activities of the human spirit which are much richer when they are done in community. It is no doubt a fine thing to enjoy a long-playing record of some great symphony, played by some great orchestra under some master conductor, in one's own room, but the impact of it in such circumstances is nothing to the impact it will make upon us when we are in some great concert-hall and in human living contact with others who are also thrilling to it. Just because we are made as we are, nothing will really take the place of worshipping together.

(iv) There are bound to come times in life and in the affairs of men when Christian action is necessary, when witness must be made to some Christian principle, when action must be taken in connection with some Christian effort, when support must be given to some good cause, and opposition registered to some evil force. At such times the joint action of Christians is supremely necessary, and that action cannot come except through the Church. There are times at which, unless Christians can act together, the forces of good will lack the dynamic they ought to have, and the forces of evil will be unchecked when they might have been halted. If the work of Christ is to be done, there are times when the Church must do it, and the Christian will necessarily wish to be part of the Church which is the agent and the instrument of Christ.

It is still true that 'God knows nothing of solitary religion', and that the Christian without the Church and the Church without the Christian cannot fully exist.

It will be better if at this point we pause to look at a question which is fundamental to our whole discussion. Did Jesus ever mean to found a Church at all? Was the Church ever within the view and the intention of Jesus? There are many scholars who would very decidedly answer, No. There are many who think that Jesus looked forward to his own immediate return in power, that he looked forward to the immediate and the catastrophic destruction and end of things as they are. When he sent his disciples out on their preaching tour, he said to them, as Matthew tells: 'You will not have gone through all the towns of Israel before the Son of Man comes' (Matthew 10.23). 'Truly,' he said, 'I say to you, there are some standing here who will not taste death before they see the Son of Man coming in his kingdom' (Matthew 16.28). There are scholars who, relying on sayings of Jesus such as these, insist that Jesus saw no time at all intervening between his death and his return in power, and the end of time and of the world, and the emergence of the rule and reign of God.

But we must not forget that there are just as many sayings in the Gospels which see the coming of the kingdom in terms of growth, like evolution in nature (cf. Mark 4.26–9); and there are just as many sayings which look forward to a process in which all men all over the world will hear the message of the gospel (Matthew 24.14; 28.19; Acts 1.8).

But even if we were to leave this question in suspense, there are certain facts which we must take into account.

(i) It is quite certain that Jesus took steps to surround himself with a group of men whom he had invited to follow him (Mark 1.16–20; 2.13–14). Even in his lifetime he made himself the centre of a society of men who were pledged to him, even though that society consisted of only a few.

(ii) That society was composed of men who were by obligation different from the rest of men. They were to be the lights of the world and the salt of the earth, and their lives were to be so lovely that when men saw them, their thoughts would be turned to God (Matthew 5.13–16). Jesus not only chose a group of men, but expected from them a distinctive mode of life which would differentiate them from other people.

(iii) His group was to be an expanding group; it was their task and duty and function to persuade others to enter into the same relationship with Jesus into which they had entered (Matthew 10.5–7). They were not a closed group; they were a group the reason for whose existence, whose ultimate task, was to gather all men into the fellowship of Jesus Christ (Matthew 28.19).

(iv) To put it in another way, this group was meant to have an effect upon the world. It was to be the leaven which leavened the whole lump; it was to be the little mustard seed from which the greater plant was to grow (Matthew 13.31–3). This chosen group was not only a group to whom things had happened, it was also a group through which things were to happen to other people; and ultimately, to all men.

In principle it does not make any difference whether this was to happen in a very short time or in a very long time. In either case the fact remains that Jesus chose certain men, and that out of them he formed a society whose purpose was to exist in close fellowship with himself and to bring others by preaching and by teaching and by example into that same fellowship; and surely therein we have the picture of the nature and the function of the Church. This is not in the least to argue that Jesus either foresaw or intended the vast ecclesiastical structure which the Church was to become, but it is to say that he did create, and envisage the continuance of, a group of people in fellowship with himself and in fellowship with each other, and commissioned to bring others into the same fellowship.

When we have arrived at this stage in our picture of the Church, we can lay something down which is very simple, but very fundamental and very illuminating. The word *Church* is derived from the Greek word *kuriakon* which literally means *belonging to the Lord*; but in its beginning and in its essence that which belongs to the Lord is not a building but a fellowship of people. Nowadays we freely use the word *church* to describe a building. There is not a single instance of that usage of the word in the New Testament; it always means a group of people pledged and dedicated to Jesus Christ and to each other. It was in fact to be very many years before the Church possessed any buildings. The Church was poor; and still more the Church was illegal; it was impossible for it to have any buildings; when the Christian groups met, they met in a room in a house. In any thinking about the Church it is fundamental to remember this. It will mean too that we will get closest to discovering the essential nature of the Church by studying the names by which the early Christians were called. If the Church is people, what kind of people were these people of whom the Church was composed?

(i) The word *Christian* does not occur often in the New Testament. It originated in Antioch. 'In Antioch for the first time the disciples were called Christians' (Acts 11.26). The word is used again in the New Testament in Acts 26.28 and in 1 Peter 4.16. The fact that the name originated in Antioch is significant. Antioch was notorious for its ability to produce nicknames. No one, not even the Emperor himself, was immune from the ribald wit of the Antiochenes. Centuries later the Emperor tried to turn the clock back and bring back the old ways and the old gods. He himself returned to the wearing of a beard and the Antiochenes promptly nicknamed him The Goat! Nothing was sacred to the jesting citizens of Antioch.

There is then little doubt that the name *Christian* was originally a nickname. In Latin the word is *Christiani* and in Greek *Christianoi*. The suffix *-iani* in Latin and *-ianoi* in Greek mean *belonging to the party of*. In English we use the suffixes *-ite* and *-er* in much the same way. So in the Victorian days the Liberal party could be called Gladstonites; and in the early days the Christians were mockingly called Christers.

The word Christian began as a nickname – these Christ-folk! And the Christians took a name given in mockery and made it a name than which the world knows none greater. And this name lays down the first and most important fact about the Christian – the essential thing about the Christian is his relationship to Christ. He is first and foremost a Christ-man.

(ii) One of the commonest names for the Christian is the name *saint* (1 Corinthians 1.2; 2 Corinthians 1.1; Philippians 1.1). The word is *hagios*, and as we have already seen, this word saint, *hagios*, can also be translated as *holy*. *Saints* is an unfortunate translation, because nowadays that word paints the picture of a long-robed, long-haired, pale-faced figure in a stained-glass window, a model of piety and propriety. We have only to read the history of the early Church to see that the Church members were in fact anything but like that, and that they were just as liable to get into trouble and just as liable to cause trouble as Church people are today. But we have already seen the basic meaning of this word *hagios*. Basically it describes that which is *different*. Therefore the Church member, the Christian, is the one who is different. And wherein does that difference lie?

It lies in that phrase which occurs more than eighty times in Paul's letters, in the phrase *in Christ*. The Church member is different because he is *in Christ*. He never forgets the presence of Christ; he walks for ever with Christ; he makes no decision without consulting the guidance of Christ; he attempts no task without the help of Christ; he is in Christ just as really as he is in the air he breathes. The difference is that the life of the Christian is lived in Christ and with Christ.

(iii) A third and very common title given to the Christians is *disciple* (e.g. Acts 6.1). Disciple, *discipulus* in Latin and *mathētēs* in Greek, literally means a *learner*. If God is infinite and if his riches are unsearchable, there can be no such thing as a static Christianity. For the Christian there are always new wonders to discover, new mysteries to know, new heights to scale, new horizons to beckon. It is exactly its rigidity that is the fault of so much Christianity. Of course it is true that for the Christian there is the one unchanging fact of the love of God in Jesus Christ; but the wonder, the meaning, the implications, the method of that one great fact are enough to keep any man studying and thinking and learning for ever.

(iv) Often in the New Testament Christians are called *believers* (Acts 5.14; Romans 4.11; 1 Timothy 4.12). The verb *to believe* is in Greek *pisteuō*, and the noun for *faith* is *pistis*, and clearly the two Greek words are closely connected; *to believe* and *to have faith* mean exactly the same thing. What then is this faith, this belief, which is the very essence of the Christian religion?

– Faith means the settled conviction that certain things are true. It means unswerving intellectual belief in certain facts. Unless we in the first place believe that God is the loving Father of men, we will not turn to him at all. If we believed that God was quite indifferent. we would not turn to him, for we would be well aware that in that case he would not even notice that we had turned. If we believed that God was nothing but holy justice and righteousness we would not turn to him, for we would know that we could expect nothing but condemnation. The very beginning of the Christian faith is the conviction of the loving fatherhood of God.

– Faith is very far from stopping at intellectual belief. Faith means committing the whole of life to that which we believe to be true. A man may well be intellectually convinced of the truth of something, and may yet not allow his intellectual conviction to have any effect on his life and conduct. For instance, there is many a man who is intellectually convinced that smoking and lung cancer have some connection with each other, and who yet continues to smoke. He has not allowed his intellectual belief to affect his conduct. This is exactly what James meant when he said that faith without works is dead (James 2.26). The devils, he said, are intellectually convinced of the existence of God; they are even convinced that they are under the condemnation of God, but for all that they remain devils (James 2.19).

– If this is so, it will be true to say that real Christian belief comes in the end from experience. It comes from acting on the assumption that the demands and the promises of God in Christ are true, and thereby experiencing that they are true. Faith is born from the experience which is begotten from taking the risk of really being Christian.

– In the last analysis, faith is faith in a person. We began by saying that faith is the conviction that certain things about God are true. But to whom do we owe our knowledge of these truths about

God? We owe that knowledge to Jesus Christ; and we cannot and
will not believe what Jesus says about God, unless we first believe
that he has the right to say it. Faith therefore ultimately goes back
to trust in Jesus Christ. Faith is basically the reaction of the human
soul in trust to Jesus Christ.

(v) One of the very commonest of words for the Christian in the
New Testament is the word *brother*. The Christians are the brothers (Acts
15.3; 17.14; 18.18). This is an idea to which we shall later have to return.
But we must note now as one of the fundamental facts about the
Christian faith that Christianity puts a man into a new relationship not
only with God but also with his fellow men. Jesus Christ effects a double
reconciliation in the life of the man who accepts him as Saviour and
Lord; he reconciles him to God and he reconciles him to his fellow men.
This is something that no one ever laid down with more urgency than
the John of the Fourth Gospel and the Letters. 'By this all men will know
that you are my disciples, if you have love one for another' (John 13.35).
'We know that we have passed out of death into life, because we love the
brethren.... Anyone who hates his brother is a murderer' (1 John
3.14–15). 'If anyone says, I love God, and hates his brother, he is a liar'
(1 John 4.20). A society in which there is no love may be many things,
but it cannot be a Church. A congregation in which dispeace, dissension
and division reign, has forfeited all right to the name of Church.

(vi) The Christians are those who are God's beloved (Romans 1.7).
'To all God's beloved in Rome,' Paul writes. The word that Paul uses for
beloved is the word *agapētos*, and this is exactly the same word as the divine
voice uses to describe Jesus at his baptism (Matthew 3.17) and at his
transfiguration (Matthew 17.5). It is as if through Jesus Christ we are in
the same relationship to God as Jesus Christ.

The sense of being loved necessarily does two things to a man. First,
it fills him with a sense of quite undeserved privilege. He is in amaze-
ment and gratitude that, being such as he is, he is loved as he is.
Secondly, it fills him with an overwhelming sense of obligation, for
somehow or other he has to strive for ever after to be worthy of being
loved. He will never achieve that worthiness, but he is under continuous
obligation to try to achieve it.

The Christian is the man who knows the privilege and the responsibility of being loved by God.

(vii) Very frequently (e.g. Philippians 1.1) the Christian is called the *doulos* of Christ. Usually this word is translated *servant* in English translations, but literally and properly its meaning is *slave*. *Kurios*, *lord*, is the supreme New Testament title of Jesus, and *doulos* is the correlative of *kurios*. *Kurios* describes the person who has absolute rights and control over someone else. *Doulos* describes the servant who has no rights of his own. To call the Christian the *doulos*, the slave of Christ says two things.

- It lays down the absolute authority of Jesus Christ over the Christian. In the ancient world a slave was very different from a modern employee. In the ancient world a slave was classified as a thing; he was, so far as his master was concerned, in Aristotle's famous phrase, a living tool. His master had absolute power over him, even the power of life and death. A slave had no will of his own; and a slave had no time of his own. A slave had no possessions of his own; in Roman law even a slave's children belonged to the master who owned him.

  No one would ever think of Jesus Christ as treating any person as a thing; but it is true that the Christian has no will of his own; the Christian has no time of his own; the Christian has no possessions of his own; he is the possession body and soul of Jesus Christ. This title slave does stress and underline the absolute authority of Christ over the Christian, and the absolute submission of the Christian to Christ.

- But there is another side to this. There is a sense in which *doulos*, slave, is the proudest title in the Bible. The *doulos*, the servant, of God is the supreme title of the great men of the Old Testament. Moses is called the *doulos* of God oftener than anyone else (e.g. Exodus 14.31); David has this title second only to Moses (e.g. 2 Samuel 7.5, 8); it is given to Abraham (Genesis 26.24); to Joshua (Judges 2.8); to Caleb (Numbers 14.24); to Elijah (2 Kings 9.36); to Jacob (Isaiah 44.1, 2); to Job (Job 1.8); to Isaiah (20.3); to all the prophets (Amos 3.7). To be called the *doulos* of God is to walk in the greatest of all successions.

  After all, it could not be otherwise. The whole relationship between Christ and the Christian lies within the context of love; and love's one delight is unreservedly to serve the one it loves. In such a case service is not servitude but privilege; and it is so with the Christian and Christ.

Christian, saint, the one who is different, disciple, believer, brother, God's beloved, the slave of Christ – these are the titles of the Christian, and it is of such that the Church is composed.

We now turn to look at some of the collective titles for the Church, at some of the titles for the Church as a whole, and we shall find them equally significant and equally illuminating.

(i) The Church is described as *the flock of God* (Acts 20.28–9; 1 Peter 5.2–3; cf. Matthew 26.31; Luke 12.32). This is a picture which has a long history; it goes back to Old Testament times, for in the Old Testament the nation of Israel is often called the flock of God (Psalm 23.1; 77.20; 78.52; 80.1; 100.3; Isaiah 40.11; Jeremiah 13.17; 23.2–3; Zechariah 10.3). It is implicit in Jesus' picture of himself as the Good Shepherd (John 10.1–18), and in the Parable of the Lost Sheep (Luke 15.3–7; Matthew 18.10–14).

In any terms the picture of the Church as the flock of God is a lovely picture, but it is even lovelier when it is set against its Palestinian background. The pasture land of Judaea is no more than a narrow ridge like the backbone of the country. There were no walled fields, and the pasture land either plunged in cliffs down to the Dead Sea or fell away in infertile valleys through the Shephelah to the Mediterranean coast. The wandering sheep would certainly perish, and even on the pasture land itself grass was sparse and wells and springs were few and far between. The result of this was that in Palestine a flock was never to be seen without its shepherd. Day and night the shepherd was on constant guard; without his constant and unsleeping care the sheep would certainly starve or wander to disaster.

The picture of the Church as the flock of God underlines the twin facts of God's unceasing care for his Church, and of the Church's complete dependence upon God. In the picture of the flock we see at one and the same time the love of God and the need of man.

(ii) More than once in Acts the Church is called a *hairesis*. It is usually so called by the enemies of Christianity, and the word is usually translated as *sect*. This word *hairesis* appears in English as the word *heresy*; and in fact it is used in that sense in the letters of Paul (1 Corinthians 11.19; Galatians 5.20; cf. 2 Peter 2.1). It is used of the Church in Acts 24.5, 14 and 28.22, and is not necessarily a bad word at all. It is used in Acts to describe both the party of the Sadducees and of the Pharisees (Acts 24.5,

14; 26.5). In secular Greek is can regularly be used to describe a philosophic school; and it has something to tell us about the Church, even if it is applied to the Church by the Church's enemies.

The word *hairesis* comes from the verb *hairein*, which means *to choose*, and *hairesis* literally means *an act of choosing*. It is in fact precisely here that Christianity differed from the religions of the ancient world. For the most part in the ancient world a man's religion depended on his nationality. A Jew accepted the Jewish religion because he was a Jew. A Roman or an Athenian accepted the gods of the state and carried out the prescribed worship simply because he was a citizen of Rome or Athens and it was dangerous not to give the gods of the state their due place and their due honour. But a man always became a Christian absolutely of his own free choice. That is exactly where the word *hairesis* fits the Christian religion. Unless a man's entry into the Church is the result of a definite act of decision and of a deliberate choice, it is nothing at all. This word *hairesis* at least conserves the truth that the members of the Church are those whom God has chosen and those who have chosen God.

(iii) Sometimes the Church is likened to a *building*. You are God's building, Paul writes to the Church at Corinth (1 Corinthians 3.9). Peter develops this building picture when he sees the individual Christians as individual, living stones built into the structure of a spiritual house of which the cornerstone is Jesus Christ (1 Peter 2.4–7).

There are two great thoughts in the picture of the Church as a building. First, it gives us the truth that in the Church each individual Christian has a place, like the stones in a house, and the removal of any injures both the beauty and the strength of the structure. Secondly, it gives us the truth that the whole structure will necessarily collapse if the cornerstone is removed, and the cornerstone is Jesus Christ. The Church is composed of people built into, and held together by, Jesus Christ.

That picture of the Church reminds us of the saying of the Spartan king. He had boasted that no nation in the world had walls like Sparta. But when a visitor came to visit Sparta he saw no walls at all, and asked the Spartan king where the walls were. The Spartan king pointed at his bodyguard of magnificent Spartan soldiers: 'These', he said, 'are the walls of Sparta, and every man of them a brick.' In exactly the same way, the Christian is the living stone built into the structure of the Church.

(iv) A more intimate name for the Church than any of these is *the household and the family of the faith*. Through Jesus Christ the Christian, once a stranger, becomes a member of the household of God (Ephesians 2.19). We are to do good to all men, especially to those who belong to the household of faith (Galatians 6.10). The first letter to Timothy speaks of the household of God which is the Church of the living God (1 Timothy 3.15).

If this is so, it means that in any Church Christians are related to God and related to each other in love; and if this is so, it means that a Church which is divided by disputes, or a Church which has become a legalistic debating society has ceased to be a Church.

(v) But there is for the Church a title more intimate even than that. Sometimes the Church is called *the bride of Christ*. It is Paul's claim that he has betrothed the Corinthian Church to Christ as a pure bride to her one husband (2 Corinthians 11.2). The Church is the Bride of the Lamb (Revelation 19.7; 21.2, 9). We have the same thought in the passages in which Jesus is referred to as the bridegroom. So he is called by John the Baptist (John 3.29), and so he calls himself (Matthew 9.15).

This is a picture with a very ancient history. It goes back to the Old Testament in which again and again we find the picture of the nation of Israel as the bride of God. 'Your Maker is your husband,' said Isaiah to Israel, 'the Lord of hosts is his name' (Isaiah 54.5). 'As the bridegroom rejoices over the bride, so shall your God rejoice over you' (Isaiah 62.5) 'Turn, O backsliding children, saith the Lord; for I am married unto you' (Jeremiah 3.14 AV). God's voice comes to the nation through Hosea: 'I will betroth you to me for ever; I will betroth you to me in righteousness and in justice, in steadfast love, and in mercy; I will betroth you to me in faithfulness; and you shall know the Lord' (Hosea 2.19, 20).

This picture is common in the Old Testament, and it begets two other ways of speaking which often offend the fastidiousness of modern ears.

First, this is why spiritual infidelity is described in terms of physical adultery. 'You have played the harlot,' says Hoses, 'forsaking your God' (Hoses 9.1). This is why again and again in book after book of the Old Testament we get in the AV the description of Israel as going a-whoring after strange gods (Exodus 34.15, 16; Leviticus 20.5, 6; Numbers 15.39; Deuteronomy 31.16; Judges 8.27, 33; 1 Chronicles 5.25; Psalm 73.27; Ezekiel 23.30). It may be that this is a metaphor which strikes oddly on modern ears; but to the Old Testament writers it was natural, fitting and inevitable. If Israel was the bride of God, then infidelity to God might fitly and expressively be expressed in terms of adultery. This comes into the New Testament in the phrase: 'an evil and adulterous generation' (Matthew 12.39; 16.4; Mark 8.38). And here too it has the meaning of being unfaithful to God.

Secondly, this line of thought gives rise to an adjective which in the Old Testament is applied often to God and which again modern ears do not much like. In the Old Testament God is often called a *jealous* God (Exodus 20.5; Deuteronomy 4.24; Joshua 24.19; Nahum 1.2; Zechariah 1.14; 8.2). This word can be understood if we think in terms of Israel as the bride of God, and God as the lover of Israel. No lover could ever bear to share his loved one with someone else; love is necessarily exclusive. And when the Bible speaks of God as a jealous God it is thinking of God as the passionate lover of the souls of men.

(vi) We now come to look at a title of the Church which is full of meaning but about which there is a certain doubt that needs investigation. This is the title *The New Israel,* or *The Israel of God.*

The difficulty about this title is that it is mainly based on Galatians 6.16 and there is a doubt about the exact translation of that verse. Let us set down that verse in three different translations. First, the Authorized Version:

> And as many as walk according to this rule, peace be on them, and mercy and upon the Israel of God.

Second, the Revised Standard Version:

> Peace and mercy be upon all who walk by this rule, upon the Israel of God.

The New English Bible:

> Whoever they are who take this principle for their guide, peace and mercy be upon them, and upon the whole Israel of God!

We see that both the AV and the NEB have an *and*; and in their translation it would be possible to hold that the blessing is pronounced upon two groups of people, first, on all who walk according to this rule, and secondly, on the Israel of God. It would then be possible to hold, as some scholars do, that the phrase 'the Israel of God' is not simply an alternative title for the whole Christian Church, but that it is a description of the faithful remnant of the national Israel, that part of Israel which remained true to God and which accepted the Christian religion. This remnant of Israel, this part of Israel which accepted Christ, is then regarded as the true Israel, the Israel of God. On the other hand the RSV omits the *and,* and in that case 'the Israel of God' is another way of describing *all who walk by this rule,* and 'the Israel of God' is then a real title of the Christian Church.

We must first see how this ambiguity arises. The Greek word for *and* is *kai,* and there is a *kai* in Greek between the two expressions. But the word *kai* can be used in two ways; it can be used simply to add one thing to another, as it is commonly used in English, but it can also be used to introduce a clause or expression which is an explanation and a definition of the one that has gone before. This second kind of *kai* has a technical name; it is called the epexegetic or explanatory *kai,* and it can well be translated, 'I mean'. There is a good example of this in Revelation 2.2. In the AV that verse runs: 'I know thy works *and* thy labour and thy patience.' The RSV has: 'I know your works, your toil and your fortitude. The NEB has: 'I know all your ways, your toil and your fortitude.' These two translations give the meaning simply by omitting the first *and.* But the construction really is that that which comes after the first *and* is an explanation and definition of the word *works,* and a full translation is: 'I know your works, I mean your toil and your fortitude.'

Now we return to our Galatian passage. The question is, does the *and,* the *kai,* in it *add* or *explain*? Are there two different groups, first, all who walk by this rule, *and,* second, the Israel of God? Or, is there simply one group of people, and is the translation: 'Peace and mercy upon all who walk by this rule, I mean,' or, 'that is, the Israel of God'? The Greek will bear either meaning equally well. Unquestionably it would be a loss to Christian thought and theology if we could no longer think of the Church in terms of the new Israel. Since we cannot be certain how the Galatians passage should be taken, we can only decide the matter by looking at the general thought of Paul in regard to Israel and the Christian Church.

There is no doubt at all that Paul consistently draws a distinction between the spiritual and the physical Israel. 'Not all who are descended from Israel belong to Israel,' he said (Romans 9.6). 'He is not a real Jew who is one outwardly, nor is true circumcision something external and physical. He is a real Jew who is one inwardly, and real circumcision is a matter of the heart, spiritual and not literal' (Romans 2.28–9). 'If you are Christ's, then you are Abraham's offspring' (Galatians 3.29). 'We are the true circumcision, who worship God in spirit, and glory in Christ Jesus, and put no confidence in the flesh' (Philippians 3.3). From all this it is quite clear that it is in complete accordance with the thought of Paul to think of the Church as the new and the true Israel, the Israel of God. We are perfectly justified in retaining this expression as one of the titles of the Church. What then is its significance?

– It clearly anchors Christianity firmly in history, and it clearly maintains the unbreakable link with the past. The revelation of God is an historical revelation. Christianity is not a breach and a break with the past; it is a continuation and a development of the past. To put it in another way, the New Testament could not have come without the Old Testament to precede it. Christianity cannot without loss to itself cut itself adrift from its historical past. The Jewish nation had its irreplaceable part to play in the revelation of God, and this title will make certain that the Christian Church does not forget the rock from which it was hewn. It will remind the Church of what is at one and the same time its debt and its duty to Judaism; and as a corollary it will remind the Christian that anti-semitism is one of the most unjustifiable of all sins.

– But secondly the title 'the *new* Israel' makes it clear that Christianity is above all racial distinctions. John the Baptist reminded the Jews of his day that they must not think that they had nothing to fear from God simply because they were descendants of Abraham (Matthew 3.9; Luke 3.8). For some Israelites did indeed believe that descent from Abraham ensured salvation. 'All Israel has a part in the world to come,' said the Rabbinic saying. Abraham is depicted as sitting at the gate of Gehenna to turn back any Jew who might mistakenly find his way there. The merits of Abraham were so mighty and far-reaching that they would avail even for a man who was otherwise morally and spiritually dead.

But the concept of the new Israel makes it quite clear that no man is entitled by race to any special favour in the sight of God.

The saving fact is not membership of any race or breed; it is a relationship to God, made possible for every man through the work of Jesus Christ. The idea of the new Israel introduces the conception of a Church which is a unity in which the barriers are down, and in which what matters is not a man's race or colour or nationality but his personal relationship to God.

- It may well be that it is the third significance within this title which is the most important of all. If the Christian Church is the new Israel, it must mean that the promises and the privileges and the responsibilities of Israel have been inherited by the Christian Church. And this must mean that to read the Old Testament prophecies as political and nationalistic prophecies telling the future of the nation of Israel must necessarily be an error. If the Christian Church be the new Israel, then the prophecies must be spiritual truth and must be fulfilled in the Church.

And it is exactly here that there comes challenge and even threat. Israel was the holy nation, the chosen people; and the failure of Israel lay precisely in her mistaken interpretation of the word *chosen*. Far too often the word was interpreted in terms of *privilege*. It is exactly this thinking of chosenness in terms of privilege that the prophets condemned. Jeremiah fulminates against the people who confidently hold that, because the Temple of the Lord is in Jerusalem, nothing can happen to destroy the city (Jeremiah 7). The chosenness was a chosenness for responsibility and for service and not for privilege, or rather, to put the matter more accurately, the service was the privilege. It was just because of this misconception that Judaism was never a missionary faith; and it was just because of this that Judaism thought of the choice of the Jews as involving the rejection of the Gentiles. Of course, there were voices and great voices on the other side, but for the most part orthodox Judaism regarded the choice of the Jews as involving the rejection, and even destruction, of the Gentiles. What the new Israel inherits is the task, once committed to Israel and now given to the Church, of being the instrument of God to bring all nations to himself.

(vii) We have left to the end the greatest and the most significant of all the titles of the Church. In Paul's letters the Church is called *the Body of Christ*. There are two closely interconnected titles by which the Church is called.

The Church is called quite simply *a body* or *the body*, or, if it is not directly so called, it is likened to a body.

> As in one body we have many members, and all the members do not have the same function, so we, though many, are one body in Christ, and individually members one of another (Romans 12.4).

> Because there is one loaf we who are many are one body, for we all partake of the same loaf (1 Corinthians 10.17).

> For just as the body is one and has many members, and all the members of the body, though one, are one body, so it is with Christ (1 Corinthians 12.12).

> The purpose of Christ in regard to Jew and Gentile is that he might reconcile us both to God in one body through the cross, thereby bringing the hostility to an end (Ephesians 2.16).

> There is one body and one Spirit (Ephesians 4.4).

> Let the peace of Christ rule in your hearts, to which indeed you were called in the one body (Colossians 3.15).

When Paul used the metaphor of the body to depict the unity of the Church he was using a picture which had often been used before. Marcus Aurelius warns his readers that when they go out in the morning they must expect to meet inquisitive, ungrateful, violent, treacherous, envious, uncharitable men. But in spite of that they must never be angry with anyone and they must never hate anyone, for all men are kin to each other. 'We have come into the world to work together like feet, like hands, like eyelids, like the rows of the upper and lower teeth' (*Meditations* 2.1). Socrates tried to bring together two friends who had quarrelled by reminding them of the unity of the body. 'What if a pair of hands refused the office of mutual help for which God made them, and tried to thwart each other; or if a pair of feet neglected the duty of working together, for which they were fashioned and took to hampering each other?' (*Memorabilia* 2.3.18). Justinian says: 'Throughout its many members the state is formed into one body.'

The most famous use in ancient literature of the metaphor of the body comes from the history of Livy (2.32). At an early stage of Roman history the state of Rome was split in two. There was a complete cleavage between the plebeians (the common people) and the patricians (the aristocracy). So serious had this become that the plebeians had withdrawn from the city altogether, and had refused to take part in its life, and the life and business of the state had consequently been brought to a standstill. The senate sent Menenius Agrippa to the people to try to persuade them to be of a better mind, and it was then that he made a famous speech and in it used this metaphor of the body:

> At a time when the members of the human body did not as at present all unite in one plan, but each member had its own scheme and its own language, the other parts were provoked when they saw that the fruits of all their care, of all their toil and service were applied to the use of the stomach, and that the stomach meanwhile remained at its ease and did nothing but enjoy the pleasures provided for it. They therefore conspired together that the hand should not bring food to the mouth, that the mouth should not receive it if offered, and that the teeth should not chew it. They wished by these angry measures to subdue the stomach through hunger. But the result was that the members themselves and the whole body with it were reduced to the last stage of decay. From this it appeared that the office of the stomach was not confined to a slothful idleness, that it not only received nourishment but supplied it to the others, conveying to every part of the body that blood on which depend our life and vigour, by distributing it equally through the veins, after having brought it to perfection by digesting the food.

Here there is the same picture, and the same conclusion that unless there is unity a body cannot exist, and unless there is unity a Church cannot exist.

But this picture of the unity of the Church tells us not only that unity is in itself a necessity for the life of the Church; it also tells the kind of unity that it must be. It is unity but it is not uniformity. The duty and the function and the appearance and the work of the members of the body are not the same. In fact, as Paul says, a body that was composed of one member would not be a body at all. Quintilian the Roman orator said exactly the same thing: 'I would not that the body should be all eyes, lest the other members should lose their office' (1 Corinthians 12.17; Quintilian, *Institutes of Oratory* 8.5). The unity is a unity in difference. Someone has illustrated it in this way. Suppose a group of people want to sing. They can do one of three things. They can all sing different tunes, and then the result will be merely an unpleasant noise. They can all agree to sing the same tune and the result will be unison singing, which is better, but which is not the best. They can divide themselves into sopranos, contraltos, tenors and basses, and those in each part can sing their own line of the harmony, and the result is best of all.

This is what the unity of the Church ought to be like. It ought to be very far from being a case of flat uniformity in which all differences are ruled out. It ought to be a unity in which all the differences are gathered into a larger harmony. There will always be those who wish elaboration in worship and those who wish simplicity; there will always be those who are happy in a cathedral and those who are happy in a bare and austere little hall; there will always be those who are conservative in their theology and those who are liberal; there will always be those who are fundamentalist in their approach to Scripture and those who are not. But Christian unity does not mean the obliteration of all differences; it means the harmonizing of all differences in a larger unity; it means concentration on the Christ who unites rather than on the systems and the theologies which divide. This much is true, that a divided Church has lost the right to be called a Church.

There are few congregations which have not had in them at one time or another people who are characteristically troublemakers and disturbers of the peace; there are few Churches which have not at some time been divided into parties and divisions. There have been few discussions on Christian unity which have not been obstructed and sometimes destroyed by those who intolerantly insist that they and their communion alone have the right creed or the right ecclesiastical structure. When divisions such as these arise we would do well to remember that, as the New Testament sees it, there are few graver and more serious sins than destroying the unity of what ought to be the united body of the Church.

There are two kinds of tolerance. There is the tolerance of the man who is tolerant because he does not care, who is tolerant because he has no strong beliefs or principles, who is tolerant because he does not think the issue matters, who is tolerant because he is too mentally and spiritually lazy to take a stand on anything. For that kind of tolerance the

Church can never have any use. But there is the tolerance which comes from the certainty that God fulfils himself in many ways, the tolerance which refuses to be arrogant enough to believe that any man has an exclusive grasp of the whole truth, the tolerance which is quite sure that a great many things on the circumference of the faith can be left fluid so long as the centre – which is Christ – is right, the tolerance which cannot bring itself to believe that any ecclesiastical system is necessary for salvation, the tolerance which can say as John Wesley did: 'Is your heart as my heart? Then give me your hand.'

Those who have been, and who are still, responsible for the divisions within the Church and within individual congregations have much to answer for. The Church ought to be a united body but the body which should be united is disintegrated into fragments. And since it is so, the weakness and the ineffectiveness of the Church are as inevitable as they are tragic.

Before we leave the idea of the Church as a unity there is one other passage at which we must look. It is a passage of the utmost importance, and yet it has more than a tinge of doubt about it. Its importance comes from the fact that it is part of the earliest account of the Lord's Supper, and part of what is commonly called our warrant for the sacrament. The passage is in 1 Corinthians 11.29. The Authorized Version unquestionably was the translation of a Greek text which is late and incorrect. In this passage Paul is pleading that the Christian sacrament should be engaged in in the right spirit. And above all those are condemned who take part in it, as the AV has it, *not discerning the Lord's body*. A glance at any modern translation, with the single exception of the Roman Catholic translation of Ronald Knox, will show that the words *the Lord's* are no part of the true text. The true Greek text is *not discerning the body*, as the Revised Version, the Revised Standard Version, Weymouth, Moffatt, Kingsley Williams, Goodspeed and the New English Bible will show.

Even if we omit the words *the Lord's*, it is still quite possible that the words refer to the body of Jesus, and that the condemnation is upon those who do not discern the real meaning of the bread, that in fact it is for faith nothing other than the body of Christ. Moffatt and the NEB leave no doubt that they mean this. They omit the words *the Lord's*, but they spell the word *Body* with a capital B, thereby making it clear that they believe that it is the body of Christ which is in question.

But there is another interpretation of this saying which is at least as possible as this. When we turn back to the beginning of the chapter to discover the situation out of which Paul's instruction arose, we find that the trouble was that the Church of Corinth was split into sects and cliques and factions. 'When you assemble as a Church, I hear that there are divisions among you' (1 Corinthians 11.18). When they meet to share in their Common Meal, in the Love Feast, there is no fellowship and there is no sharing; each little group isolates itself selfishly; there are some who have far too much, and there are others who have far too little (1 Corinthians 11.20–2). It is immediately after that, in the next verse, that Paul begins to give instructions as to how the Lord's Supper should be eaten.

Now, it is against this background that we have to interpret the saying that it is a dangerous and a sinful thing to eat the Lord's Supper *not discerning the body*. And if this is taken and read in its context, it is at least possible that the words *not discerning the body* do not at all refer to the symbolism of the bread of the sacrament, but *refer to the unity of the Church*; and that the condemnation is upon those who come to the sacrament completely forgetting, or completely ignoring the fact that the Church is a body and that therefore sects, divisions, parties, cliques are a sin, and that a service marked by them is a travesty, and even a blasphemy.

It is more than likely, we believe indeed that it is highly probable, that this is a grim and terrible warning to those who partake of the sacrament of the Lord's Supper and who at the same time are responsible for disunity in the Church, to those who ignore the fact that the Church is a body, to those who refuse to discern the body, the essential, necessary unity of the Church. And if we take this passage in that way, we come face to face with the awesome thought that the sacrament of the Lord's Supper, as it is observed and celebrated in the modern Church, may be not a sacrament but a blasphemy, because it is precisely in it that the divisions of the Church are most apparent, most acute, and most difficult to heal. It may be that we Christians have no right to celebrate the sacrament at all until we can celebrate it in love together.

However that may be, there is no doubt that the New Testament regards the Church as a body, a unity in diversity, and that only when that unity obtains, is the Church a Church in reality and not only in name.

There is a story of Kagawa the great Japanese Christian, which vividly sums up this matter. 'I speak English very badly,' Kagawa once said, 'and when I say "denomination" some people think I am saying "damnation". I am not surprised. To me, they are very much the same thing.' It may be that the sin of denominationalism is the greatest sin of the modern Church.

Finally, let us see those things upon which according to the New Testament this unity is based.

— There is one body because there is one Lord, one faith, one God and Father of all (Ephesians 4.4–6). That is to say, this unity is based on a common loyalty, a common belief, and a common membership of the family of God.

— This unity exists in the Holy Spirit. There is one Spirit (Ephesians 4.4; 1 Corinthians 12.13). The Spirit is, as it were, the common atmosphere in which the body lives, and the common life-giving air which the body breathes.

— This unity is sacramentally based. We are all baptized into one body (1 Corinthians 12.13); because we have all partaken of the one loaf, we are all members of the one body (1 Corinthians 10.17). It is part of the tragedy of the modern situation that the very sacraments which were meant to be the focus of unity have become the centre of difference.

— This unity is eschatologically directed. Before all Christians there is one hope (Ephesians 4.4). For all Christians life moves to one goal and to one end. They are on a common journey to a common destination, inspired and upheld by a common hope.

Whatever be the actual state of the Church, however much the Church is in fact divided and fragmented, there is no doubt that it was meant to be as real and living a unity as a body, in which the parts are all for one and one for all. And this is to say that anything which divides the unity of the Church is against God's vision of the Church and God's purpose for the Church, and anything which unites its broken fragments is bringing the Church nearer to the desire of God. Christians in every branch of the Church should be working and praying for the day when every part of the Church will retain its own characteristics, its own gifts and its own traditions, and yet all the parts will have that unity and that harmony and that togetherness which come from the realization that the Christ who unites is infinitely more important than the creeds and the structures which divide.

We turn now to the second and the even more important way in which the Church is called a body. The Church is called *the Body of Christ*.

> Now you are the Body of Christ, and individually members of it (1 Corinthians 12.27).

> God has put all things under the feet of Jesus Christ and has made him the head over all things for the Church, which is his Body, the fulness of him who fills all in all (Ephesians 1.23).

> The spiritual gifts which are given within the Church are given for the equipment of the saints, for the work of the ministry, for the building up of the Body of Christ (Ephesians 4.12).

> No man ever hates his own flesh, but nourishes it and cherishes it, as Christ does the Church, because we are members of his Body (Ephesians 5.29–30).

> He is the head of the Body, the Church (Colossians 1.18).

> The reason for the drift into error is the failure to hold fast to the Head, from whom the whole Body, nourished and knit together through its joints and ligaments, grows with a growth that is from God (Colossians 2.19).

In these passages the Church is called the Body of Christ. There are certain New Testament scholars who go a very long way towards making this phrase identify the Church and the Risen Christ. J. A. T. Robinson says: 'To say that the Church is the Body of Christ is no more a metaphor than to say that the flesh of the incarnate Jesus ... is the Body of Christ.' Karl Ludwig Schmidt says: 'Christ is the *ekklesia*.... Ecclesiology and Christology are identical.' Oscar Cullmann says: 'The resurrection Body of Christ is identical with the Church.' Dietrich Bonhoeffer says: 'The fellowship of the baptized is a body which is identical with Christ's own Body ... Jesus Christ is at once himself and his Church ... Christ *is* the Church.' Bruce Kenrick writes: 'The Church receives the very flesh and blood of Jesus Christ. She becomes nothing less than the Body of Christ. His life is her life. His nature is her nature. His being is her being. Christ is the Church.'

There is a dangerously loose use of language in these statements. It is very difficult to understand what exactly they mean by the word *is*. If we say that Christ *is* the Church, can then the Church redeem the world? If the life of the Church is the life of Christ, is the Church pre-existent and eternal? If the nature of the Church is the nature of Christ, does that mean that the Church is divine and sinless?

Further, never in the New Testament is there any identification of the Church and Jesus Christ. The Church worships Christ, prays to Christ, awaits Christ, follows Christ, serves Christ, calls Christ Lord. Christ in the letters of Paul is in fact not identical with the Church; he is the Head of the Church (Colossians 1.18; 2.19; Ephesians 1.22–3; 4.15). As Vincent Taylor puts it: 'The name "the Head" asserts Christ's inseparability from the Church, but excludes his identity with it.' What then does the New Testament mean when it calls the Church the Body of Christ?

We will get a very valuable approach to this question in the Letter to the Ephesians. E. F. Scott saw in that Letter two great facts. First, it is God's wish to reconcile this disintegrated and warring universe to himself (Ephesians 1.10); and God's agent in that task of reconciliation is Jesus Christ. Secondly, Jesus lived and died to effect this reconciliation of men to God, but the story of what he has done and the offer of the reconciliation he brought about has to be made to all men; and that is the task of the Church. And that is to say that Jesus Christ's instrument of reconciliation is the Church. God's agent of reconciliation is Jesus Christ; Jesus Christ's instrument of reconciliation is the Church. In this sense the Church is the Body of Christ, for it is through the Church that Jesus Christ works.

The part of the Church in this matter comes out in Ephesians 1.23. There the Church is called the Body of Christ, *the fulness of him who fills all in all.* The word for fulness is *plērōma*, which can be either active or passive. Passively, it can mean *that which is filled by*; actively, it can means *that which fills up*. So here the Church can be described as that which is filled by Jesus Christ, or as that which fills up Jesus Christ. Now here it is much more natural, so far as the Greek goes, to take *plērōma* in the active sense; the Church is that which fills up Christ. *Plērōma* is used in Greek for the crew of a ship, for the cargo of Noah's ark, for the duty of a cup-bearer in filling a cup, for the tradesmen and professional people necessary to make up the population of a city. In this sense – and we believe it is the sense here – the English word for *plērōma* is *complement*; *the Church is the complement of Christ.*

We have in Colossians 1.24 a saying which illuminates this line of thought. There Paul speaks of his sufferings for the Church completing what is lacking in the afflictions of Christ. This is a startling saying. How can there be anything lacking in the afflictions of Christ? A physician or a surgeon or a scientist may make a great discovery which will save the lives, or ease the pain, or lighten the labour of many people; but that discovery remains ineffective until there are people who are prepared to take it out of the hospital and out of the operating-theatre and out of the laboratory into the whole world; and undoubtedly those who take the discovery out to men complete the work of the one man who made it. Just so, the work of Christ is completed in his life and in his death; but that work remains ineffective until men know of it and accept it and appropriate it. And how can they hear without a preacher? (Romans 10.14). The work of the Church is to bring to men the good news of the work of God in Christ. If in doing that the preacher or the missionary or the teacher suffers, then he is filling up, completing the sufferings of Christ. Christ performed his perfect work of reconciliation; the Church must tell the whole world of it; and therein the Church is the agent, the body, the complement of Christ.

Immediately a thought leaps to the mind. Does this mean that Jesus Christ is literally dependent on the Church? That is precisely and exactly what it does mean. Chrysostom, commenting on this passage, says: 'See how Paul brings Christ in as needing the Church.' 'Such is Christ's love for the Church that he, as it were, regards himself as incomplete, unless he has the Church united to him as a body.'

However startling the dependence of Christ on men may appear to be, it is demonstrably true. There is a sense in which we can speak of the divine helplessness. If Jesus Christ wants a child taught, nothing will teach that child, unless some man or woman is prepared to do so. If Jesus Christ wants a land evangelized, the purpose of Christ is frustrated, unless men and women are prepared to go out into the world and preach the gospel. Jesus Christ is not now here in the body, although he is powerfully here in the Spirit and in his risen presence; if, therefore, he wants anything done in this world he has to get a man or a woman to do it for him. That is the real sense in which the Church is the Body of Christ. To say that the Church is the body of Christ is to say that we must be hands through which he can work, we must be voices through which

he can speak, we must be feet with which he can travel, we must be the
agents he can send and the instruments he can use.

> He has no hands but our hands
>   To do his work today,
> He has no feet but our feet
>   To lead men in his way.
> He has no voice but our voice
>   To tell men how he died,
> He has no help but our help
>   To lead men to his side.

There remains only one thing to be said. We came to the conclusion that
plērōma in Ephesians 5.23, when it is used of the Church in relation to
Jesus Christ, is best taken actively, and understood as meaning that the
Church is the complement of Jesus Christ. That is true, but it often happens that Greek makes use of the necessary ambiguity which resides in
some of its words, and it is extremely probable that it does so here, and
the *plērōma* is to he taken *both* actively and passively. What the word will
then mean is that the Church is the instrument or agent which fills up
Christ and is the complement of Christ, but it can never be that until it
itself is filled with Christ and until Christ and his Spirit and his power
reside in it. In order to fill up Christ the Church must be filled by Christ,
and then indeed it becomes his body through which he can act on earth.

The Church has many titles but the greatest of all is the Body of
Christ, for therein there are enshrined the twin truths that the Church is
the agent of Jesus Christ and the dwelling-place of Jesus Christ.

CHAPTER EIGHTEEN

In the Communion of Saints

Although this article of the creed expresses a truth and an experience which were always at the heart of the Church, it is nonetheless true that it was very late in making its appearance as an actual part of the creed. It is in fact not until midway through the sixth century that this phrase first appears in the creed. And it may well be true to say that even today it is the article of the creed about the meaning of which people are most vague.

In Greek the communion of Saints is *koinōnia hagiōn*; and this word *koinōnia* is one of the most beautiful words in the Greek language. Long before it was taken into the Christian vocabulary, it was used extensively by the great Greek writers. It describes any partnership, any fellowship, any activity or experience or relationship in which people come together; the essential meaning of the word is togetherness, and always with the idea at the back of it that that fellowship is for mutual benefit and good in the widest sense of the term. It is worthwhile analyzing the many spheres in which it is used in Greek language and thought.

(i) It is regularly used of the *marriage relationship*. Aristotle calls marriage a *koinōnia,* a fellowship, a partnership (*Politics* 1334 b 33). In a marriage contract in the papyri two people take each other *pros biou koinōnian,* for partnership, for fellowship, to share all life (BGU 4.1051.9).

(ii) It is regularly used to describe *a business relationship*. In the papyri a man denies that he has any *koinōnia* with his brother; he declares that he has no business partnership with him (P.Ryl.2.117.16). It describes a relationship in which two people pool their resources to work together for their common profit and their common good.

(iii) It describes a partnership in *education*. Plato in the *Republic* lays it down that in his ideal state men and women are to share a common way of life (*Republic* 466 c). They are to have the same education and the same activities and opportunities in life and living. In the ancient world the woman was entirely uneducated and secluded; Plato has his vision of a state where men and women will share equally in the privileges and the responsibilities of the state.

(iv) It describes the *social life* of the community. Plato in legislating for the community notes that in the dealings (*koinōnia*) and the intercourse (*homilia*) between citizens, injuries are likely frequently to occur (*Laws* 861 E). The word describes the community life which people are bound to live when they are members of the same society.

(v) With Aristotle *koinōnia* is a favourite *political* word. His definition of a state is that it is a political *koinōnia* (*Politics* 1252 a 7). A state is a fellowship of people living and working and acting together in a common unity. 'A state', he says, 'is a partnership (*koinōnia*) of clans and villages in a full independent life' (*Politics* 1281 a 1). The state is a fellowship in which certain laws and obligations are accepted in order that life may be fuller and freer for all.

(vi) It is used in the *international* sense. Thucydides lays it down that friendship between men and a league (*koinōnia*) between states depends on honesty of purpose and likeness of outlook (Thucydides 3.10). *Koinōnia* is an alliance of people who have a common goal and a common mind, made for a common purpose.

(vii) It is the word which expresses the very essence and foundation of *friendship*. 'Where there is no *koinōnia*, no fellowship, there can be no friendship' (*Gorgias* 507 E). The basis of friendship is this fellowship in which two people have learned to share, that each may have more by giving to each other.

(viii) Lastly, even in secular Greek *koinōnia* has a religious flavour. It is the word used for *fellowship with God*. Epictetus lays it down that even in the body, even in the world of space and time, the good man has his heart set on *koinōnia* with Zeus, on fellowship with God (*Discourses* 2.19.27).

Beyond a doubt *koinōnia* came into the Christian vocabulary with a great background, for it is the word of togetherness in every sphere of life.

Let us now look more directly at this phrase *the communion of saints*. But before we turn to these interpretations we must remember one other preliminary fact. The word *saints* is used here, as usual, in its New Testament sense and not in its modern sense. The saints are not those who have the word 'Saint' prefixed to their names; they are not the famous examples of holiness and piety who have been canonized into saints in the ecclesiastical sense of the term. The saints are, as we have seen in the last chapter, the *hagioi,* the members of the Church. They are those who have separated themselves and who have made themselves different by dedicating their lives to Jesus Christ, even if they still have their very human faults and failings. They are not so much the people who *are* different as they are the people who with the help of Jesus Christ are *trying* to be different and to be Christlike.

(i) The first and the simplest interpretation of the phrase *the communion of saints* takes it to be a description of *the way in which Christian people in mutual care and love share everything with each other.* This caring and sharing have always been the mark of the Church when it was truly Christian.

It was the mark of the life of the early Church. All those who believed had all things in common. There was not a needy person in the Christian fellowship, for those who had possessions sold them and gave the money to the apostles to use for the common good (Acts 2.44–5), just as Barnabas sold the estate he owned and brought the money to the apostles and handed it over to them (Acts 4.34–7). The Christians were like the members of a body. Each member had care for every other member. The need of one was the need of all and the suffering of one was the suffering of all (1 Corinthians 12.25–6). There was in the Church a true sympathy in which each felt for and with all the others. When the Jerusalem Christians were in need the Christians of Antioch were quick to send to their help (Acts 11.27–30).

The best example of all of this is Paul's scheme to help the Church at Jerusalem. The Jerusalem Church was a poor Church and Paul organized a collection from the younger Churches for the Church at Jerusalem (2 Corinthians 8.1–5; 9.1; Romans 15.25–8). This was Paul's way of clearly and practically demonstrating the communion of saints, the fellowship of caring and sharing which should be the mark of the Church. A Church which has forgotten, not the obligation, but the privilege of sharing has lost the mark of a Christian Church.

(ii) Sometimes the word *hagiōn* in this article has been taken to be neuter and not masculine; it would then mean: 'I believe in the fellowship in sacred things; I believe in the privilege of the Christian in sharing in holy things.' 'I believe', as it has been put, 'in our joint participation in holy things.' So Peter Abelard took this to refer to the sharing in the holy things of the altar, that is, in the sanctified bread and wine of the sacrament.

Sometimes we call the sacrament of the Lord's Supper quite simply The Communion. That sacrament was meant to be the *kionōnia*, the act of sharing and of fellowship *par excellence*. It was meant to be an act and an occasion where above all places on earth men and women have fellowship (*kionōnia*). communion with one another and with God.

And so in this article of the creed we are again face to face with the tragedy of the Church. In the old catechism known as Nowell's Catechism the master is asked by the learner why the Church's belief in the communion of saints comes immediately after the belief in the Holy Catholic Church; and the answer is that 'this parcel (*pars*, part) doth somewhat more plainly express the conjoining and society that is among the members of the Church, than which there can be none nearer.' It is the tragedy of the Church that it has been marked by division and disunity rather than by this supreme unity which ought to be the closest of all unities. We should surely regard it as an astonishing and a shocking thing to go on repeating a creed which in action we deny, and to go on affirming a belief which our practice bluntly and flatly contradicts. It is time that we remembered that the Communion Table or Altar, as the case may be, belongs to no branch of the Church, but to our Lord, and that any believer in him has the privilege of a share in holy things.

However, neither of these two interpretations is what might be called the Church's orthodox and traditional interpretation of this article.

Nicetas, one of the early fathers, writes as follows: 'What is the Church but the congregation of all saints? Patriarchs, prophets, apostles, martyrs, all the just who have been, are, or shall be, are one Church, because sanctified by one faith and life, marked by one Spirit, they constitute one body. Believe, then, that in this one Church you will attain the communion of saints.' In this definition the communion of saints is defined as the fellowship that all Christians have with one another, those in this world, and those who have passed into the world beyond, and those who will yet be, those in the Church militant in this earth and those in the Church triumphant in heaven. That is true, but the communion, the fellowship, which the saints enjoy is even wider than that. Pearson has given the fullest analysis of this and we follow his headings.

(i) The Christian has communion, fellowship, *koinōnia*, with *God the Father*. Abraham was called the friend of God (James 2.23). We are the children of God (1 John 3.1). We are partakers of the divine nature (2 Peter 1.14). If Christ is the vine and we are the branches the Father is the vinedresser (John 15.1)

Somewhere H. G. Wells drew a picture of a big business man who was on the very verge of a nervous breakdown. His doctor told him that the only way he could save his sanity was by finding fellowship with something bigger than himself, fellowship with God. 'What?' he said. 'Me – have fellowship with that up there? I would as soon think of cooling my throat with the milky way or shaking hands with the stars.' To him fellowship with God was unthinkably impossible. It is precisely that fellowship with the God who is called Father which, through Jesus Christ, is open to every Christian.

(ii) The Christian has fellowship, communion, *koinōnia*, with *Jesus Christ the Son*. Our fellowship, writes John, is with the Father and with his Son Jesus Christ (1 John 1.3). We are called into the fellowship of God's Son, Jesus Christ our Lord (1 Corinthians 1.9). The friendship, the presence and the fellowship of Jesus Christ are open to every Christian.

(iii) The Christian has fellowship, communion, *koinōnia*, with the *Holy Spirit*. In the blessing it is the love of God, the grace of our Lord Jesus Christ, and the fellowship of the Spirit which are invoked upon us (2 Corinthians 13.14). The Christian is God's temple and God's Spirit dwells in him (1 Corinthians 3.16). It is our participation, our fellowship in and with the Spirit, which alone can give us fellowship with one another (Philippians 2.1).

(iv) The Christian has fellowship, communion, *koinōnia*, with *the holy angels*. The angels are ministering spirits sent to serve for the sake of those who are to obtain salvation (Hebrews 1.14). The angels are glad when one sinner repents and comes back to God (Luke 15.10). There may be a certain unreality for many people in this idea now, but there are times when it can become very real. Alan Walker in a book called *Everybody's Calvary* recounts the experience of a young minister. He had been preaching in a tiny village country chapel, and he invited the people to stay for Communion. Only two stayed. He was a little depressed and discouraged at so very small a congregation. So he went on with the ancient ritual a little dully and dejectedly. And then in the course of it he came to the passage: 'With angels and archangels and with all the company of heaven, we worship and adore thy glorious name.' He paused; the wonder gripped him. 'Angels and archangels and all the company of heaven ... God forgive me,' he said, 'I did not know I was in that company.' It is well that sometimes we should remind ourselves that heaven lies about us.

(v) We have fellowship, communion, *koinōnia*, with all the saints within the Church. It is just here that there has been dispute about this article of the creed. There are those who wished, and those who still wish, to limit the word saints to those who truly have holiness. This is an old dispute, going back to the days of the great persecution, when there were some who would have debarred for ever from the Church those whose courage had failed and who had sought safety, however penitent they might be. There are some who, as it has been put, have in them 'that false Puritanism which was dissatisfied with the *permixtum corpus* of the Catholic Church.'

Pearson draws an analogy from the people of Israel. The people of Israel were God's chosen people; they were the holy people. Now quite clearly they were not all holy and they were not all such as God's people ought to be; but even in spite of that their membership of the chosen nation, the holy people, bound them together in the one whole. The Church, while it is the Church on earth, cannot be anything other than a mixture. The dragnet brought in things of every kind (Matthew 13.47). Until God's good time the wheat and the tares were to grow together; there was a time when to separate them could do nothing but harm and damage (Matthew 13.24–30). The Catholic Church has room for all. H. B. Swete suggests two reasons why we must still have fellowship even with those who are very unsatisfactory saints. First, it is not in human power, nor is it within human right, to draw a dividing line. That can only be done by God. Secondly, you cannot eject those who need it most from the power and the operation of the Holy Spirit within the Church and from the Christian fellowship in which the influence of Christ has its greatest opportunity to play upon them.

There have always been two conceptions of the Church. There has been that of the gathered Church in which personal holiness was a precondition of fellowship; there has been that of the catholic Church, which opened its arms to all who would come. There are arguments on both sides, but it may not be untrue to say that the conception of the gathered Church has tended to produce a certain arrogance and intolerance, a certain self-righteousness and a certain forgetfulness that we must not judge lest we be judged; and it is certainly true that the main tradition of the Church has always seen the Church as inclusive rather than as exclusive. The fellowship of the saints includes fellowship with those who have little claim to saintliness.

(vi) The Christian has fellowship communion, *koinōnia*, with *those who have departed from this life and who are in the presence of God*. We have come, as the writer to the Hebrews puts it, 'to Mount Zion, and to the city of the living God, the heavenly Jerusalem, and to innumerable angels in festal gathering, and to the assembly of the firstborn who are enrolled in heaven, and to a judge who is God of all, and to the spirits of just men made perfect' (Hebrews 12.22–3). The foundation of the union between Christian and Christian is Jesus Christ, and therefore that union cannot be removed by death. Hugh Burnaby speaks of 'the intimate union and conjunction between all believers with one another in Christ – a union not broken by death.' As Charles Wesley wrote:

> One family we dwell in him,
> One Church, above, beneath,
> Though now divided by the stream,
> The narrow stream of death.

For the Christian nothing will be more real than the fellowship of the unseen cloud of witnesses who compass him about (Hebrews 12.1). Not least in the communion of saints is the communion with those whom we have loved and lost awhile.

So then we believe in the communion of saints. We believe that we have fellowship and communion with the Father, the Son and the Holy Spirit; we believe that we can be conscious of the power of heaven around us and about us; we believe that we have the fellowship with all the members of the Church on earth, and that that fellowship is inclusive rather than exclusive; and we believe that we have fellowship with those who have departed this life to be with God.

CHAPTER NINETEEN

In the Forgiveness of Sins

All the great historic creeds have a double aspect. They have a positive aspect and they have a negative aspect. In their positive aspect they state the faith of the Church; in their negative aspect they contradict some error, some deviation from the belief of the Church. When a belief is stated firmly and unequivocally in a creed there is at least a likelihood that it is inserted because there are those who refuse to accept it, or who pervert it. A. C. McGiffert holds strongly that it is so with this article of the Apostles' Creed.

There is no possible doubt that the early Church preached and offered to men the forgiveness of sins. Repentance and remission of sins is to be preached to all nations beginning from Jerusalem (Luke 24.47). The offer is that men should repent and turn again that their sins may be blotted out (Acts 3.19). 'Through this man', says Paul, 'forgiveness of sins is proclaimed to you' (Acts 13.38). In the first recorded sermon Peter says: 'Repent and be baptized every one of you in the name of Jesus Christ for the remission of your sins' (Acts 2.38). It is Ananias' invitation to Paul: 'Be baptized, and wash away your sins' (Acts 22.16). John preached a baptism of repentance for the forgiveness of sins (Mark 1.4), and the proclamation of Jesus is: 'My son, your sins are forgiven' (Mark 2.5). There is no doubt that the original Christian message had as its very centre and focus the proclamation that in and through Jesus Christ the forgiveness of sins was offered to men.

But a curious thing happened. In the Christian literature immediately following the New Testament the forgiveness of sins was not stressed. The writers who follow the New Testament are known as the Apostolic Fathers. That literature consists of the Letters of Ignatius, Barnabas, Clement, Polycarp, the Letter to Diognetus, the Shepherd of Hermas, and the Teaching of the Twelve Apostles. The Forgiveness of sins is mentioned six times in Barnabas, only once each in Hermas, the Teaching of the Twelve Apostles, and the seven Letters of Ignatius, not at all in Polycarp or Second Clement. At this stage God is the law-giver and the judge; what is stressed is the ethical demand of Christianity and the necessity of being different from the world. The demand of the Church is rigorous; ecclesiastical discipline is severe; and there is excommunication without restoration for serious offences. Even within New Testament times there is the first sign of this in Hebrews. 'It is impossible to restore again to repentance those who have once been enlightened, who have tasted the heavenly gift, and have become partakers of the Holy Spirit, and have tasted the goodness of the word of God, and the powers of the age to come, if they then commit apostasy, since they crucify the Son of God on their own account and hold him up to contempt' (Hebrews 6.4–6). If a man spurns the Son of God, if he profanes the blood of the covenant by which he was sanctified, if he outrages the Spirit of grace, then the vengeance of God will deal with him, and it is a terrible thing to fall into the hands of the living God (Hebrews 10. 26–31). There was no doubt that repentance and baptism brought forgiveness for sins committed prior to baptism, but with post-baptismal sin the situation was very different; there was no forgiveness for that.

But then again the pendulum slowly swung. There came – perhaps there had to come – a new view of the Church. As McGiffert puts it, there came the idea that the Church is not so much a community of saints as it is the ark of salvation, containing both good and bad, and outside of which salvation is not possible. Previously the aim had been to exclude the unworthy; now the aim is that they should come in and find the salvation which they could not find anywhere else. There is here a conflict of views which still exists, the conflict between the idea of the gathered Church, the Church as an exclusive body of saints, and the idea of the inclusive Church, the Church into which the sinner is invited to come, sinner as he is, that he may find salvation.

At this stage there was as yet no canonical New Testament and the proof texts for the more merciful view had to be drawn from the Old Testament, and they were there to find. 'The Lord, the Lord, a God merciful and gracious, slow to anger, and abounding in steadfast love and faithfulness' (Exodus 34.6). 'Have I any pleasure in the death of the wicked, says the Lord God, and not rather that he should turn from his way and live?' (Ezekiel 18.23). But the books of the New Testament were gaining authority and they too could be quoted. Was not Jesus himself the friend of tax-collectors and sinners? (Matthew 11.19). Was it not forbidden to root recklessly out of the ground the tares, lest the good be destroyed with the bad? Was not that something which had to be left to the judgement and the decision of God? (Matthew 13.39). 'Be ye merciful,' said Jesus, 'even as your Father is merciful' (Luke 6.36). We must not judge others lest we ourselves be judged (Luke 6.37). Jesus told the stories of the woman and the coin, the shepherd and the sheep, the father and the rebellious son (Luke 15). 'Who are you', said Paul, 'to pass judgement on the servant of another?' (Romans 14.4). It is Paul's plea that the trouble-maker in Corinth should be received back into the Church (2 Corinthians 2.6–7). 'The blood of Jesus cleanses us from all sin' (1 John 1.7).

So the emphasis changes. Up until this time a man who had committed post-baptismal sin was excluded and excommunicated from the Church. True, he was in the hands of God, and God might forgive him if he so willed, but from the Church he was shut out. But then there came the change. Callixtus, who was bishop of Rome from AD 217–22, issued an edict declaring that he would pardon all post-baptismal sin, except murder and apostasy, if the sinner showed true repentance and did due penance. As we have already put it, the Church was no longer the exclusive community of the saints; it was the inclusive ark of salvation. The Church was no longer to be regarded as holy because it was composed solely of holy people; it was to be regarded as holy because it could make people holy and because in it there resided the grace which could enable all who would come to find salvation. As Callixtus put it, 'The Church has the power to forgive sin' (*habet potestatem ecclesia delicta donandi*: Tertullian *De Pud, 21*).

Very naturally there were those who were bitterly opposed to any such laxity; those who wished to maintain the old rigour and the old severity and the old discipline. As far as the official doctrine and belief of the Church was concerned, the wider view of mercy prevailed and this became the orthodox belief of the Church; but although the opposition lost the day from the point of view of official belief, it was never totally silenced and it was never completely eliminated, and to this day there are those for whom the Church is still the gathered community of saints.

This is the background of this article of the Apostles' Creed; and this background explains the position in the creed which this article holds. It comes immediately after the statement of belief in the Holy Catholic Church, because it was believed that it was precisely within the Church that this forgiveness was to be found.

In point of fact in the other creeds there are slightly expanded versions of this article which tie it indissolubly to the Church. In the Creed of Jerusalem it runs: 'I believe in one baptism of repentance for the remission of sins.' In the Creed of Constantinople it runs: 'We confess one baptism for the remission of sins.' As soon as this article of the creed is definitely attached to baptism it is definitely attached to the Church. Cyprian has it *remissionem peccatorum per sanctam ecclesiam*, the remission of sins comes through the holy Church (*Ep.* 69, 70). The Church thus becomes the vehicle through which forgiveness comes to men.

So then the existence of this article in the creed summarizes a development in the thought of the Church about itself. The Church began by calling on men to accept the gift of forgiveness which, on repentance, was made possible by the work of Jesus Christ. Placed as a small community in a pagan world the Church began by stressing its difference from the world; and that emphasis brought into the Church an uncompromising ethical demand and disciplinary rigour which turned it towards the aim of becoming a community of saints from which the sinner was excluded. Perhaps inevitably the Church swung away from that, and began to think of itself as the community in which saints could be made. It began to be more interested in a man's potential sainthood than in his actual performance. It therefore became the place where a man might find forgiveness, where he found amendment when he failed, where he found strength for his struggle at least as much as reward for his victory. And so Pearson rightly sums up this article when he says that it means: 'I believe that forgiveness of sins is to be obtained in the Church of Christ.'

It will be well before we go further to see just what the Bible means by sin. And the best way to find that out is to look at the various words which are used for sin.

In the Old Testament there is one group of words and three separate words which are most commonly used.

(i) We begin with a group of three words which all have the same basic meaning. There is the word *chet*, which occurs more than thirty times. Hide thy face from my *sins* (Psalm 51.9). He does not deal with us according to our *sins* (Psalm 103. 10). There is the word *chataah*, which is much rarer, occurring about seven times. Blessed is he whose *sin* is covered (Psalm 32.1). There is the word *chattath*, which occurs about 170 times. Remember not the *sins* of my youth (Psalm 25.7).

These three words all have the same root meaning; basically they all – like the New Testament *hamartia*, as we shall go on to see – mean a failure, a missing of the mark. Essentially all these words describe sin as man's failure to be what he was meant to be and what he should have been. The Bible has the highest possible view of man. In the Creation story God says: 'Let us make man in our image, after our likeness' (Genesis 1.26). And sin may well be said to be man's failure to reach the object and the purpose for which he was created. As G. K. Chesterton put it: 'Whatever else is true of man, man is not what he was meant to be.' So, then, in the first place sin is failure.

(ii) The second word is the word *avon*, which occurs in the Old Testament about 220 times, and which is usually translated in the AV as *iniquity*. 'For thy name's sake, O Lord, pardon mine iniquity' (Psalm 25.11).

Two things are to be noted about this word. First, the basic idea of it is distortion or perversion. It thinks of sin as that which distorts and perverts what is right. Secondly, the word *avon* does not so much describe a definite individual act; but rather a quality attaching to an act. It is rather the quality and the character of distortion and perversion. Now such a quality necessarily has results and consequences. The personal consequence of it is *guilt*, and that is very often what *avon* means, and that is how the newer translations often translate it. For instance, in the text that we have already cited, the RSV translation rightly is: 'For thy name's sake, O Lord, pardon my *guilt* for it is great' (Psalm 25.11). Further, guilt has necessary consequences. The consequence of guilt is *punishment*, and this also *avon* can mean. It is Cain's cry: 'My *punishment* is greater than I can bear' (Genesis 4.13).

(iii) The third word is the word *pesha*, which occurs more than eighty times. The basic meaning of it is rebellion. It is the same word as is used in 1 Kings 12.19: 'So Israel has been *in rebellion* against the house of David to this day.' Elihu says of Job: 'He adds *rebellion* to his sin' (Job 34.37).

This word thinks of sin as rebellion against God; it thinks of sin as the refusal to submit, the insistence on taking one's own way, the forgetfulness on the part of the creature that he is a creature and that he ought humbly to submit to his Creator.

(iv) The fourth word is *resha*. *Resha* describes rather a state than an act. It is the state of *wickedness* which is the result of habitual sin. It is the exact opposite of righteousness. Abraham asks God: 'Wilt thou indeed destroy the righteous with the *wicked*?' (Genesis 18.23). It is the state of sin into which a sinning man eventually comes.

So then in the Old Testament sin is failure; sin is perversion; sin is rebellion; sin is the state in which sinning finally leaves a man.

Now we turn to the New Testament. In the New Testament there is one group of two similar words, and there are eight main words for sin.

(i) First, there is the word *hamartia*, which occurs in the New Testament more than 170 times. It is the word which Luke uses in the Lord's Prayer; 'Forgive us our sins' (Luke 11.4). It is the great Pauline word for sin; and Paul uses it for sin as an individual act, for sin as a state and quality, and for sin as an almost personified malign power which tries to hold sway over man. *Sin* came into the world through one man, and death through sin (Romans 5.12). Let not *sin* reign in your mortal bodies (Romans 6.12). It is no longer I that do it, but *sin* which dwells within me (Romans 7.17).

Secondly, there is the word *hamartēma*. It is much rarer, occurring in the New Testament only five times. In all cases it means a definite individual act of sin. Every *act of sin* will be forgiven to men except the sin against the Holy Spirit (Mark 3.28).

There is no doubt as to the meaning of *hamartia*. *Hamartia* was originally a shooting word. It described what happened when the shot arrow or the hurled javelin missed the target. Sin is the failure to be what we should have been and what we ought to have been, what we could have been and what we might have been.

The effect of the biblical conception of sin is startling. It effectively 'detheologizes' sin. For long enough sin may be to a man a theological concept which has little or nothing to do with him. Even if he gets past that stage, he will very likely think of sin in terms of robbery, murder, theft, adultery, drunkenness – things with which the outwardly respectable – and that is most people – have nothing to do. But if sin is regarded in terms of failure to hit the mark, then sin is personalized, universalized, and detheologized. There will be few who will claim that they have been as good a father or a mother, a son or a daughter, as they might have been. There will be few who will claim that they have done whatever job they have to do as well as they might. There will be few who will claim that their personal relationships with other people have been all that they could have been. There will be few who will claim that they have made of life all that life could have been. This conception of sin places all men fairly and squarely under sin. And, be it remembered, this is by far the most central biblical conception of sin in both the Old and the New Testament.

(ii) The second New Testament word is the word *parabasis*. *Para* means *across*; and *basis* is the verbal noun from *baino*, which means *to go*. *Parabasis* is *a stepping across*. The idea is that there is a line drawn between good and bad, and to step across that line is to sin. As Paul has it: 'Where there is no law, there is no *transgression*' (Romans 4.15). The word occurs six times in the New Testament and the consistent and correct translation of the AV is *transgression*, which is simply the Latinized form of the Greek word *parabasis*, for *trans* means across, and *gredior* means *I go*.

Parabasis introduces another emphasis into the idea of sin: the emphasis of sin against knowledge. No man is guilty if he transgresses a law of the existence of which he was not aware. No man can be blamed for not obeying something which he never had the chance to know. But it is also to be remembered that, though a man is not responsible for an ignorance which he could not avoid, he is responsible for the neglect of a knowledge which he could have known. It is no defence to say: 'I never knew,' if the knowledge in question was open and attainable.

Parabasis is the word which forcibly reminds us of the responsibility of privilege. A savage cannot be blamed for doing that for which a civilized man might be condemned. A man brought up in circumstances which hardly give him a chance to be good cannot be blamed for something for which a man brought up with all the privileges might well be held guilty. The greater the privilege the greater the responsibility. The more our knowledge, the better our chance in life, the greater our privilege, the more serious our transgression.

(iii) The third New Testament word for sin is *paraptōma*. Here again we have *para* meaning *across*; and *ptōma* is the noun from the verb *piptein*, which means *to fall*. Basically the word ought rather to mean to slip or to stumble across a line. It is used more than twenty times in the New Testament.

In the case of this word the AV is curiously varied in its translation. It is translated *fall* in Romans 11.11, 12; *fault* in Galatians 6.1; James 5.6; *offence* in Romans 4.25, 5.15–20; *sin* in Ephesians 1.7; 2.5; *trespass* in Matthew 6.14, 15; 18.25; Mark 11.25, 26; 2 Corinthians 5.19; Ephesians 2.1; Colossians 2.13. The practice of the RSV is to translate *parabasis* by *transgression* and *paraptōma* by *trespass*.

In actual usage there seems to be little distinction between the two words. If their root meaning is pressed, then the difference is that *paraptōma* is less deliberate than *parabasis*. *Parabasis* would be the conscious and deliberate stepping across the line between right and wrong, in full knowledge that the step was being taken; *paraptōma* would be the slipping across the line through inadvertence and the failure to be on the watch. In secular Greek *paraptōma* means rather a *slip* or a *blunder*. It is used by Polybius for an error in judgement; by Longinus for a grammatical solecism, a slip-up in style. There are two interesting usages in the papyri. It is used there for an accidental error in the payment of an account. And there is a papyrus which lays down in regard to weighing scales that only so much margin must be allowed for *error*, and *error* is *paraptōma*. The background of this word and its root meaning would tend to indicate that the meaning of the word is a slip, a blunder, a stumble through want of care and watchfulness rather than a deliberate step into sin.

Eternal vigilance is the price of liberty and it is also the price of goodness.

(iv) The fourth word for sin is *anomia*. *Nomos* is *law* and *a-* is the prefix meaning *without*; and *anomia* is *lawlessness*. This is the word which occurs in one of the most famous definitions of sin in the New Testament in 1 John 3.4. There the AV has: 'Sin is the transgression of the law.' But the newer translations (RSV, Moffatt, NEB) all have: 'Sin is lawlessness.' The kindred word *paranomia* occurs once in 2 Peter 2.16 where it is used of the conduct of Balaam, where the AV translates *iniquity*, the NEB *offence*, and the RSV *transgression*.

It might well be said that these are the most deliberate words for sin. A man cannot be consciously lawless unless he knows the law and has made up his mind to disregard it or defy it. Lawlessness is the sin of the man who is impatient of all restraint, who thinks that, whatever may be true of other people, laws were not made for him and that he is superior to the law, who, knowing society's way, takes his own way, and who, being aware of God's laws, goes out on his own self-chosen path. This is the sin of the man who knows the right and who does the wrong. It is the sin of the man who in the pride of his heart makes his own will and his own desires the final law. *Anomia* implies the enthronement of self and the dethronement of God.

(v) The fifth word for sin is *asebeia*, which occurs six times in the New Testament. The idea of *asebeia* is that it is the characteristic of conduct which is the opposite of reverence and of piety. *Asebeia* thinks of a man's conduct specially as it affects God. It is the irreverence which denies and refuses to God the honour and the respect which should be his. So it is used in the Pastoral Epistles: 'Avoid such godless chatter, for it will lead into more and more *ungodliness*' (2 Timothy 2.16). In Paul's indictment it is one of the sins which are characteristic of the pagan world (Romans 1.18) in all its terrible immorality.

(vi) The sixth word for sin is *adikia*. *Dikē* is the accepted standard by which a man ought to live. *Adikia* is the refusal to accept that standard. The AV often translates it unrighteousness. The modern translations vary in the twenty-five instances of the word. The RSV has *wrong-doing* in 1 John 5.17; *wickedness* in Romans 1.29 and 3.5; *wrong* in 1 Corinthians 13.6; *iniquity* in 2 Timothy 2.19; *unrighteousness* in 1 John 1.9. A still further translation is introduced by the NEB, which has *injustice* in Romans 1.29 and 3.5.

Two things are near the heart of this word's meaning. First, as we have said, *dikē* is the Greek word for the standard, whatever it may be in different places, by which men agree to live. Therefore *dikē* comes to mean *justice,* as justice is understood in any particular place. It is therefore true that *injustice* is often the best translation of *adikia*. Secondly, because of this, just as *asebeia* is characteristically sin against God in its attitude, *adikia* is sin against men in its attitude. The verb *adikein* can mean quite simply to hurt; and *adikia* is that attitude of injustice which hurts and injures its fellow men. It is not altogether a true distinction, but it is not altogether wrong to say that *asebeia* hurts God and *adikia* hurts men.

(vii) The seventh word for sin is *opheilēma*. It only occurs once (Matthew 6.12), but that occurrence is of great importance for it is in the Lord's Prayer in the petition: 'Forgive us our debts.' The verb *opheilein* means to *owe a debt. Opheilēma* is that which is *owed*, that which the debtor *ought* to pay, that which is *due*, that which is our *duty* to give.

Sin is a failure in duty to God; and it must always be remembered that the debt we owe to God is not only the debt we owe to a law-giver and to a judge; it is the obligation that we owe to the love than which none can be greater.

(viii) The eighth word for sin is the word *parakoē*. We may best see the meaning of *parakoē* from a study of the verb with which it is connected, *parakouein. Parakouein* has an interesting development in meaning. It begins by meaning to hear imperfectly or indistinctly, as a man hard of hearing might hear. There is first of all what we might call the involuntary meaning of the word in which it means to *misunderstand*. But there is also the deliberate meaning of the word in which it means to refuse to hear, to *disobey* or to *ignore. Parakouein* seems to have begun by meaning a quite accidental and involuntary inability to hear, and then to have gone on to mean a deliberate unwillingness and refusal to listen. So then *parakoē* means disobedience, the deliberate refusal to hear the voice of conscience and of God. It is used three times in the New Testament. By one man's *disobedience* many were made sinners (Romans 5.19). God is ready to punish every *disobedience* (2 Corinthians 10.6). Every transgression and *disobedience* of and to the law has its punishment (Hebrews 2.2). *Parakoē* is the deliberate and self-induced deafness which stifles and silences the voice of God, from whatever source from within or without it may come to a man. The proverb says that there are none so blind as those who will not see, and it is equally true that there are none so deaf as those who will not hear.

(ix) There is one last word at which we may look for it may well introduce still another element into the picture. Paul was rebuking the litigious Corinthians for their liking for going to law. As the AV has it, he says: 'There is utterly a *fault* among you, because ye go to law with one another.' The RSV more correctly has: 'To have law-suits at all with one another is *defeat* for you' (1 Corinthians 6.7). The word is *hēttēma* and it means any kind of defeat. In point of fact it is the technical word for losing a law-suit, and Paul is playing on the word. To go to law at all for a Christian is to lose the case. The NEB loses the metaphor but keeps the meaning: 'Indeed, you already fall below your standard in going to law with one another at all.'

Here is still another idea. Sin is defeat; sin is a man's better knowledge and better self being conquered by that which is below the Christian standard. Sin is goodness worsted in the contest with evil.

These then are the words for sin in the Old and the New Testaments, and surely the effect of the study of them is to make us realize the truth of Paul's sweeping statement: 'All have sinned, and fall short of the glory of God' (Romans 3.23). Man's destiny was to be in the likeness of God, and there is none who has achieved it.

We have now to go on to see how man can be forgiven for his sins. We begin with what we may call man's share in the process of forgiveness.

The one thing which is consistently connected with forgiveness is *repentance*. In Greek the word repentance bears its meaning on its face. The word is *metanoia*, which literally means an *after-thought*. An after-thought is generally a changed thought, just as we speak about having second thoughts about something. If in our after-thought, if on our second thoughts, we see that we have made a very grave mistake, then the after-thought brings with it sorrow, regret and remorse. And, if the sorrow is anything more than a mere passing emotion, it will bring with it an accompanying change of action in which we try to make amends for the mistaken action of the past. So then we may say that repentance involves three stages. It involves, first, new thoughts about some action or situation; regret for the mistake that has been made or the wrong that has been done; determination to amend life in the future and not to make the same mistake or to commit the same sin again. With this summary in our minds let us now go to the New Testament to see what it has to say about the connection of repentance with the forgiveness of sins.

(i) Repentance is the very basis and foundation of the Christian message. The initial invitation of Jesus was 'Repent and believe in the gospel' (Mark 1.15). Even before Jesus arrived on the scene the preparation for his coming was John's baptism which was a baptism of repentance for the remission of sins (Mark 1.5). According to Luke the commission of the Risen Christ was that his disciples should preach repentance and forgiveness of sins in his name to all nations (Luke 24.47). Paul sums up the message he preached throughout the years in Ephesus as a summons to Jew and Greek to repentance to God and faith in our Lord Jesus Christ (Acts 20.21). According to the writer to the Hebrews the most elementary stage of the Christian religion, a stage which those to whom he wrote should long ago have left behind, consists in repentance from dead works and faith toward God (Hebrews 6.1). It is clear that repentance belongs to the very essence of the Christian faith, that repentance is indeed something without which the Christian faith cannot begin at all.

(ii) God's delay in exercising judgement and in withholding the last times is nothing other than the offering to men of a last opportunity to repent. God's kindness is not intended to be an excuse for men to remain as they are; God's kindness is designed to lead men to repent (Romans 2.4). The end of all things is delayed simply in order that all should repent (2 Peter 3.9). Life is designed and prolonged for no other reason than to lead men to repent. In and through every event of life God is pleading with men to repent.

(iii) It is sorrow at our previous way of life and our previous mistakes that leads to repentance. The Corinthians at Paul's rebuke and appeal were grieved into repenting. There is a godly grief which produces a repentance that leads to salvation (2 Corinthians 7.9–10).

There is a very real sense in which the way to repentance is through self-loathing and self-disgust. To come to hate one's present way and one's present self is the way to a new way and a new self. O. Henry has a story of a young man who went from a little village to the great city. In the village he had been brought up in the innocence of a good home and of a good school. In the city he had taken to petty crime and had become a sharp trickster and a pick-pocket and a confidence man. He was well pleased with himself. There had been a girl in the old village days; he had sat beside her in school; he had known her and loved her; but that was a boy and girl affair which belonged to the limbo of the past. Then one day just after he had done a smart job in picking a pocket, quite by chance he saw this girl in the great city. She did not see him, but he saw her. She was just as fresh and sweet and innocent and pure as she had been in the old days when he had known her in the village. He looked at her in all her innocent purity; he looked at himself in all his cheap and tawdry petty crime. He leaned his forehead against the coolness of an iron lamp post. 'God,' he said, 'how I hate myself.' That is precisely the first step to repentance, the realization of what we are and the self-disgust which comes from that realization.

How does that self-realization come? It too is the gift of Jesus. Peter said that it was the function of Jesus to give Israel repentance and forgiveness of sins (Acts 5.31). It is not only salvation that Jesus gives; he also gives the repentance which leads to it. And he does so by opening a man's eyes to a life of beauty which he had never glimpsed before and in comparison with which his own looks soiled and drab. Jesus Christ sets a man's life in the light of his own life, and in the light of that comparison a man can say like Peter: 'Depart from me, for I am a sinful man, O Lord' (Luke 5.8). Jesus Christ wakens that godly sorrow by compelling a man to see himself as he is.

(iv) The only proof that repentance is real is the proof of an amended life. The consistent demand is for fruits which will match the repentance (Matthew 3.8; Luke 3.8; Acts 26.20). The repentance which is confined to words and to emotions is not real. Words of repentance have to be guaranteed by amended deeds; the emotion of regret has to be worked out in action. Repentance is no easy, sentimental, emotional thing in which we say we are sorry and go away and do the same thing again; repentance involves the humiliating experience of self-examination and the determination to be changed.

(v) Repentance, as the New Testament sees it, is intimately connected with two things.

- It is connected with truth. God, writes the author of the Pastoral Epistles, may perhaps grant that they will repent and come to know the truth (2 Timothy 2.25). It is tragically easy for a man to live under a delusion. He can be deluded about himself and he can be deluded about where real happiness lies. Repentance is really seeing things as they are and to see things as they are is to see them in the light of Jesus Christ.

- It is connected with life. God, as Peter said, granted the Gentiles repentance unto life (Acts 11.18) To repent is clearly to leave one life behind and to enter into another life. And the life to which repentance leads is the real life.

Repentance in the New Testament is frequently connected with something else: with the forgiveness of sins. Repentance, baptism and the forgiveness of sins are frequently all connected together. John the Baptist was baptizing with water for repentance (Matthew 3.11; Acts 13.24; 19.4). He was preaching a baptism of repentance for the forgiveness of sins

(Mark 1.4; Luke 3.3). The apostolic summons to the people was: 'Repent and be baptized every one of you in the name of Jesus Christ for the remission of your sins' (Acts 2.38) The invitation of Ananias to the newly converted Paul was 'Be baptized and wash away your sins' (Acts 22.16).

Three things are to be remembered about baptism in the very early Church, the Church of New Testament times.

First, as we have seen earlier, it was necessarily adult baptism. Secondly, baptism was an absolutely definite act of decision; the decision once and for all to break with the old way of life and to accept the new. Thirdly, baptism was commonly by total immersion. It was not necessarily so because sometimes total immersion for practical reasons would be impossible, but it normally was. And in total immersion the symbolism of real washing and real cleansing, and the symbol of dying and rising again is much more vivid.

Baptism was the act of decision; and baptism symbolized the cleansing grace of God and the death to the old life and the resurrection to the new.

It was not that the early Church regarded baptism as something magical and miraculous; it was that in the moment of baptism a man was involved in a situation and in a ritual in which it was easy for him to appropriate the cleansing and the forgiveness offered to him in Jesus Christ. Baptism was the moment of the appropriation of the grace of God.

So then on the human side the forgiveness of sins was indissolubly connected with that repentance in which a man sorrowed for the past and reached out to a new future; and it was appropriated in the moment of baptism which was the moment of decision in all its dramatic vividness.

What exactly does this forgiveness of sins consist of? We shall come best at its meaning by looking at the words and ideas which are used to describe it in both Testaments. We begin with the Old Testament.

The Old Testament has three main words in which it describes the forgiveness of sins. There is the word *kaphar*, which literally means *to hide*. The picture in it is that sin is hidden, put out of sight. The commonest translation of it in the AV is *to make atonement for*. The idea is that sin is put out of sight and thus man and God are at one again. The second of the words is *nasa*. It literally means *to lift up* or *to lift away*. Sin is a burden, and forgiveness lifts it away from a man. The third is *salach*, which means *to send away*. Sin begets debt; sin merits punishment; sin involves guilt. But in forgiveness the debt and the punishment are remitted, sent away.

The words are not really distinguishable in translation, and in an English translation of the Old Testament it is impossible to know which is being used. In Psalm 78.38, 'Yet, he being compassionate *forgave* their iniquity', the word is *kaphar*; in Moses' prayer in Exodus 32.32, 'But now if thou wilt *forgive* their sin', the word is *nasa*; in Jeremiah 31.34, 'I will *forgive* their iniquity', the word is *salach*. Covering, lifting away, sending away – the three ideas all express the same thing, the forgiveness of sin.

In Judaism the forgiveness of sin is connected with sacrifice. And in a sense the sacrifice was the substitute for the sinner. For instance, in the ritual for the Day of Atonement, before the scapegoat is sent off into the wilderness, the priest puts his hand on its head and so to speak transfers to it the sin of the people, and it goes out into the wilderness bearing that sin. But in its highest and its purest form Judaism certainly never thought of any sacrifice as such atoning for sin and removing man's guilt. Judaism at its highest always held that the only thing which can find forgiveness is the penitent heart. 'The sacrifice acceptable to God is a broken spirit; a broken and contrite heart, O God, thou wilt not despise' (Psalm 51.17) is of the very essence of Judaism. Without true penitence and repentance the most costly sacrifice was unavailing; and the sacrifice itself was no more than the material proof and guarantee of the penitence of the heart. By the offering of the sacrifice the suppliant only wished to prove that his penitence went beyond words and was truly real.

We now turn to the New Testament, and, when we do so, we find that the New Testament's vocabulary of forgiveness is amazingly rich and varied.

(i) The commonest New Testament word for forgiveness is the noun *aphesis* and the corresponding verb *aphiēmi*. The apostolic invitation is: 'Repent, and be baptized every one of you for the *forgiveness* of your sins' (Acts 2.38). This is the word which is used in connection with the baptism of John (Mark 1.4). In God's Son we have redemption and the *forgiveness* of sins (Colossians 1.14). 'Take heart, my son,' Jesus said to the paralytic, 'your sins are forgiven' (Matthew 9.2).

The word quite literally means to send away; it then goes on to mean to set free, as cattle are set free in a field, as doves are set free to fly away, as people are set free from some captivity to go their own way. Quite naturally it then goes on to mean to acquit of a charge. It is used of remitting tribute and taxation, and of excusing from some duty. Its main meaning is therefore *the remission of a debt*, which a man ought to have paid and which he could not have paid. Forgiveness absolves a man from the debt to God into which his sins had put him. *Aphesis* is man's liberation from the awful liability to God in which his sin had involved him.

(ii) It is at this point, thus early in our consideration of these New Testament words, that we must take the word *charizesthai*. *Charizesthai* means *to give out of grace as an absolutely free gift*. It is used in Colossians 2.13 'God has *forgiven* us all our trespasses.' It is used of forgiveness both divine and human: 'As the Lord has *forgiven* you, so you also must *forgive* (Colossians 3.13; cf. Ephesians 4.32).

The point of this word, and it is of the very essence of the Christian gospel, is that forgiveness is not something which can be earned or merited or achieved; it is the free gift of the grace of God and a man can do no more than take in humble gratitude that which is offered to him.

(iii) Twice a very vivid word is used of the forgiveness of sins. In Acts 3.19 Peter invites his hearers to repent and to turn again that their sins may be *blotted out*; and in Colossians Paul says that Christ has *cancelled* the bond that stood against us (Colossians 2.14). In both cases the word is *exaleiphein*, which means *to wipe* or *to sponge off*. In the ancient world writing was done on a substance called papyrus, which was made from the pith of the bulrush; in ancient ink there was no acid; it therefore did not bite into the paper, but, as it were, lay on the surface. With a sponge and water writing could quite literally be sponged or wiped off, and so the writing was obliterated and the papyrus left absolutely clean. So because of Jesus Christ, because of what he was and did, the slate is wiped clean and the record is completely expunged.

(iv) There is another New Testament expression which is kin to this. The writer to the Hebrews contrasts the sacrifices which the Levitical priests have to make with the sacrifice which Jesus Christ made. The sacrifices of the Levitical priests have to be made over and over again; the sacrifice of Jesus Christ is made once, finally and for all. As the AV has it, Christ appeared *to put away* sin by the sacrifice of himself (Hebrews 9.26). The RSV retains this translation. Moffatt and the NEB both have *to abolish sin*. In Greek the phrase is *eis athetēsin tēs hamartias*. *Athetēsis* is the noun from the verb *athetein*, and *athetein* is used of cancelling an agreement, of annulling a contract, of abrogating a law. It means to render something inoperative and ineffective and to make it no longer binding and authoritative. In forgiveness the claim of sin is ended, the power of sin is broken, the authority of sin is cancelled. In forgiveness the forgiven man enters into a life in which sin has lost its power and its penalty.

(v) One of the simplest of all the ideas meets us in the name of Jesus. Mary was told to call her son Jesus, 'for he will *save* his people from their sins' (Matthew 1.21). The Greek verb to save is *sōzein*; salvation is *sotēria*; and Jesus is *sōtēr*, the Saviour (John 4.42).

This group of words has two inter-related ideas. First, there is the idea of *rescue* and of *deliverance* in danger. The soldier Apion writes home to his father Epimachus in a papyrus letter that he gives thanks to his god Serapis that Serapis *saved* him (*sozein*) when he was in peril in the storm at sea. These words describe rescue in a situation in which life itself is in danger. So in forgiveness a man is rescued from the perilous situation into which his sin has brought him; he is rescued from that which threatens him with nothing less than the death of the soul.

Secondly, this group of words has to do with *healing* and with *health*. In regard to health *sozein* can mean quite simply *to heal* or *to cure*. Jesus says to the woman who touched him in the crowd: 'Daughter, your faith has *saved*, i.e. *cured*, you' (Mark 5.34). In the papyrus letters one of the commonest of all requests is for information about the correspondent's *soteria*, about his or her *health*. Forgiveness then brings to a man health of life and health of soul. Sin is the sickness of the soul; sin is that which takes the health out of life. In forgiveness sin is defeated and man is restored to health of soul.

(vi) The idea of rescue and deliverance leads us very naturally on to another conception which is connected with forgiveness, the conception of *liberation* and of *freedom*. The New Testament has two words specially connected with this idea.

The first is the word *luein*, which means *to loose*. It occurs in Revelation 1.5. The RSV speaks of him who loves us and who has *freed* us from our sins; Moffatt has, has *loosed* us from our sins; the NEB has, *freed* us from our sins. The idea is that of freeing from shackles and fetters. The idea is that man is bound by the chains of his sin, and in forgiveness these chains are loosed and he is able to go free. Forgiveness is the knocking off of the fetters with which sin binds a man.

(It will be noted that here the AV has *washed* us from our sins. The word for *to free* is *luein* and the word for to wash is *louein*; the pronunciation is exactly the same; the two words are not infrequently confused. Both readings exist in this passage, but *luein*, *to set free*, is to be preferred as the modern translations show.)

The second of these words is *eleutheroun*, which means *to liberate* or *to set free* or *to give freedom to*. Paul speaks of the Christian as having been *set free* from sin (Romans 6.18, 22). 'The spirit of life in Jesus Christ has *set me free* from the law of sin and death' (Romans 8.2). In this case the picture is from slavery. Man as he is is the slave of sin, under the tyranny of sin, sold under sin (Romans 7.14). In forgiveness man is liberated from sin; sin has no more dominion over him, sin cannot lord it over him any more (Romans 6.14). Forgiveness brings freedom from the shackles and liberation from the tyranny of sin.

(vii) There is another group of words which also have a common picture in them. The simplest is the word *apolouein*, which simply means *to wash*. Ananias says to Paul after Paul's conversion: 'Rise and be baptized, and *wash away* your sins' (Acts 22.16). This is the simplest idea of all. In the forgiveness of Jesus Christ the sinner finds that which can cleanse him from the dirt, the stain, the pollution of sin.

A little more elaborate are the words which are connected with *katharos*, which means *pure*. The blood of Jesus *cleanses* us from all sin (1 John 1.7). The word is *katharizein*, which means to make *katharos*, to make pure. The man who slips back into the old impure ways forgets that he has been cleansed from sin (2 Peter 1.9). The expression here is *lambanein katharismon*, to receive *purification*. Such a man forgets that he has received purification and proceeds to pollute himself all over again. When Jesus had *made purification* for sins he sat down at the right hand of the Majesty on high (Hebrews 1.3). Here the expression is *poieisthai katharismon*, which is quite literally to make *purification* for sins.

The point about all these words is this. The word *katharos* in the Old Testament specially does not usually mean *morally* pure, although that is involved. It far more usually means *ritually* pure, that is, in a state and condition in which it is possible to approach God. The man who is *katharos* is free from any of that ritual uncleanness which debars him from the worship and the presence of God.

(viii) Sometimes the New Testament speaks quite simply about sin being *taken away*. Two verbs are used, *hairein* and *aphairein*. Jesus is the lamb of God who *takes away* the sin of the world (John 1.29). Paul quotes from Jeremiah the saying about the new covenant which God will make when he *takes away* the sins of the people (Romans 11.27; Jeremiah 31.33). It is impossible, says the writer to the Hebrews, that the blood of bulls and goats should *take away* sins (Hebrew 10.4). This is like John Bunyan's picture of the pilgrim, whose burden, when he came up with the cross, was rolled away. This means quite simply that when a man is forgiven his sins are removed. As the Psalmist has it: 'As far as the east is from the west, so far does he remove our transgressions from us' (Psalm 103.12). Forgiveness involves the lifting from off our backs of the burden of sin.

(ix) It will be remembered that this idea of lifting away the burden of sin is also an Old Testament idea and that it is contained in the Hebrew word *nasa*; another of the Old Testament ideas recurs in the New Testament, the idea of hiding or covering sin, which is the same idea as is in the Hebrew word *kaphar*. In Greek the word is *epikaluptein* or *kaluptein*, the first of which means *to cover over*, and the second simply *to cover*. Paul quotes Psalm 32.1-2: 'Blessed are those whose iniquities are forgiven (*aphiēmi*), and whose sins are *covered*' (Romans 4.7). Love *covers a* multitude of sins (1 Peter 4.8). To bring back a sinner from the error of his ways is to do something which will *cover* a multitude of sins (James 5.20). In forgiveness a man's sins are covered, so that God puts them out of his sight and never looks at them again.

(x) There is a group of words which are all rendered *expiation* or *propitiation*. God put forward Jesus as an *expiation* by his blood (Romans 3.25), where the word is *hilastērion*. Jesus Christ is the *expiation* (*hilasmos*) for our sins (1 John 2.2; 4.10). Jesus Christ is the perfect High Priest, who came *to make expiation* (*hilaskesthai*) for the sins of the people (Hebrews 2.17). At the back of all these words there is a sacrificial picture. Now the essence of a sacrifice is that by it and through it the interrupted relationship with God is restored. Because of what Jesus is and did in forgiveness the interrupted relationship between man and God is restored. Through his sacrifice man and God come together again.

(xi) This brings us finally to two great pictures in the thought of Paul which tell of what happens in forgiveness. The first is the picture of *justification*. Since we are *justified* by faith we have peace with God (Romans 5.1). One thing makes it clear that the New Testament is not using this word *justify* in the normal English sense of the term. If we justify a person, we find reasons to prove that he was right and correct to act as he did. But in Romans 4.5 Paul speaks about God who justifies the ungodly. Now quite certainly God does not produce reasons to prove that the ungodly man is right to be as he is. We must look for some other meaning of the word. In Greek the word translated *to justify* is *dikaioun*. Greek verbs which end in *-oun* do not mean *to make* a man something; they mean *to reckon, account, treat* a man as something; and to say that God *justifies* the ungodly is to say that God treats the sinner as if he had been a good man. Here is the very essence of the gospel. This is exactly what the father did with the rebellious son in the parable; he treated him as if he had never been away. God in his astonishing mercy, instead of treating the sinner like a criminal, treats him as if he had been a good man. In forgiveness we discover that, if we return to God, we return not to an avenging king, not to an offended judge, but to a loving father who treats his erring child with all the love that by rights should only go to a good man. In forgiveness we learn the amazing truth that, sinners as we are, God still loves us as if we had been altogether good. That is what justification means.

(xii) So we come to the last of the pictures. It is the picture *of reconciliation*. Jesus, says Paul, through whom we have now received our reconciliation (Romans 5.11). God through Christ reconciled us to himself (2 Corinthians 5.18–20). The word is *katallagē*; and this is the regular word of the bringing together of two people who have drifted apart and who have become estranged. It is to be noted – and to this we shall return – that the New Testament never speaks of God being reconciled to us, but always of us being reconciled to God; the drifting away and the estrangement were all on our side; the love of God was ever constant and unceasing and undefeated. In forgiveness we find ourselves once again friends with God. In forgiveness we come home and we find that the everlasting arms are open to receive us, and we are no longer estranged from God.

Such then is the New Testament vocabulary of forgiveness. It is a rich and varied vocabulary for a great and precious experience; and the wide variety of it, and the many-sidedness of its pictures is the proof that in whatever situation a man is, from wherever he starts out, there is a way to forgiveness for him and whatever his need it will be met in the forgiveness of God.

There now arises one question which every Christian is bound to ask. *What is the part that Jesus plays in the forgiveness of sins?* In what way is the forgiveness of sins connected with what he was and what he did?

We may begin by noting quite generally that the New Testament gives us ample evidence out of Jesus' own mouth as to why he came into this world. In the Gospels the phrase 'I came' or its equivalent is often to be heard on his lips.

There are certain hard and stern sayings on his lips. He came not to bring peace but a sword, and the result of his coming would be a cleavage and a division which would cut across the nearest and the dearest of earthly ties (Matthew 10.34–9). The very fact that Jesus Christ demands decision must mean that some will accept him and some will reject him. The very fact that he demands a loyalty which surpasses all earthly loyalties must mean that there are bound to be tensions. Decision for Christ may well mean the cleavage from those who will not make the same decision. He came to cast fire on the earth (Luke 12.49), and in the New Testament fire always stands at least in part for judgement. There is that in life and in the world which the coming of Jesus Christ must necessarily destroy. He came for judgement. 'For judgement I came into this world' (John 9.39). Yet at the same time he did not come for judgement. 'I did not come to judge the world but to save the world' (John 12.47). The explanation of the apparent contradiction is that Jesus came with the sole intention of saving the world. But confrontation with Jesus demands a decision Every man must have a reaction to Jesus Christ. If his reaction is that his heart runs out to Jesus Christ, then it is well; if his reaction is dislike, resentment, evasion, then by that reaction he has condemned himself. If a man finds nothing lovely in Jesus Christ, then he stands, not condemned by Jesus Christ, but self-condemned.

But even these hard sayings are the results and the consequences of the fact that Jesus came with an offer so great that a man refuses it at the peril of his soul. So now we turn to the great and gracious sayings.

(i) Jesus came for *revelation*. 'I have come as a light into the world' (John 12.46). He came to shed the revealing light on man, on life, on the world, on God. The revelation of the true involves the revelation of the false. There cannot be one without the other. Jesus came with the revealing light in which a man may see himself and see God.

(ii) Jesus came for *fulfilment* and not for destruction. 'I have come not to abolish the law and the prophets but to fulfil them' (Matthew 5.17). He came not to destroy the hopes of men but to fulfil them. He came to be that which all the seeking of man had sought and never found, that to which all the searching of man had pointed and had never reached, that for which the heart of man had always hoped but had never attained. In him man's haunting dream of God came true.

(iii) Jesus came with an *invitation* to those who needed it most. 'I came, not to call the righteous, but sinners to repentance' (Matthew 9.13). Like a wise and compassionate doctor his great interest was in those who were sick in soul and who knew it. He came with a special invitation precisely to those whom men despised and condemned. A man will never seek a cure until he realizes that he is ill; Jesus could not penetrate the resisting armour of those who were conscious of their own goodness; but the way to the hearts of those who were bitterly conscious of their own sin was wide open to him.

(iv) Jesus came with a *search*. 'The Son of Man came to seek and to save the lost' (Luke 19.10). He was like the shepherd who went out to search for and to rescue those who had taken the wrong way and who were lost far away from God (Luke 15.3–7). In this he had reversed the common Jewish attitude, for Jewish orthodoxy would have said that there is joy in heaven when sinners perish from the earth, whereas Jesus said that there was joy in heaven when one lost sinner was found and brought home.

(v) Finally there is one all-important fact. According to the Fourth Gospel Jesus said: 'I have come in my Father's name' (John 5.43). There were two ways in which this saying may be interpreted.

– In Hebrew the *name* does not stand only for the name by which a person is called; it stands for the nature and the character of the person so far as they are known and revealed. When the Psalmist said: 'Those who know thy name put their trust in thee' (Psalm 9.10), he did not mean that those who know the name by which God is called, the name Jahweh, put their trust in him; he meant that those who know the nature and the character of God as he is, have no difficulty in trusting him. If we interpret this saying of Jesus along these lines it means that Jesus is saying: 'I have come to you in and with the nature and the character of God. In me you see what God is like.' And this is true.

— In Greek the phrase *in the name of* has an almost technical usage. There is a papyrus which tells of the accession of an Emperor and the attendant ceremonies. The ceremonies in a village are being recorded; and it is said that the elders of the village offered sacrifice for the welfare of the Emperor in *the name of the whole village*. There the meaning is as *representing*. If we take this line of interpretation it will mean that Jesus is saying: 'I have come representing, as the representative of, God.'

In point of fact both interpretations come in the end to much the same, for they both mean that in Jesus we see the character and the nature and the action of God. And the supremely important thing about this is that it means that in Jesus' attitude to sin and to the sinner we see the attitude of God to the sin and the sinner. When we see Jesus dealing with the sinner, we can say: 'This is the way in which God himself deals with sin and with the sinner.'

Given, then, that there is this close connection with Jesus and the forgiveness of sins, wherein does that connection lie?

It may well be that at the end of the day we shall have to be content with the attitude of Rufinus in his exposition of the creed. Rufinus in effect says that no one can explain the wonder of the forgiveness of sins; you can only accept it. 'As regards the forgiveness of sin,' Rufinus says, 'a bare act of faith ought to be sufficient. Who would search for cause or explanation when a prince's bounty is in question? An earthly monarch's generosity is scarcely a fit subject for argument. Then is God's largesse going to be argued about by presumptuous human beings?' As Rufinus sees it, we should be lost in wonder, love and praise – and we should leave it at that. But even if we cannot come at the whole truth, we may still try to find part of the truth.

(i) It may be that the simplest explanation is that our forgiveness was won by the fact that Jesus Christ bore the punishment that should have fallen on us. This is the view which Pearson puts forward at its sharpest in his *Exposition of the Creed*. We outline his argument and his point of view:

Sin is characteristically transgression of the law (1 John 3.4). Sin is 'to do what God forbiddeth and to omit that which God commandeth.' If this be so, sin causes guilt. And guilt is 'a debt or obligation to suffer a punishment proportionate to the iniquity of the sin'. Now there can be no forgiveness of sin and no remission of this penalty without shedding of blood (Hebrews 9.22). Therefore the blood of Christ must be involved in the forgiveness of sins. His dying for our sins 'was suffering death as a punishment taken upon himself to free us from the punishment due unto our sins'. God laid on him the iniquity of us all (Isaiah 53.6). He who knew no sin was made sin for us (2 Corinthians 5.21).

Forgiveness, then, involves 'the reconciliation of an offended God, and a satisfaction unto a just God'. God was offended by our sins and Christ by his death reconciled God to men. 'He which before was angry with us upon the consideration of Christ's death became propitious unto us.' 'Christ did render God propitious unto us by his blood who before was offended with us for our sins.' Reconciliation is 'kindness after wrath', and it was this that Christ produced in God. 'God was most certainly offended before he gave us a redeemer.' 'The punishment which Christ who was our surety endured was a full satisfaction to the will and justice of God.' His suffering and death was accepted 'in full compensation and satisfaction for the punishment which was due' to be inflicted on us.

Here forgiveness by substitution is stated at its sharpest and most definite. God was angry with men; the only thing that would appease that anger was the infliction of the punishment due to sin; that punishment should have been inflicted on us; it was in fact inflicted on Jesus Christ; and thus the anger of God was turned to mercy. It was the sacrifice of Christ which turned God's wrath to love.

(ii) There is no doubt at all that the New Testament does see the death of Jesus as a sacrifice for sin. When Paul was stating the basic and fundamental and essential Christian message which had been passed on to him, the very first article in it is, 'Christ died for our sins' (1 Corinthians 15.3). The Letter to the Ephesians speaks of Christ giving himself up as a sacrifice and an offering to God (Ephesians 5.2). The writer to the Hebrews says that we have been sanctified by the offering of the body of Jesus Christ once and for all (Hebrews 10.10).

Although the actual words *sacrifice* and *offering* are not often used, the idea is there all through the New Testament. Christ died for the ungodly, and it was while we were yet sinners that he died for us (Romans 5.6, 8). We must do nothing to injure or ruin the man for whom Christ died (Romans 14.15). Christ died for all (2 Corinthians 5.14, 15). He who knew no sin was made sin for us (2 Corinthians 5.21). Christ became a curse for us (Galatians 3.13). He experienced death for all (Hebrews 2.9). He offered for all time a single sacrifice for sin (Hebrews 10.12). Christ suffered for us; he bore our sins in his body on the tree (1 Peter 2.21, 24). He died for sins once and for all, the righteous for the unrighteous (1 Peter 3.18).

Most definite of all these sayings is the saying in which Jesus says that he came to give his life a ransom (*lutron*) for many (Mark 10.45; Matthew 20.28). But there are certain facts to be noted before we can come at the full meaning of this idea.

- Again and again the New Testament does not speak of Jesus *being sacrificed* but of him *giving himself* for us. The normal sacrificial victim is an animal whose share in the event of sacrifice is passive and involuntary. Whatever Jesus did, he willingly and consciously chose to do. The Lord Jesus Christ who *gave himself* for our sins, says Paul (Galatians 1.4). The Son of God, he says, who loved me and *gave himself* for me (Galatians 2.20). He *gave himself* up as an offering and a sacrifice for us (Ephesians 5.2). Christ loved the Church and *gave himself up* for it (Ephesians 5.25). He *gave himself* as a ransom for all (1 Timothy 2.6). He *gave himself* for us (Titus 2.14). He *laid down* his life for us (1 John 3.16), and the greatest love of all is the love which makes a man lay down his life for his friends (John 15.13).

- The sacrificial character of the death of Jesus is underlined in the words spoken at the Last Supper. His body is broken for them; his blood is shed for many (Mark 14.24; Luke 22.20; 1 Corinthians 11.24). 'The bread I shall give for the life of the world is my flesh' (John 6.51). In particular this emerges in the Pauline version of the saying with the cup: 'This cup is the new covenant in my blood' (1 Corinthians 11.25). A covenant is a relationship between two people, and the covenant of which Jesus speaks is the new relationship between God and man. This, he says, is *in my blood*. It is entirely likely that the *in* (*en*) translates the Hebrew word *be, at the price of*. And, if that be so, Jesus was saying: 'This cup stands for the new relationship between God and man made possible at the cost of my blood, at the price of my death.' Here again Jesus is saying that he was voluntarily giving his life to establish a relationship between man and God which was otherwise impossible.

— We have to add still another fact to this. There are places in the New Testament, and they are very important places, where it is quite clear that the initiative, the dynamic, the motive power behind the whole process of man's salvation is the love of God. It was because God so loved the world that he gave his Son (John 3.16). He did not spare his own Son but gave him up for us all (Romans 8.32). So far from there being behind this process an angry and offended God, there is a God in whose heart there is such a passion of love that he gives his Son to mend the terrible and tragic situation.

It is further a most significant fact that, as we have seen, nowhere in the New Testament is it ever said that God is reconciled to men, but always that men are reconciled to God. While we were enemies we were reconciled to God by the death of his Son (Romans 5.10). God was in Christ reconciling the world to himself. The appeal of the gospel is: 'Be reconciled to God' (2 Corinthians 5.19–20). It was the aim of Jesus to reconcile both Jew and Gentile to God (Ephesians 2.16). It was God's aim through Jesus Christ to reconcile all things to himself. Men who were once estranged, hostile, sinning, Jesus Christ has reconciled in the body of his flesh by his death (Colossians 1.20–2). There is no instance of any statement in the New Testament in which it is said that God is reconciled to men; the reconciliation is always of man to God. The picture of an angry and an offended God does not come from the New Testament.

— To all this there must be added still one other extremely important fact. The New Testament speaks of Jesus Christ giving his life *for* men in one way or another, between twenty and thirty times. In every case but one the preposition used in Greek for *for* is *huper*, which means *for the sake of*, on *behalf of*, and not *instead of*, which would be *anti*. In only one saying is *anti* used and that is in the saying that Jesus came to give his life a ransom *for* many (Mark 10.45; Matthew 20.28). The evidence overwhelmingly states that Jesus did not suffer and die *instead of us*; he suffered and died *for the sake of us*. And in the one case in which *anti* is used the meaning is rather that he paid for us a price that we ourselves could never have paid;

he paid the price instead of us. When we go to the New Testament itself we find that the evidence that the death of Jesus was in substitution for us is almost non-existent.

So then, when we examine the evidence of the New Testament, we find that to all intents and purposes there is no evidence for the picture of an offended God and there is no evidence that God punished Jesus instead of us.

And surely in all reverence we may say this: that if God punished Jesus instead of us to satisfy his outraged justice, then in what would be an intolerable paradox he satisfied his justice by an act of staggering injustice, for he punished the one person in this universe who was totally innocent.

(iii) How then has the element of sacrifice which unquestionably does attach to the death of Christ to be explained? It comes from the fact that all the early thinkers were Jews, and they could only explain their experience of Jesus Christ in the terms that they knew. For a Jew sacrifice had only one function – it was through sacrifice that the relationship between man and God was restored when that relationship was lost, broken and interrupted by sin, and that relationship could not be restored in any other way.

To us the sacrifice of animals is quite alien and quite strange; but what we can clearly and unequivocally say is that *it cost the life and death of Jesus Christ to restore the lost relationship between God and man.* But how? If God does not need to be pacified, if God is not outraged justice at all, if at the back of all this, there stands the wondrous love of God, wherein the necessity of the death of Christ?

The truth, as usual with truth, is very simple. Before Jesus came no man knew what God was like; men thought of God as king and judge, as justice and holiness, as wrath and vengeance; but they never conceived of the supreme wonder of the love of God. So in Jesus Christ God comes to men, and he says: 'I love you like that.' When we see Jesus healing the sick feeding the hungry being the friend of outcasts and sinners this is God saying: 'I love you like that.' When we see Jesus still refusing to do anything but love even when men betray and insult and revile him this is God saying: 'I love you like that.' And if Jesus had stopped before the cross it would have meant that there was some point beyond which the love of God would not go, but because Jesus, having loved men, loved them to the end, it means that there is nothing which can alter the love of God. It means that God in Jesus Christ says: 'You can betray me; you can hate me; you can misjudge me; you can scourge me; you can crucify me; and nothing you can do can alter my love.' No man ever thought of God like that and no man ever could have thought of God like that. This is staggeringly new and utterly undiscoverable by any human means. Only Jesus Christ could tell men that. And therefore it is most literally true to say that *it cost the life and death of Jesus Christ to reconcile men to God.* Had it not been for the life and the death and the cross of Christ, no man would ever have known what God is like.

And so the essence of Jesus is not that he altered God, not that he changed a wrathful and offended God into a loving and forgiving God, but that he died to show men what God is always like, not that he should threaten us into a prudential response, but that at the sight of him we should be moved and compelled to love him as he first loved us. Jesus came not to persuade God to forgive us, but to tell us that God in his love has forgiven us, and that all that we can do is in wondering gratitude to accept the forgiveness of sins, which it cost the cross to make known to us.

CHAPTER TWENTY

In the Resurrection of the Body

For many people in every age of the Church this has been one of the most difficult articles in the creed. If it is difficult as it stands, it is still more difficult when it is translated literally, for in the Greek what is believed in is *anastasis sarkos*, and in the Latin *resurrectio carnis*, which both mean literally, not the resurrection of the *body*, but the resurrection of the *flesh*. Somehow the word *flesh* sounds even more crudely physical and materialistic than the word *body*. *And*, further, very largely due to Paul's use of the word, the word flesh has always had an atmosphere of evil about it; the flesh is the source of that weakness both physical and moral which can bring life to ruin; the flesh is that which is subject to the dangerous temptations; the flesh is that part of man which gives sin its bridgehead, and which is most vulnerable to the assaults of evil. In Paul it is largely true to say that the flesh is human nature without God.

Up until 1543 this article did in fact read in the English creeds, 'I believe in the resurrection of the flesh', and the first appearance of the form, 'I believe in the resurrection of the body' is in a book entitled *A Necessary Doctrine and Erudition for any Christian Man*, commonly called *The King's Book*, published in that year. And it is to be noted that to this day in the Baptismal Service in the Book of Common Prayer, the creed in its interrogative form, that is to say in the form in which it is put to the adult person to be baptized, this section still reads: 'And dost thou believe in the Holy Ghost; the Holy Catholick Church; the Communion of Saints; the resurrection of the flesh; and everlasting life after death?'

It is further to be noted that the phrase *the resurrection of the flesh* is not a scriptural phrase at all. The word for resurrection, *anastasis*, occurs about forty times in the New Testament. It is used eight times of the resurrection of Jesus. When it is used of men it appears simply as *the resurrection* fourteen times; eleven times it is accompanied by *nekrōn* or *tōn nekrōn,* which means the resurrection of the dead; twice it appears as the resurrection *ek nekrōn* or *ek tōn nekrōn,* which means the resurrection from the dead or from among the dead. On five occasions it has descriptive phrases attached to it: the resurrection of the just (Luke 14.14); the resurrection of life and the resurrection of judgement (John 5.29); the resurrection of the just and of the unjust (Acts 24.15); the first resurrection (Revelation 20.5, 6). Typical occurrences of the words are: *resurrection* alone, Matthew 22.23, 28, 30; Mark 12.18, 23; Luke 20.27, 33; John 11.24, 25; Acts 17.18; 23.8; 2 Timothy 2.18; *resurrection of the dead,* Matthew 22.31; Acts 17.32; 23.6; 24.21; 26.23; 1 Corinthians 15.12, 13, 21, 42; *resurrection from the dead,* Luke 20.35; Acts 4.2. Scripture does not speak either of the resurrection of the body or of the resurrection of the flesh.

The only passages in Scripture which come near to this at all are Job 19.26, where the Greek version – not the Hebrew – has: 'Thou wilt raise up my flesh', and Psalm 16.9: 'My flesh also shall rest in hope.' Where then does this idea of the resurrection of the flesh come from and why is it so prominent and emphatic in this creed?

(i) The resurrection of the body was a standard Jewish belief in the time between the Testaments. In those days the Jews in their captivities and their humiliations dreamed of the day when God would intervene and vindicate them and show that they were his own peculiar people. Clearly it was only just that those who had suffered would also be rewarded, and so the belief arose that they with their bodies would be resurrected to share in the final triumph and joy and judgement. The promise in Enoch is: 'And in those days will the earth also give back those who are treasured up within it, and Sheol also will give back that which it has received, and Hell will give back that which it owes' (Enoch 51.1–2). Fourth Esdras has it: 'The earth gives up again they that rest in her, the dust returns them that sleep in her, the chambers deliver up the souls that were committed unto them' (4 Esdras 7.32-3). Even within the Old Testament itself we get this note: 'Thy dead shall live again; their bodies shall rise. O dwellers in the dust, awake and sing for joy!' (Isaiah 26.19).

In Judaism between the Testaments and contemporary with the New Testament there was a strong belief in the resurrection of the body. This belief could even extend to the length of believing that a man would be resurrected in the clothes in which he was buried, for which reason, we are told, there were Rabbis who gave the minutest instructions about the clothes in which their dead bodies were to be buried.

Here then is a positive influence behind the insertion of this article into the creed. But creeds, as we know, are almost always worked out to defend the faith against the attacks of some heresy. If then the Apostles' Creed emphatically declares its belief in the resurrection of the body, we can quite certainly conclude that there were those who attacked that belief. Were there such people at the time that the creed was composed?

(ii) It was characteristic of Greek thought to despise the body. The Greek thinkers thought of the body as the greatest handicap to the attainment of true knowledge and true goodness. 'The body', said the Orphics away back in the 6th century BC, 'is a tomb.' Philolaus said that the body is a house of detention in which the soul is imprisoned. The study of philosophy, said Plato, is nothing other than the study of dying and of being dead – and the assumption is that the body will not survive death. Epictetus said that he was a poor soul shackled to a corpse. Seneca talks of the detestable habitation of the body, and of the vain flesh in which the soul is imprisoned.

Now this is why the Greeks believed in the immortality of the soul, and the one thing they aimed at was the destruction of the body, for this meant the liberation of the soul. It is precisely against that way of thinking that this article of the creed is directed.

(iii) This type of thought reached its peak in Gnosticism, which, as we have seen in Chapter 4, began from the conviction that there are two realities in the world, both equally eternal: spirit and matter. But in this matter there is a flaw; the world is made out of bad stuff. Which means that the body too is essentially evil, incurably evil; and that all a man can hope and pray for is the total obliteration of the body and the survival of pure spirit. A belief like that would regard the resurrection of the body as the worst possible thing that could happen.

Now this Gnostic belief is the very reverse of Christian belief. The Christian believes that God created man body, soul and spirit; and that body, soul and spirit all belong to God. The Christian does not believe that there is one part of man which is beyond salvation and fit only for obliteration; the Christian believes that man can be saved as a whole; the Christian believes – and to this we will later return-that a man can glorify

God with his body, that his body can be a sacrifice to God, that his body can become nothing less than the temple and the dwelling-place of the Holy Spirit (1 Corinthians 6.19-20; Romans 12.1).

We must now go on to see how the Greek and Gnostic ideas reacted on Christian belief and on Christian theology, and what errors this line of thought produced.

There were undoubtedly in the Church those who held the Greek view of the immortality of the soul rather than the resurrection of the body. Justin Martyr refers in condemnation to 'those who say that there is no resurrection of the dead, and that their souls, when they die, are taken to heaven' (*Dialogue with Trypho* 80). Against this belief the Church set its face. Justin (*On the Resurrection* 8) makes the point this way: man is a composite creature; he is body and soul; you cannot say of the body, 'This is the man', and no more can you say of the soul, 'This is the man'. Man is body and soul together. And God calls *man* to resurrection, not a part of man but the *whole* man. Therefore, to say that only the soul is immortal is to say that only a part of man can be redeemed and enter into life eternal. It is therefore necessary in the very essence of Christianity to believe in the resurrection of the body. In a sense this belief in the immortality of the soul rather than in the resurrection of the body was not one of the supremely dangerous deviations; it was an error, but it was not as serious an error as those at which we must go on to look.

That the error was there is clear. Polycarp counts as 'the first-born of Satan' the man who says that there is 'neither resurrection nor judgement' (*To the Philippians* 7). Irenaeus, holding the belief that man is made in the image of God (Genesis 1.27), says that those who despise the body therefore despise the workmanship of God. These men may be reluctant to believe in the resurrection of the body, but the day will come when they will rise in the body to receive their own judgement and condemnation (*Against Heresies* 1.22.1). He makes another interesting point: Jesus himself in the sacrament of the Lord's Supper speaks of giving his body and his blood as the means of salvation. His body was a human body, and how can we despise that through which salvation comes to men? (*Against Heresies* 5.2.2).

It is clear how real and troubled an issue this was within the early Church.

There is a verse in the New Testament itself which will provide us with an approach to the even more serious errors. In 2 Timothy 2.18 we read of those who hold that 'the resurrection is past already'. It is here that the really dangerous error emerges. How could these mistaken thinkers say that the resurrection was past already, that the resurrection had already taken place? They did so in two ways.

(i) There were those who regarded the resurrection of man as a purely spiritual experience which can happen here and now. There were those who regarded a man's resurrection as happening on the day when he came to a knowledge of the truth in Jesus Christ. Tertullian speaks of those who believed that a man's resurrection took place on the day of his baptism. On that day a man is reanimated by access to the truth; he has dispersed the death of ignorance; he has burst forth from the sepulchre of the old man; he has put on Christ (*Concerning the Resurrection of the Flesh* 19). This kind of belief had already emerged in Philo, the Jewish thinker, who held, for instance, that the translation of Enoch was Enoch's conversion from a lower to a higher moral stage of life (*Concerning Abraham* 3.4).

It is possible to support this interpretation of our resurrection from the Pauline view of baptism, in which Paul speaks of us as dying and rising with Christ, of being buried with him in baptism and rising with him to newness of life (Romans 6.5-11). But it is abundantly clear from the rest of his writings that though Paul could write like this about the spiritual experience of baptism, he still believed intensely in the resurrection of the body after death. To support the doctrine that resurrection is a spiritual experience undergone in baptism is to make the mistake of isolating one passage in Paul and of failing to take into account the whole tenor of his thought.

This was bad enough when the resurrection was held to come through baptism into Jesus Christ; it was infinitely worse when there emerged heretics who taught that baptism into *them* produced the resurrection in men. Irenaeus tells us that Simon and the Carpocratians hold that the resurrection from the dead is simply an acquaintance with the truth which they taught (*Against Heresies* 2.31.2). Simon Magus (Acts 8) became in the early Church the man who was considered to be the great arch-heretic. He had a kind of successor called Menander, and this type of belief was particularly connected with Menander. Irenaeus says of him that he claimed that 'his disciples obtain the resurrection by being baptized into him, and can die no more, but remain in possession of immortal youth' (*Against Heresies* 1.23.5). Tertullian says that he taught that all who partake of his baptism become immortal, incorruptible, instantaneously invested with resurrection-life' (*Concerning the Soul* 50). Justin Martyr says that he persuaded his followers that they would never die (*First Apology* 26).

Here was extremely dangerous teaching. It might be possible to 'demythologize' the resurrection of the body into a spiritual experience, received at baptism, when a man entered into newness of life, and shared the resurrection life of Jesus Christ. That is a not impossible interpretation; but when the resurrection came to be connected with baptism into an apparently megalomaniac heretic then this is the destruction of the faith.

(ii) But there was another interpretation of man's resurrection, which came into the Church as early as the second century and which has lasted down to the present day. It was held that a man was resurrected in his children, that he continued to live in the children whom he left in the world. This is expressed in many places in the early writings and in particular in the Acts of Paul and Thecla (14). There people are spoken of who hold that 'the resurrection has already come to pass in the children that we have, and we rise again when we come to the knowledge of the true God'. In that sentence both the beliefs of which we are thinking are summarized together. According to this belief a man has no individual continuance; he continues in his children. It is not so much the individual man who is resurrected as that mankind continues to live.

It is of course true that a man lives on in his children, but Christianity could never accept this view, because Christianity could never accept the obliteration of the individual. Christianity has always thought in concrete terms of individual men, and not in abstractions like mankind or humanity.

So, then, as we shall go on to see, again and again and again the early Church affirmed and reaffirmed its belief in the resurrection of the body as against those who held only the immortality of the soul, and those who spiritualized the whole conception, and those who saw the resurrection in the continuance of the race in their children.

But before we go on to cite the evidence for the universality of this belief, we must note that the great thinkers of the Church were not unaware of certain difficulties. Let us remember that what the creed lays down is the resurrection of the *flesh* (Greek, *sarkos*; Latin, *carnis*). Now, they were immediately confronted with the quite definite saying of Paul: 'I tell you this, brethren, flesh and blood cannot inherit the kingdom of God' (1 Corinthians 15.50). This seems bluntly and absolutely to deny the resurrection of the flesh.

Two of the ancient writers faced this problem fairly and squarely, Irenaeus *(Against Heresies* 5.9.1) and Tertullian *(On the Resurrection of the Flesh* 50). Both make largely the same point: that it is not from resurrection that the flesh is excluded, but from the *kingdom*. The flesh is resurrected certainly, but what it is resurrected to is judgement. And both make the point that now there enters into matter a power which can never be left out, and which no Christian thinker would dream of leaving out – the power of the Spirit. The promise is not to the flesh as such; for the flesh destitute of the Spirit indeed cannot inherit the kingdom of God. The promise is to the flesh quickened, made alive, vivified by the Spirit. The Spirit is still needed, in Tertullian's phrase, 'to qualify' flesh and blood for the kingdom. The fact of course is that this article of the creed must be read in a Christian context, and the Christian context is the Spirit, for the Spirit is the person in whom the Christian lives. The creed has already expressed its belief in the Holy Spirit, and the resurrection of the flesh is for the flesh which has experienced the power of the Spirit, as every true Christian must have experienced it.

In the early Church the resurrection of the flesh became an article of belief universally accepted wherever orthodoxy held sway. It was, as Justin Martyr said, something in which every right-minded Christian believed *(Dialogue with Trypho* 80). Whenever the early writers make a kind of credal statement of their beliefs, they include the belief in the resurrection of the flesh. Irenaeus expresses his belief in the coming manifestation of Christ Jesus our Lord from heaven 'to raise up anew all flesh of the whole human race' *(Against Heresies* 1.10.1).

Tertullian says: 'He will come again to take the saints to the enjoyment of everlasting life and of the heavenly promises, and to condemn the wicked to everlasting fire, after the resurrection of both these classes shall have happened, together with the restoration of their flesh' *(On Prescription Against Heresies* 13). Christ is destined, he says, to come to judge the quick and the dead through the resurrection of the flesh as well as of the spirit *(On the Veiling of Virgins* 1). God, says Theophilus of

Antioch, will raise your flesh immortal with your soul (*To Autolycus* 1.7). We believe, says Tatian, that there will be a resurrection of bodies, after the consummation of all things (*To the Greeks* 6).

Sometimes the belief in the resurrection of the flesh was used with great nobility. Sometimes it was used as the reason for purity and chastity. If the body was to be raised, if the flesh was as immortal as the spirit, then there was a new and compelling reason for using the body honourably and for keeping it pure and chaste. In 2 Clement (9.1–6) there is a notable passage which makes this plea: 'Let none of you say that the flesh is not judged and does not rise again. Understand! In what state did you receive salvation, in what state did you receive your sight, except in the flesh? We must therefore guard the flesh as a temple of God, for as you were called in the flesh, you shall also come in the flesh. If Christ, the Lord who saved us, though he was originally spirit, became flesh and so called us, so also we shall receive our reward in the flesh. Let us then love one another that we may all attain to the kingdom of God.' In the Shepherd of Hermas there is the same kind of passage: 'Guard this flesh of yours, pure and undefiled, that the spirit which dwells in it may bear it witness, and your flesh may be justified. See to it, lest the idea enter your heart that this flesh of yours is mortal, and you can abuse it in some defilement. For if you defile your flesh, you defile also the Holy Spirit.' If a man has defiled the flesh, God can forgive and God can cure, 'if for the future you defile neither the flesh nor the spirit; for both are in communion, and neither can be defiled without the other. Keep therefore both pure and you shall live to God' (The Shepherd of Hermas, *The Similitudes* 5.7.2). The idea is, says Rufinus, that each of the faithful should realize that if only he keeps his flesh clean from sin, it will be a vessel of honour, useful to the Lord and serviceable for every good work, whereas if he allows it to be sullied by sin, it will be a vessel of wrath fitted for destruction (*A Commentary on the Apostles' Creed* 43).

But it is very obvious that, while this idea is capable of a noble interpretation, it is equally possible for it to be held and stated with crude and materialistic literalism, and it was too often the cruder type of interpretation which was offered.

Rufinus in the passage which we have just quoted says that his Church, the Church of Aquileia, had added one word to the creed, and recited this article in the form: 'I believe in the resurrection of *this* flesh'.

Then he goes on: 'The word *this* of course refers to the actual flesh of
the Christian who recites the creed.' This belief came to be stated with
more and more literalism. Centuries later, Pearson in his great work *On
the Creed* was to say that God knows all the scattered bones of men
wherever they are; he knows the dust into which their bodies have
turned. He knows the ways and means by which 'this ruined fabric
should be restored; he knows how every bone should be brought to its
old neighbour-bone, how every sinew may be re-embroidered on it;
he understands what are the proper parts to be conjoined, what is the
proper gluten by which they may become united.' The belief becomes a
literal belief in the resurrection of this actual body.

All of the flesh, says Tertullian, rises again, the very flesh itself, the
whole of it (*On the Resurrection of the Flesh* 63). Tatian says: 'Even though
fire destroy all traces of my flesh, the world receives the vaporized matter; and though dispersed through rivers and seas, or torn in pieces by
wild beasts, I am laid up in the storehouses of a wealthy Lord. And,
although the poor and godless know not what is stored up, yet God the
Sovereign, when he pleases, will restore the substance that is visible to
him alone to its pristine condition' (*To the Greeks* 6). Burned, drowned,
torn in pieces, the flesh will be restored. Theophilus of Antioch uses a
strange idea. When you are ill you lose flesh; when you recover you gain
flesh. You do not know where the flesh went to and you do not know
where it comes back from! If God can do that, he can resurrect the flesh
(*To Autolycus* 1.13).

Rufinus addresses those who argue that 'human flesh rots and disintegrates or else is changed into dust; it is sometimes sucked under the sea
and dispersed under the waves', and who ask how it can ever be got
together again. He cites the analogy of a seed planted in the ground, and
in any event, he says, to doubt that this can happen is simply to doubt
the power of God. 'Each soul has restored to it, not a composite nor an
alien body, but the actual one it formerly possessed' (*A Commentary on the
Apostles' Creed* 42–3).

Justin Martyr wrote a book on this subject of which parts remain.
People will say that that which has decayed and dissolved cannot be
restored; and they will say that the flesh is the cause of infirmities and of
sin, and, if it rises, so do they. Justin argues that, either the body rises
entirely or it rises imperfectly and only in part. If the body rises only in

part, then God cannot be all-powerful, for it means that he can only raise part of the body. But if the body rises then the desires and passions of the body rise with it. But, says Justin, even in this world there are those who have conquered passion and lived in virginity; much more in the world to come. But, says the objector, what happens to bodies which were maimed and wounded? Justin answered that on earth Jesus healed men's diseases; how much more in heaven?

The most astonishing example of this literalism is, in Augustine (*The City of God* 22.20) where, among other questions Augustine discusses what is to happen to the flesh of a man who was cannibalistically eaten by another man! Even this flesh will be restored. 'The flesh of the man that was eaten shall return to the first owner from whom the famished man who ate it does but, as it were borrow it, and must repay it again.' Surely crude literalism can go no further than this.

There were not wanting those in the early Church who protested against this literalism, and notably among them was Origen (Jerome, *To Pammachius* 25). There were those who repudiated the grotesque and fantastic lengths to which all this went.

We must now ask why the early Church held so tenaciously to the belief in the resurrection of the body. One would have said that the whole climate of the age in which Christian thought grew up would have been unfavourable to this belief. True, the belief existed strongly in Palestinian Judaism, but it was completely absent from the Greek world, and even Jews who had gone out from Palestine to live in the Greek world were infected with the almost universal suspicion and even hatred of the body. Two main reasons for this belief occur frequently in the writings of the thinkers of the early Church.

(i) They believed strongly in what we might call the totality of salvation. 'The body', said Irenaeus, 'is capable of sharing salvation' (*Against Heresies* 1.27.3). We await, he says, the salvation of *the complete man,* that is of the soul and the body (*Against Heresies* 5.20.1). Justin Martyr makes the same point. God calls man to salvation, not a part of man. The body is not the man, and the soul is not the man; the man is body and soul together; therefore both will rise (*On the Resurrection* 8). The early thinkers – and rightly – could be satisfied with nothing less than a total salvation, and they would have regarded a resurrection in which the body was completely omitted as a sadly partial and truncated thing.

(ii) More than once the early thinkers make the point that it is only justice that the body should rise in order to receive the necessary rewards and punishments for that which was actually done in the body. It would be wrong, argues Pearson, to punish the soul alone, for without the body in this life the soul can neither do nor suffer anything. That which is sinned in one body cannot be reasonably punished in another. It is only just that the flesh which has lived morally should be crowned along with the soul, and that the immoral flesh should be punished along with the immoral soul, says Rufinus (*Commentary on the Creed* 43). Jerome reports Origen as saying: 'Paul's body will be that of Paul, Peter's that of Peter, and each will have his own; for it is not right that souls should sin in one body and be tormented in another, nor is it worthy of the Righteous Judge that one body should shed its blood for Christ and another be crowned' (*To Pammachius* 26).

When we ask what the early thinkers really meant by their stress on the resurrection of the body, we are bound to see that, in spite of all their occasional crude materialistic literalism, they could not really have meant the literal and physical resurrection of this body *just as it is*. We are bound to look for something other than this completely physical interpretation.

Now in one passage of the New Testament this very question is dealt with, in 1 Corinthians 15.35-50. The question is asked 'How are the dead raised? With what kind of body do they come?' Paul first uses the analogy of the seed. The seed is planted in the ground; it dies; it rises again; but the body it rises with is not in the least like the body that was buried in the ground and died. A dry, brown, wrinkled bulb is planted – a green and yellow daffodil rises from the ground. The one quite definitely and even physically comes from the other; in one sense they are the same body under different conditions – and how different the conditions make them. So Paul says there are different kinds of flesh and different kinds of bodies, the flesh and bodies of men, animals, birds, fish, celestial and terrestrial bodies. Each sphere of life has its own body. But there are two all-embracing spheres of life, the physical and the spiritual. Through our connection with Adam we are part of the physical sphere of life, and Adam was made from the dust, of the earth earthy, and so are we. But through our connection with Jesus Christ we are part of the spiritual world; and just as we bear the image of Adam the man of earth, so we shall bear the image of Jesus Christ the man from heaven. In other words, just as we have a physical body so we will also have a spiritual body; and just as the daffodil grew out of the bulb and is indissolubly connected with it, so the spiritual body grows out of the physical body and is indissolubly connected with it. Paul never describes this spiritual body; it is part of the immortal and imperishable and incorruptible glory of heaven. It is that body that we shall have. Flesh and blood cannot inherit the kingdom of God, nor does the perishable inherit the imperishable; but our connection with the life-giving Spirit of Jesus Christ takes us out of the physical world into the spiritual world.

(i) The early thinkers were right in insisting on the salvation of the total man. It is not *soul* salvation but *whole* salvation that we believe in. The body too is able to be recreated and remade and glorified by the work of Jesus Christ.

(ii) This gives the body its place. What the New Testament is always vividly aware of is the immense potentiality of the body.

Of course the body is mortal (Romans 7.24; 8.11). Of course the body can be sinful (Romans 6.6, 12; 8.10), and can be dishonoured by man's impurity and immorality (Romans 1.24). But for all that the body can be redeemed (Romans 8.23); it can be offered as a sacrifice to God (Romans 12.1); it can be the temple of the Holy Spirit (1 Corinthians 6.19); our bodies can be nothing less than members of Christ (1 Corinthians 6.15); a man can be holy in body as well as in spirit (1 Corinthians 7.34); Christ can be glorified in our bodies (Philippians 1.20); his life can be manifested in our bodies (2 Corinthians 4.10); the body can be blameless as the soul and spirit (1 Thessalonians 5.23). The incarnation, the enmanning, the enfleshing of Jesus Christ at once shows the infinite value of the body. If we believe in the resurrection of the body, if we believe that the physical body is intimately, vitally and indissolubly connected with the spiritual body, we can never despise the body again.

(iii) It may well be that language such as we have been using does not speak with any clarity to twentieth-century man. It may be that we must put this in another way – and we can.

The real truth behind the idea of the resurrection of the body is that the individual survives as an individual. It is not necessary to believe in the survival of the individual to believe in the immortality of the soul. The Stoics believed that a man's soul was a spark of God which had come to stay in a man's body, and that when a man died that spark left his body and went back to be reabsorbed in God. To them the soul was immortal but not the individual person.

The truth is that Greek and Hebrew have no word for *personality*. They could not conceive of a personality without a body – and indeed how can we? because it is through the body that the personality acts and expresses itself. In so far as we can see in our earthly position, a disembodied spirit could not act on other spirits or in any way express itself. So then in the last analysis and in unmistakable and intelligible modern words, when the creed affirms our belief in the resurrection of the body, what it is really and essentially saying is:

'I believe in the survival of the individual personality. I believe that we will neither be obliterated into nothingness, nor yet absorbed in the divine. I believe that after death you will still be you and I will still be I.' The ancient thinker said: 'I believe in the resurrection of the body', because he had no words to put it any other way; we might well say: 'I believe in the survival of the individual personality', and the ancient and the modern man might well mean exactly the same thing.

CHAPTER TWENTY-ONE

In the Life Everlasting

It is entirely fitting that the creed should culminate in the affirmation of the belief in the life everlasting. The one question which men have always asked, and which they always will ask, is: 'If a man die, shall he live again?' (Job 14.14). The one fear which is almost a universal fear is the fear of death, and there have been many who through the fear of death were subject to lifelong bondage (Hebrews 2.15). The affirmation of belief in everlasting life is a fitting climax to any statement of Christian belief.

In the New Testament it is a basic axiom of belief that there is a life to come. In its teaching life is lived on the assumption that there is another life and that there is another world. In view of this it is surprising to see that in the Old Testament there is no such steady and fixed belief.

The Old Testament believed, as we have seen, that good and bad alike went after death to the vast subterranean cavern-like world of Sheol. There the dead lived a shadowy, strengthless life. They were 'dead, limp shades', semblances of their true selves, 'bereft of strength'. They were called in Hebrew the *refa'im*, the impotent, the strengthless ones. They were like ghosts, each one of them 'the conscious wraith of the man that had been'. Sheol was barred in, and there was no exit from it. The Babylonians called it The Land Without Return. It is true that there is a kind of peace in Sheol:

> There the wicked cease from troubling,
>   and there the weary are at rest.
> There the prisoners are at ease together;
>   they hear not the voice of the taskmaster.
> The small and the great are there,
>   and the slave is free from his master
>
> (Job 3.17–19).

It is this idea that all men alike go to Sheol when they die that gives to the Old Testament its atmosphere of pessimism and despair in regard to life after death. 'In death there is no remembrance of thee; in Sheol who can give thee praise?' (Psalm 6.5). 'What profit is there in my death, if I go down to the pit? Will the dust praise thee! Will it tell of thy faithfulness?' (Psalm 30.9). 'Dost thou work wonders for the dead? Do the shades rise up to praise thee? Is thy steadfast love declared in the grave, or thy faithfulness in Abaddon? Are thy wonders known in the darkness, or thy saving help in the land of forgetfulness?' (Psalm 88.10–12). 'The dead do not praise the Lord, nor do any that go down into silence' (Psalm 115.17). 'Whatever your hand finds to do, do it with your might; for there is no work or thought or knowledge or wisdom in Sheol, to which you are going' (Ecclesiastes 9.10). 'Sheol cannot thank thee, death cannot praise thee; those who go down to the pit cannot hope for thy faithfulness' (Isaiah 38.18). Job prays that he may have a little comfort 'before I go whence I shall not return, to the land of gloom and deep darkness' (Job 10.21). 'As the cloud fades and vanishes, so he who goes down to Sheol does not come up' (Job 7.9). This despair of life after death reaches its climax in Job 14.7-12: 'For there is hope for a tree, if it be cut down, that it will sprout again, and that its shoots will not cease. Though its root grow old in the earth, and its stump die in the ground, yet at the scent of water it will bud and put forth branches like a young plant. But man dies and is laid low; man breathes his last, and where is he? As waters fail from a lake, and a river wastes away and dries up, so man lies down and rises not again; till the heavens are no more he will not awake, or be roused out of his sleep.'

J. E. Macfadyen has said that there are few nobler and more heroic sights in history than the sight of the people of Israel living greatly and doing faithfully everything that came to them, with no hope of anything worth calling life on the other side of the grave. No doubt this is so, but we should very certainly remember, when we read passages like these, that this is not the Christian gospel. This is a lower stage of belief; this is a lesser grasp of the revelation of God; this is all of truth to which men could grope their way at that stage of life and thought. It would be quite wrong to take sayings like that as the last word of the revelation of God. It is not to the Old Testament that we turn when we desire to find the full light and glory of the life to come.

But in spite of the general belief in the shadow land of Sheol, the Old Testament is not without its glimpses of something greater. Sometimes the eyes of men saw for a moment through the darkness and caught a glimpse of the life eternal; and sometimes their faith reached out instinctively and touched for a moment the idea of a real life to come. We get two such glimpses in the Psalms. The first is in Psalm 16.8–11: 'I keep the Lord always before me; because he is at my right hand, I shall not be moved. Therefore my heart is glad, and my soul rejoices; my body also dwells secure. For thou dost not give me up to Sheol, or let thy godly one see the pit. Thou dost show me the path of life; in thy presence there is fulness of joy, in thy right hand are pleasures for evermore.' The basic idea here is that the man who loves God and has faith in God's love has entered into a relationship with God which not even death can break. The glimpse of the life to come here is not founded on theological doctrine or on philosophical speculation, but on a personal relationship with God, a relationship which, just because it is with God, must necessarily be independent of life and death.

The second great Old Testament outreach of faith is in Psalm 73.21–6: 'When my soul was embittered, when I was pricked in heart, I was stupid and ignorant, I was like a beast toward thee. Nevertheless I am continually with thee; thou dost hold my right hand. Thou dost guide me with thy counsel, and afterward thou wilt receive me into glory. Whom have I in heaven but thee? And there is nothing upon earth that I desire besides thee. My flesh and my heart may fail, but God is the strength of my heart and my portion for ever.' Here there is exactly the same thought, the conviction that a personal relationship with God is necessarily a relationship which neither life nor death can break.

The most famous glimpse of the life to come in the Old Testament is in Job 19.24–7. It has become doubly famous because Handel wedded it to immortal music. Both the actual words of it in the Hebrew and the actual meaning of it in translation are uncertain; but in it Job undoubtedly expresses his confidence in the ultimate help of God. 'I know that my Redeemer (Vindicator) lives and at last he will stand upon the earth; and after my skin has been thus destroyed, then without my flesh I shall see God, whom I shall see on my side, and my eyes shall behold, and not another.' One thing is sure, Job is saying that whether in this life or in some life to come, God will never ultimately fail to vindicate the man who has put his trust in him.

There are two other Old Testament passages in which a belief in a life to come is even more definitely stated. The first is in Isaiah 26.19: 'Thy dead shall live, their bodies shall rise. O dwellers in the dust awake and sing for joy! For thy dew is a dew of light, and on the land on the shades thou wilt let it fall.' This is part of the vision of what will happen on the Day of the Lord, when the Lord himself breaks into history. The last passage is in Daniel 12.2-3, and it speaks of what is to happen, as the seer foresaw it at the end time: 'And many of those who sleep in the dust of the earth shall awake, some to everlasting life, and some to shame and everlasting contempt. And those who are wise shall shine like the brightness of the firmament, and those who turn many to righteousness like the stars for ever and ever.'

But although the Old Testament has its glimpses of a belief in the life to come, it cannot be said that such a belief became an integral part of the Jewish faith. It was in the times between the Testaments that the belief in a life to come became strong, articulate and widespread. The Book of Enoch can speak of Sheol giving back its dead (51.1-2); and in the Psalms of Solomon it is stated as standard belief (3.12): 'They that fear the Lord shall rise unto eternal life; their life shall be in the light and it will never cease.'

There are two reasons why this belief in a life to come did become part of the Jewish belief. First, there was a development in the idea of God. We can trace how men came more and more to grasp what God really is. We can see three great stages. There is the stage which is called *henotheism*. At this stage Israel believed that Jahweh was the only God for her, but she was quite willing to believe that other gods might be equally valid for other nations. So Joshua tells the Ammonites to possess what Chemosh their god has given them, and Israel will possess what Jahweh their God has given them (Judges 11.23-4). The next stage is *monotheism*. At this stage Israel came to see that Jahweh is not only the national God of Israel but the God of all the earth. This is the stage of the prophets. But there is a further stage, which has not got a name: the stage when Israel comes to see that God is not only the God of all the earth, but also the God of all the universe. Once that is seen, there can be no part of the universe which is separate from God, and therefore no room for a Sheol which is separate from God. So there emerges the idea that death cannot separate us from the God of Heaven and earth, and therefore that there is a life to come.

Secondly, the circumstances of Jewish history almost inevitably led the Jews to a belief in a life to come. They believed that God loved the Jewish nation above all nations; they believed that the children of Abraham were in a special sense his children. And yet their history was one long disaster. The Assyrians, the Babylonians, the Persians, the Greeks, the Romans – one by one the great nations of the world conquered and subjected them. There were the most savage attacks on their country, on their religion and on their lives. They were the victims of hatred, of injustice, of persecution. Clearly, there was no justice in this world. Yet, not only did they believe that God loved them, but they also believed that God was just and faithful and that God must and would keep his promises; and, if these promises were to be kept, it was absolutely necessary to bring in a new world to redress the balance of the old. If those who loved God and served him and suffered for him and died for him were ever to enter into their reward, another world and another life were sheer necessities.

So the Jews had acquired a strong belief in a life to come by the time that Jesus came into this world. But that belief was never universal. It was held by the Pharisees as a part of their orthodox belief. 'Their belief is that souls have a deathless vigour, and beneath the earth there are rewards and punishments according as they have been devoted in life to virtue or vice.' The Sadducees on the other hand denied the survival of the soul, and declared that it perished with the body and held that after death there was neither life nor reward nor punishment. But of the two beliefs that of the Pharisees was by far the most widely held (Josephus, *Antiquities,* 18.1.3, 14).

By the time of Jesus the Jewish world would at least know what Christianity was talking about when it saw all things in the light of eternity.

We now go on to look at the life to come in the thought of the Greek and Roman world to which Christianity first came. Here we find a wide range of belief. We find a wistful longing that it should be true that there is something on the other side of death; the Greeks still buried their dead with a coin in their mouths to pay the fare of the ferryman Charon across the waters of death. We also find what T. R. Glover called 'the half belief' of 'timid and of tender spirits'. But it cannot be said that any-where we find complete conviction and complete certainty, and some-times we find the whole matter dismissed as one of the fairy-tales which attract and hold only the simple and the childish in mind.

It was certainly true that the Greeks would like to have believed in a life to come, for, as Plutarch said: 'The idea of annihilation was intoler-able to the Greek mind.' Faced, he says, with the alternative of annihila-tion and a life of torment in Hades, the Greek would have chosen the torment rather than the annihilation (*On the Impossibility of Living Happily According to the Teaching of Epicurus* 1104–5). The Greek loved life and the Greek wanted to live.

The earliest Greek belief was very close to the earliest Hebrew belief. It thought of the world to come as a grey shadowy place where ghostlike figures dragged out a joyless and colourless existence. Achilles in the *Odyssey* tells Odysseus that he would rather be a hired labourer on earth, working for a man of no substance, than the king of all the dead. So Iphigenia says: 'The sweetest thing one can see is daylight. What is below is nothing. He who prays for death is mad. It is better to live wretchedly than to die in splendour (Euripides, *Iphigenia at Aulis* 1250–2). And Virgil makes the grim ferryman say to those who approach the underworld: 'This is the region of ghosts, of sleep, and drowsy night' (*Aeneid* 6.390).

The only thing that lightens this in the early days is the picture of the Elysian fields and the Isles of the Blest to which the heroes go. It is the land where there is no snow, no rain, no storm, no tears, the land where a man does not need to toil on the land or labour on the sea to win a scant livelihood, the land where the zephyr always gently blows and the flowers of gold are blazing (Homer, *Odyssey* 4.561–3; Pindar, *Olympians* 2.55.79). 'The body of man is subject to over-mastering death, but an image of life (that is, the soul) remains, for it alone cometh from the gods.' 'The happiness of the blessed is no fugitive!' (Pindar, *Fragments* 131, 134).

It is worthwhile to stop to point that as far back as Pindar men had begun to make heaven in terms of earth. In Pindar's vision of the Blessed Isles, 'Some of them delight themselves with horses and with wrestling; others with draughts and lyres; while beside them bloometh the fair flower of perfect bliss' (*Fragment* 130). Horsemanship, wrestling, music – this was heaven. And this was to be the way all down the journey of human thought. The Indian had his Happy Hunting-ground, where he could hunt to his heart's content. The Norseman had his Valhalla where he could fight terrific battles all day and rest at night to fight again. The Mohammedan, child of the desert and of a hard life, had his Paradise of sensual delights. During the war someone wrote a little poem about some prisoners-of-war who after long suffering and imprisonment and pain died and came at last to heaven. All the weary years in the prison camp they had dreamed of England. Now they had come to heaven.

> God, but it's England, someone said,
> And there's a cricket field.

Simply because men are men they can think only in the terms and the pictures of one world; they will therefore always tend to make heaven in terms of that which to them is dearest on earth – and there is no harm in that – so long as we know what we are doing.

Even when we come to later times there was never in either Greek or Roman thought any real conviction of personal immortality, even though many wistfully longed to feel that certainty. Catullus in his famous love poem pleads with Lesbia for love's delights, because, when this world is ended, there remains nothing but an endless night of sleep from which no man shall ever awake (Catullus 5). Again and again Horace grimly sees the end of life as a final end. Fate knocks at every door, and man can never extend his life beyond its destined end (*Odes* 1.4.15). All men will in the end be sent to one eternal banishment (*Odes* 2.3.27). We are even in our happiest moments oppressed with thoughts of endless night (*Odes* 4.9.28). Sallust quotes Caesar as saying in his speech against Catiline: 'Death is a relief from suffering and not a torment; it puts an end to all human woes; beyond it there is no place for sorrow or for joy' (*Catiline* 51). Juvenal declares that nowadays not even a child believes in the shades and in the underworld (*Satires* 2.149). Pliny says that the idea of a life after death is no more than a child's fairy tale to satisfy man's insatiable desire not to come to an end. It is simply what we would call a projection of a man's own desires. There is nothing after death, says Seneca, and death itself is nothing, and you will be with the unborn.

There are two writers who are typical of that ancient and agnostic world. Tacitus wrote his noble tribute to Agricola who fully deserved it, and in the last paragraph he writes: 'If there is any habitation for the spirits of the just; if, as wise men will have it, the soul that is great perishes not with the body, you may rest in peace' (*Agricola* 46). If – that is all that he can say, however willingly he would say more. Cicero in the *Tusculan Disputations* is at one moment believing and at another completely agnostic. At one moment he can say that the soul is of the same texture as God, a very emanation of the divine, and that his great hope is that at some time he will be with the great souls and the great minds of the past (1.26; 1.27, 31; 5.13); and yet at another he is reduced to saying that, even if there is nothing good in death, surely there is nothing evil (1.28). And in his sorest hour at the death of his daughter Tullia, all that he can say is 'Not to have been born were best; the earliest possible death the next best' (Quoted Lactantius 3.18.19). Cicero is typical of an age which half believed but which could never be wholly sure.

But the pagan attitude to death can be seen best of all in the epitaphs and inscriptions on graves. Again and again they show a complete pessimism. 'Enjoy thy youth, dear heart of mine. In due time other men will be born, and as for me, I shall be dead, and changed to dark earth.' 'I was not – I was born. I was – now I am not. That is the sum. If any man says other wise, he lies. I shall not be.' 'I was not – I was born. I am not. I care not. Traveller, fare you well.' 'Friend, I advise you, mix a goblet of wine and drink and crown your head with flowers; earth and the fire consume all that remains after death.' 'Hold all a mockery, nothing is our own.' 'This is the end of living and the end of life.' 'There is nothing left – for nothing awakens the dead – except to afflict the souls of whose who pass. Nothing else remains.' 'Wayfarer, do not pass my epitaph, but stand and listen, and then, when you have learned the truth, proceed. There is no boat in Hades, no ferryman Charon, no Aeacus keeper of the keys, nor any dog called Cerberus. All of us who have died and gone below are bones and ashes and there is nothing else. What I have told you is true.' And lastly we may quote the bleakest and the grimmest of all inscriptions: 'Bereaved for ever.' There is perhaps nothing which so vividly illustrates the difference between paganism and Christianity as the words that pagans and Christians wrote upon their tombs.

Other schools of thought and other thinkers of the ancient world also demand our attention:

First, there was the school which did teach immortality of a kind. The

Stoics taught the immortality of the soul, but it cannot be said that they taught anything like personal and individual immortality.

The Stoics, as we saw in Chapter 4, were thorough-going pantheists. They believed quite literally that everything was God and that God was everything. They believed that God was in himself fiery spirit, far purer and far finer than any earthly fire. Part of that fire became dull and inert and depotentiated, and that depotentiated fire became matter. But in particular a particle, a spark, a *scintilla*, of the divine fire came to rest in man's body. That spark of the divine fire was man's soul and gave him life; and when he died that spark went back to the divine fire of which it was a part and was absorbed into the divine.

It is a great thought that a man's soul is a fragment of God, a spark and particle of divine fire; it is a great thought to think that God is in everything and that we live in a world which is full of God. But for the Stoic the end was not personal immortality; it was rather the loss of individuality and personality; it was absorption in the divine.

However lovely and attractive that idea may at first sight look, it is not the Christian idea, for, as we have already seen, the Christian states his belief in the resurrection of the body, by which he means the survival of the individual person and the individual personality.

Secondly, there was the school which deliberately denied the immortality of the soul and did everything possible to make men abandon belief in it. The Epicureans completely denied that the soul is immortal or that there is any life after death.

The Epicureans believed that the supreme good of life is what they called *ataraxia*, which means *serenity*. The great enemy of serenity is *fear*. And the Epicureans believed that men are haunted by the fear of the gods and the fear of death. Epicurus then set out to produce an account of the universe which would banish the fear of death and the fear of the gods.

To this end he produced his famous atomic theory. In the beginning there was nothing but space with atoms falling through it like rain. The atoms were endowed with the power to swerve. When they swerved they collided with each other. When they collided they coagulated into masses of atoms bouncing against each other. When they bounced together and rebounded some distance away, the result was a gas. When they bounced together and rebounded a shorter distance, the result was liquids. When they bounced together and hardly rebounded at all, the result was solids. This is to say, to use Epicurus' own phrase, that everything in this world is nothing other than a fortuitous conglomeration of atoms. Everything and every person in the world are simply collections of atoms. *And so is the soul.* The soul is no different from anything else, and when death comes the atoms simply disintegrate and death is literally a return to nothingness. There is nothing to fear in death, for the soul simply disintegrates into the atoms which fortuitously came together to form it. There is no life to come, and therefore there is nothing to fear.

One of the main reasons why Epicureanism came into being was precisely as an attempt to demonstrate that the soul is not, and cannot be, immortal.

We come now to the third great system of thought. Plato believed firmly in the personal immortality of the soul, and in the dialogue called the *Phaedo* he sets out logically to prove it.

For a philosopher death is no evil. All his life he has known that the body is the greatest obstacle to thought and to peace; all his life he has tried as far as possible to rid himself of the body. Death is therefore for him a liberation and a release; it is the way to fulness of knowledge – but of course only if the soul, freed from the body, continues to survive. Plato uses a series of arguments to prove that the soul is immortal.

(i) There is the argument from the contention that everything is generated from its opposite. If a thing becomes hot, it must have been cold; if a thing becomes cold, it must have been hot. If a thing becomes weak, it must have been strong, and vice-versa. If a thing becomes greater, it must have been smaller, and vice-versa. If a person wakes, he must have been asleep, and if he sleeps, he must have been awake. What then is the opposite of life? Death. But, if life is always passing into death, then in the end there could be nothing but death, But life continues. Therefore, life must also be generated out of death. Therefore the soul will live again; and in the endless process which is of the very essence of being, life will always pass into death, and death into life.

(ii) There is the argument from the doctrine of reminiscence. Plato believed that all knowledge comes in the end not from learning, but from remembering. In the dialogue called the *Meno* there is the famous demonstration of this. Socrates has stated this doctrine of reminiscence. It is of course questioned. A slave who has had not the slightest education is brought in, and by a process of question and answer Socrates succeeds in making him prove that the square on the diagonal is double the square of the side of any square. The slave with no knowledge has achieved a geometrical proof. The argument is that he must have remembered it and that question and answer elicited the proof from his mind. Again, if you say that two pieces of wood are equal in length, where did you get the notion of equality? It must be prior to having seen the wood, prior to that of mere length. It is something already known and remembered and applied. If then we did not learn these things *in* life we must have learned them *before* life.

Therefore the soul must have pre-existed, before it came into this world. And the pre-existence of the soul before this life implies its post-existence after this life.

(iii) There is the argument of the exclusiveness of opposites. True, opposites are generated from each other, but they cannot co-exist in the same thing or person. Heat cannot exist where cold is; a number cannot be odd and even at the same time. Further, the things which go with such qualities cannot exist with the opposite quality. Snow goes with cold and cannot exist with heat. Opposites exclude each other. Now the characteristic of the soul is life; that is its distinguishing attribute. And that of which life is the characteristic cannot admit death, but must be imperishable. The soul is immortal because it contains the principle of imperishableness, and that excludes death.

Finally Plato uses two quite general arguments.

(iv) The aspiration of the soul after another state of being is a fore-taste of immortality. The soul does desire another life, free of the body. The desire of the soul is to fly away and to be with God, Plato says in the *Theaetetus*, 'and to fly to God is to be like God'. The immortal longings are the proof of immortality.

(v) Finally, there is the moral argument. There is need of retribution, if there is to be justice. Since God is just, and since the principle of justice is at the heart of the universe, there must be some life in which justice is done.

Here then is the Platonic argument. It is summed up in what is really not an argument, but an affirmation of faith: 'There can no evil happen to a good man in life or in death.' We may not at times be impressed by the Platonic arguments, for this is not something about which we can

construct a neat argument and write at the end of it QED. But the *Phaedo*
is one of the great works of the reverently seeking mind. As someone
said of it, it is the noblest offering ever laid on the altar of human hope,
and we must remember that it was the argument Socrates put forward in
prison an hour before his death.

We have now looked at the matter of life after death historically, and we
must go on to look at it personally. Death is a universal fact of life. Birth
and death are the two great experiences through which every man must
go, and from which none is exempt. But there are different attitudes to
death. An American journalist set down as the first article in his personal creed: 'Never to allow myself to think of death.' But whether or not a
man will allow himself to think of death, death will force itself upon his
attention. There were certain principles which the famous chancellor Sir
Thomas More was not prepared to abandon, and it was fairly clear that
his fidelity to them would provoke the king's displeasure and so result in
his own death. He seemed to be quite unaware of the danger of his position. Once the Earl of Norfolk reminded him how close he walked to
death. Sir Thomas answered: 'Then in good faith between your grace
and me there is but this, that I shall die today, and you tomorrow.' To him
it was no more than a universal fact that all men must die. Dr Johnson
wrote of a certain time in the life of Swift: 'The thoughts of death rushed
upon him at this time with such incessant importunity that they took
possession of his mind, when he first waked for many hours together.'

For some there is the fear of death. 'Is not the fear of death natural to
man?' Boswell asked Johnson. 'So much so, sir,' said Johnson, 'that the
whole of life is but keeping away the thoughts of it.' John Mactaggart
was one of the brilliant but short-lived Scottish men of letters. He once
wrote: 'Ever since the night on which my mother told me that there
would come a day on which I would die and be covered with cold mould
in a grave, I have been haunted with the thought.' There are always those
who are all their lives in bondage to the fear of death (Hebrews 2.15).

For some there has been the attraction of death as an escape from a life
which has become too complicated or too exhausting to endure. Rupert
Brooke was one of the great poets who perished all too young in the
1914–18 war. He had loved the beauty of the earth and the joy of living.
Before he went overseas to France a lady gave him a little charm which she

said would bring him luck and keep him safe. 'Yes,' he wrote back, 'but what luck is we'll wait and see; I can well see that life might be great fun; but I can well see that death might be an admirable solution.' For some death might seem to be the solution of all the problems. That almost legendary figure T. E. Lawrence once said: 'O Lord, I am so tired. I want to lie down to sleep, to die. To die is best because there is no reveille.' When life becomes intolerable, then death may look like the way out. 'The gods', said the Stoics, 'gave men life, but they gave them the even greater gift of being able to take their own lives away.'

Finally, there are those who have faced death with joy, because they regarded death as the way to a still greater life. F. B. Meyer a very short time before his death wrote to a friend: 'I have just heard to my surprise that I have only a few more days to live. It may be that before this reaches you I shall have entered the palace. Don't trouble to write; we shall meet in the morning.' Hugh McKail was one of the most steadfast of the Covenanters. He was captured and condemned to death. He was to die in four days' time. He was led through the streets of Edinburgh to the Tolbooth and the crowds wept for the pathos of his fate. But his own face shone. 'Good news,' he said, 'I am within four days of enjoying the face of Christ.' For him death was indeed the gateway to eternal life.

Can we then find any proofs to help to convince the mind that there is a life after death? Can we reasonably believe? Before we go on to look at the reasons which invite us to believe that there is a life after death, we ought to face the arguments of those who say that there is no such thing.

(i) There are those who say that there can never be any proof of a life after death. If by proof we mean an undeniable chain of logical argument, then there is no proof. If by proof we mean the kind of proof that we can get by weighing, counting and measuring visible and tangible things, then again there is no proof. But there are remarkably few things which can be proved in that way. Nothing could be proved about beauty, goodness, truth, honour, honesty, love by these methods. If on the other hand by proof we mean the production of reasons which move the mind to accept something and the heart to believe in it, then we shall see that there are such proofs.

(ii) It is claimed that the belief that the dead live comes from such phenomena as dreams in which we see again people who hive died, and that the belief in the soul comes from the fact that in dreams we can see ourselves in places far from where our body lies; it is claimed that the belief in a life after death emerges as a kind of extension of the idea of naturally sleeping and waking, and the idea that sleep is a kind of temporary death. Even if this were so – and it is not proved that it is so – it would not invalidate the idea. It is quite possible for people to arrive at a true idea in ignorance and in superstition and in partial knowledge, long before they have arrived at a stage of progress when they can arrive at it for the right reasons. The origin of an idea neither proves nor disproves the truth of the idea.

(iii) It is claimed that the idea of living after death simply means that we live on in our children and in those who come after us, that immortality is, as it were, corporate and not personal. Or that we live on in the effect of the things we do, that we do leave something permanent in the world. No doubt both these things are true, but they do not constitute immortality in any real sense of the term. Long ago Huxley said that if you fling a stone into the ocean the waves go out and out and out illimitably, and so the effects of our selves and of our deeds may well go out illimitably; but, as Huxley went on to say, no one would ever think of claiming that the stone which caused the illimitable waves was personally immortal. To live on in those who come after and to live on in our deeds and influences is not immortality in any real sense of the term.

(iv) It has even been claimed that belief in immortality is unethical, because it makes a man undervalue this life, and regard it as important, not in itself, but only as a means to an end. It is perfectly true that too much thinking about heaven and too little thinking about earth has produced at times a wrong otherworldliness. But it is also true that life is full of things which are stages to something else but which never lose their own value. Childhood, youth, manhood, age, are all stages leading to each other, yet all are important in themselves. In all study and learning, each part and each class and each stage leads to the next without in the least losing its own value. The fact that a thing leads beyond itself, so far from necessarily devaluating it, gives it, if properly looked at, a new and wider value.

(v) It has been argued by a thorough-going materialism that there is neither mind nor soul to survive. The older materialism held two principles. First, there are in the world seventy elements and everything that is made is made from them by a process of one into the other by means of motion. Secondly, there is the principle of the conservation of energy which means that in the world there is just so much energy and no more. Everything happens by the motion and combination of the elements which are material. Always a cause produces an effect for material reasons Everything is to be explained by physical and material actions and re-actions. Now it is said that the brain is made of 3,000,000,000 particles; these particles are material, and everything that happens in the brain is simply the result of the actions and the reactions of these particles. There is no such thing as mind; there is only mechanism. Man is simply a machine working according to certain physical and mechanical laws. Everything that has ever happened would have happened for purely phys-ical reasons. What this leaves out of sight altogether is the something extra which sees all this and which forms the conscious centre around which all this moves. Even if this could be proved – and it cannot be proved – nothing will remove from a man the conviction that he is a responsible creature making his own decisions and not a machine in the grip of law.

Having dealt with the arguments against, we now turn to the positive reasons which can be adduced to enable us to believe that there is a life after death.

(i) When we go to the Bible itself, we find only one such formal argu-ment, and it appears almost incidentally on the lips of Jesus himself. He was in the midst of an argument with the Sadducees. The Sadducees did not believe in the resurrection of the dead. Further, the Sadducees accepted as Scripture only the Pentateuch, the Law, the first five books of the Old Testament, and they had long insisted that from these books no evidence could be drawn that there was a life after death. Jesus point-ed out to them that in the Pentateuch itself God is called the God of Abraham and of Isaac and of Jacob. Now God is clearly the God of the living and not of the dead. Therefore Abraham, Isaac and Jacob must still be alive, and therefore there is such an event as the resurrection of the dead (Matthew 22.31-2; Mark 12.26–7; Luke 20.37-8). This argument was greeted with astonishment, for Jesus was the first to disprove the Sadducean argument that the only part of the Scripture which they accepted contained no evidence at all for the resurrection of the dead.

It may well be that the form of this argument does not seem to us very convincing, but it must be remembered that on this occasion Jesus was meeting the Sadducees on their own ground and arguing with them on their own terms. He was quite deliberately using their own method of argument in order to convince them of their error by their own methods. Even if the argument does not seem very convincing to the modern mind, it was entirely convincing, and indeed unanswerable, for the people to whom it was addressed.

(ii) The one modern argument which is persuasive and convincing is what is known as *the teleological argument*. This argument begins from what is in fact an affirmation of faith. It begins from the assumption that this is a reasonable universe; that the universe has a *telos*, an end, and therefore a purpose in it. Given that initial assumption of faith the argument is wellnigh unanswerable.

The argument exists in many forms. It may be said to be the argument from the nature of the world and the nature of man. We shall look at it as two of its exponents state it.

First, it is Kant's argument. Reason, Kant says, lays it down that absolute obedience to the moral law is the *highest* good; such obedience is virtue. Reason also lays it down that the *completest* good is when virtue and happiness are united. But if virtue is perfect obedience to the moral law, then in this life it is never completely attainable, nor can it be attainable in any finite period, because of the opposition of man's animal, impulsive and passional nature to this moral imperative. This must mean that the complete good, the union of virtue and happiness, is not realizable in this life. Therefore immortality is a necessity if ever the supreme ends of practical reason are to become possible. To put this very simply, in this life man can never become what reason says he ought to become, and what he is meant to become; and therefore there must be another life so that man may complete his *telos*, his end. If ever man is to become what he is meant to be, this life is not enough.

Secondly, it is stated much more generally by James Ward. 'Within the whole range of the wide world's literature we find no more constant theme than this disparity between man's possibilities and aspirations on the one hand, and the narrow scope afforded them in the brief scope of the present life on the other.' A reasonable universe demands another life. If 'the fulfilment of the potentialities of finite personality is part of the purpose of the universe' it involves life beyond death.

It would not be a reasonable universe if progress is for no other purpose than annihilation, if aspirations are sent only to haunt, and if potentialities are never in the nature of things to be realized. This is exactly what Browning put into verse in *Abt Vogler*:

> There shall never be lost one good! What was, shall live as before;
> The evil is null, is nought, is silence implying sound;
> What was good shall be good, with, for evil, so much good more;
> On earth the broken arcs; in the heaven, a perfect round.
> All we have willed or hoped or dreamed of good shall exist;
> Not in its semblance, but itself; no beauty, nor good, nor power
> Whose voice has gone forth, but each survives for the melodist
> When eternity affirms the conception of an hour.
> The high that proved too high, the heroic for earth too hard,
> The passion that left the ground to lose itself in the sky,
> Are music sent up to God by the lover and the bard;
> Enough that he heard it once we shall hear it by-and-by.

In a reasonable universe it is not reasonable to suppose that progress exists to end in nothingness, that potentiality exists never to become actuality, that aspiration must be for ever unrealized.

(iii) But what we have been saying does not in the end depend on a view of the universe and of man; it depends on a view of God. Long ago Plutarch said that belief in providence and belief in immortality stand or fall together. As Benjamin Jowett said: 'If God is perfect, he must will that all other beings should partake of that perfection which he himself is. In the words of the *Timaeus*, he is good, and therefore he desires that all other things should be as like him as possible.'

In the Christian conception of God two attributes exist side by side, God's justice and God's love, and both of them demand another life. Bertrand Russell somewhere imagines that God grew tired of the angels and created a race called men. He deliberately beset them with pains and difficulties to see how they would react. Man of the gallant spirit uses them to climb upwards and thanks God for them as opportunities. And then one day God will laugh and say: 'A good play! Some day I must do it again. Meanwhile – enough! The jest is ended!' And God will brush the whole matter into annihilation. Somewhere Thomas Hardy describes God as, 'the dreaming, dark, dumb thing that turns the handle of the idle show'. If it is possible to describe God in these terms, then clearly there is no necessity to postulate any life to come. But if he is justice and love, then life to come becomes a necessary assumption.

It is necessary in justice. It is necessary to redress the balance of this world. As one of the ancient writers said, if there is no life to come, 'that would be good news for evil men'. The moral government of the universe demands a life to come. Mellone speaks about 'the desire to live to see the meaning of the apparently undeserved sufferings of life'. Nor is this merely a selfish desire, for a man desires this for far more than himself. We have only to look at this life, to see that, if God is justice, it is clearly an unfinished story.

It is necessary in love. The most tragic thing in life is not death in old age. There is nothing to lament when a man has to die 'his work accomplished and the long day done'. The most tragic thing is when death comes so soon that a life has never had time to blossom and to grow. If there be no place where such a life finds its fulfilment, then it does not seem possible to believe in either the love or the justice of God.

We may put this very simply, for this is not a matter so much of theology and philosophy as it is of faith. Alistair McLean tells of a gentle Highland lady dying in a Glasgow slum. She had come from a farm in the Hebrides. Once life had been very comfortable for her, but misfortune had struck. She had had to come to the city, and the city air had slowly killed her and now she was dying in the most wretched circumstances. 'God will make it up to me,' she said. 'I know his will and I shall see the flowers again.'

Even a non-Christian can accept the teleological argument for a life to come, on the grounds that this is a reasonable universe, even if that assumption is itself an act and affirmation of faith. But the real argument for the life to come, at least for a Christian, depends on the character of God as it is seen in the face of Jesus Christ, and in the conviction that a God of justice and of love cannot end things when this life ends.

Whenever we allow our minds to think about the life everlasting, it is almost impossible not to ask the question, What happens immediately when we die? The odd thing is that to that very basic question the New Testament itself gives no definite, certain or cut and dried answer. It can in fact be said to give a number of different answers.

We may note in the first place that in the very earliest days, immediately following upon the death and the resurrection of Jesus, it was hardly a question which arose. In those first days the Church expected the return of Christ immediately, any day, any hour; certainly, they thought, within their own lifetime, and so the question was not so much, What happens when a man dies? as, What happens when Jesus Christ comes again? But it became clear that the coming of Jesus Christ was to be long delayed, or that the whole matter of his coming would have to be re-thought, and then the question of what happens after death became an insistent and universally relevant question.

The doubt in the answer to that question is not doubt as to what *ultimately and finally* happens; the doubt is as to what *immediately* happens. It may be said that the answers – and all of them can be supported by quotations from the New Testament – fall into four different groups.

(i) The first answer is that immediately after death there is a waiting time and a sleep of the soul, after which there comes the general resurrection and the final judgement. This was in fact the belief of Luther, who held that 'souls remain in a state of unconsciousness between death and resurrection.'

This view is supported by the number of times in the New Testament those who have died are said to be *asleep*. It is said that at the crucifixion 'the tombs were opened, and many bodies of the saints who had fallen asleep were raised' (Matthew 27.52). Jesus refers to Lazarus as having fallen asleep and says that he is going to waken him out of sleep (John 11.11). Paul speaks of the Corinthian dead as having fallen asleep (1 Corinthians 11.30), and he uses the same expression as a general term for those who have died (1 Corinthians 15.6, 20). In 1 Thessalonians the dead are called 'those who are asleep', and they are said to sleep in Jesus (1 Thessalonians 4.13–14).

(ii) The second view is that of Millennarianism, the evidence for which is to be found only in Revelation 20. As we have seen in Chapter 15, Millennarianism holds that the end of the world will come, as it were in two stages. There will first of all be a resurrection of the martyrs of those who died for their faith. This resurrection will last for a thousand years, a millennium, and during this time the Devil will be bound and the saints will reign gloriously with Christ. At the end of it the Devil will be released; there will be one last and final conflict at the end of which the Devil will be thrown into the lake of fire. Then the general resurrection will come, the final judgement, and the casting of the wicked also into the lake of fire.

There were those in the early Church who took all this literally. There was a tendency for the thousand-year reign of the saints to be thought of in very material terms, as a kind of continual banquet in a world of luxuriant fertility, and even by the fourth century this was a view which orthodox belief had discarded. In Egypt, Dionysius came upon an otherwise excellent man called Nepos who interpreted the Millennium in terms 'of bodily luxury upon this earth' (Eusebius, *The Ecclesiastical History* 7.241.). Cerinthus was one of the most famous of all heretics; he was a contemporary of the apostle John in Ephesus. Eusebius says of him: 'The doctrine that he taught was this: that the kingdom of Christ will be an earthly one. And as he himself was devoted to the pleasures of the body and altogether sensual in his nature, he dreamed that the kingdom would consist of those things which he desired, namely in the delights of the belly and sexual passion; that is to say, in eating and drinking and marrying, and in festivals and sacrifices and the slaying of victims, under the guise of which he thought he could indulge his appetites with a better grace' (Eusebius, *The Ecclesiastical History* 7.25.3). Even the great theologian Irenaeus was a Millennarianist, and he transmits what he alleges to be a saying of Jesus: 'The days shall come in which vines shall grow, each having ten thousand branches, and in each branch ten thousand twigs, and in each true twig ten thousand shoots, and in each one of the shoots ten thousand clusters, and on every one of the clusters ten thousand grapes, and every grape when pressed will give twenty measures of wine.' So every grain of wheat would give ten pounds of the finest flour, and every fruit tree would produce in similar proportions (Irenaeus, *Against Heresies* 5.33.3). The moon was to be as bright as the sun, and the sun ten times brighter than any earthly sun; there would be no sorrow, and no labour, and a table always spread with food; the wicked would be destroyed, or any who remained would become the slaves of the righteous.

We may well leave this doctrine aside, for it ought to have been clear from the beginning that it is dangerous to found a doctrine on a literal acceptance of the apocalyptic pictures of the Revelation; and in any event Millennarianism, however enthusiastic its devotees may have been or may be, has never been part of the main stream of Christian belief.

(iii) The third view holds that there is a long period between death and the final judgement, but seems at least to admit the possibility of things happening within that period.

One famous passage has been pressed into the service of this view. As the AV has it, Jesus said: 'In my Father's house are many mansions' (John 14.2). The RSV has it: 'In my Father's house are many rooms.' In Greek the word is *monai*, and in Latin *mansiones*. Now it is quite true that both these words can mean abiding-places, places in which to stay; but it is equally true that both these words are the regular and technical words for the stages, the stopping-places, the stations on a journey. It could be held that what Jesus said is that there are many *stages* in his Father's house. The great protagonist of this view – he quotes this text from John to prove it – is Origen (*De Principiis* 2.11.8). He says that the saints, when they die, go to some place on this earth which is called Paradise; there they are instructed as in a classroom or school. Those who are pure in heart and practised in perception rise up and pass through the air until they reach the kingdom of heaven, having gone through the various spheres or stages. These stages are the *monai* which Jesus speaks about.

Here is a definite picture of training, instruction, progress. There are very many who have been attracted by this picture. In another place Origen speaks of them going through punishments and disciplines and being instructed by the angels until in the end they reach the truly heavenly place (*De Principiis* 1.6.3). Someone has asked the question: 'Have you ever known anyone good enough to go straight to heaven, or anyone bad enough to go straight to hell?' How indeed would we answer this question of ourselves?

(iv) Finally, there is the view which holds that immediately upon death, with no intermediate state at all, with neither a sleep nor a probation, the soul passes either to blessedness or to shame.

This view too can be strongly supported from the New Testament. Jesus' saying to the penitent thief is: 'Truly, I say to you, today you will be with me in paradise' (Luke 23.43). Paul's instinctive desire is to depart and to be with Christ, which is far better (Philippians 1.23). Men must die once, says the writer to the Hebrews, and after that comes judgement (Hebrews 9.27). It is even here and now that the unseen cloud of witnesses compass us about (Hebrews 12.1), and that cloud of witnesses can hardly mean anything other than the saints in glory. Still further, it is

Paul's conviction that nothing in life or in death can separate him from the love of God in Christ Jesus his Lord (Romans 8.38–9), which would seem to show that he did not think in terms of a long sleep and then an awakening, but of a life lived here and hereafter in the presence of his Risen Lord.

It is by no means easy to extract from the New Testament any kind of clear and coherent statement of what happens after death. That there is a life after death the New Testament is never in any doubt. From beginning to end the Christian life is lived in the awareness of that which is beyond; but when that life begins and what it is like we are not given definitely to know – and it could not be otherwise, for we have always to walk by faith and not by sight. And it is for that reason that we turn now to examine the idea of *eternal life*.

We may begin by noting one simple point. The AV confuses the two words *everlasting* and *eternal*, using sometimes the one and sometimes the other to translate the same Greek word. It will be far better *always* to use the word *eternal*, for we shall come to see that, whatever else is true of this kind of life it is very much more than a life which simply lasts for ever. It is *quality* of life even more than it is *quantity* of life.

Let us first of all try to catch something of the meaning of this word *eternal*. *Eternal* translates the Greek adjective *aiōnios*. *Aiōnios* comes from the noun *aiōn*. In Greek this word *aiōn* is what might be called an expanding word. It can mean simply a man's *life-time*, and so Herodotus can speak of ending one's *aiōn*, coming to the end of one's life (Herodotus 1.32). It moves on in time and it can mean a *generation*. It moves on still further to mean *a very long space of time*, gaining the idea of *for ever*. So it was the prayer that the power of the Emperor might last *eis ton aiōna*, for ever.

There are two uses of the word which will effectively illustrate its meaning. One is a Jewish use, which of course was based on Hebrew. The Jews divided all time into two ages, the one the age of this present world, the other the golden and eternal age of God which would begin when time and this world as we know them come to an end through the action of God. So the Jew could speak of this present *aiōn*, and the *aiōn* which is to come. Even in this use, *aiōn* means, as it were the life-time of a world and in the second sense it is the life-time of a world which has no end.

The second thing which reveals the meaning of this word comes directly from the adjective derived from the word *aiōn, aiōnios.* We can see that *aiōnios* can mean *belonging to the life-time of a man,* at its shortest, *belonging to a generation,* as it begins to expand, and finally *belonging to nothing less than the life-time* of a world, and that in connection of a world which will have no end. Now it was this last meaning which became the characteristic meaning of the word. As Milligan has put it, *aiōnios* describes 'a state wherein the horizon is not in view'.

Now it is just at this stage that something, so to speak, happened to this word *aiōnios.* Plato began to use it of a kind and mode of being which is not of this world at all, of a kind of life which is more than human life. He said, for instance, that the soul and the body are indestructible, but they are not *aiōnios,* not eternal (*Laws* 904 A). There is something more than just infinite extension of time in *aiōnios.* Most suggestive of all, in the *Timaeus* (37 D) he speaks of the creation of the world. He says that God created the world, but the one thing in the nature of things that God could not do was to make the world *aiōnios,* 'he could not attach eternity to time', and so the world is only 'a moving image of eternity'. That which is *aiōnios* has no beginning and no ending; it has no becoming and changing and altering, it is always itself, always one and indivisible, always the same. It has no becoming older or younger; it has no past, present and future. It always *is,* unalterably, unchangeably the same. We begin now to see the meaning of this word *aiōnios,* which for want of a better word we have to translate *eternal.* In one word, it describes the life of God. The only person in the universe who can properly be called *aiōnios* is God. Eternal life is the life of God, and to have eternal life is to share the life of God. Here we are at the very heart of the matter. Eternal life is nothing less than God's life.

The New Testament has much to say about eternal life, and we have enough material to build up our picture of it.

(i) Eternal life is both the promise and the gift of God. God who never lies promised this eternal life ages ago (Titus 1.2). What God has promised is eternal life (1 John 2.25). But eternal life is more than promised; it is given by God. The gift of God is eternal life (Romans 6.23). God gave us eternal life (1 John 5.11). Eternal life is not a human achievement, although man has his part to play in the attainment of it; it is the promise and the gift of God.

(ii) Eternal life is altogether bound up with Jesus Christ. It is the free gift of God in Christ Jesus our Lord (Romans 6.23). God gave us eternal life and this life is in his Son (1 John 5.11). Jesus gives the water which is like a spring welling up inside a man to eternal life (John 4.14). He is the divine food which gives a man eternal life (John 6.27, 54). His words are the words of eternal life (John 6.68). He not only gives eternal life (John 17.2), he is eternal life (1 John 5.20).

(iii) This eternal life comes to a man through different channels.

– It comes through knowledge. Eternal life is to know God and Jesus Christ whom God has sent (John 17.3). But we must be careful to understand what this knowledge is. There is certainly an intellectual side to it, but there is far more. There are two kinds of knowledge. There is the knowledge of facts and theories, the knowledge which the mind can discover and retain. But there is a knowledge which is the result of a personal relationship. We say of a person: 'I know him very well indeed.' And that expression indicates a close and personal relationship of heart to heart. There is a world of difference between *knowing about* and *knowing*. There are any number of people whom we *know about*, but whom we do not *know*. We can know about a person without ever having met him at all; we can only know a person when we are in intimate fellowship with him. It is a significant fact that the Bible uses the word *know* of the sexual relationship between two people (Genesis 4.1). It is in that act that human relationship reaches its most intimate stage. Eternal life does not come through theologically *knowing about* God; it comes through the establishment through Jesus Christ of a personal relationship with God.

– It comes through what the New Testament calls belief or believing. It is repeatedly said that the man who believes in Jesus Christ has eternal life (John 3.15–16; 5.24; 6.40, 47; 1 John 5.13; 1 Timothy 1.16). What do we mean by this word *believe*? When we are urged to believe, what is it that we are being urged to do? Belief has three elements in it in the Christian sense of the term.

First, it has unquestionably an intellectual element. We cannot believe unless we know the claims that Jesus Christ has made; we must in the first place *know about* him before we can *know* him. We must know the offer and the claims he makes and we must know how they were substantiated by his life and actions.

Secondly, we must be convinced that these claims are true. Unless there is reasonable evidence for a claim we cannot really and truly believe that it is true.

Thirdly, there are, however, two ways in which evidence can come. It can come by the presentation of certain facts to the mind; or it can come through personal experience. It can come, perhaps will most frequently come, by a combination of both ways. It will come by the hearing of the facts first, and the experiencing of them afterwards. Our knowledge of Christ comes from the personal experience of what his presence and his fellowship can do for us when we accept his offers and his claims and commit the whole of life to them.

It is the belief which knows and experiences and which commits itself to that knowledge and experience which finds eternal life.

– There is the part of *preaching*. In Titus (1.2–3) we read of the eternal life which God long ago promised, and which at the proper time was manifested in his word 'through the preaching with which I have been entrusted by command of God our Saviour'. The means, as it were, through which people are introduced to eternal life, is the preaching of the gospel. The design of preaching is to lead men into the experience of eternal life, to bring them into contact with the promised life of God. And once that is realized by the preacher it must mean an end of all trivialities and the beginning of that proclamation by which men are confronted with Christ and his claims.

– There are the *sacraments*. There is no doubt that the Fourth Gospel thinks of the close connection of eternal life with the sacraments. In that Gospel we find Jesus depicted as saying: 'He who eats my flesh and drinks my blood has eternal life' (John 6.54). There is no doubt that this is a reference to the sacrament of the Lord's Supper. In that sacrament we are enabled through the elements of bread and wine to enter into such a real and close relationship to Jesus Christ that it can be for us the way to the experience of the life of God.

(iv) We have already stressed the fact that eternal life is a promise and a gift of God, but for all that it is not without its demands on men.

– It demands *obedience*. It is the commandment of God which is eternal life (John 12.50) Jesus is the source of eternal salvation to all who obey him (Hebrews 5.9). Just as a man cannot receive health unless he does what his physician tells him, so he cannot find eternal life unless he is obedient to the Lord of life.

— It demands true *loyalty*. It is by fighting the good fight of faith that a man can lay hold on the eternal life to which he was called (1 Timothy 6.12). It is those who hear and who follow who receive eternal life (John 10.27–8). Eternal life can only be found by linking our life with the life of Jesus Christ, and that is something of which the consequences can never be easy.

— There is an *ethical* demand on the man who would enter into eternal life. Sanctification, the road to holiness, and eternal life go together (Romans 6.22). It comes to those who are patient in well-doing (Romans 2.7). It comes to the man who has the gift of perseverance to the end of the day. It cannot come to the man who hates his brother, for the man who hates his brother is no better than a murderer and cannot have eternal life (1 John 3.15). It comes in the end to those who keep themselves in the love of God (Jude 21).

Eternal life is the good life. No man can share the life of God without the holiness which God alone can give to him.

(v) Eternal life is the reward of the man who is prepared to adventure his life for Christ. The man who loves his life will lose it, and the man who is prepared to lose it will keep it to eternal life (John 12.25). Eternal life is not found by hoarding life but by spending it.

(vi) Paul connects righteousness with eternal life (Romans 5.21). For Paul righteousness and justification are the same thing; and they both mean that new relationship with God into which a man can freely enter through Jesus Christ. When Paul spoke of justification and when John spoke of eternal life they both meant the same thing.

So then we can see something of the riches of eternal life. Basically, eternal life is nothing other than the life of God. It is in one sense the promise and the gift of God, but it brings its own conditions which a man must satisfy.

One thing that emerges quite clearly is something that we noticed at the very beginning. We began by saying that there was much more to eternal life than simply life that went on for ever. It is quite obvious that life which went on for ever would not necessarily be a blessing; it might well be a curse.

The Greeks had a parable of this. There was, they told, a mortal lad called Tithonus with whom Aurora the goddess of the dawn fell in love. The gods were sympathetic to her love, and Zeus, the king of the gods, offered her any gift she might choose for her mortal lover. She asked that Tithonus might live for ever. She was a goddess and she remained for ever young; but, although Tithonus was not to die, she had forgotten to ask for him the gift of eternal youth, and he grew older and older and could not die so that life was a torture and a weariness for him. It is true that eternal life involves life which lasts for ever, but to that idea of quantity there is added the far more important idea of quality, for eternal life is the life of God himself.

It is in terms of eternal life that we must think of the life to come, and, when we do so, certain things become clear.

(i) We do not need to wait for eternal life until we are dead. We can possess it here and now. Within this world of space and time we can enter into that relationship with God which is eternal life. Even here and now we can share the life which is the life of God.

(ii) This is the great argument for a life beyond the grave. If we enter into a relationship with God, that relationship is bound to be a relationship which lasts for ever simply because God is God. Human relationships can be and are broken. People drift apart; distance separates them and the old intimacy is gone. Death comes between. But none of these things can happen with God. To be in a relationship with God of which the essence is love is necessarily to be in a relationship which cannot end because God cannot end.

(iii) But this idea of eternal life here and now will also mean that the life to come is necessarily a continuation of this life. This relationship with God is something which must continue. There is no necessity to think of a long sleep or a long interim period. This relationship is something which can begin on this plane and which will continue on another plane unbroken and uninterrupted.

(iv) But we may say something still more. To understand things in this way is to open the possibility – perhaps the necessity – of growth and development even in the life to come. Man's relationship with God can never be static. For man there must always be more of God to know. In this world there are the things which interrupt that relationship and which limit it and frustrate it. In the life to come we may believe that we shall grow steadily and uninterruptedly closer and closer to God, for even in heaven no man can reach the end of God.

(v) We may finally say that this is one of the subjects which we can never speak about as if we knew everything. There are things which we must be content not to know; we may experience the beginning and we can be confident that the end will be beyond our dreams.

In this matter Paul is our guide and he speaks at his highest not like a theologian but like a poet. 'Now', he says, 'we see through a mirror dimly, but then face to face. Now I know in part; then shall I understand fully, even as I have been fully understood' (1 Corinthians 13.12). 'What no eye has seen nor ear heard, nor the heart of man conceived, what God has prepared for those who love him' (1 Corinthians 2.9).

What we may say with confidence is that the Christian is a child of eternity who can know eternal life here and now, and who will one day know in full the life of God.

CHAPTER TWENTY-TWO

The Apostles' Creed Today

Now that we have thought and studied our way through the Apostles' Creed it is inevitable that we should ask, What ought to be the position of the Apostles' Creed today? What standing should it have in the Church and in the belief of the individual Christian?

It may well be that our first instinct will be to say that it ought to be discarded. It is close on eighteen hundred years old. The Church has come a long way in experience and in thought since the latter half of the second century. There are unquestionably difficulties in the Apostles' Creed for the modern mind. It is a fact of history that all the great creeds of the Church have what we might call an apologetic basis, and that they were wrought out to face the particular theological dangers of their time. It may well be that a first reaction today is that it is high time that there was a restatement of faith, made against a twentieth-century background, made in twentieth-century terms, and made specifically for twentieth-century man. It was indeed with some such thoughts as these in my mind that I myself set out on the examination of this creed. But there are formidable difficulties, and there is not a little to be said on the other side. Let us look at some of these difficulties.

(i) There is the obvious practical difficulty that it would be to all intents impossible to construct a modern statement of belief to which any one Church, let alone all the Churches, would be likely to agree. To try to construct any such creed would in fact lay bare the things which divide, far more than state the things which unite. It may be natural to long for such a creed stated in modern terms; it will probably prove impossible ever to construct it

(ii) Now if this be so, and we believe that it is so, it is inevitable that our creeds must be symbolic rather than concrete, and that they must be poetical rather than theological. They must be such that they do not tie people to a belief as definite as a mathematical formula; they must rather leave room for movement. They must leave room for experience to interpret them. They must say things in pictures rather than in exact formulation.

I once heard a friend of mine say a very significant thing, half in jest and half in earnest, or, if one may be paradoxical, half in jest and wholly in earnest. He is the kind of person who is an adventurous and often a disturbing thinker; he is notable for his challenge to orthodoxy rather than his support of it. We were discussing the need for a new and modern creed, and any one of us would have been prepared to wager a large sum that this person would have wished to sweep away the Apostles' Creed and to substitute something up-to-date in its stead. What he did say was this: 'By all means let us keep the Apostles' Creed. The Church must never be allowed to produce a modern and up-to-date creed, for, if they do, they'll expect us to believe in it!'

That statement may sound completely cynical – but it is not. The point at issue is this. If a creed was constructed in definite and concrete terms, in terms which left no room for interpretation, in terms which left a man no alternative between accepting the thing as it stood and rejecting it as it stood, something very valuable would be lost. And worse – a yard-stick would be evolved which would open the way to all kinds of heresy trials, and in which orthodoxy could be stated with the exactitude of a mathematical formula. It seems at least to us that we are far better with a situation in which the truth is stated symbolically, poetically, pictorially, a situation within which there is room to move, a situation in which orthodoxy is not so much a strait-jacket as an atmosphere in which a man's mind has room to think, a situation in which a man does not have all his thinking done for him but in which, so to speak, an area is defined, and within that area his mind is free to move.

G. H. C. Macgregor wrote in his commentary on John that John's doctrine of the Holy Spirit is a protest against all fixity of dogma. In John's Gospel Jesus says that the Holy Spirit will teach them all truth, will bring all things to their remembrance, will take of the things of Christ and show them to them, will tell them things which at the moment they could not bear (John 14.26; 16.12–14). This means that belief in the Christian sense of the term can never be a static thing; it must always be dynamic. It can never be fossilized; it must be living.

This does not mean that a Christian can finish up by believing anything; it means that there is an area of thought in which Jesus Christ is supreme, but within that area the discovery of truth must always be an adventure and an exploration. If that be so, Christian truth can never be stated in a series of cut-and-dried, unaltering and unalterable statements; it can far better be stated in a series of symbols and pictures which can expand through thought and interpretation under the guidance of the Holy Spirit.

This is very obviously true of the Apostles' Creed. There are three items in the Apostles' Creed round which the difficulties mainly arise – the Virgin Birth, the Descent into Hades and the Resurrection of the Body. When we look closely at these three items of the creed, we see that each of them is symbolically and pictorially and even poetically conserving a truth which the Christian faith would lose at its peril. The doctrine of the Virgin Birth is conserving the truth that, however Jesus came into this world, his coming was due to the direct action of God. We may explain the fact as we will, the fact remains. The doctrine of the Descent into Hades is conserving the truth that Jesus was really and truly dead, that his death was no mere appearance, that he did die and experience death as all men experience it. We may state this fact in any kind of picture and in any kind of symbolism; we may state it in what are Jewish ideas of life and death and the afterworld; but however we state it and whatever symbol we use, the fact remains. The doctrine of the Resurrection of the Body is conserving the truth that salvation is the salvation of the total man, that personality survives, that after death we are neither obliterated nor absorbed in the Divine, but that we remain individual personalities. We can express that as we will; the picture and the symbolism do not matter; it is the truth behind them which is the one important thing. In every case the symbol and the picture contain the underlying and essential truth.

There is a basic reason behind this: a proposition stated with cut-and-dried precision cannot expand. It can be accepted or rejected. It can be false or true. It can be adequate in one age of thought and inadequate in the next. But its characteristic is that it is fixed. On the other hand a symbol, a picture, a poetical expression is capable of almost infinite expansion. It can be the vehicle of a growing truth which is almost limitless.

So we come to our conclusion. We shall always need to rethink and to restate the truth. Every age and every generation will need to do its own thinking and its own stating. The process of reappropriating the truth is endless and must continue so long as there is a man with a mind to think. But it may be that we should keep the Apostles' Creed not so much as a test and a yardstick of orthodoxy but rather as a symbolic and pictorial and poetical setting forth of these truths which we must always rethink and restate for ourselves.

The Church had a creed long before it had the Apostles' Creed. It was very short and very sufficient. It was the uncompromising statement JESUS CHRIST IS LORD (Romans 10.9; Philippians 2.11). It is in the light of this prior statement that all subsequent creeds have to be read. So long as we are certain of the lordship of Jesus Christ, we can rethink and reinterpret all statements about the Christian faith, and in the Apostles' Creed we have a symbolic statement of the faith which in the light of the lordship of Jesus Christ and under the guidance of the Holy Spirit is dynamically expandable in every age.